Silver Burdett & Ginn

MATHEMATICS

AUTHORS

SENIOR SERIES AUTHORS
Lucy J. Orfan • Bruce R. Vogeli

SENIOR PROBLEM SOLVING AUTHORS
Stephen Krulik • Jesse A. Rudnick

Sadie C. Bragg • Ruth I. Champagne • Gerald A. Goldin • Edith E. Grimsley
Deborah B. Gustafson • John F. LeBlanc • William D. McKillip • Fernand J. Prevost

SILVER BURDETT & GINN
MORRISTOWN, NJ • NEEDHAM, MA
Atlanta, GA • Cincinnati, OH • Dallas, TX • Menlo Park, CA • Deerfield, IL

Table of Contents

Theme: The Sea

Addition Facts

Mr. James turns on the 2 flashing red lights of the lighthouse. Then he turns on the 3 fixed white lights. How many lights does he turn on in all?

Add to find how many in all.

$$
\underset{\text{addend}}{2} + \underset{\text{addend}}{3} = \underset{\text{sum}}{5}
\qquad
\begin{array}{r}
2 \leftarrow \text{addend} \\
+3 \leftarrow \text{addend} \\
\hline
5 \leftarrow \text{sum}
\end{array}
$$

Mr. James turns on 5 lights.

CLASSWORK

Find each sum.

1. $\begin{array}{r} 3 \\ +5 \\ \hline \end{array}$
2. $\begin{array}{r} 1 \\ +9 \\ \hline \end{array}$
3. $\begin{array}{r} 2 \\ +8 \\ \hline \end{array}$
4. $\begin{array}{r} 7 \\ +6 \\ \hline \end{array}$
5. $\begin{array}{r} 4 \\ +7 \\ \hline \end{array}$
6. $\begin{array}{r} 2 \\ +5 \\ \hline \end{array}$
7. $\begin{array}{r} 9 \\ +4 \\ \hline \end{array}$

8. $5 + 6 = \square$

9. $8 + 9 = \square$

10. $5 + 9 = \square$

11. $7 + 8 = \square$

Find each sum.

1. 4
    +3

2. 2
    +9

3. 8
    +3

4. 2
    +6

5. 3
    +1

6. 6
    +5

7. 9
    +5

8. 8
    +5

9. 4
    +6

10. 5
    +5

11. 6
    +1

12. 6
    +8

13. 8
    +4

14. 7
    +2

15. 3
    +7

16. 8
    +7

17. 6
    +6

18. 7
    +3

19. 4
    +2

20. 9
    +6

21. 2
    +2

22. 3
    +6

23. 2
    +1

24. 5
    +4

25. 3
    +3

26. 5
    +8

27. 8
    +1

28. 7
    +7

29. 1
    +4

30. 8
    +8

31. 7
    +1

32. 3
    +9

33. 1
    +5

34. 9
    +9

35. 9
    +7

36. 6 + 3 = □   37. 4 + 9 = □   38. 4 + 4 = □   39. 3 + 8 = □

40. 8 + 6 = □   41. 1 + 1 = □   42. 7 + 9 = □   43. 7 + 5 = □

Write three addition facts for each sum.

★ 44. 9   ★ 45. 14   ★ 46. 16   ★ 47. 11   ★ 48. 15   ★ 49. 13   ★ 50. 12

APPLICATION

51. Lindsay sketched 5 sea gulls on the rocks. Then she drew 7 more sea gulls. How many sea gulls did she draw in all?

★ 52. The lighthouse has 5 lights. The lights can be red or white. Write all the different combinations of red and white lights the lighthouse can have.

Addition Properties

In *Sea Pup Again* by Archie Binns, Clint and Buster caught an octopus. It had 6 arms hanging over the side. Another 2 arms were tangled in a net. How many arms did the octopus have in all?

You can write the addition example in two ways.

$$\begin{array}{r} 6 \\ +2 \\ \hline 8 \end{array} \qquad \text{or} \qquad \begin{array}{r} 2 \\ +6 \\ \hline 8 \end{array}$$

The octopus had 8 arms.

▶ The order in which numbers are added does not change the sum.

$$\begin{array}{r} 4 \\ +5 \\ \hline 9 \end{array} \qquad \begin{array}{r} 5 \\ +4 \\ \hline 9 \end{array}$$

$$3 + 4 = 7$$
$$4 + 3 = 7$$

▶ The sum of any number and 0 is that number.

$$\begin{array}{r} 8 \\ +0 \\ \hline 8 \end{array} \qquad \begin{array}{r} 0 \\ +6 \\ \hline 6 \end{array}$$

$$2 + 0 = 2$$
$$0 + 5 = 5$$

CLASSWORK

Add.

1. $\begin{array}{r} 9 \\ +6 \end{array}$ $\begin{array}{r} 6 \\ +9 \end{array}$

2. $\begin{array}{r} 3 \\ +0 \end{array}$ $\begin{array}{r} 0 \\ +3 \end{array}$

3. $\begin{array}{r} 4 \\ +7 \end{array}$ $\begin{array}{r} 7 \\ +4 \end{array}$

4. $\begin{array}{r} 2 \\ +8 \end{array}$ $\begin{array}{r} 8 \\ +2 \end{array}$

5. $7 + 0 = \square$
   $0 + 7 = \square$

6. $8 + 3 = \square$
   $3 + 8 = \square$

7. $5 + 8 = \square$
   $8 + 5 = \square$

8. $9 + 4 = \square$
   $4 + 9 = \square$

4

Add.

1. $\begin{array}{r} 3 \\ +7 \end{array}$	2. $\begin{array}{r} 7 \\ +3 \end{array}$	3. $\begin{array}{r} 5 \\ +9 \end{array}$	4. $\begin{array}{r} 9 \\ +5 \end{array}$	5. $\begin{array}{r} 4 \\ +8 \end{array}$	6. $\begin{array}{r} 8 \\ +4 \end{array}$	7. $\begin{array}{r} 0 \\ +4 \end{array}$
8. $\begin{array}{r} 9 \\ +9 \end{array}$	9. $\begin{array}{r} 9 \\ +0 \end{array}$	10. $\begin{array}{r} 6 \\ +6 \end{array}$	11. $\begin{array}{r} 0 \\ +0 \end{array}$	12. $\begin{array}{r} 7 \\ +7 \end{array}$	13. $\begin{array}{r} 1 \\ +0 \end{array}$	14. $\begin{array}{r} 8 \\ +8 \end{array}$
15. $\begin{array}{r} 5 \\ +2 \end{array}$	16. $\begin{array}{r} 7 \\ +1 \end{array}$	17. $\begin{array}{r} 8 \\ +7 \end{array}$	18. $\begin{array}{r} 6 \\ +5 \end{array}$	19. $\begin{array}{r} 1 \\ +8 \end{array}$	20. $\begin{array}{r} 5 \\ +5 \end{array}$	21. $\begin{array}{r} 0 \\ +8 \end{array}$

22. $9 + 8 = \square$　　23. $8 + 9 = \square$　　24. $2 + 7 = \square$　　25. $7 + 2 = \square$

26. $6 + 4 = \square$　　27. $4 + 4 = \square$　　28. $5 + 0 = \square$　　29. $6 + 8 = \square$

Write two addition facts for each pair.

30. 6, 7　　　　31. 9, 2　　　　32. 5, 7　　　　33. 7, 8

34. 0, 9　　　　35. 3, 6　　　　36. 7, 9　　　　37. 8, 6

Use each input number. Follow the rule, if given, to find each output number.

Rule: Add 2.

	Input	Output
	5	7
38.	6	
39.	7	
40.	8	
41.	9	

Rule: Add 7.

	Input	Output
	6	13
42.	3	
43.	9	
44.	5	
45.	8	

Find the rule.

	Input	Output
★ 46.	2	7
	7	12
	3	8
	6	11
	4	9

APPLICATION

47. Clint found 3 arrowheads at Fisherman's Harbor. Buster did not find any. How many arrowheads did they find?

★ 48. Buster caught 2 small fish and 3 large fish. Clint caught 3 small fish and 2 large fish. How many fish did each catch? How many fish did they catch together?

5

Adding Three or More Numbers

The clouds are made of 3 clam shells.
The beach umbrella is made of 5 ark shells.
The sailboats are made of 4 conch shells.

Add to find how many shells were used
in the picture.

```
 3               3
 5   >8          5   +4 ↓   You can
+4     +4 ↓      12         add down.
        12
```

```
 3         3
 5   >9    You can
+4     +    add up.
        12
```

▶The way in which numbers are grouped does not
change the sum.

Another Example

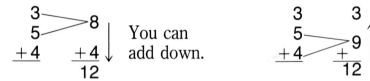

$(2 + 6) + 3 = \square$ $2 + (6 + 3) = \square$ Work inside the
                              ( ) first.

$8 \quad + 3 = 11$ $2 + \quad 9 \quad = 11$

CLASSWORK

Add.

```
1.   4      2.   6      3.   7      4.   5      5.   6      6.   5      7.   4
     2           2           1           1           3           1           2
    +6          +4          +5          +7          +6           3           1
                                                                +2          +6
```

8. $3 + 2 + 4 = \square$ 9. $6 + 1 + 3 = \square$ 10. $5 + 4 + 5 = \square$

Add.

1.   2
   3
+2
	2. 4
	   1
	+3
		3. 2
		   2
		+5
			4. 4
			   3
			+3
				5. 4
				   1
				+7
					6. 3
					   1
					+6
						7. 7
						   2
						+5

8.   5
   2
+6
	9. 5
	   2
	+7
		10. 6
		   1
		+8
			11. 7
			   2
			+4
				12. 2
				   5
				+3
					13. 8
					   1
					+7
						14. 6
						   2
						+7

15. 3
   4
   0
+5
	16. 2
	   1
	   5
	+3
		17. 4
		   3
		   1
		+4
			18. 3
			   2
			   0
			+7
				19. 4
				   3
				   2
				+0
					20. 3
					   2
					   3
					+1
						21. 5
						   1
						   1
						+7

22. $4 + 2 + 5 = \square$

23. $5 + 1 + 8 = \square$

★ 24. $2 + 3 + 1 + 4 + 5 = \square$

★ 25. $3 + 0 + 5 + 1 + 2 + 7 = \square$

APPLICATION

26. Carlos collected 2 cone shells, 5 scallop shells, and 3 wedge shells. How many shells did he collect?

★27. Karen used 4 shells each for the ball and boat in her picture. Then she used another 3 shells to make a fish. How many shells did Karen use in her picture?

═══ MENTAL ARITHMETIC ═══

When you add three or more numbers, look for a sum of 10.

  4
  3   4 + 6 = 10
+6   10 + 3 = 13
13

$5 + 2 + 5 = 12$
$5 + 5 = 10$
$10 + 2 = 12$

1. 2
  1
+8
	2. 3
	  7
	+2
		3. 5
		  4
		+6
			4. 8
			  2
			+3
				5. 5
				  1
				  5
				+3
					6. 4
					  3
					  1
					+6
						7. 7
						  1
						  3
						+2

8. $3 + 0 + 1 + 7 = \square$

9. $3 + 4 + 2 + 6 = \square$

Subtraction Facts

There were 9 fish in Lee's net. Then 2 fish jumped out. How many fish were left?

Subtract to find how many are left.

$$9 - 2 = 7$$
↑
difference

$$\begin{array}{r} 9 \\ -2 \\ \hline 7 \end{array} \leftarrow \text{difference}$$

There were 7 fish left.

Lee's father caught 2 fish. How many more fish can he catch without going over the limit of 10 fish?

Subtract to find how many more.

$$\begin{array}{r} 10 \\ -2 \\ \hline 8 \end{array}$$

Lee's father can catch 8 more fish.

CLASSWORK

Find each difference.

1. $\begin{array}{r} 8 \\ -3 \\ \hline \end{array}$
2. $\begin{array}{r} 3 \\ -2 \\ \hline \end{array}$
3. $\begin{array}{r} 10 \\ -3 \\ \hline \end{array}$
4. $\begin{array}{r} 12 \\ -4 \\ \hline \end{array}$
5. $\begin{array}{r} 14 \\ -9 \\ \hline \end{array}$
6. $\begin{array}{r} 9 \\ -3 \\ \hline \end{array}$
7. $\begin{array}{r} 7 \\ -2 \\ \hline \end{array}$

8. $6 - 2 = \square$
9. $11 - 2 = \square$
10. $13 - 5 = \square$
11. $15 - 8 = \square$

Find each difference.

1. $\begin{array}{r} 7 \\ -5 \\ \hline \end{array}$	**2.** $\begin{array}{r} 5 \\ -2 \\ \hline \end{array}$	**3.** $\begin{array}{r} 4 \\ -3 \\ \hline \end{array}$	**4.** $\begin{array}{r} 3 \\ -1 \\ \hline \end{array}$	**5.** $\begin{array}{r} 7 \\ -4 \\ \hline \end{array}$	**6.** $\begin{array}{r} 12 \\ -6 \\ \hline \end{array}$	**7.** $\begin{array}{r} 14 \\ -7 \\ \hline \end{array}$
8. $\begin{array}{r} 17 \\ -8 \\ \hline \end{array}$	**9.** $\begin{array}{r} 18 \\ -9 \\ \hline \end{array}$	**10.** $\begin{array}{r} 13 \\ -7 \\ \hline \end{array}$	**11.** $\begin{array}{r} 7 \\ -6 \\ \hline \end{array}$	**12.** $\begin{array}{r} 11 \\ -7 \\ \hline \end{array}$	**13.** $\begin{array}{r} 14 \\ -5 \\ \hline \end{array}$	**14.** $\begin{array}{r} 15 \\ -9 \\ \hline \end{array}$
15. $\begin{array}{r} 11 \\ -6 \\ \hline \end{array}$	**16.** $\begin{array}{r} 13 \\ -9 \\ \hline \end{array}$	**17.** $\begin{array}{r} 15 \\ -6 \\ \hline \end{array}$	**18.** $\begin{array}{r} 16 \\ -7 \\ \hline \end{array}$	**19.** $\begin{array}{r} 9 \\ -5 \\ \hline \end{array}$	**20.** $\begin{array}{r} 11 \\ -3 \\ \hline \end{array}$	**21.** $\begin{array}{r} 13 \\ -8 \\ \hline \end{array}$
22. $\begin{array}{r} 14 \\ -8 \\ \hline \end{array}$	**23.** $\begin{array}{r} 10 \\ -6 \\ \hline \end{array}$	**24.** $\begin{array}{r} 4 \\ -2 \\ \hline \end{array}$	**25.** $\begin{array}{r} 16 \\ -8 \\ \hline \end{array}$	**26.** $\begin{array}{r} 13 \\ -4 \\ \hline \end{array}$	**27.** $\begin{array}{r} 13 \\ -6 \\ \hline \end{array}$	**28.** $\begin{array}{r} 12 \\ -9 \\ \hline \end{array}$

29. $11 - 9 = \square$ **30.** $8 - 6 = \square$ **31.** $12 - 5 = \square$ **32.** $9 - 4 = \square$

33. $17 - 9 = \square$ **34.** $11 - 5 = \square$ **35.** $12 - 3 = \square$ **36.** $11 - 8 = \square$

Solve.

★**37.** The sum of two numbers is 15. Their difference is 3. What are the numbers?

★**38.** The sum of two numbers is 11. Their difference is 5. What are the numbers?

APPLICATION

39. Myra caught 5 fish. Her brother cleaned 3 of them. How many fish were left to clean?

40. Ben wants to catch 8 fish for the family's dinner. He caught 5 fish. How many more fish does he need to catch?

41. Mr. Taris saw 12 sponges growing around a rock. With a long pole he pulled up 8 sponges. How many sponges remained?

★ **42.** Ms. Sun dives for sponges. She put 6 sponges in a bag. Then she picked 5 more sponges. As she put them in the bag, 4 sponges floated away. How many sponges are in the bag?

More About Subtraction

Mrs. Simon is an oceanographer. She studies
samples of sea life. How many more sea horses
than starfish did she collect?

Subtract to compare.

$$\begin{array}{r} 8 \\ -5 \\ \hline 3 \end{array}$$

You can use addition to check subtraction.

$$\begin{array}{r} 8 \\ -5 \\ \hline 3 \end{array}$$ These should be the same. $$\begin{array}{r} 3 \\ +5 \\ \hline 8 \end{array}$$

She collected 3 more sea horses than starfish.

There are special properties of zero for subtraction.

► When 0 is subtracted from any number,
the difference is that number.

$$\begin{array}{r} 4 \\ -0 \\ \hline 4 \end{array} \qquad \begin{array}{r} 7 \\ -0 \\ \hline 7 \end{array} \qquad \begin{array}{l} 2 - 0 = 2 \\ 9 - 0 = 9 \end{array}$$

► When a number is subtracted from
itself, the difference is 0.

$$\begin{array}{r} 5 \\ -5 \\ \hline 0 \end{array} \qquad \begin{array}{r} 6 \\ -6 \\ \hline 0 \end{array} \qquad \begin{array}{l} 3 - 3 = 0 \\ 8 - 8 = 0 \end{array}$$

CLASSWORK

Subtract. Check by adding.

1. $\begin{array}{r} 9 \\ -9 \\ \hline \end{array}$ 2. $\begin{array}{r} 1 \\ -1 \\ \hline \end{array}$ 3. $\begin{array}{r} 4 \\ -4 \\ \hline \end{array}$ 4. $\begin{array}{r} 8 \\ -0 \\ \hline \end{array}$ 5. $\begin{array}{r} 10 \\ -7 \\ \hline \end{array}$ 6. $\begin{array}{r} 14 \\ -6 \\ \hline \end{array}$ 7. $\begin{array}{r} 6 \\ -5 \\ \hline \end{array}$

8. $3 - 0 = \square$ 9. $15 - 7 = \square$ 10. $2 - 2 = \square$ 11. $12 - 7 = \square$

Subtract. Check by adding.

1.	2.	3.	4.	5.	6.	7.
6	7	10	5	9	8	0
-0	-7	-5	-0	-7	-4	-0

8.	9.	10.	11.	12.	13.	14.
5	8	16	11	6	7	8
-5	-7	-9	-7	-4	-0	-8

15. $10 - 8 = \square$ 16. $9 - 0 = \square$ 17. $3 - 3 = \square$ 18. $14 - 9 = \square$

19. $13 - 8 = \square$ 20. $10 - 3 = \square$ 21. $17 - 9 = \square$ 22. $11 - 8 = \square$

Use each input number. Follow the rule, if given, to find each output number.

Rule: Subtract 3.

	Input	Output
	3	0
23.	4	
24.	5	
25.	6	
26.	7	

Rule: Subtract 6.

	Input	Output
	8	2
27.	12	
28.	6	
29.	15	
30.	11	

Find the rule.

	Input	Output
★ 31.	3	3
	6	6
	4	4
	8	8
	7	7

APPLICATION

Use the table to answer the questions.

32. How many more crabs than coral were collected?

33. How many more sand dollars than sea urchins were collected?

34. An oceanographer wants to study 10 samples of sea anemones. How many more samples does he need?

★ 35. How many more sand dollars and sea anemones were collected than coral?

SAMPLES OF SEA LIFE COLLECTED	
TYPE	NUMBER
CORAL	9
SAND DOLLAR	8
SEA ANEMONE	6
SEA URCHIN	8
CRAB	12

Related Facts

This ship has 11 sails. There are 5 sails up and 6 sails down.

You can write four related facts using three different numbers.

$$\begin{array}{r} 5 \\ +6 \\ \hline 11 \end{array} \qquad \begin{array}{r} 6 \\ +5 \\ \hline 11 \end{array} \qquad \begin{array}{r} 11 \\ -\ 5 \\ \hline 6 \end{array} \qquad \begin{array}{r} 11 \\ -\ 6 \\ \hline 5 \end{array}$$

Related facts help you find missing numbers in a number sentence.

$16 - \square = 9$ **Think** $9 + 7 = 16$
so $16 - 7 = 9$

CLASSWORK

Find each missing number.

1. $3 + 6 = \square$
   $6 + 3 = \square$
   $9 - 3 = \square$
   $9 - 6 = \square$

2. $7 + 5 = \square$
   $5 + \square = 12$
   $12 - \square = 7$
   $\square - 7 = 5$

3. $4 + \square = 13$
   $9 + \square = 13$
   $\square - 4 = 9$
   $13 - \square = 4$

4. $14 - \square = 6$
   $6 + \square = 14$
   $\square - 6 = 8$
   $8 + \square = 14$

5. $7 + \square = 15$

6. $9 - \square = 2$

7. $9 + \square = 17$

8. $13 - \square = 8$

Find each missing number.

1. $3 + 7 = \square$
   $7 + 3 = \square$
   $10 - 3 = \square$
   $10 - 7 = \square$

2. $3 + \square = 11$
   $8 + \square = 11$
   $11 - \square = 8$
   $\square - 8 = 3$

3. $\square + 7 = 13$
   $7 + 6 = \square$
   $\square - 6 = 7$
   $13 - \square = 6$

4. $\square - 4 = 5$
   $5 + \square = 9$
   $9 - \square = 4$
   $\square + 5 = 9$

5. $9 + \square = 11$

6. $12 - \square = 4$

7. $15 - \square = 9$

8. $8 + \square = 16$

★ 9. $(7 + 5) - 7 = \square$

★ 10. $(8 - 3) + 3 = \square$

Write the letter of the correct answer.

11. Which fact is related to
    $2 + 8 = 10$?
    a. $10 - 4 = 6$ b. $3 + 7 = 10$
    c. $10 - 2 = 8$ d. $0 + 8 = 8$

12. Which fact is related to
    $12 - 6 = 6$?
    a. $4 + 8 = 12$ b. $6 + 6 = 12$
    c. $12 - 7 = 5$ d. $6 - 6 = 0$

Write the related facts for each.

13. 2, 6, 8

14. 5, 9, 14

15. 4, 6, 10

16. 5, 5, 10

Write two number sentences for each story.

17. A ship had 5 sails. Two were torn in a storm. How many were left to use? A sailor repaired the sails. Then how many sails were there?

★ 18. Four sailors were on deck. Three more came. How many were there? Then four went away. How many were left?

CALCULATOR

2, 3, 4, 5, 6, 7

1. Choose any two numbers and $\boxed{+}$ or $\boxed{-}$ to show a fact.

2. Use the answer and $\boxed{+}$ or $\boxed{-}$ to show a related fact.

Fast Facts

Add as fast as you can.

1. 2 +3	2. 4 +6	3. 5 +1	4. 6 +3	5. 0 +8	6. 2 +9	7. 8 +5
8. 9 +4	9. 5 +5	10. 3 +4	11. 1 +2	12. 3 +7	13. 7 +9	14. 4 +2
15. 8 +3	16. 7 +6	17. 3 +5	18. 9 +8	19. 4 +9	20. 1 +7	21. 6 +2
22. 7 +2	23. 0 +9	24. 4 +8	25. 2 +8	26. 4 +4	27. 6 +7	28. 9 +6
29. 9 +2	30. 6 +6	31. 8 +9	32. 7 +4	33. 2 +5	34. 1 +9	35. 3 +9
36. 5 +4	37. 8 +6	38. 7 +8	39. 9 +9	40. 4 +3	41. 0 +5	42. 9 +5
43. 3 +3	44. 0 +0	45. 6 +5	46. 6 +8	47. 1 +8	48. 7 +5	49. 4 +0
50. 8 +8	51. 3 +1	52. 6 +8	53. 6 +1	54. 7 +7	55. 2 +0	56. 9 +7
57. 1 +1	58. 6 +9	59. 7 +3	60. 2 +2	61. 7 +0	62. 1 +4	63. 8 +9

Subtract as fast as you can.

1. 8
− 5

2. 11
− 4

3. 8
− 1

4. 16
− 8

5. 11
− 9

6. 4
− 1

7. 12
− 3

8. 11
− 6

9. 6
− 2

10. 9
− 7

11. 13
− 6

12. 9
− 1

13. 5
− 0

14. 8
− 6

15. 12
− 7

16. 8
− 3

17. 8
− 7

18. 15
− 9

19. 13
− 5

20. 8
− 8

21. 10
− 2

22. 13
− 9

23. 8
− 4

24. 9
− 8

25. 14
− 8

26. 16
− 7

27. 10
− 4

28. 5
− 3

29. 7
− 5

30. 9
− 6

31. 11
− 8

32. 17
− 8

33. 10
− 3

34. 6
− 1

35. 18
− 9

36. 14
− 7

37. 10
− 9

38. 9
− 5

39. 15
− 7

40. 12
− 5

41. 8
− 0

42. 13
− 8

43. 17
− 9

44. 10
− 5

45. 12
− 8

46. 14
− 9

47. 7
− 4

48. 11
− 6

49. 13
− 7

50. 10
− 8

51. 3
− 2

52. 14
− 6

53. 13
− 4

54. 11
− 7

55. 6
− 3

56. 2
− 0

57. 16
− 9

58. 15
− 6

59. 9
− 3

60. 12
− 9

61. 15
− 8

62. 14
− 5

63. 9
− 2

Problem Solving

FINDING FACTS FROM PICTURES

Here are four steps you should follow to become a better problem solver.

Some people are going on a boat ride. Each person must have a life jacket. How many more children can go on the boat ride?

Use the four steps to help solve the problem.

THINK **What is the question?**

How many more children can go on the boat ride?

What are the facts?

Look at the picture. Some of the facts are in the picture. There are 3 children on the boat. The sign says there are 8 life jackets for children.

PLAN **How can the answer be found?**

Subtract the number of children on the boat from the number of life jackets for children.

$$8 - 3 = \square$$

SOLVE **Carry out the plan. Do the work and find the answer.**

$$\begin{array}{r} 8 \\ -3 \\ \hline 5 \end{array}$$

5 more children can go on the boat ride.

LOOK BACK **Did you answer the question? Is your arithmetic correct? Does your answer make sense?**

Yes. $3 + 5 = 8$. All 8 children will have life jackets.

Use the picture on page 16 to answer 1–6.

1. How many life jackets are there for adults?

2. How many adults are already on the boat?

3. How many more adults can go on the boat ride?

4. How many people are on the boat already?

5. How many more children than adults are already on the boat?

★6. How many more people can go on the boat ride?

Use the picture to answer 7–12.

7. How many sailboats are in the race?

8. Which boat is leading?

9. Which boat is last?

10. Which boat is third?

11. If 3 more boats enter the race, how many boats will there be?

★12. There are 4 people each on the red and yellow boats. There are 3 people each on the blue and green boats. How many people are sailing in all?

═══ CREATE YOUR OWN PROBLEM ═══

Look at the picture of an underwater scene. Make up 2 problems using facts from the picture.

Hundreds

The digits 0, 1, 2, 3, 4, 5, 6, 7, 8, and 9 are used to write numbers.

The divers found 238 gold coins of buried treasure.

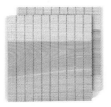

2 hundreds   3 tens   8 ones

number in standard form   238
- read   2 hundred 38
- word name   two hundred thirty-eight

The place-value table gives the value of each digit.

HUNDREDS	TENS	ONES
2	3	8
↓	↓	↓
200	30	8

Another Example

number in standard form   705
- read   7 hundred 5
- word name   seven hundred five

CLASSWORK

Read each number. Give the value of the digit 6.

1. 642   2. 56   3. 963   4. 610   5. 67

Write each number in standard form.

6. 4 hundred 25   7. 9 hundred 18

8. six hundred seventy-two 9. three hundred forty-five

18

PRACTICE

Give the value of the digit 3.

1. 536
2. 341
3. 237
4. 83

Write each number in standard form.

5. 5 hundred 10
6. 9 hundred 26
7. one hundred nineteen
8. 2 hundred 15
9. forty-one
10. 8 hundred 40
11. six hundred ninety-two
12. twenty-six
13. seventy-four
14. 6 hundred 6
15. three hundred five
16. two hundred

Write each word name.

17. 284
18. 68
19. 972
20. 107

Find the number.

★21. 3 tens more than 24

★22. 5 hundreds more than 475

APPLICATION

Use the treasure map to answer the questions.

23. How far is it from the boat wreck to the rocks?

24. It is forty-nine steps between what two points?

★25. How many steps is it from the rocks to the treasure?

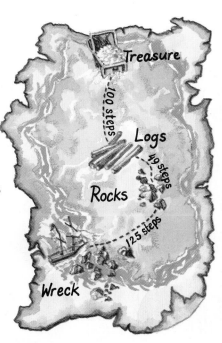

Mixed Practice

1. 5
   +8

2. 3
   +5

3. 15
   − 6

4. 9
   +7

5. 7
   +5

6. 18
   − 9

7. 14
   − 8

8. 9
   −2

9. 17
   − 9

10. 7
    +7

11. 9
    +0

12. 7
    +4

13. 11
    − 3

14. 9
    +9

15. 8 + 7 = □

16. 16 − 8 = □

17. 4 + 9 = □

18. 6 + 5 = □

19. 7 − 0 = □

20. 4 + 8 = □

21. 5 − 5 = □

22. 15 − 7 = □

23. 0 + 6 = □

24. 10 − 3 = □

Thousands

The U.S.S. *Nautilus* was the first submarine to travel under the North Pole. The trip from Alaska to the Greenland Sea covered 2,628 kilometers.

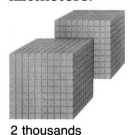 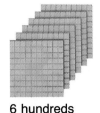 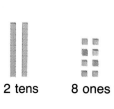

| 2 thousands | 6 hundreds | 2 tens | 8 ones |

number in standard form   2,628
- read   2 thousand, 628
- word name   two thousand, six hundred twenty-eight

The value of a digit depends on its place in the number.

THOUSANDS			ONES		
hundreds	tens	ones	hundreds	tens	ones
		2,	6	2	8
		↓	↓	↓	↓
		2,000	600	20	8

Numbers are separated by commas into groups of three digits called **periods.**

Another Example

number in standard form   5,407
- read   5 thousand, 407
- word name   five thousand, four hundred seven

CLASSWORK

Read each number. Give the value of the digit 3.

1. 2,315
2. 4,036
3. 813
4. 3,127
5. 930

Write each number in standard form using commas.

6. 2 thousand, 531
7. 8 thousand, 19
8. nine thousand, eight hundred sixty
9. four thousand, seven hundred five

Give the value of the digit 6.

1. 8,761
2. 6,415
3. 956
4. 1,603
5. 2,367

6. 6,044
7. 3,689
8. 2,106
9. 7,864
10. 621

Write each number in standard form using commas.

11. 4 thousand, 862
12. 5182

13. 6 thousand, 17
14. 3 thousand, 9

15. nine thousand, two hundred thirty-seven

16. two thousand, one hundred six
17. eight hundred twelve

★ 18. fifteen hundred
★ 19. sixteen hundred forty-eight

Write the word name.

20. 1,275
21. 349
22. 8,671
23. 9,018
24. 4,103

Write the numbers in standard form.

25. William Beebe built a bathysphere to help him explore underwater. He was lowered nine hundred eight meters into the ocean.

★ 26. The *Alvin* was the world's first deep-diving submarine. In nineteen hundred sixty-five it dove one thousand, eight hundred meters into the ocean.

APPLICATION

LOGICAL THINKING

1. My ones digit is 3. My tens digit is 5 more than my ones digit. My hundreds digit is 2 less than my tens digit. My thousands digit is 4 more than my ones digit. What number am I?

2. My tens digit is 7. My ones digit is 3 less than my tens digit. My thousands digit is 1 more than my tens digit. My hundreds digit is the same as my ones digit. What number am I?

Ten Thousands, Hundred Thousands

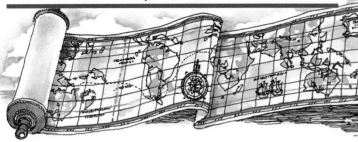

Ferdinand Magellan was captain of the first ships to sail around the world. The trip took 3 years and covered 81,449 kilometers.

number in standard form   81,449
- read   81 thousand, 449
- word name   eighty-one thousand, four hundred forty-nine

THOUSANDS			ONES		
h	t	o	h	t	o
	8	1,	4	4	9

The expanded form shows the value of each digit in the number.

81,449 = 80,000 + 1,000 + 400 + 40 + 9

Another Example

number in standard form   237,506
- read   237 thousand, 506
- word name   two hundred thirty-seven thousand, five hundred six
- expanded form   200,000 + 30,000 + 7,000 + 500 + 6

CLASSWORK

Read each number. Give the value of the digit 5.

1. 256,134   2. 45,106   3. 538,729   4. 11,506

Write each number in standard form using commas.

5. thirty-four thousand, seven hundred eleven

6. one hundred fifty thousand, nine hundred sixty-two

7. 30,000 + 8,000 + 600 + 20 + 7

8. 500,000 + 40,000 + 9,000 + 30 + 1

22

Give the value of the digit 7.

1. 137,256   2. 70,184   3. 722,199   4. 623,071

Write each number in standard form using commas.

5. nineteen thousand, four hundred fifty-two

6. seventy-two thousand, eighty-one

7. five thousand, twelve

8. one hundred fifty-six thousand, seven hundred twenty-four

9. six hundred thousand, nine hundred eleven

10. 90,000 + 6,000 + 80 + 7

11. 300,000 + 80,000 + 1,000 + 500 + 40

★12. 200 + 7,000 + 5 + 60,000

★13. 9 + 1,000 + 40 + 600,000 + 800

Write each number in expanded form.

14. 87,145   15. 63,508   16. 120,974   17. 406,208

Match.

18. 40,208   a. four thousand, twenty
19. 402,080   b. forty thousand, two hundred eight
20. 4,020   c. four hundred twenty
21. 402   d. four hundred two thousand, eighty
22. 420   e. four hundred two

APPLICATION

CALCULATOR

Take the 4 out of each number by subtracting. What number do you subtract? What is the new number?

1. 248,105   2. 46,793   3. 51,247   4. 403,166

Comparing and Ordering Numbers

The average depth of the Indian Ocean is 3,960 meters. The average depth of the Atlantic Ocean is 3,677 meters. Which ocean has the greater average depth?

▶Compare the digits in each place, starting at the left.

THOUSANDS			ONES		
h	t	o	h	t	o
		3,	⑨	6	0
		3,	⑥	7	7

same ←⌐

9 > 6

so 3,960 > 3,677 and
3,677 < 3,960

> means is greater than
< means is less than

The Indian Ocean has the greater average depth.

List these numbers in order from least to greatest.

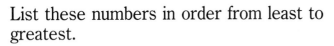

7,841   17,106   7,835

▶To order numbers, compare them two at a time.

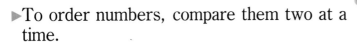

7,841 < 17,106   The number with fewer digits is less.
7,835 < 7,841
7,835 < 7,841 < 17,106   The numbers are in order from least to greatest.

CLASSWORK

Compare. Use >, <, or = for ●.

1. 67 ● 76

2. 281 ● 279

3. 981 ● 1,000

4. 73,804 ● 73,804

5. 340 ● 346

6. 1,525 ● 1,524

List these numbers in order from least to greatest.

7. 651   639   1,207

8. 29,244   33,996   28,051   6,124

Compare. Use >, <, or = for ●.

1. 72 ● 81

2. 415 ● 472

3. 526 ● 526

4. 1,856 ● 931

5. 6,804 ● 7,680

6. 358 ● 97

7. 499 ● 479

8. 22,365 ● 22,365

9. 4,112 ● 4,211

10. 8,332 ● 51,001

11. 7,682 ● 7,632

12. 9,284 ● 9,284

13. 19,145 ● 19,146

14. 2,393 ● 2,393

15. 18,370 ● 8,475

16. 26,412 ● 2,641

17. 584 ● 5,840

18. 6,700 ● 67,000

List these numbers in order from least to greatest.

19. 826   1,014   815

20. 13,170   12,961   13,042

21. 16,100   4,527   4,552   6,893

22. 9,486   21,496   10,179   21,396

23. 570   75   7,537   57

24. 24,986   2,948   29,486   294

Give the number that is 100 less.

★25. 3,615

★26. 18,426

★27. 37,194

★28. 5,904

Give the number that is 1,000 more.

★29. 4,290

★30. 21,575

★31. 19,783

★32. 641

APPLICATION

33. Which ocean has the greatest depth?

34. Which ocean has the least depth?

35. Write the depths in meters from the table in order from least to greatest.

★36. Use > or < to compare the depths of the Arctic and Indian oceans.

DEEPEST SPOT	
Ocean	Depth in Meters
Arctic	5,450
Atlantic	8,648
Indian	7,725
Pacific	11,033

Rounding Numbers

On the Spot News reported there were about 20 sailboats in the race. Brian counted 17 sailboats.

The news reporter used a rounded number. Rounded numbers tell *about* how many.

17 is between 10 and 20.
17 is closer to 20.
17 rounded to the nearest ten is 20.

Round 321 to the nearest hundred.

321 is between 300 and 400.
321 is closer to 300.
321 rounded to the nearest hundred is 300.

Round 650 to the nearest hundred.

650 is halfway between 600 and 700. When a number is halfway, round it to the greater number.
650 rounded to the nearest hundred is 700.

CLASSWORK

Round to the nearest ten.

1. 12   2. 19   3. 15   4. 13   5. 18   6. 11

Round to the nearest hundred.

7. 310   8. 350   9. 386   10. 675   11. 628   12. 656

26

Round to the nearest ten.

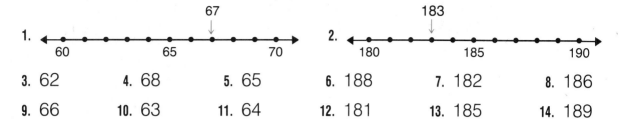

1.

2.

3. 62   4. 68   5. 65   6. 188   7. 182   8. 186

9. 66   10. 63   11. 64   12. 181   13. 185   14. 189

Round to the nearest hundred.

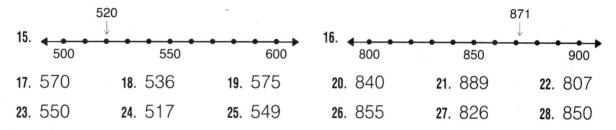

15.

16.

17. 570   18. 536   19. 575   20. 840   21. 889   22. 807

23. 550   24. 517   25. 549   26. 855   27. 826   28. 850

Use the digits 3, 5, and 8. Write the number that rounds as shown.

★ **29.** 500   ★ **30.** 600   ★ **31.** 900   ★ **32.** 840

APPLICATION

Round the given information.

33. There are 243 people watching the race. About how many people is that, rounded to the nearest hundred?

34. There are 68 people working as crews on the sailboats. Rounded to the nearest ten, about how many people are in the race?

═══ LOGICAL THINKING ═══

A news reporter received the following information on a sailboat race.
Find the order in which these boats finished.

Dolphin finished in second place.
The Wave came in last.
Smile came in two places before *The Wave*.
Happy Time finished before *Dolphin*.
America finished after *Smile*.

More Rounding

To the nearest hundred, about how many beach umbrellas were rented?

►To round a number, follow these steps.

DUNE'S RENTALS
136 UMBRELLAS
RENTED TODAY

Step 1	Find the rounding place.	1̲36
Step 2	Look at the digit to the right. If it is less than 5, leave the digit in the rounding place unchanged.	1̲36 ↓ 3 < 5
	If it is 5 or more, increase the digit in the rounding place by 1.	
Step 3	Change each digit to the right of the rounding place to 0.	100

About 100 umbrellas were rented.

Another Example

Round 3,684 to the nearest thousand.

Step 1 3̲,684
↓

Step 2 3̲,684 6 > 5   Round to the next thousand.

Step 3 4,000

Round money the same way you round other numbers.

$352 — to the nearest hundred dollars → $400
$1,475 — to the nearest hundred dollars → $1,500
$1,475 — to the nearest thousand dollars → $1,000

CLASSWORK

Round to the nearest hundred.

1. 409   2. 538   3. 2,463   4. 652   5. $881   6. $4,129

Round to the nearest thousand.

7. 7,452   8. 2,631   9. 41,770   10. 9,483   11. $13,522   12. $5,319

Round to the nearest ten.

1. 42   2. 86   3. 55   4. 171   5. 329   6. 94

Round to the nearest hundred.

7. 265   8. 531   9. 1,412   10. 829   11. 2,754   12. 145

13. 608   14. 337   15. 555   16. 6,483   17. 928   18. 3,986

Round to the nearest thousand.

19. 2,143   20. 8,602   21. 13,457   22. 11,813   23. 6,521

24. 1,904   25. 47,256   26. 4,499   27. 5,723   28. 50,798

Round to the nearest hundred dollars in 29–33.
Round to the nearest thousand dollars in 34–38.

29. $428   30. $159   31. $245   32. $3,519   33. $8,451

34. $1,543   35. $6,098   36. $4,849   37. $12,450   38. $19,829

Use the digits 1, 3, 5, and 7.

★ 39. Give the greatest number possible that rounds to 4,000.

★ 40. Give the least number possible that rounds to 4,000.

APPLICATION

41. Dune's Rentals had 36 surfboards rented out. Rounded to the nearest ten, about how many surfboards were rented?

42. The beach food stand had $438 in the cash register. About how much money is that, rounded to the nearest hundred dollars?

★ 43. Over the weekend 11,835 people went to the beach. About how many people is that, rounded to the nearest ten thousand?

Millions

How many kilograms of fish were caught in Hawaii?

AMOUNT OF FISH CAUGHT	
State	Kilograms of Fish
Alabama	11,250,000
California	312,750,000
Georgia	9,000,000
Hawaii	6,300,000
Maine	97,650,000

number in standard form   6,300,000
- read   6 million, 300 thousand
- word name   six million, three hundred thousand
- expanded form   6,000,000 + 300,000

MILLIONS			THOUSANDS			ONES		
h	t	o	h	t	o	h	t	o
		6,	3	0	0,	0	0	0

There were 6,300,000 kilograms of fish caught in Hawaii.

Another Example

number in standard form   218,304,760
- read   218 million, 304 thousand, 760
- word name   two hundred eighteen million, three hundred four thousand, seven hundred sixty
- expanded form   200,000,000 + 10,000,000 + 8,000,000 + 300,000 + 4,000 + 700 + 60

CLASSWORK

Read each number. Give the value of the digit 7.

1. 2,741,385   2. 376,800,000   3. 7,190,054

Write each number in standard form using commas.

4. 12468307   5. 3 million, 41 thousand, 206

6. seven million, four hundred twenty-six thousand, fifteen

7. four hundred eight million, fifty-one thousand, six hundred

8. 50,000,000 + 3,000,000 + 100,000 + 2,000 + 800 + 70

PRACTICE

Give the value of the digit 5.

1. 25,140,000
2. 3,750,600
3. 54,186,922

4. 8,561,007
5. 160,342,518
6. 593,176,404

Write each number in standard form using commas.

7. 3216543
8. 20783604
9. 7 million

10. 14 million, 312 thousand, 657

11. two million, one hundred sixteen thousand, four hundred ten

12. three million, five hundred thousand, forty-nine

13. twenty-six million, thirteen thousand, two hundred five

14. one hundred million, six hundred four thousand, fifty-two

15. 3,000,000 + 600,000 + 50,000 + 8,000 + 700 + 4

★16. 200 + 10 + 5 + 4,000 + 90,000

★17. 1 + 50,000,000 + 3,000 + 4,000,000

★18. 40,000 + 300 + 9,000,000 + 100,000,000 + 2,000

Write each number in expanded form.

19. 6,145,820
20. 37,061,024
21. 200,403,890

Write the greatest and least numbers using each digit once.

★22. 3, 2, 5, 4, 7, 9, and 1
★23. 6, 8, 3, 4, 1, 7, 2, and 5

APPLICATION

Use the table on page 30.

24. Which state had the greatest amount of fish caught?

25. Which state had the least amount of fish caught?

26. Which state had eleven million, two hundred fifty thousand kilograms of fish caught?

★27. Which states had more than ten million kilograms of fish caught?

Problem Solving

SKILLS AND STRATEGIES REVIEW A Diving Bell

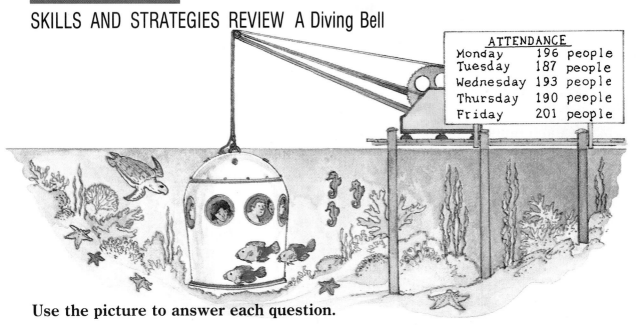

ATTENDANCE		
Monday	196	people
Tuesday	187	people
Wednesday	193	people
Thursday	190	people
Friday	201	people

Use the picture to answer each question.

1. How many seahorses are there?

2. How many starfish are there?

3. Are there more seahorses or more parrot fish?

4. Are there more starfish or more seahorses?

5. How many starfish and seahorses are there in all?

6. How many more starfish are there than sea turtles?

7. How many parrot fish and sea turtles are there in all?

8. If 3 seahorses swim away, how many will be left?

9. What was the attendance for Tuesday?

10. What was the attendance for Thursday?

11. On what day did the most people go down to see the fish?

12. On what day did the fewest people go down to see the fish?

13. Did more people attend on Wednesday or Thursday?

14. Is it true that about 100 people came on Tuesday?

★ 15. The diving bell holds 12 people. There were 4 empty seats on each of 2 trips. How many people used the bell in 2 trips?

★ 16. The attendance for Saturday was 100 more people than the attendance for Thursday. What was the attendance for Saturday?

Problem Solving

WHAT IF . . . ?

Seashells $3 each

Model Anchors $4 each

Postcards 5 for $1

T-shirts $7 each

Pennants $2 each

Use the picture to answer each question.

1. How much does 1 seashell cost?

2. How much does a T-shirt cost?

3. How much do 5 postcards cost?

4. How much does 1 pennant cost?

5. Which costs more, a seashell or a model anchor?

6. Which costs more, a pennant or a seashell?

What if Stan bought 1 T-shirt and 1 seashell?

7. How much would he spend in all?

8. How much more would he spend for the T-shirt than the seashell?

What if Clara had $10?

9. Could she buy 2 model anchors?

10. Could she buy 2 T-shirts?

11. Could she buy 2 pennants and 5 postcards?

12. How much money would she have left if she bought 1 seashell?

What if seashells cost $2 each and model anchors cost $5 each?

★ 13. How much would 4 seashells and 1 model anchor cost?

★ 14. Bonnie had $5 and bought 1 seashell. Does she have enough money left to buy 10 postcards?

33

Add or subtract. pages 2–11

1. $\quad 3$ $+4$	2. $\quad 8$ $+4$	3. $\quad 10$ $-\ 5$	4. $\quad 14$ $-\ 7$	5. $\quad 13$ $-\ 7$	6. $\quad 9$ -0	7. $\quad 18$ $-\ 9$
8. $\quad 9$ $+8$	9. $\quad 5$ $+9$	10. $\quad 7$ -7	11. $\quad 15$ $-\ 6$	12. $\quad 12$ $-\ 8$	13. $\quad 6$ $+8$	14. $\quad 16$ $-\ 8$

15. $1 + 4 + 8 = \square$ 16. $4 + 2 + 7 = \square$ 17. $5 + 4 + 0 = \square$

Write the related facts for each. pages 12–13

18. 2, 6, 8 19. 7, 8, 15 20. 4, 6, 10 21. 7, 9, 16

Give the value of the digit 8. pages 18–23, 30–31

22. 8,342,976 23. 148,601 24. 47,835

Write each number in standard form. pages 18–23, 30–31

25. $200,000 + 30,000 + 1,000 + 400$

26. one million, fifty thousand, six hundred eighteen

Compare. Use $>$, $<$, or $=$ for ●. pages 24–25

27. 178 ● 187 28. 3,850 ● 3,849 29. 48,629 ● 48,629

Round each number to the underlined place. pages 26–29

30. $\underline{6}50$ 31. $\underline{4}1$ 32. $\underline{2},321$ 33. $\underline{6},998$ 34. $3\underline{4},750$

Solve. pages 16–17, 32–33

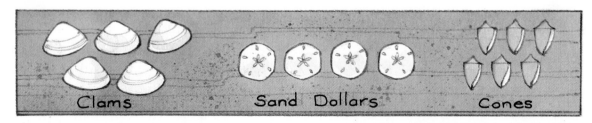

Clams   Sand Dollars   Cones

35. How many items are in the collection?

36. How many more cone shells than sand dollars are there?

Add or subtract.

1. $\begin{array}{r} 9 \\ -9 \\ \hline \end{array}$

2. $\begin{array}{r} 8 \\ +8 \\ \hline \end{array}$

3. $\begin{array}{r} 7 \\ +5 \\ \hline \end{array}$

4. $\begin{array}{r} 6 \\ -0 \\ \hline \end{array}$

5. $\begin{array}{r} 11 \\ -\ 4 \\ \hline \end{array}$

6. $\begin{array}{r} 3 \\ +8 \\ \hline \end{array}$

7. $\begin{array}{r} 15 \\ -\ 7 \\ \hline \end{array}$

8. $\begin{array}{r} 2 \\ +9 \\ \hline \end{array}$

9. $5 + 8 = \square$

10. $2 + 3 + 6 = \square$

Write the related facts for each.

11. 3, 7, 10

12. 4, 8, 12

Give the value of the digit 7.

13. 127,543

14. 1,781,002

15. 37,450,601

Write each number in standard form.

16. two million, one hundred forty thousand, fifteen

17. $700,000 + 4,000 + 60 + 2$

Compare. Use >, <, or = for ●.

18. 21,401 ● 21,399

19. 8,279 ● 8,379

Round each number to the underlined place.

20. 2̲5

21. 3̲,500

22. 2,8̲42

23. 27̲,418

Solve.

24. How many beach umbrellas and sailboats are there?

25. How many more surfboards than sailboats are there?

Janice caught 5 fish, Justin caught 3, and Sam caught 4. They gave away 7 fish. How many fish are left?

NAMES FOR NUMBERS

Make believe you live in a place where everything is small. In that place, there are only 4 names that can be used for numbers.

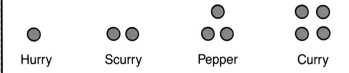

Hurry   Scurry   Pepper   Curry

When people see one object, they say *Hurry*. If there are four objects, they say *Curry*.

To name the number of eyes you have, you would say *Scurry*.

How would you name the number of fingers on one hand?

The only number words you can use are *Hurry, Scurry, Pepper,* and *Curry*. Here are some of the possible names.

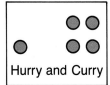

Hurry and Curry

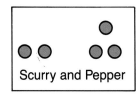

Scurry and Pepper

Hurry and Scurry and Scurry

1. Write other names for the number of fingers on one hand. What is the longest name you can give?

2. How would you name the number of days in one week?

3. Make up other questions about numbers. Have a friend name the number.

4. Make up your own names for numbers and teach them to a friend.

ROMAN NUMERALS

The Roman numeral system uses symbols to name numbers.

I	V	X	L
1	5	10	50

C	D	M
100	500	1,000

You show the numbers by adding and subtracting the symbols.

I   I   I
1 + 1 + 1 = 3

X   V   I   I
10 + 5 + 1 + 1 = 17

When I appears before V or X, subtract 1.
IV
5 − 1 = 4

When X appears before L or C, subtract 10.
XC
100 − 10 = 90

When C appears before D or M, subtract 100.
CD
500 − 100 = 400

I	II	III	IV	V	VI	VII	VIII	IX
1	2	3	4	5	6	7	8	9
X	XX	XXX	XL	L	LX	LXX	LXXX	XC
10	20	30	40	50	60	70	80	90
C	CC	CCC	CD	D	DC	DCC	DCCC	CM
100	200	300	400	500	600	700	800	900
M								
1,000								

Write the standard number for each.

1. LXIV

2. CCXXII

3. DCLVI

4. MMI

5. XLVII

6. LXXIX

7. CXCV

8. MDLII

Write the Roman numeral for each.

9. 28

10. 319

11. 1,986

12. 731

13. 54

14. 185

15. 427

16. 1,342

17. Write the year Columbus discovered America in Roman numerals.

18. Write the year you were born in Roman numerals.

INTRODUCING THE CALCULATOR

A calculator is a tool. A person can use a calculator to do mathematics calculations quickly and accurately.

When the calculator is on, numbers and commands are entered by pressing keys. This is **input.** The results are called **output.** The output is shown in a display.

When we press 9 $+$ 6 $=$, the display shows 15 . The output is 15.

When we press 1 7 $-$ 8 $=$, the display shows 9 .

To clear away all entries, press C . To clear away the last number entered, press CE .

Tell what the output will be.

1. $14 - 7 =$ 2. $6 + 8 =$ 3. $9 + 7 =$

4. $5 + 2 + 8 =$ 5. $19 - 2 =$ 6. $6 + 3 + 5 =$

WITH A CALCULATOR

1. Try exercises **1–6** with a calculator.

2. How does each output compare with your answer?

★ 3. On Your Own: Press 7 $+$ 8 C $=$

Press 7 $+$ 8 CE 6 $=$

Press 2 $+$ 4 $+$ 3 $+$ 8 CE 1 $=$

INTRODUCING THE COMPUTER

A person can use a computer to solve many different kinds of problems. A computer can do mathematics computations over and over with great speed and accuracy.

Monitor

Screen

CPU

Keyboard

To use a computer we need:

● an **input** device, usually a keyboard

● a **central processing unit (CPU),** which works with the information

● an **output** device, usually a monitor

Input   To subtract 15 − 8, we type the command PRINT 15 − 8.

Process   When we press RETURN or ENTER , the CPU computes the answer.

Output   Then the answer is displayed on the screen.

PRINT 15 - 8
7

PRINT 6 + 7
13

If we type PRINT 6 + 7, and press RETURN or ENTER , the output is 13.

Tell what the output will be.

1. PRINT 16 - 7   2. PRINT 8 + 5   3. PRINT 6 + 3 + 7

4. PRINT 10 + 3   5. PRINT 14 - 8   6. PRINT 8 + 2 + 1 + 5

AT THE COMPUTER

1. Input the commands in 1-6 on a computer.

2. How does each output compare with your answer?

★3. On Your Own: Use PRINT commands to give other output. Try adding and subtracting long lists of numbers.

Choose the correct answer. Write A, B, C, or D.

1. $9 + 2 = \square$

   A 7   C 13

   B 11   D not given

2. $8 + 5 = \square$

   A 13   C 3

   B 11   D not given

3. $5 + \square = 5$

   A 1   C 3

   B 0   D not given

4. $6 + 8 + 3 = \square$

   A 12   C 13

   B 10   D not given

5. $15 - 7 = \square$

   A 8   C 7

   B 22   D not given

6. What fact is related to $7 + 8 = 15$?

   A $15 + 8 = 23$ C $8 + 7 = 15$

   B $7 + 15 = 22$ D not given

7. What fact is related to $5 + 4 = 9$?

   A $9 - 4 = 5$ C $4 + 9 = 13$

   B 549   D not given

8. What is the value of 5 in 4,592?

   A 5,000   C 50

   B 500   D not given

9. What is the value of 7 in 57,943?

   A 70,000   C 700

   B 7,000   D not given

10. Compare. 583 ● 843

    A >   C =

    B <   D not given

11. Compare. 4,386 ● 4,387

    A >   C =

    B <   D not given

12. Round 393 to the nearest hundred.

    A 400   C 390

    B 395   D not given

Use the picture for 13 and 14.

13. How many fish are there?

    A 2   C 4

    B 6   D not given

14. How many more fish are there than birds?

    A 2   C 4

    B 6   D not given

Adding and Subtracting Whole Numbers

Exploring Patterns

The shaded squares in a crossword puzzle display patterns.

- Describe some patterns that you notice in this crossword puzzle.
- Discuss other everyday situations where you see patterns in a grid.

C	A	B	S		S	T	Y		A	B	E	T
A	L	O	T		T	O	E		C	O	R	E
R	E	A	R		A	D	A		I	D	L	E
S	C	R	E	E	N		R	E	D	Y	E	D
			A	N	D		V	I	C			
S	I	C	K		F	O	R	E	C	A	S	T
E	T	A			O	R	E			S	E	A
C	A	S	T	I	R	O	N		S	T	E	P
		T	O	R			D	O	T			
P	L	A	T	E	S		E	N	A	M	E	L
I	O	N	A		T	A	R		V	I	V	A
N	O	E	L		I	C	E		E	D	E	N
A	N	T	S		R	E	D		S	I	N	E

WORKING TOGETHER

Work with a partner.

1. Use different strategies to find the number of blue squares in each design without counting all of them. Record your work in an organized way.

2. Explore and record different ways to find the number of white squares in each design.

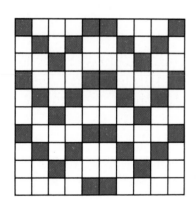

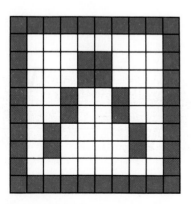

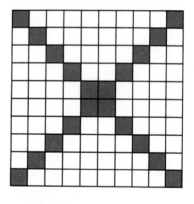

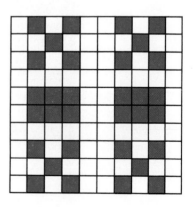

1. Share the records you made. Compare the different methods students used to find the number of blue squares in each drawing.

   - How are they the same?

   - How are they different?

   - Are some methods more efficient than others? Give examples and explain why.

   - Choose a strategy that someone used to find the number of blue squares in one of the designs. Would this strategy be efficient for the other designs? Why or why not?

2. Discuss some different strategies that you used to find the number of white squares in one of the designs.

THINKING IT THROUGH

1. Cut out a 10 × 10 section of grid paper. Make patterns by shading some of the squares. Ask others to explain their methods for finding the number of shaded squares in your drawing.

2. Discuss how patterns make it easier to find the number of squares without counting all the squares.

Adding Two-Digit Numbers

In the 1800s the Sioux Indians made tepees from buffalo hides. One family had 27 hides. Then they got 19 more. How many hides did they have in all?

Add to find how many in all.

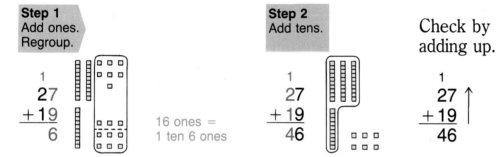

Step 1
Add ones.
Regroup.

$$\begin{array}{r} 1 \\ 27 \\ +19 \\ \hline 6 \end{array}$$

16 ones =
1 ten 6 ones

Step 2
Add tens.

$$\begin{array}{r} 1 \\ 27 \\ +19 \\ \hline 46 \end{array}$$

Check by adding up.

$$\begin{array}{r} 1 \\ 27 \\ +19 \\ \hline 46 \end{array}$$

They had 46 hides.

Sometimes you must regroup ones and tens.

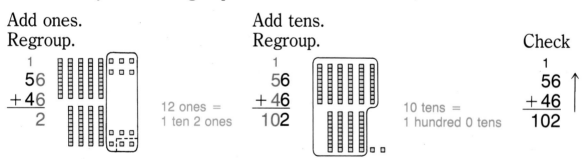

Add ones.
Regroup.

$$\begin{array}{r} 1 \\ 56 \\ +46 \\ \hline 2 \end{array}$$

12 ones =
1 ten 2 ones

Add tens.
Regroup.

$$\begin{array}{r} 1 \\ 56 \\ +46 \\ \hline 102 \end{array}$$

10 tens =
1 hundred 0 tens

Check

$$\begin{array}{r} 1 \\ 56 \\ +46 \\ \hline 102 \end{array}$$

CLASSWORK

Add. Check by adding up.

1. $\begin{array}{r} 53 \\ +24 \end{array}$
2. $\begin{array}{r} 7 \\ +21 \end{array}$
3. $\begin{array}{r} 58 \\ +27 \end{array}$
4. $\begin{array}{r} 77 \\ +47 \end{array}$
5. $\begin{array}{r} 98 \\ +12 \end{array}$
6. $\begin{array}{r} 94 \\ +59 \end{array}$

7. $27 + 6 = \square$ 8. $7 + 96 = \square$ 9. $35 + 21 = \square$ 10. $99 + 26 = \square$

Add. Check by adding up.

1. $\begin{array}{r}31\\+60\end{array}$	2. $\begin{array}{r}32\\+33\end{array}$	3. $\begin{array}{r}24\\+56\end{array}$	4. $\begin{array}{r}8\\+44\end{array}$	5. $\begin{array}{r}63\\+17\end{array}$	6. $\begin{array}{r}29\\+18\end{array}$
7. $\begin{array}{r}51\\+52\end{array}$	8. $\begin{array}{r}73\\+78\end{array}$	9. $\begin{array}{r}79\\+53\end{array}$	10. $\begin{array}{r}67\\+11\end{array}$	11. $\begin{array}{r}96\\+88\end{array}$	12. $\begin{array}{r}48\\+70\end{array}$
13. $\begin{array}{r}38\\+68\end{array}$	14. $\begin{array}{r}19\\+87\end{array}$	15. $\begin{array}{r}92\\+\ 9\end{array}$	16. $\begin{array}{r}46\\+73\end{array}$	17. $\begin{array}{r}68\\+49\end{array}$	18. $\begin{array}{r}39\\+84\end{array}$
19. $\begin{array}{r}34\\+\ 8\end{array}$	20. $\begin{array}{r}75\\+86\end{array}$	21. $\begin{array}{r}89\\+59\end{array}$	22. $\begin{array}{r}5\\+95\end{array}$	23. $\begin{array}{r}43\\+43\end{array}$	24. $\begin{array}{r}69\\+85\end{array}$

25. $5 + 69 = \square$ 26. $42 + 65 = \square$ 27. $93 + 9 = \square$ 28. $18 + 36 = \square$

29. $4 + 47 = \square$ 30. $64 + 71 = \square$ 31. $57 + 4 = \square$ 32. $62 + 48 = \square$

Find each missing digit.

★33. $\begin{array}{r}3\blacksquare\\+\blacksquare5\\\hline 78\end{array}$	★34. $\begin{array}{r}\blacksquare6\\+3\blacksquare\\\hline 83\end{array}$	★35. $\begin{array}{r}\blacksquare5\\+7\blacksquare\\\hline 113\end{array}$	★36. $\begin{array}{r}9\blacksquare\\+\blacksquare6\\\hline 149\end{array}$	★37. $\begin{array}{r}9\blacksquare\\+\blacksquare9\\\hline 198\end{array}$

APPLICATION

38. A Sioux stretched a buffalo hide on the ground to dry. She pounded 18 sticks along the edge of the hide. There were 16 more sticks to use. How many sticks did she use in all?

★40. Quickfoot and 2 neighbors made new tepees. Quickfoot's tepee needed 18 hides. Each neighbor's tepee needed 12 hides. How many hides were needed for the 3 tepees?

39. One Sioux girl found 86 sticks to use for drying hides. Another girl found 45 sticks. How many sticks did they find in all?

Adding Three or More Numbers

In the "Little House" books, Laura Ingalls Wilder tells how her family traveled by covered wagon. How many miles did they travel in the three days?

Day	Miles
July 19, 1884	12
July 20, 1884	9
July 21, 1884	13

Add to find how many miles they traveled.

Step 1
Add ones.
Regroup.

Step 2
Add tens.

Check

```
  1          1          1
 12         12         12 ↑
  9          9          9  |
+13        +13        +13  |
  4         34         34
```

They traveled 34 miles in three days.

Find 35 + 89 + 26 + 7.
Line up ones and tens.

Add ones.
Regroup.

Add tens.
Regroup.

Check

```
  2          2          2
 35         35         35 ↑
 89         89         89  |
 26         26         26  |
+ 7        + 7        + 7  |
  7        157        157
```

CLASSWORK

Add. Check by adding up.

1.	2.	3.	4.	5.	6.
30	51	46	32	47	6
16	9	53	18	9	15
+22	+27	+19	60	16	8
			+24	+71	+24

7. 4 + 23 + 41 = ☐

8. 8 + 25 + 34 + 9 = ☐

46

Add. Check by adding up.

1.	54 22 +13	2.	13 24 +40	3.	61 23 +14	4.	47 16 +29	5.	9 28 +38	6.	19 66 + 8
7.	34 51 +23	8.	75 30 +62	9.	67 42 + 9	10.	56 87 +31	11.	77 38 25 +18	12.	18 26 41 +93
13.	30 47 9 +26	14.	7 21 36 + 8	15.	76 31 27 +92	16.	43 9 98 +60	17.	62 21 37 9 +52	18.	75 34 36 28 +52

19. $36 + 51 + 8 = \square$

20. $6 + 15 + 43 = \square$

21. $48 + 67 + 5 + 56 = \square$

22. $9 + 27 + 90 + 8 = \square$

★ **23.** Write 1, 3, 5, 7, 9, 11, 13, 15, or 17 in each circle so that the sum on each side is 30. Use each number only once.

APPLICATION

24. Manly made 3 payments to buy a plow. The first payment was $27. The second was $13 and the last was $15. How much did the plow cost?

★ **25.** Laura and Manly took an afternoon buggy ride. They rode 12 miles to Lake Thompson. Then they rode to Spirit Lake 15 miles away. If they followed the same route home, how far did they ride?

Adding Three-Digit Numbers

Naturalists have found 435 kinds of cactus in Mexico. In Arizona they identified 289 other kinds. How many kinds of cactus did they find in all?

Add to find how many kinds of cactus in all.

Step 1
Add ones.
Regroup.

$$\begin{array}{r} 1 \\ 435 \\ +289 \\ \hline 4 \end{array}$$ 14 ones = 1 ten 4 ones

Step 2
Add tens.
Regroup.

$$\begin{array}{r} 11 \\ 435 \\ +289 \\ \hline 24 \end{array}$$ 12 tens = 1 hundred 2 tens

Step 3
Add hundreds.

$$\begin{array}{r} 11 \\ 435 \\ +289 \\ \hline 724 \end{array}$$

They found 724 kinds of cactus in all.

Another Example

Add ones.
Regroup.

$$\begin{array}{r} 1 \\ 976 \\ +548 \\ \hline 4 \end{array}$$

Add tens.
Regroup.

$$\begin{array}{r} 11 \\ 976 \\ +548 \\ \hline 24 \end{array}$$

Add hundreds.
Regroup.

$$\begin{array}{r} 11 \\ 976 \\ +548 \\ \hline 1,524 \end{array}$$ 15 hundreds = 1 thousand 5 hundreds

CLASSWORK

Add and check.

1. $\begin{array}{r} 426 \\ + 54 \\ \hline \end{array}$

2. $\begin{array}{r} 357 \\ +459 \\ \hline \end{array}$

3. $\begin{array}{r} 787 \\ +661 \\ \hline \end{array}$

4. $\begin{array}{r} 638 \\ +894 \\ \hline \end{array}$

5. $\begin{array}{r} \$7.96 \\ + 8.59 \\ \hline \end{array}$

6. $251 + 69 = \square$

7. $\$588 + \$428 = \square$

8. $789 + 99 = \square$

48

Add and check.

1. 86
   + 305

2. 235
   + 473

3. 394
   + 529

4. $9.74
   + 7.33

5. 115
   + 9

6. 272
   + 569

7. 523
   + 79

8. 456
   + 757

9. $3.14
   + .96

10. 539
    + 784

11. 689
    + 558

12. 864
    + 338

13. 797
    + 537

14. $5.82
    + 4.78

15. $9.97
    + 8.98

16. 339
    97
    + 553

17. $498
    648
    + 536

18. $6.79
    7.68
    + .65

19. 938
    9
    + 82

20. 736
    492
    + 988

21. $142 + $159 = □

22. 754 + 58 = □

23. 999 + 1 = □

24. 57 + 765 = □

25. 8 + 996 = □

26. $2.15 + $.98 = □

27. 63 + 259 = □

28. 5 + 807 = □

29. $.67 + $5.84 = □

★ 30. Each letter names a digit. The same letter always names the same digit. Find as many different answers as you can.

ONE
+ ONE
I WON

APPLICATION

CALCULATOR

Add these pairs of three-digit numbers.

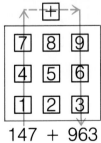

147 + 963

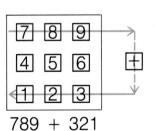

789 + 321

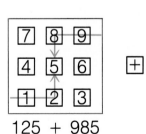

125 + 985

Do you get the same sum each time?
What sum do you get? Find 5 more pairs
of three-digit numbers that have this sum.

Estimating Sums

The newspaper headline has used an estimate. It is based on actual numbers that have been rounded.

▶To estimate a sum, round the greatest number to its greatest place. Round each number to that place. Then add.

411 is the greater number.
The greatest place is hundreds.

Round to the nearest hundred.

178	rounds to	200
+411	rounds to	+400
		600 estimated sum

600 BURROS ADOPTED
Grand Canyon National Park reported that 178 wild burros were flown out of the canyon in the spring and 411 in the fall. Individuals and families across the country adopted the burros.

About 600 burros were adopted.

More Examples

a. Estimate 67 + 43.

67 is the greater number.
Round to the nearest ten.

67	rounds to	70
+43	rounds to	+40
		110

b. Estimate $235 + $82.

235 is the greater number.
Round to the nearest hundred dollars.

$235	rounds to	$200
+ 82	rounds to	+100
		$300

CLASSWORK

Estimate each sum.

1. 47
   +24

2. 68
   +35

3. 428
   +372

4. $561
   + 783

5. $468
   + 73

6. 81 + 7 = ☐

7. $112 + $155 = ☐

8. 61 + 853 = ☐

50

Estimate each sum.

1. 43
  +76

2. 81
  +67

3. 45
  +30

4. 52
  +84

5. $79
  + 25

6. 423
  +181

7. 360
  +318

8. 609
  +540

9. 394
  +462

10. $535
  + 951

11. 24
  + 8

12. 9
  +87

13. 316
  + 54

14. 73
  +208

15. $763
  + 91

16. $36 + $78 + $13 = ☐

17. 45 + 8 + 61 = ☐

18. 639 + 283 + 570 = ☐

19. 178 + 66 + 319 = ☐

★20. 81 + 7 + 52 + 9 = ☐

★21. 65 + 536 + 81 + 60 = ☐

Estimate each sum. Find the exact sum with a calculator. Then compare the sums.

22. 317 + 478 = ☐

23. 132 + 91 + 727 = ☐

24. 581 + 236 = ☐

25. 453 + 76 + 84 = ☐

APPLICATION

26. Roy and Kathleen adopted two burros. One burro weighs 484 pounds. The other burro weighs 512 pounds. About how much is the total weight of the burros?

★27. The animal fund used donations of $395 for each burro it handled. It cost the fund another $575 to handle each burro. Estimate the cost for handling each burro.

MENTAL ARITHMETIC

Here is an easy way to add numbers in your head.

23 + 59 = ☐ **Think** 23 + 60 = 83
Subtract 1 from 83 to get the answer.
83 − 1 = 82, so 23 + 59 = 82.

Find each sum.

1. 57 + 29 = ☐

2. 99 + 14 = ☐

3. 73 + 35 = ☐

4. 199 + 27 = ☐

5. 89 + 101 = ☐

6. 210 + 190 = ☐

Adding Greater Numbers

Jonathan's family followed a route along the Oregon Trail. How far did they travel from Independence to Oregon City?

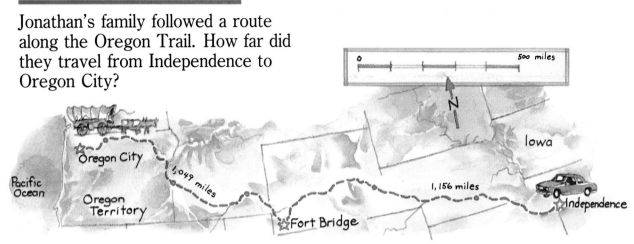

Add to find the total distance.

Step 1 Add ones. Regroup.	**Step 2** Add tens. Regroup.	**Step 3** Add hundreds.	**Step 4** Add thousands.

Step 1	Step 2	Step 3	Step 4
1	1 1	1 1	1 1
1,156	1,156	1,156	1,156
+1,049	+1,049	+1,049	+1,049
5	05	205	2,205

Jonathan's family traveled 2,205 miles.

Estimate to be sure the answer makes sense.

Round to the nearest thousand.

1,156	rounds to	1,000
+1,049	rounds to	+1,000
		2,000

The exact sum and estimate are close. The answer makes sense.

CLASSWORK

Add. Check by adding up.

1. 6,521
   +2,734

2. 5,478
   +1,379

3. $9,240
   +   875

4. 15,045
   +66,786

5. $189.46
   +   37.92

Add. Estimate to be sure each answer makes sense.

6. 1,987 + 2,495 = ☐

7. 35,408 + 7,821 = ☐

Add. Check by adding up.

1. 3,186
  +2,505

2. 4,361
  +1,724

3. $643.91
  +   56.37

4. 3,756
  +6,624

5. $785.64
  + 467.96

6. 9,625
  +2,688

7. 1,987
  59,988
  + 3,654

8. 46,755
  28,959
  +10,078

9. $778.16
  344.79
  + 22.53

10. 5,689 + 879 = ☐   11. 359 + 7,847 = ☐

12. $9,425 + $96 = ☐   13. 21,310 + 695 = ☐

Add. Estimate to be sure each answer makes sense.

14. 9,376
  +2,103

15. 35,831
  +63,131

16. 4,304
  + 967

Compare. Use >, <, or = for ●.

★ 17. 312 + 4,375 ● 3,946 + 872

★ 18. 9,290 + 45,125 ● 28,170 + 26,245

APPLICATION

19. In one year, 3,296 people traveled along the Oregon trail. Another year, 4,085 people followed it. How many people traveled this trail in two years?

★ 20. The O'Grady family spent $97.50 during the first week of their vacation. They spent $256.50 the second week. Estimate how much money they spent in all.

1. $7 + 6 + 0 = ☐$

2. $5 + 1 + 8 = ☐$

3. $13 - 6 = ☐$

4. $11 - 5 = ☐$

5. $19 - 0 = ☐$

6. $28 - 28 = ☐$

7. $8 + ☐ = 11$

8. $12 - ☐ = 6$

9. $☐ + 5 = 12$

10. $☐ - 8 = 6$

11. $☐ + 4 = 13$

12. $☐ - 9 = 7$

13. $8 + ☐ = 17$

14. $☐ - 3 = 8$

Compare. Use >, <, or = .

15. 17 ● 175

16. 46 ● 64

17. 650 ● 605

18. 5,001 ● 5,010

Problem Solving

WHICH OPERATION?

You must know which operation to use
to solve a problem.

Two rafts are on a trip going down the river.
There are 24 people in the first raft. There are
19 people in the second raft. How many people
are on the trip?

THINK   **What is the question?**

How many people are on the trip?

What are the facts?

First raft: 24 people
Second raft: 19 people

PLAN   **How can you find the answer?**

Decide which operation to use. There
are 2 groups of people. Join the groups
to find how many in all. Add to find
the answer.

$$24 + 19 = \square$$

SOLVE   **Carry out the plan. Do the work
and find the answer.**

$$
\begin{array}{r}
1 \\
24 \\
+19 \\
\hline
43
\end{array}
$$

There are 43 people on the trip.

**LOOK
BACK**   **Have you answered the question?
Is your arithmetic correct?
Does your answer make sense?**

Yes. 24 + 19 is about 20 + 20,
or 40. The answer makes sense.

Tell which operation you would use to answer each question. Then solve the problem.

1. In the raft, 4 people wore blue hats, 6 people wore white hats, and 5 people wore brown hats. How many people in all wore hats?

2. There are 11 rafts that need a safety check. Janet will check 5 of them, and Tim will check the rest. How many rafts will Tim check?

3. Gary gives out the life preservers. He gave 43 to adults and 62 to children. How many life preservers did he give out in all?

★ 4. There were 90 people waiting to take the raft ride. By noon 60 people had taken the ride. How many were still waiting?

In these problems, ▲, ■, and ● take the place of numbers. Write a number sentence for each. The first one is done for you.

5. Lucy had ■ postcards. She bought ▲ more. How many postcards does she have now?
Answer: ■ + ▲ = ☐

6. There were ● mugs and ▲ key rings in the souvenir shop. How many more mugs than key rings were there?

7. Marva's job is to sell tickets for the raft ride. She started the day with ■ tickets. She sold ▲ tickets. How many tickets were left?

8. Sheila takes pictures of the riders. She took ▲ pictures on Monday, ■ on Tuesday, and ● on Wednesday. How many pictures did she take in all?

═══ CREATE YOUR OWN PROBLEM ═══

One raft had 18 adults and 6 children in it. There were 7 adults and no children in the second raft. Make up an addition problem and a subtraction problem using this information.

Subtracting

Paul raises sheep in South Dakota. He sheared 23 pounds of wool from his ram and 12 from his ewe. How many more pounds did he get from the ram?

Subtract to find how many more.

Step 1
Subtract ones.

```
  23
- 12
───
   1
```

Step 2
Subtract tens.

```
  23
- 12
───
  11
```

Check by adding.

```
  11
+ 12
───
  23
```

Paul got 11 more pounds of wool from the ram.

Subtract money the same way you subtract other numbers.

Find $4.97 − $1.73.

```
  $4.97
−  1.73
```
Line up the decimal points.

```
  $4.97
−  1.73
──────
  $3.24
```
Write the dollar sign and decimal point in the answer.

CLASSWORK

Subtract. Check by adding.

1.
```
  54
− 23
```

2.
```
  286
− 172
```

3.
```
  $6.45
−  5.03
```

4.
```
  7,984
− 6,422
```

5.
```
  9,679
− 8,617
```

6. 587 − 62 = ☐

7. 4,765 − 531 = ☐

8. 648 − 227 = ☐

9. $.95 − $.53 = ☐

10. $6.25 − $.15 = ☐

11. $19.54 − $8.31 = ☐

Subtract. Check by adding.

1. $\begin{array}{r} 46 \\ -12 \end{array}$	2. $\begin{array}{r} 38 \\ -11 \end{array}$	3. $\begin{array}{r} 53 \\ -23 \end{array}$	4. $\begin{array}{r} 79 \\ -33 \end{array}$	5. $\begin{array}{r} 97 \\ -\ \ 4 \end{array}$
6. $\begin{array}{r} 632 \\ -102 \end{array}$	7. $\begin{array}{r} \$8.26 \\ -\ 4.06 \end{array}$	8. $\begin{array}{r} 917 \\ -\ 11 \end{array}$	9. $\begin{array}{r} \$7.48 \\ -\ 7.45 \end{array}$	10. $\begin{array}{r} 975 \\ -\ \ 4 \end{array}$
11. $\begin{array}{r} 3,796 \\ -2,560 \end{array}$	12. $\begin{array}{r} 7,598 \\ -2,328 \end{array}$	13. $\begin{array}{r} \$96.87 \\ -\ \ 4.37 \end{array}$	14. $\begin{array}{r} 8,793 \\ -6,051 \end{array}$	15. $\begin{array}{r} 5,498 \\ -\ \ 15 \end{array}$
16. $\begin{array}{r} 8,594 \\ -4,470 \end{array}$	17. $\begin{array}{r} 9,767 \\ -9,644 \end{array}$	18. $\begin{array}{r} 8,799 \\ -8,526 \end{array}$	19. $\begin{array}{r} 9,687 \\ -\ \ 356 \end{array}$	20. $\begin{array}{r} 7,969 \\ -2,569 \end{array}$

21. $96 - 5 = \square$ 22. $485 - 35 = \square$ 23. $5,287 - 103 = \square$

24. $\$.84 - \$.21 = \square$ 25. $\$6.64 - \$.52 = \square$ 26. $\$18.39 - \$4.08 = \square$

Write the next two numbers in each.

★27. 85, 74, 63, $\square$, $\square$

★28. 136, 106, 76, $\square$, $\square$

APPLICATION

29. The rancher moved a herd of 855 sheep to new pastures. The sheepdog rounded up the sheep that wandered away. There were 820 sheep still in the herd. How many sheep had wandered away?

★30. Randy spins and dyes the wool that is sheared. She has 16 bundles of dyed wool and 32 bundles of undyed wool. She used 12 bundles to make a sweater. How much is left?

LOGICAL THINKING

1. When you subtract me from 87, you get 23. What number am I?

2. When you add me to 36, you get 79. What number am I?

3. When you subtract me from 44, you get me. What number am I?

Subtracting with Regrouping

Until 1957, buildings over 15 stories could not be built in Los Angeles, California. The 32-story city-hall building was allowed to go over the limit. How many stories higher than the limit was the city hall?

32 − 15 = ☐

Step 1
Not enough ones.
Regroup 1 ten.

$$\begin{array}{r} {\scriptstyle 2\,12} \\ \cancel{3}\,\cancel{2} \\ -1\,5 \\ \hline \end{array}$$

3 tens 2 ones = 2 tens 12 ones

Step 2
Subtract ones.

$$\begin{array}{r} {\scriptstyle 2\,12} \\ \cancel{3}\,\cancel{2} \\ -1\,5 \\ \hline 7 \end{array}$$

Step 3
Subtract tens.

$$\begin{array}{r} {\scriptstyle 2\,12} \\ \cancel{3}\,\cancel{2} \\ -1\,5 \\ \hline 1\,7 \end{array}$$

The city hall was 17 stories higher than the limit.

Find 50 − 36.

Not enough ones.
Regroup 1 ten.

$$\begin{array}{r} {\scriptstyle 4\,10} \\ \cancel{5}\,\cancel{0} \\ -3\,6 \\ \hline \end{array}$$

Subtract ones.

$$\begin{array}{r} {\scriptstyle 4\,10} \\ \cancel{5}\,\cancel{0} \\ -3\,6 \\ \hline 4 \end{array}$$

Subtract tens.

$$\begin{array}{r} {\scriptstyle 4\,10} \\ \cancel{5}\,\cancel{0} \\ -3\,6 \\ \hline 1\,4 \end{array}$$

Check

$$\begin{array}{r} {\scriptstyle 1} \\ 1\,4 \\ +3\,6 \\ \hline 5\,0 \end{array}$$

CLASSWORK

Subtract. Check by adding.

1. $\begin{array}{r} 34 \\ -15 \\ \hline \end{array}$
2. $\begin{array}{r} 53 \\ -27 \\ \hline \end{array}$
3. $\begin{array}{r} 60 \\ -36 \\ \hline \end{array}$
4. $\begin{array}{r} 40 \\ -\ 9 \\ \hline \end{array}$
5. $\begin{array}{r} 96 \\ -39 \\ \hline \end{array}$
6. $\begin{array}{r} 86 \\ -\ 8 \\ \hline \end{array}$

7. 26 − 7 = ☐   8. 54 − 47 = ☐   9. 61 − 8 = ☐

58

Subtract. Check by adding.

1. 30 −12	2. 43 −18	3. 51 −22	4. 37 − 9	5. 61 −24	6. 52 −26
7. 61 −26	8. 50 −11	9. 33 −17	10. 80 − 3	11. 65 −37	12. 81 −27
13. 72 −33	14. 64 − 6	15. 83 −44	16. 70 −28	17. 75 −68	18. 92 −39
19. 70 −57	20. 85 −29	21. 92 −17	22. 91 −89	23. 66 −48	24. 52 −44

25. 83 − 59 = ☐   26. 76 − 9 = ☐   27. 42 − 8 = ☐

28. 71 − 5 = ☐   29. 88 − 79 = ☐   30. 30 − 7 = ☐

Follow the rule to find each missing number.

Rule: Subtract 9.

	Input	Output
	25	16
31.	39	
32.	43	
33.	50	
34.	67	

Rule: Subtract 25.

	Input	Output
	52	27
35.	57	
36.	84	
37.	78	
38.	63	

Rule: Subtract 15.

	Input	Output
★ 39.		25
★ 40.		17
★ 41.		3
★ 42.		18
★ 43.		47

APPLICATION

44. The First Interstate Bank building in Los Angeles has 62 floors. Dan's office is on the 45th floor. How many floors below the top floor is his office?

★ 45. Karen's office is on the 53rd floor. She takes the express elevator to the 40th floor. Then the elevator stops on the next 5 floors. How many more floors to Karen's office?

Subtracting Three-Digit Numbers

Sue looked up the climate of Arizona. How many more clear days than rainy days did Tucson have in this year?

	Number of Days	
	Clear	Rainy
Flagstaff	154	96
Phoenix	226	38
Tucson	214	53
Yuma	212	15

Step 1
Subtract ones.

```
  2 1 4
-   5 3
      1
```

Step 2
Not enough tens.
Regroup 1 hundred.

```
    1 11
  2 1̶ 4
-   5 3      2 hundreds 1 ten =
      1      1 hundred 11 tens
```

Step 3
Subtract tens.

```
    1 11
  2 1̶ 4
-   5 3
    6 1
```

Step 4
Subtract hundreds.

```
    1 11
  2 1̶ 4
-   5 3
  1 6 1
```

There were 161 more clear days than rainy days in Tucson.

Find 573 − 186.

Not enough ones.
Regroup 1 ten.
Subtract ones.

```
   6 13
  5 7̶ 3̶      7 tens 3 ones =
- 1 8 6      6 tens 13 ones
        7
```

Not enough tens.
Regroup 1 hundred.

```
     16
   4 6̶ 13
  5̶ 7̶ 3̶      5 hundreds 6 tens =
- 1 8 6      4 hundreds 16 tens
        7
```

Subtract tens.

```
     16
   4 6̶ 13
  5̶ 7̶ 3̶
- 1 8 6
      8 7
```

Subtract hundreds.

```
     16
   4 6̶ 13
  5̶ 7̶ 3̶
- 1 8 6
    3 8 7
```

CLASSWORK

Subtract. Check by adding.

1. 783
    −267

2. 649
    −192

3. 846
    − 59

4. $7.12
    − 5.94

5. 816
    −527

6. 538 − 71 = □   7. $3.53 − $3.49 = □   8. 913 − 76 = □

Subtract. Check by adding.

1. 518
   −276

2. 747
   −359

3. $483
   − 169

4. 774
   −256

5. 435
   − 83

6. 845
   −127

7. 850
   −243

8. 981
   − 48

9. $817
   − 293

10. $3.28
    − 1.36

11. 719
    −468

12. 745
    −159

13. $2.31
    − 1.64

14. 748
    − 49

15. 620
    −597

16. 826 − 85 = ☐

17. 810 − 6 = ☐

18. 535 − 28 = ☐

19. 444 − 8 = ☐

20. 958 − 79 = ☐

21. $467 − $398 = ☐

Choose the correct number sentence and solve.

22. There are 365 days in one year. Phoenix had 226 clear days one year. How many days were not clear?

    a. 356 + 226 = ☐   b. 365 − 139 = ☐

    c. 365 − 226 = ☐   d. 36 + 26 = ☐

Find each missing digit.

★23. 4▮6
     −38▮
      92

★24. ▮25
     −6▮7
      208

★25. 3▮6
     − 8▮
     ▮61

★26. 9▮2
     −▮5▮
      78

★27. ▮5▮
     −3▮7
      253

Use the table at the top of page 60.
Tell which operation you would use to solve
each problem. Then solve.

28. How many more clear days did Tucson have than Flagstaff?

29. How many fewer rainy days than clear days did Yuma have?

30. How many days were clear or rainy in Flagstaff that year?

★31. How many days that year were not clear or rainy in Tucson?

Subtracting Across Zeros

The director hired 205 people for the western movie. Then 87 of them took other jobs. How many people were left?

Subtract to find how many were left.

Step 1
Not enough ones.
There are no tens.
Regroup 1 hundred.

```
  1 10
  2 Ø 5
 -  8 7
```

Step 2
Regroup 1 ten.
Subtract ones.

```
      9
  1 1Ø 15
  2 Ø 5
 -  8 7
      8
```

Step 3
Subtract tens.

```
      9
  1 1Ø 15
  2 Ø 5
 -  8 7
    1 8
```

Step 4
Subtract hundreds.

```
      9
  1 1Ø 15
  2 Ø 5
 -  8 7
  1 1 8
```

There were 118 people left.

Find 400 − 115.

Not enough ones.
There are no tens.
Regroup 1 hundred.

```
  3 10
  4 Ø 0
 -1 1 5
```

Regroup 1 ten.
Subtract ones.

```
      9
  3 1Ø 10
  4 Ø Ø
 -1 1 5
      5
```

Subtract tens.

```
      9
  3 1Ø 10
  4 Ø Ø
 -1 1 5
    8 5
```

Subtract hundreds.

```
      9
  3 1Ø 10
  4 Ø Ø
 -1 1 5
  2 8 5
```

CLASSWORK

Subtract and check.

1.
```
  304
 -174
```

2.
```
  405
 -367
```

3.
```
  $4.00
 - 1.68
```

4.
```
  $7.06
 - 5.08
```

5.
```
  800
 - 82
```

6. 203 − 59 = ☐

7. 600 − 587 = ☐

8. 700 − 8 = ☐

Subtract and check.

1. 205
  −138
	2. 501
	  −347
		3. 700
		  −351
			4. $400
			  − 86
				5. 605
				  −527

6. 407
  −264
	7. 500
	  −360
		8. $8.01
		  − 7.93
			9. 100
			  − 87
				10. 706
				  −457

11. 804
  − 97
	12. 900
	  −183
		13. 502
		  −308
			14. $2.00
			  − 1.27
				15. 602
				  −409

16. $600 - 29 = \square$

17. $409 - 36 = \square$

18. $700 - 99 = \square$

19. $\$3.06 - \$1.49 = \square$

20. $500 - 7 = \square$

21. $900 - 91 = \square$

Find each missing number.

★ 22. $600 - \square = 215$

★ 23. $\square - 419 = 67$

★ 24. $803 - \square = 246$

APPLICATION

25. There were 800 feet of film on the roll for a western movie. Then 267 feet were shot on the trail. How many feet of film were left on the roll?

★ 26. In one scene, the trail boss and 23 cowboys rounded up 100 head of cattle. How many more cattle than people were in the scene?

=== LOGICAL THINKING ===

This is a magic square. The sum along each row, column, and diagonal is the same. Fill in the missing numbers to complete this magic square.

		206
	200	
194		182

Estimating Differences

One Saturday morning 218 people visited the National Cowboy Hall of Fame. That afternoon 493 people came. About how many more people visited in the afternoon?

When you do not need an exact answer, you can estimate.

▶ To estimate a difference, round the greater number to its greatest place.

Round each number to that place. Then subtract.

493 is the greater number. The greatest place is hundreds.

Round to the nearest hundred.

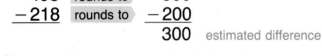

493	rounds to	500
− 218	rounds to	− 200
		300 estimated difference

About 300 more people visited in the afternoon.

More Examples

a. Estimate 72 − 29.

72 is the greater number.
Round to the nearest ten.

72	rounds to	70
− 29	rounds to	− 30
		40

b. Estimate $613 − $87.

613 is the greater number.
Round to the nearest hundred dollars.

$613	rounds to	$600
− 87	rounds to	− 100
		$500

CLASSWORK

Estimate each difference.

1. 72
   − 39

2. 58
   − 42

3. 603
   − 125

4. 598
   − 287

5. $208
   − 90

6. 57 − 8 = □

7. 264 − 200 = □

8. $735 − $89 = □

Estimate each difference.

1. 51 − 28	2. 66 − 17	3. 82 − 50	4. 91 − 32	5. 76 − 9
6. 309 − 127	7. 461 − 182	8. 518 − 367	9. 276 − 104	10. $893 − 456
11. 42 − 27	12. 947 − 200	13. 673 − 497	14. 32 − 7	15. $162 − 74
16. 926 − 89	17. 244 − 63	18. 536 − 72	19. 318 − 52	20. $829 − 76

21. 83 − 19 = ☐

22. $808 − $334 = ☐

23. 67 − 9 = ☐

24. 432 − 173 = ☐

★25. 956 − 94 = ☐

★26. 961 − 53 = ☐

Estimate each difference. Find the exact difference with a calculator. Then compare the differences.

27. 726 − 199 = ☐

28. 561 − 354 = ☐

29. 215 − 86 = ☐

30. 482 − 75 = ☐

★31. 954 − 276 = ☐

★32. 983 − 97 = ☐

APPLICATION

33. Patrick's family traveled 382 miles to visit the National Cowboy Hall of Fame. Gregory's family traveled 815 miles. About how much farther did Gregory's family travel?

★34. Patrick bought a poster for $4.65 and a cowboy hat for $8.29. About how much change would Patrick get from $20?

Subtracting Greater Numbers

The crew is drilling for oil. They have already gone 3,589 feet. Study the diagram to see where the oil is. How much farther will they have to drill to strike oil?

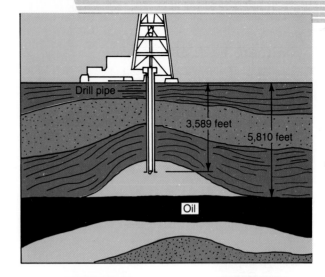

Drill pipe

3,589 feet

5,810 feet

Oil

Subtract the number of feet they have already drilled from the number of feet to the oil.

Step 1 Not enough ones. Regroup. Subtract ones.	Step 2 Not enough tens. Regroup. Subtract tens.	Step 3 Subtract hundreds.	Step 4 Subtract thousands.

Step 1
```
    0 10
  5,8 7̶ 0̶
 -3,5 8 9
        1
```

Step 2
```
        10
    7̶ 0̶ 10
  5,8 7̶ 0̶
 -3,5 8 9
      2 1
```

Step 3
```
        10
    7̶ 0̶ 10
  5,8 7̶ 0̶
 -3,5 8 9
    2 2 1
```

Step 4
```
        10
    7̶ 0̶ 10
  5,8 7̶ 0̶
  3,5 8 9
  2,2 2 1
```

They must drill 2,221 feet farther to reach oil.

Estimate to be sure the answer makes sense.

Round to the nearest thousand.

```
  5,810   rounds to    6,000
 -3,589   rounds to   -4,000
                       2,000
```
The exact difference and estimate are close. The answer makes sense.

CLASSWORK

Subtract. Check by adding.

1.
```
  3,446
 -1,072
```

2.
```
  4,685
 -2,737
```

3.
```
  6,707
 -  948
```

4.
```
  $372.43
 - 158.79
```

5.
```
  58,005
 -39,243
```

Subtract. Estimate to be sure each answer makes sense.

6. 6,082 − 1,875 = ☐

7. 22,104 − 17,518 = ☐

Subtract. Check by adding.

1. 6,731
   − 1,470

2. 7,488
   − 2,752

3. 2,567
   − 1,038

4. 4,026
   − 1,118

5. $86.17
   − 18.58

6. 13,419
   − 12,130

7. 34,056
   − 11,242

8. $312.41
   − 80.29

9. $357.28
   − 238.09

10. 64,824
    − 43,375

11. 8,752 − 193 = ☐   12. 6,972 − 89 = ☐   13. 58,174 − 9,236 = ☐

★14. 103,278 − 66,154 = ☐   ★15. 275,044 − 138,720 = ☐

Subtract. Estimate to be sure each answer makes sense.

16. 8,750
    − 3,568

17. 7,443
    − 2,651

18. 3,077
    − 558

19. $28,135
    − 16,409

20. 39,060
    − 8,271

APPLICATION

21. An oil well can pump 21,380 barrels of oil weekly in good weather. In bad weather, production falls to 3,750 barrels weekly. How much more oil is produced weekly in good weather than in bad?

★22. A floating oil derrick drilled 790 feet the first month. The next month it drilled 1,083 feet. How much farther will it have to drill to reach 3,800 feet?

CALCULATOR

Pick a 4-digit number that does not have the same digit in every place.   4,297

Scramble the digits.   9,247

Subtract the smaller number from the larger.

9,247 − 4,297 = 4,950

Add the digits of your answer.   4 + 9 + 5 + 0 = 18

If you get a 2-digit number, add those digits.   1 + 8 = 9

The sum will always be 9.

Make up some numbers of your own and try it.

Problem Solving

SKILLS AND STRATEGIES REVIEW Rodeo

"Smiley" Gabe won three events at the rodeo. He won $75 in the wagon race, $50 in the barrel jumping contest, and $50 in the lasso contest.

Tell which operation you would use to find each answer.
Then solve the problem.

1. How much money did Smiley win at the rodeo?

2. How much more did Smiley win for the wagon race than for the lasso contest?

3. Smiley finished the wagon race in 87 seconds. Cal finished in 93 seconds. How many more seconds did Cal take to finish the race?

4. The souvenir shop at the rodeo sold a total of 248 bandanas. This was 89 more than they sold last year. How many bandanas did they sell last year?

5. There were 37 men, 18 women, and 12 children entered in the events at the rodeo. How many people were entered in all?

6. The shop clerk counted 275 cowboy posters and 137 horse posters. How many posters were there altogether?

7. Rachel spent $4.50 for a ticket to the rodeo. Then she bought a poster for $5.89. How much did Rachel spend in all?

8. An active horse eats about 92 pounds of hay a week. Chestnut has eaten 45 pounds of hay so far this week. How much more hay should Chestnut eat this week?

★ 9. The hamburger stand owner sold 1,100 hamburgers for the day's show. There were 810 adults and 390 children at the show. Could each person have had a hamburger?

★ 10. Joel drove 87 miles from home to the rodeo. After the rodeo he drove 21 miles to the store, then 73 miles home. How many more miles was his trip home than his trip going?

The target shows how many points you score. You lose 2 points if you miss the target. Each person gets 5 chances.

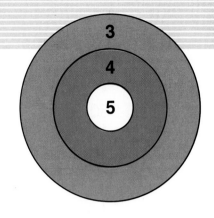

Read and solve each problem.

11. Luke hit the red area 2 times, the blue area 2 times, and the white area once. What was his score?

12. Annie hit the red area once, the blue area 3 times, and missed the target once. What was her score?

13. Buster scored 1 white and 4 blues. Reva scored 4 whites, but she missed the target on her last try. Who won?

14. What is the highest score you can get with 5 chances? What is the lowest score you can get if you hit the target 5 times?

15. Find 2 ways that 21 points can be scored.

★ 16. How can 11 points be scored?

═══ SOMETHING EXTRA ═══

Then

A man bought a horse for $40. After paying $15 for keeping him, he sold him for $75. How much did he make?†

Now

Louis bought a used car for $700. He spent $200 to fix it. Then he sold the car for $1,350. How much did he make?

†*Ray's Modern Intellectual Arithmetic*
(New York: American Book Company, 1877), p. 28, #16.

CHAPTER REVIEW

Add. Check by adding up. pages 44–49, 52–53

1. 42
    +31

2. $50.16
    + 16.23

3. 25
    +46

4. 476
    +314

5. 6,392
    +2,427

6. 50
    35
    +12

7. 42
    8
    +71

8. $931
    677
    + 809

9. 544
    267
    +920

10. 882
    45
    +731

11. $.27 + $.51 = ☐

12. $9.37 + $.11 = ☐

13. 7,935 + 6,114 = ☐

Estimate each sum. pages 50–51

14. 23
    +44

15. 59
    +61

16. 451
    +549

17. 360
    +178

18. 28
    +731

19. 14 + 57 = ☐

20. 7 + 35 = ☐

21. 878 + 450 = ☐

Subtract. Check by adding. pages 56–63, 66–67

22. 43
    −21

23. $5.74
    − 2.61

24. 9,628
    −3,317

25. 52
    −25

26. 747
    −190

27. $8.71
    − 1.93

28. 500
    − 69

29. 901
    −257

30. 2,162
    −1,834

31. 59,396
    −24,903

32. $.58 − $.24 = ☐

33. $4.69 − $.42 = ☐

34. 3,915 − 1,856 = ☐

Estimate each difference. pages 64–65

35. 54
    −13

36. 92
    −28

37. 854
    −397

38. 704
    − 82

39. 610
    −378

40. 87 − 22 = ☐

41. 297 − 130 = ☐

42. 798 − 450 = ☐

**Tell which operation you would use to solve
the problem. Then solve.** pages 54–55, 68–69

43. Ms. Corio bought a bracelet that cost $12.75. She gave the salesperson $15.00. What was her change?

44. Mr. Corio bought cuff links and a tie clip. The cuff links cost $13.50. The tie clip cost $8.95. How much did he pay in all?

Add. Check by adding up.

1. 34
    +12

2. 91
    +72

3. $5.34
    + 1.22

4. 974
    +543

5. 2,078
    +5,432

6. $.35 + $.52 = ☐

7. 113 + 32 + 469 = ☐

8. 242 + 453 + 703 = ☐

9. $27.56 + $73.02 = ☐

Estimate each sum.

10. 27 + 38 = ☐

11. 142 + 51 = ☐

12. 504 + 278 = ☐

Subtract. Check by adding.

13. 87
    − 46

14. 73
    − 29

15. $2.43
    − 1.19

16. 700
    −545

17. 5,791
    −2,768

18. $.92 − $.61 = ☐

19. 803 − 337 = ☐

20. 1,508 − 1,029 = ☐

Estimate each difference.

21. 67 − 24 = ☐

22. 298 − 137 = ☐

23. 551 − 430 = ☐

Tell which operation you would use to solve the problem. Then solve.

24. The rancher and his workers sheared 48 sheep in the morning. In the afternoon, they sheared 43 sheep. How many sheep did they shear altogether?

25. Last year the rancher had 745 sheep. This year he has 830 sheep. How many more sheep does he have this year than last year?

Melinda went shopping. She bought a blouse for $6.95 and a pair of socks for $1.98. She paid for her purchases with a twenty-dollar bill. How much change did she receive?

SECRET CODES

You can write secret codes by matching the alphabet to a number pattern.

A	B	C	D	E	F	G	H
1	2	4	5	7	8	10	11

Complete this pattern for the rest of the alphabet and decode the message.

4	22	5	7	28

1	26	7

8	31	20

Make up a number pattern and enter it on your own secret decoder.

You will need:

- 2 oaktag circles
- a ruler
- a hole punch
- a paper fastener
- a sharp pencil

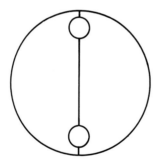 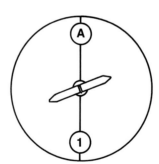

Draw a line dividing one of the circles in half. Punch two holes in the circle as shown. Put this circle on top of the other circle. Place a paper fastener through the centers of the two circles.

Print the letter *A* in the top window and its code number in the bottom window. Then turn the circle until the *A* disappears. Print *B* and its code number. Do this for the rest of the alphabet.

Send a friend a coded message.

MENTAL ARITHMETIC

You can use these steps to find mentally that
100 − 33 = 67.

$$100 - 33 = \square$$

$$1 + \underline{99 - 33}$$

$$\underline{1 + \quad 66}$$

$$67 \qquad\qquad 100 - 33 = 67$$

▶To subtract any two-digit number from 100:

1. Subtract the two-digit number from 99.   2. Add 1 to your answer.

Here is another way to find 100 − 33 = 67.

$$100 - 33 = 67$$

subtract   subtract
from 9   from 10

9 − 3 = 6 tens   10 − 3 = 7 ones

▶To subtract a two-digit number that does not
end in 0 from 100:

1. Subtract the tens digit from 9.   2. Subtract the ones digit from 10.

To play the cross-out game:

a. Copy the digits 0−9 on a piece of paper.

b. Subtract each number from 100 mentally by one of the methods.

c. Cross out the digits that are in the answer.

d. If you are correct, you should cross out each digit exactly once.

Subtract from 100.	Cross out the digits in the answer.
1. 70	0 1 2 3
2. 54	
3. 75	4 5 6 7
4. 81	
5. 13	8 9

Subtract from 100.	Cross out the digits in the answer.
6. 49	0 1 2 3
7. 10	
8. 72	4 5 6 7
9. 36	
10. 27	8 9

Choose the correct answer. Write A, B, C, or D.

1. $8 + 6 = \square$

   A 15   C 2

   B 14   D not given

2. $\square + 9 = 9$

   A 0   C 9

   B 1   D not given

3. $17 - 9 = \square$

   A 10   C 8

   B 26   D not given

4. What fact is related to
$6 + 7 = 13$?

   A $13 - 6 = 7$ C $6 + 1 = 7$

   B $7 - 6 = 1$ D not given

5. What is the value of 8 in 9,843?

   A 8,000   C 80

   B 800   D not given

6. What is the value of 9 in 93,476?

   A 9,000   C 90,000

   B 900   D not given

7. Compare. 3,629 ● 362

   A >   C =

   B <   D not given

8. Round $7,777 to the nearest thousand.

   A $7,000   C $9,000

   B $8,000   D not given

9. $26 + 8 + 34 = \square$

   A 58   C 78

   B 130   D not given

10. $567 + 489 = \square$

   A 1,056   C 946

   B 78   D not given

11. $324 - 265 = \square$

   A 159   C 59

   B 89   D not given

12. $\$5.00 - \$1.72 = \square$

   A $6.72   C $4.72

   B $3.28   D not given

Use the picture for 13 and 14.

13. How many hats are there in all?

   A 8   C 5

   B 3   D not given

14. How many more baseball hats are there than cowboy hats?

   A 3   C 2

   B 5   D not given

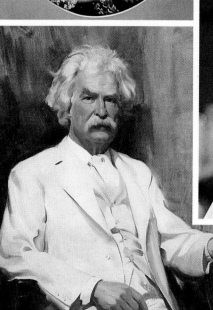

Theme: Famous Americans

2 and 3 as Factors

Casey Jones drove a locomotive that had 5 sets of wheels. There were 2 wheels in each set. How many wheels did the locomotive have in all?

Each set has the same amount. Multiply to find how many in all.

5 × 2 = 10
↑   ↑   ↑
factor   factor   product

$$\begin{array}{r} 2 \leftarrow \text{factor} \\ \times 5 \leftarrow \text{factor} \\ \hline 10 \leftarrow \text{product} \end{array}$$

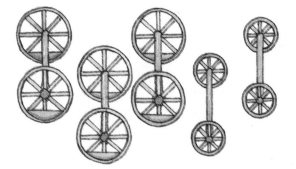

The locomotive had 10 wheels in all.

Another Example

How many keys are there in all? There are 4 rings. There are 3 keys on each ring.

4 × 3 = 12

$$\begin{array}{r} 3 \\ \times 4 \\ \hline 12 \end{array}$$

There are 12 keys in all.

CLASSWORK

Find each product.

1.	2.	3.	4.	5.	6.	7.
3	2	3	2	3	3	2
×5	×6	×8	×9	×6	×7	×4

8. 1 × 3 = ☐   9. 3 × 2 = ☐   10. 7 × 2 = ☐   11. 9 × 3 = ☐

Find each product.

| 1. 3 $\times 3$ | 2. 2 $\times 5$ | 3. 3 $\times 8$ | 4. 2 $\times 6$ | 5. 3 $\times 1$ | 6. 3 $\times 4$ | 7. 2 $\times 1$ |

| 8. 2 $\times 2$ | 9. 3 $\times 2$ | 10. 2 $\times 8$ | 11. 3 $\times 9$ | 12. 2 $\times 3$ | 13. 3 $\times 7$ | 14. 2 $\times 9$ |

| 15. 2 $\times 7$ | 16. 3 $\times 6$ | 17. 2 $\times 8$ | 18. 3 $\times 5$ | 19. 3 $\times 3$ | 20. 2 $\times 1$ | 21. 2 $\times 4$ |

22. $2 \times 2 = \square$ 23. $2 \times 3 = \square$ 24. $8 \times 3 = \square$ 25. $6 \times 2 = \square$

26. $7 \times 3 = \square$ 27. $5 \times 3 = \square$ 28. $5 \times 2 = \square$ 29. $8 \times 2 = \square$

Choose the correct number sentence and solve.

30. A steam locomotive has 9 sets of wheels. Each set has 2 wheels. How many wheels does the locomotive have in all?

 a. $9 - 2 = \square$

 b. $18 - 2 = \square$

 c. $9 + 2 = \square$

 d. $9 \times 2 = \square$

31. Todd has a model train with 4 boxcars and 3 passenger cars. How many cars does the model train have in all?

 a. $12 - 4 = \square$

 b. $4 \times 3 = \square$

 c. $4 + 3 = \square$

 d. $4 - 3 = \square$

Compare. Use $>$, $<$, or $=$ for ●.

★ 32. $4 \times 2 ● 9$ ★ 33. $7 \times 3 ● 20$ ★ 34. $6 \times 2 ● 12$

★ 35. $16 ● 5 \times 3$ ★ 36. $6 \times 3 ● 8 \times 2$ ★ 37. $4 \times 3 ● 6 \times 2$

APPLICATION

38. A train made 8 stops. At each stop it picked up 3 bags of mail. How many bags of mail were picked up in all?

★ 39. The towns of Adam and Barnville are 9 miles apart. A train makes 2 round trips between the towns each day. How many miles does the train travel each day?

4 and 5 as Factors

Johnny Appleseed spread seeds to plant apple trees wherever he went. Johnny planted 3 rows of trees, with 4 trees in each row. How many trees did he plant?

$3 \times 4 = \square$

3 groups of 4

$3 \times 4 = 12$

$$\begin{array}{r} 4 \\ \times 3 \\ \hline 12 \end{array}$$

Johnny planted 12 trees.

Another Example

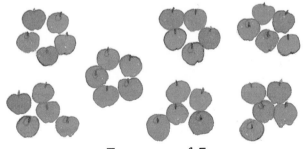

7 groups of 5

$7 \times 5 = 35$

$$\begin{array}{r} 5 \\ \times 7 \\ \hline 35 \end{array}$$

CLASSWORK

Multiply.

1. $\begin{array}{r} 4 \\ \times 6 \\ \hline \end{array}$
2. $\begin{array}{r} 5 \\ \times 5 \\ \hline \end{array}$
3. $\begin{array}{r} 4 \\ \times 5 \\ \hline \end{array}$
4. $\begin{array}{r} 5 \\ \times 7 \\ \hline \end{array}$
5. $\begin{array}{r} 5 \\ \times 9 \\ \hline \end{array}$
6. $\begin{array}{r} 4 \\ \times 1 \\ \hline \end{array}$
7. $\begin{array}{r} 5 \\ \times 3 \\ \hline \end{array}$

8. $8 \times 5 = \square$
9. $2 \times 4 = \square$
10. $4 \times 5 = \square$
11. $9 \times 4 = \square$

Multiply.

1. $\begin{array}{r} 5 \\ \times 2 \\ \hline \end{array}$	2. $\begin{array}{r} 4 \\ \times 4 \\ \hline \end{array}$	3. $\begin{array}{r} 5 \\ \times 1 \\ \hline \end{array}$	4. $\begin{array}{r} 4 \\ \times 8 \\ \hline \end{array}$	5. $\begin{array}{r} 5 \\ \times 8 \\ \hline \end{array}$	6. $\begin{array}{r} 4 \\ \times 5 \\ \hline \end{array}$	7. $\begin{array}{r} 5 \\ \times 3 \\ \hline \end{array}$
8. $\begin{array}{r} 4 \\ \times 9 \\ \hline \end{array}$	9. $\begin{array}{r} 4 \\ \times 6 \\ \hline \end{array}$	10. $\begin{array}{r} 5 \\ \times 7 \\ \hline \end{array}$	11. $\begin{array}{r} 4 \\ \times 7 \\ \hline \end{array}$	12. $\begin{array}{r} 5 \\ \times 4 \\ \hline \end{array}$	13. $\begin{array}{r} 4 \\ \times 3 \\ \hline \end{array}$	14. $\begin{array}{r} 5 \\ \times 6 \\ \hline \end{array}$
15. $\begin{array}{r} 5 \\ \times 9 \\ \hline \end{array}$	16. $\begin{array}{r} 4 \\ \times 5 \\ \hline \end{array}$	17. $\begin{array}{r} 5 \\ \times 5 \\ \hline \end{array}$	18. $\begin{array}{r} 4 \\ \times 2 \\ \hline \end{array}$	19. $\begin{array}{r} 4 \\ \times 4 \\ \hline \end{array}$	20. $\begin{array}{r} 5 \\ \times 2 \\ \hline \end{array}$	21. $\begin{array}{r} 4 \\ \times 1 \\ \hline \end{array}$

22. $5 \times 4 = \square$ 23. $1 \times 5 = \square$ 24. $9 \times 4 = \square$ 25. $5 \times 3 = \square$

26. $7 \times 4 = \square$ 27. $2 \times 4 = \square$ 28. $8 \times 5 = \square$ 29. $6 \times 5 = \square$

Write each pair of numbers.

★ 30. The sum is 12.
The product is 35.
What are the two numbers?

★ 31. The difference is 6.
The product is 27.
What are the two numbers?

APPLICATION

32. It takes 5 apples to make 1 serving of Mrs. Chapman's applesauce. How many apples are needed for 8 servings?

★ 33. Johnny gave each of 7 pioneers 5 seeds to plant trees. He gave 9 other pioneers 4 seeds each. How many trees could all of these pioneers plant?

=== VISUAL THINKING ===

Follow the pattern. How many dots will be on the next picture? Draw the next picture.

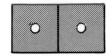 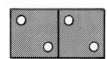 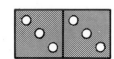 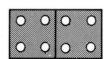

Multiplication Properties

A picture of Abraham Lincoln's head appears on the penny. These Lincoln pennies show some properties of multiplication.

▶The order in which numbers are multiplied does not change the product.

$$\begin{array}{r} 3 \\ \times 2 \\ \hline 6 \end{array}$$

2 rows of 3
$2 \times 3 = 6$

$$\begin{array}{r} 2 \\ \times 3 \\ \hline 6 \end{array}$$

3 rows of 2
$3 \times 2 = 6$

▶The product of any number and 1 is that number.

▶The product of any number and 0 is 0.

$$\begin{array}{r} 1 \\ \times 3 \\ \hline 3 \end{array}$$

$3 \times 1 = 3$

$$\begin{array}{r} 0 \\ \times 3 \\ \hline 0 \end{array}$$

$3 \times 0 = 0$

CLASSWORK

Multiply.

1. $\begin{array}{r} 6 \\ \times 2 \\ \hline \end{array}$
2. $\begin{array}{r} 8 \\ \times 4 \\ \hline \end{array}$
3. $\begin{array}{r} 5 \\ \times 1 \\ \hline \end{array}$
4. $\begin{array}{r} 0 \\ \times 7 \\ \hline \end{array}$
5. $\begin{array}{r} 8 \\ \times 3 \\ \hline \end{array}$
6. $\begin{array}{r} 6 \\ \times 4 \\ \hline \end{array}$
7. $\begin{array}{r} 1 \\ \times 2 \\ \hline \end{array}$

8. $4 \times 7 = \square$ 9. $1 \times 7 = \square$ 10. $5 \times 9 = \square$ 11. $0 \times 6 = \square$

Multiply.

1.	2.	3.	4.	5.	6.	7.
8 ×1	1 ×1	1 ×4	7 ×4	8 ×0	9 ×4	9 ×3

8.	9.	10.	11.	12.	13.	14.
6 ×5	9 ×1	0 ×3	1 ×6	4 ×0	9 ×5	5 ×5

15.	16.	17.	18.	19.	20.	21.
7 ×2	8 ×2	6 ×3	7 ×3	9 ×2	6 ×1	8 ×5

22. $1 \times 5 = \square$ 23. $4 \times 8 = \square$ 24. $0 \times 1 = \square$ 25. $0 \times 9 = \square$

26. $4 \times 6 = \square$ 27. $0 \times 0 = \square$ 28. $7 \times 1 = \square$ 29. $1 \times 8 = \square$

Find each missing number.

★30. $\square \times 4 + 4 = 4$

★31. $4 \times \square - 4 + 4 = 4$

APPLICATION

Write a multiplication sentence for each.

32. How many Lincoln heads would there be on 8 Lincoln pennies?

33. How many Indian heads would there be on 6 Lincoln pennies?

Solve.

★34. In Ellen's collection of coins she has 4 rows of 6 Indian pennies. She has 3 rows of 8 Lincoln pennies. Does she have more Indian or more Lincoln pennies?

★35. Brian placed 18 pennies in rows of 6 pennies each. How else can he place the pennies with the same number in each row?

LOGICAL THINKING

The skate bank has 5 times as many pennies as the pig bank.

The skate bank has 24 more pennies than the pig bank.

How many pennies are in each bank?

6 and 7 as Factors

Benjamin Franklin organized the first fire company in America. In those days, horses pulled fire wagons.

It took 6 horses to pull 1 fire wagon. How many horses did it take to pull 8 fire wagons?

$8 \times 6 = \square$

$8 \times 6 = 48$

$$\begin{array}{r} 6 \\ \times 8 \\ \hline 48 \end{array}$$

It took 48 horses to pull 8 fire wagons.

Benjamin Franklin also organized the first public library.

9 groups of 7

$9 \times 7 = 63$

$$\begin{array}{r} 7 \\ \times 9 \\ \hline 63 \end{array}$$

CLASSWORK

Find each product.

1. $\begin{array}{r} 7 \\ \times 8 \\ \hline \end{array}$
2. $\begin{array}{r} 6 \\ \times 9 \\ \hline \end{array}$
3. $\begin{array}{r} 6 \\ \times 4 \\ \hline \end{array}$
4. $\begin{array}{r} 7 \\ \times 7 \\ \hline \end{array}$
5. $\begin{array}{r} 7 \\ \times 9 \\ \hline \end{array}$
6. $\begin{array}{r} 6 \\ \times 6 \\ \hline \end{array}$
7. $\begin{array}{r} 6 \\ \times 7 \\ \hline \end{array}$

8. $2 \times 7 = \square$ 9. $8 \times 6 = \square$ 10. $5 \times 6 = \square$ 11. $4 \times 7 = \square$

Find each product.

1.	2.	3.	4.	5.	6.	7.
6 ×9	5 ×8	3 ×7	7 ×7	9 ×0	6 ×7	3 ×5

8.	9.	10.	11.	12.	13.	14.
5 ×4	8 ×2	7 ×8	4 ×6	6 ×8	3 ×9	8 ×4

15.	16.	17.	18.	19.	20.	21.
6 ×6	9 ×2	7 ×9	0 ×6	1 ×7	5 ×7	7 ×6

22. $1 \times 6 = \square$ 23. $9 \times 6 = \square$ 24. $7 \times 7 = \square$ 25. $0 \times 5 = \square$

26. $3 \times 6 = \square$ 27. $5 \times 7 = \square$ 28. $0 \times 8 = \square$ 29. $4 \times 9 = \square$

★ 30. $(2 \times 3) \times 4 = \square$ ★ 31. $3 \times (3 \times 3) = \square$ ★ 32. $(4 \times 2) \times 6 = \square$

Follow the rule to find each missing number.

Rule: Multiply by 5.

	Input	Output
	7	35
33.	3	
34.	0	
35.	8	
36.	6	

Rule: Multiply by 7.

	Input	Output
	2	14
37.	7	
38.	1	
39.	6	
40.	5	

Rule: Multiply by 9.

	Input	Output
41.	5	
42.	2	
43.	6	
44.	4	
45.	7	

APPLICATION

46. There were 5 fire trucks sent to put out the fire. Each truck carried 6 fire fighters. How many fire fighters were there in all?

★ 47. The librarian had 61 science books. She put 8 books on each of 7 shelves. The rest of the books were put on display. How many science books were put on display?

8 and 9 as Factors

Martha Berry began a school for poor boys in Georgia. The children helped build the school, and they grew their own food.

There were 9 rows of vegetables. Each row had 8 plants. How many plants were there in all?

$9 \times 8 = 72$

$$\begin{array}{r} 8 \\ \times 9 \\ \hline 72 \end{array}$$

There were 72 plants in all.

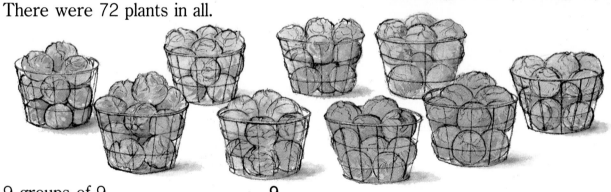

9 groups of 9

$9 \times 9 = 81$

$$\begin{array}{r} 9 \\ \times 9 \\ \hline 81 \end{array}$$

CLASSWORK

Find each product.

1. $\begin{array}{r} 8 \\ \times 5 \\ \hline \end{array}$
2. $\begin{array}{r} 9 \\ \times 7 \\ \hline \end{array}$
3. $\begin{array}{r} 9 \\ \times 4 \\ \hline \end{array}$
4. $\begin{array}{r} 8 \\ \times 7 \\ \hline \end{array}$
5. $\begin{array}{r} 8 \\ \times 4 \\ \hline \end{array}$
6. $\begin{array}{r} 9 \\ \times 6 \\ \hline \end{array}$
7. $\begin{array}{r} 8 \\ \times 8 \\ \hline \end{array}$

8. $9 \times 8 = \square$
9. $7 \times 9 = \square$
10. $4 \times 8 = \square$
11. $5 \times 9 = \square$

PRACTICE

Find each product.

1.	2.	3.	4.	5.
9 ×5	7 ×9	8 ×1	9 ×0	9 ×3

6.	7.	8.	9.	10.
6 ×8	9 ×6	4 ×7	7 ×7	8 ×3

11.	12.	13.	14.	15.
6 ×7	9 ×9	8 ×2	3 ×9	0 ×8

16. $8 \times 7 = \square$ 17. $7 \times 1 = \square$

18. $9 \times 6 = \square$ 19. $2 \times 9 = \square$

Find each missing number.

★ 20. $(9 \times 8) + 9 = \square$ ★ 21. $(7 \times 9) - 8 = \square$

★ 22. $(6 \times 9) + (3 \times 9) = \square \times 9$

APPLICATION

23. One classroom in the school has 8 rows of desks. There are 5 desks in each row. How many desks are there in the classroom?

24. One year there were 9 boys in the graduating class. There were twice as many boys in the beginning class. How many boys were in the beginning class?

25. The children planted 6 peach trees and 9 plum trees. How many more plum trees than peach trees did they plant?

★ 26. Four boys in one class each spent 2 hours a day taking care of the cows. How many hours a week did these boys spend taking care of the cows?

Mixed Practice

1. 24
  +13

2. $.60
  − .14

3. 127
  +201

4. 609
  − 85

5. $4.27
  + 1.95

6. $50.50
  − 11.98

7. $75.48
  + 10.77

8. $8 + 39 = \square$

9. $465 + 155 = \square$

10. $305 - 78 = \square$

11. $4,060 - 5 = \square$

12. $\$6,718 + \$9 = \square$

Round to the nearest hundred.

13. 476   14. 839

15. 650   16. 349

17. 2,730   18. 5,399

19. 8,150   20. 1,075

Missing Factors

Marion bought 24 stamps of famous American women. She bought 4 of each kind. How many different kinds of stamps did she buy?

Find what number times 4 equals 24.
$\Box \times 4 = 24$

To find the missing factor, count by 4's.

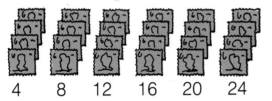

| 4 | 8 | 12 | 16 | 20 | 24 |

You need 6 groups of 4 for 24 stamps.

Marion bought 6 different kinds of stamps.

0, 4, 8, 12, 16, 20, . . .
are called multiples of 4.

A **multiple** of 4 is any product that has 4 as a factor.

You can list the multiples of a number to help you find a missing factor.

More Examples

a. $\Box \times 6 = 18$ **Think**
$0 \times 6 = 0$
$1 \times 6 = 6$
$2 \times 6 = 12$
$\boxed{3 \times 6 = 18}$

3 is the missing factor.

b. $8 \times \Box = 32$ **Think**
$8 \times 0 = 0$
$8 \times 1 = 8$
$8 \times 2 = 16$
$8 \times 3 = 24$
$\boxed{8 \times 4 = 32}$

4 is the missing factor.

CLASSWORK

Find each missing factor.

1. $\Box \times 1 = 8$
2. $\Box \times 4 = 20$
3. $9 \times \Box = 0$
4. $3 \times \Box = 21$

5. $6 \times \Box = 30$
6. $\Box \times 7 = 42$
7. $8 \times \Box = 40$
8. $\Box \times 9 = 54$

Find each missing factor.

1. $8 \times \square = 0$ 2. $\square \times 8 = 24$ 3. $5 \times \square = 30$ 4. $\square \times 9 = 45$

5. $2 \times \square = 14$ 6. $\square \times 6 = 48$ 7. $4 \times \square = 28$ 8. $3 \times \square = 27$

9. $\square \times 5 = 15$ 10. $\square \times 8 = 64$ 11. $8 \times \square = 56$ 12. $\square \times 1 = 5$

13. $4 \times \square = 24$ 14. $5 \times \square = 40$ 15. $\square \times 9 = 72$ 16. $\square \times 8 = 32$

★17. $\square \times 9 = 6 \times 3$ ★18. $3 \times \square = 4 \times 6$ ★19. $4 \times 9 = \square \times 6$

Find the next four multiples of each.

20. 0, 3, 6, . . .   21. 0, 5, 10, . . .   22. 0, 7, 14, . . .

23. 0, 6, 12, . . .   24. 0, 9, . . .   25. 0, 8, . . .

APPLICATION

26. Fred put 30 stamps of famous Americans on one page of his album. There were 6 rows of stamps. How many stamps were in each row?

★27. Amos bought 4 sets of red stamps with 8 stamps in each set. He bought 3 sets of blue stamps with 9 stamps in each set. How many stamps did he buy in all?

MENTAL ARITHMETIC

An even number is a multiple of 2.

An odd number is not a multiple of 2.

An even number ends in 0, 2, 4, 6, or 8.

1. Name the digits that can appear in the ones place of an odd number.

2. Name five even numbers between 25 and 35.

3. Name five odd numbers between 50 and 60.

Problem Solving

WHAT IS MISSING?

Sometimes an important fact is missing from a problem. You may need more information to solve the problem.

One morning 9 cars went to Hyde Park. Each car had the same number of people. How many people went to the park?

THINK　**What is the question?**

How many people went to the park?

What are the facts?

There are 9 cars. Each car had the same number of people.

What is missing?

The number of people in each car. Suppose each car had 4 people in it. Now solve the problem.

PLAN　**What operation should be used?**

Multiply the number of cars by the number of people in each car.

$$9 \times 4 = \square$$

SOLVE　**Do the work and find the answer.**

$$\begin{array}{r} 4 \\ \times 9 \\ \hline 36 \end{array}$$

There were 36 people who went to the park.

LOOK BACK　**Is your arithmetic correct?**

Check by adding.

$$4 + 4 + 4 + 4 + 4 + 4 + 4 + 4 + 4 = 36$$

The answer is correct.

Tell what fact is missing in each problem.

1. The Lee family had a picnic while they were at Hyde Park. They needed 3 tables to seat everyone. How many people were at the Lees' picnic?

2. The Lee family played softball with the Wilson family. The winning team won by 6 runs. What was the final score of the softball game?

A fact is missing in each problem. Choose the fact needed to solve the problem from the list at the right. Then solve the problem.

Problems

3. Some children went for a boat ride. They rented 6 boats. How many children went boating?

4. They rented the boats for 3 hours. How much did they pay for each boat?

5. The children counted the animals along the shore. How many animals did they see?

6. Seven people took photographs at the Roosevelt house. How many photographs were taken?

Facts

a. They saw 5 deer, 4 squirrels, and 3 beavers.

b. They caught 5 fish.

c. Each boat held 3 children.

d. They returned home at 6:00 that evening.

e. Each person took 8 photographs.

f. Boats rent for $2 an hour.

=== CREATE YOUR OWN PROBLEM ===

A bicycle shop in Hyde Park has 16 bicycles for rent. On Saturday morning, some bicycles were rented for the whole day. Six more bicycles were rented after lunch. Make up a problem that is missing a fact. Then make up a fact and solve the problem.

Dividing by 2 and 3

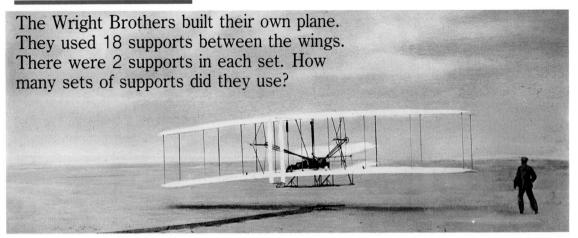

The Wright Brothers built their own plane. They used 18 supports between the wings. There were 2 supports in each set. How many sets of supports did they use?

Divide to find how many equal sets.

$$18 \div 2 = 9 \leftarrow \text{quotient}$$
$$\uparrow \qquad \uparrow$$
dividend　　divisor

$$\overset{9 \leftarrow \text{quotient}}{2)\overline{18}}$$
$$\qquad \uparrow \quad \uparrow$$
divisor　dividend

They used 9 sets of supports.

A travel agent reserved 24 plane seats for a tour group. There are 3 seats in each row. How many rows did the travel agent reserve?

$$24 \div 3 = \square$$

When you divide, think of a related multiplication fact.

Think　$\square \times 3 = 24$
$$8 \times 3 = 24 \qquad \overset{8}{3)\overline{24}}$$
$$24 \div 3 = 8$$

The travel agent reserved 8 rows.

CLASSWORK

Find each quotient.

1. $4 \div 2 = \square$

2. $12 \div 3 = \square$

3. $18 \div 3 = \square$

4. $2)\overline{16}$　　5. $3)\overline{21}$　　6. $2)\overline{12}$　　7. $3)\overline{15}$　　8. $3)\overline{6}$　　9. $2)\overline{14}$

Find each quotient.

1. $6 \div 2 = \square$ 2. $12 \div 2 = \square$ 3. $9 \div 3 = \square$

4. $10 \div 2 = \square$ 5. $3 \div 3 = \square$ 6. $21 \div 3 = \square$

7. $24 \div 3 = \square$ 8. $18 \div 2 = \square$ 9. $27 \div 3 = \square$

10. $2\overline{)10}$ 11. $2\overline{)8}$ 12. $2\overline{)12}$ 13. $3\overline{)6}$ 14. $3\overline{)24}$ 15. $2\overline{)18}$

16. $2\overline{)4}$ 17. $3\overline{)15}$ 18. $2\overline{)16}$ 19. $3\overline{)21}$ 20. $3\overline{)9}$ 21. $3\overline{)27}$

22. $3\overline{)9}$ 23. $2\overline{)18}$ 24. $2\overline{)6}$ 25. $2\overline{)14}$ 26. $3\overline{)24}$ 27. $2\overline{)2}$

28. $3\overline{)6}$ 29. $3\overline{)12}$ 30. $2\overline{)16}$ 31. $3\overline{)18}$ 32. $3\overline{)15}$ 33. $2\overline{)10}$

Choose the correct number sentence and solve.

34. A small airline company has 12 planes. They keep 3 planes in each hangar. How many hangars do they use?

    a. $3 \times 12 = \square$

    b. $12 + 3 = \square$

    c. $3 \div 12 = \square$

    d. $12 \div 3 = \square$

35. One week, 9 pilots made 3 flights each. How many flights were made in all?

    a. $9 + 3 = \square$

    b. $9 \times 3 = \square$

    c. $9 - 3 = \square$

    d. $9 \div 3 = \square$

Find each missing number.

★36. $\square \div 2 = 6$ ★37. $18 \div \square = 9$ ★38. $\square \div 3 = 1$

APPLICATION

39. There were 8 seats in the plane. Each row had 2 seats. How many rows of seats were in the plane?

★40. Steve has 5 sets of wing supports. Each set has 2 supports. His model plane needs 18 supports. How many more sets must he order?

91

Dividing by 4 and 5

Arthur Mitchell is teaching 20 dancers at the Dance Theater of Harlem. The dancers in the class form 4 equal groups.

How many dancers are there in each group?

Divide to find how many in each group.

$20 \div 4 = \square$

Think of a related multiplication fact.

Think
$$4 \times \square = 20$$
$$4 \times 5 = 20$$
$$20 \div 4 = 5$$

There are 5 dancers in each group.

More Examples

a. Divide 45 by 5. $5\overline{)45}$

Think $\square \times 5 = 45$
$9 \times 5 = 45$ $5\overline{)45}^{9}$

b. Divide 28 by 4. $4\overline{)28}$

Think $\square \times 4 = 28$
$7 \times 4 = 28$ $4\overline{)28}^{7}$

CLASSWORK

Divide.

1. $35 \div 5 = \square$　　　2. $12 \div 4 = \square$　　　3. $25 \div 5 = \square$

4. $5\overline{)10}$　　5. $4\overline{)24}$　　6. $4\overline{)8}$　　7. $5\overline{)15}$　　8. $4\overline{)4}$　　9. $5\overline{)40}$

Divide.

1. $9 \div 3 = \square$ 2. $21 \div 3 = \square$ 3. $16 \div 4 = \square$

4. $30 \div 5 = \square$ 5. $27 \div 3 = \square$ 6. $36 \div 4 = \square$

7. $4\overline{)16}$ 8. $5\overline{)45}$ 9. $4\overline{)36}$ 10. $5\overline{)30}$ 11. $5\overline{)20}$ 12. $4\overline{)20}$

13. $4\overline{)32}$ 14. $5\overline{)5}$ 15. $5\overline{)35}$ 16. $3\overline{)24}$ 17. $4\overline{)4}$ 18. $2\overline{)14}$

19. $3\overline{)15}$ 20. $4\overline{)24}$ 21. $5\overline{)40}$ 22. $2\overline{)12}$ 23. $5\overline{)25}$ 24. $4\overline{)28}$

25. $5\overline{)30}$ 26. $4\overline{)32}$ 27. $4\overline{)36}$ 28. $5\overline{)45}$ 29. $4\overline{)16}$ 30. $3\overline{)18}$

Solve.

★31. $(32 \div 4) \times 2 = \square$ ★32. $(3 \times 8) \div 4 = \square$

APPLICATION

33. A dance school has 35 classes a week. The school has 5 teachers. Each teacher teaches the same number of classes. How many classes does each teacher teach?

★34. Paula must take 18 classes in ballet and 14 in modern dance. She has 4 weeks to complete this assignment. She wants to take the same number of classes each week. How many classes must she take each week?

=== MENTAL ARITHMETIC ===

| $3 \times 5 = 15$ | $5 \times 3 = 15$ | $15 \div 3 = 5$ | $15 \div 5 = 3$ |

These are 4 related facts.

Give 3 related facts for each.

1. $36 \div 4$ 2. 2×6 3. $35 \div 5$ 4. 3×7

Dividing by 6 and 7

The fourth grade class collected 18 pictures of astronauts. They can display 6 pictures in a row on their bulletin board. How many rows do they need to show all the pictures?

$18 \div 6 = \square$
Since $3 \times 6 = 18$,
then $18 \div 6 = 3$.

They need 3 rows.

There are 28 pages on space exploration in the social studies book. The class reads 7 pages a day. How many days will it take to read all the pages?

$28 \div 7 = \square$
Since $4 \times 7 = 28$,
then $28 \div 7 = 4$.

It will take 4 days.

CLASSWORK

Divide.

1. $54 \div 6 = \square$

2. $49 \div 7 = \square$

3. $14 \div 7 = \square$

4. $6\overline{)36}$ 5. $7\overline{)21}$ 6. $6\overline{)48}$ 7. $7\overline{)28}$ 8. $6\overline{)30}$ 9. $7\overline{)35}$

Divide.

1. $7 \div 7 = \square$　　　　**2.** $24 \div 4 = \square$　　　　**3.** $42 \div 7 = \square$

4. $48 \div 6 = \square$　　　　**5.** $30 \div 6 = \square$　　　　**6.** $56 \div 7 = \square$

7. $6\overline{)24}$　　**8.** $6\overline{)42}$　　**9.** $7\overline{)63}$　　**10.** $6\overline{)18}$　　**11.** $5\overline{)40}$　　**12.** $6\overline{)6}$

13. $7\overline{)42}$　　**14.** $6\overline{)12}$　　**15.** $7\overline{)28}$　　**16.** $6\overline{)36}$　　**17.** $7\overline{)63}$　　**18.** $6\overline{)30}$

19. $6\overline{)54}$　　**20.** $5\overline{)25}$　　**21.** $5\overline{)30}$　　**22.** $7\overline{)14}$　　**23.** $4\overline{)36}$　　**24.** $6\overline{)24}$

25. $5\overline{)45}$　　**26.** $7\overline{)35}$　　**27.** $6\overline{)42}$　　**28.** $7\overline{)21}$　　**29.** $7\overline{)49}$　　**30.** $4\overline{)28}$

Follow the rule, if given, to find each missing number.

Rule: Divide by 6.

	Input	Output
31.	48	
32.	24	
33.	36	
34.	54	
35.	12	

Rule: Divide by 5.

	Input	Output
36.	15	
37.	40	
38.	30	
39.	45	
40.	25	

Find the rule.

★ **41.**

Input	Output
56	8
42	6
28	4
35	5
63	9

APPLICATION

Solve each problem. If a fact is missing, tell what it is.

42. Danny has 42 spaceship stickers. How many groups of 6 stickers can Danny make?

★ **44.** Olivia wants to put 54 spaceship stickers equally on 6 pages of an album. She can put 3 stickers in each row. How many rows of stickers will Olivia put on each page?

43. Mrs. Klein arranged the pictures in 6 rows. Each row had the same number of pictures. How many pictures were in each row?

Dividing by 8 and 9

Lee and Jamie collect baseball cards.

Lee puts 56 baseball cards into 8 equal piles. How many cards are in each pile?

$56 \div 8 = \square$

Since $8 \times 7 = 56$,
then $56 \div 8 = 7$.

There are 7 cards in each pile.

Jamie puts 54 baseball cards into 9 equal piles. How many cards are in each pile?

$54 \div 9 = \square$

Since $9 \times 6 = 54$,
then $54 \div 9 = 6$.

There are 6 cards in each pile.

CLASSWORK

Find each quotient.

1. $18 \div 9 = \square$ 2. $56 \div 8 = \square$ 3. $54 \div 9 = \square$

4. $8\overline{)16}$ 5. $9\overline{)27}$ 6. $9\overline{)45}$ 7. $8\overline{)32}$ 8. $9\overline{)63}$ 9. $8\overline{)48}$

Find each quotient.

1. $81 \div 9 = \square$ 2. $48 \div 8 = \square$ 3. $35 \div 7 = \square$

4. $45 \div 9 = \square$ 5. $30 \div 6 = \square$ 6. $54 \div 9 = \square$

7. $8\overline{)16}$ 8. $8\overline{)40}$ 9. $9\overline{)72}$ 10. $9\overline{)36}$ 11. $8\overline{)64}$ 12. $8\overline{)8}$

13. $9\overline{)81}$ 14. $4\overline{)32}$ 15. $6\overline{)54}$ 16. $8\overline{)72}$ 17. $4\overline{)16}$ 18. $9\overline{)27}$

19. $6\overline{)42}$ 20. $7\overline{)56}$ 21. $8\overline{)64}$ 22. $7\overline{)63}$ 23. $9\overline{)18}$ 24. $7\overline{)49}$

25. $6\overline{)48}$ 26. $9\overline{)63}$ 27. $5\overline{)45}$ 28. $8\overline{)24}$ 29. $9\overline{)36}$ 30. $8\overline{)56}$

Find each answer.

★ 31. $(9 \div 3) + (3 \div 3) = \square$ ★ 32. $(32 \div 8) + (24 \div 8) = \square$

★ 33. $(9 + 3) \div 3 = \square$ ★ 34. $(32 + 24) \div 8 = \square$

APPLICATION

35. Mr. Ames has 81 baseball cards for 9 children to share equally. How many cards will each child get?

★ 36. The students spent a total of $66 at the baseball game. Each of 9 students bought programs at $2 a piece. The rest was spent on baseball caps that cost $8 each. How many students bought baseball caps?

★ 37. Jamie had 32 cards. He gave 2 for 1 in 3 exchanges. He got 3 for 1 in 2 exchanges. How many cards did he have then?

CALCULATOR

In each multiplication sentence the letter stands for the same number. Find the number.

1. $a \times a \times a = 64$

2. $b \times b \times b \times b = 16$

3. $c \times c \times c = 27$

Write each missing number.

4. $\square \div 4 \div 4 \div 4 = 1$

5. $\square \div 2 \div 2 \div 2 \div 2 = 1$

6. $\square \div 3 \div 3 \div 3 = 1$

Division Properties

When Joe Boepple invented his button-cutting machine, buttons were made from shells. Today most buttons are made from plastic.

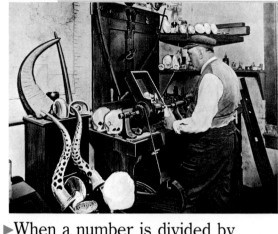

▶When a number is divided by 1, the quotient is that number.

4 in all   1 group
↓   ↓
4   ÷   1   =   4

▶When a number is divided by itself, the quotient is 1.

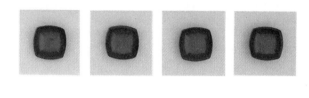

4 in all   4 groups
↘   ↓
4   ÷   4   =   1

▶When 0 is divided by any number (except 0), the quotient is 0.

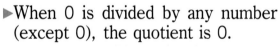

0 in all   4 groups
↓   ↓
0   ÷   4   =   0

▶You cannot divide by 0.

There are no groups. So we cannot find how many are in each group.

4 ÷ 0 is not possible.

CLASSWORK

Find each quotient.

1. $4 \div 1 = \square$ 2. $0 \div 4 = \square$ 3. $1 \div 1 = \square$

4. $1\overline{)2}$ 5. $1\overline{)0}$ 6. $1\overline{)3}$ 7. $9\overline{)9}$ 8. $7\overline{)0}$ 9. $5\overline{)5}$

Find each quotient.

1. $8 \div 8 = \square$ 2. $0 \div 4 = \square$ 3. $2 \div 1 = \square$

4. $7 \div 1 = \square$ 5. $3 \div 3 = \square$ 6. $5 \div 5 = \square$

7. $2\overline{)0}$ 8. $1\overline{)1}$ 9. $5\overline{)0}$ 10. $3\overline{)3}$ 11. $1\overline{)4}$ 12. $8\overline{)0}$

13. $6\overline{)6}$ 14. $1\overline{)7}$ 15. $8\overline{)8}$ 16. $1\overline{)6}$ 17. $3\overline{)0}$ 18. $1\overline{)9}$

19. $1\overline{)5}$ 20. $9\overline{)0}$ 21. $1\overline{)6}$ 22. $2\overline{)2}$ 23. $1\overline{)7}$ 24. $6\overline{)0}$

Compare. Use >, <, or = for ●.

★ 25. $25 \div 1 ● 1 \times 25$ ★ 26. $12 \div 1 ● 20 \div 1$ ★ 27. $0 \div 50 ● 0 \div 10$

APPLICATION

28. Bill needs 3 wooden buttons. How many cards does he need?

29. Lisa needs 6 pearl buttons. How many cards does she need?

★ 30. The tailor needs 6 gold buttons for each of 9 jackets. How many cards must he buy to have buttons for all the jackets? How many buttons will be left after the tailor sews the buttons on each jacket?

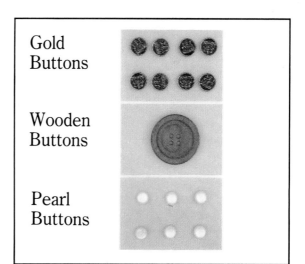

Gold Buttons

Wooden Buttons

Pearl Buttons

===== MENTAL ARITHMETIC =====

Find each missing number mentally.
Use the division properties.

1. $78 \div 1 = \square$ 2. $0 \div 63 = \square$ 3. $\square \div 127 = 1$

4. $\square \div 130 = 0$ 5. $21 \div 21 = \square$ 6. $\square \div 1 = 89$

Fast Facts

Multiply as fast as you can.

1. 4 ×3
2. 2 ×8
3. 5 ×5
4. 6 ×6
5. 2 ×5
6. 5 ×0
7. 4 ×7

8. 9 ×3
9. 3 ×5
10. 2 ×2
11. 6 ×3
12. 7 ×7
13. 3 ×8
14. 7 ×3

15. 6 ×1
16. 8 ×7
17. 5 ×6
18. 3 ×9
19. 4 ×5
20. 8 ×4
21. 4 ×4

22. 3 ×3
23. 8 ×9
24. 9 ×4
25. 6 ×8
26. 3 ×7
27. 5 ×2
28. 1 ×8

29. 2 ×9
30. 9 ×7
31. 6 ×7
32. 3 ×4
33. 0 ×9
34. 6 ×4
35. 8 ×2

36. 4 ×8
37. 5 ×3
38. 7 ×5
39. 5 ×8
40. 3 ×2
41. 9 ×5
42. 8 ×8

43. 9 ×9
44. 7 ×4
45. 9 ×2
46. 4 ×2
47. 6 ×9
48. 5 ×1
49. 7 ×6

50. 8 ×6
51. 2 ×7
52. 4 ×1
53. 9 ×8
54. 7 ×8
55. 2 ×6
56. 6 ×5

57. 5 ×9
58. 0 ×8
59. 5 ×7
60. 8 ×1
61. 8 ×3
62. 7 ×9
63. 4 ×9

Divide as fast as you can.

1. $2\overline{)12}$ 2. $6\overline{)36}$ 3. $2\overline{)4}$ 4. $3\overline{)18}$ 5. $5\overline{)20}$

6. $8\overline{)32}$ 7. $9\overline{)45}$ 8. $7\overline{)28}$ 9. $9\overline{)63}$ 10. $8\overline{)8}$

11. $4\overline{)36}$ 12. $6\overline{)6}$ 13. $7\overline{)21}$ 14. $8\overline{)56}$ 15. $3\overline{)12}$

16. $5\overline{)10}$ 17. $9\overline{)18}$ 18. $5\overline{)30}$ 19. $2\overline{)14}$ 20. $8\overline{)40}$

21. $7\overline{)56}$ 22. $8\overline{)72}$ 23. $3\overline{)9}$ 24. $4\overline{)12}$ 25. $7\overline{)35}$

26. $2\overline{)8}$ 27. $1\overline{)9}$ 28. $6\overline{)48}$ 29. $3\overline{)27}$ 30. $9\overline{)36}$

31. $3\overline{)15}$ 32. $7\overline{)42}$ 33. $3\overline{)6}$ 34. $5\overline{)40}$ 35. $7\overline{)63}$

36. $9\overline{)81}$ 37. $4\overline{)16}$ 38. $7\overline{)49}$ 39. $2\overline{)16}$ 40. $8\overline{)48}$

41. $9\overline{)54}$ 42. $5\overline{)25}$ 43. $4\overline{)4}$ 44. $4\overline{)24}$ 45. $8\overline{)64}$

46. $6\overline{)18}$ 47. $9\overline{)27}$ 48. $6\overline{)42}$ 49. $1\overline{)6}$ 50. $5\overline{)0}$

51. $1\overline{)3}$ 52. $5\overline{)20}$ 53. $8\overline{)0}$ 54. $3\overline{)24}$ 55. $6\overline{)54}$

56. $6\overline{)24}$ 57. $9\overline{)72}$ 58. $2\overline{)18}$ 59. $5\overline{)35}$ 60. $3\overline{)21}$

61. $4\overline{)32}$ 62. $4\overline{)0}$ 63. $8\overline{)24}$ 64. $7\overline{)7}$ 65. $5\overline{)45}$

Problem Solving

SKILLS AND STRATEGIES REVIEW   Americans in Space

**Each problem is missing an important fact.
Tell what fact is missing. Find the fact
in the table. Then solve the problem.**

Moon Mission	Astronauts	Hours Walking on the Moon
Apollo 11	Neil Armstrong	2 hours
	Edwin Aldrin	2 hours
Apollo 12	Charles Conrad	8 hours
	Alan Bean	7 hours
Apollo 14	Alan Shepard	14 hours
Apollo 15	David Scott	18 hours
	James Irwin	18 hours
Apollo 16	John Young	20 hours
	Charles Duke	20 hours
Apollo 17	Eugene Cernan	22 hours
	Harrison Schmitt	22 hours

1. Apollo 11 landed on the moon on July 16, 1969. Neil Armstrong and Edwin Aldrin were the first Americans to walk on the moon. How many hours in all did they spend walking on the moon?

2. Alan Bean and Charles Conrad each walked on the moon twice during the Apollo 12 mission. Conrad spent the same number of hours on each of his walks. How long was each walk?

3. Alan Shepard walked on the moon for a total of 14 hours. How many more hours did Eugene Cernan spend walking on the moon than did Alan Shepard?

4. David Scott walked on the moon for 18 hours. Which Apollo astronauts spent more time walking on the moon than Scott did?

5. If Alan Shepard had walked on the moon 6 hours longer, would he have spent the same amount of time walking on the moon as Harrison Schmitt did?

★ 6. If Neil Armstrong had walked on the moon 7 times and each walk had lasted 2 hours, would he have spent as much time walking on the moon as David Scott did?

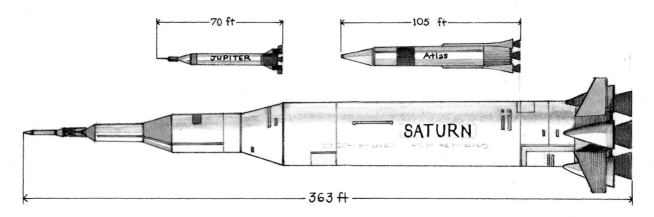

70 ft

JUPITER

105 ft

Atlas

SATURN

363 ft

Use the picture to solve each problem.

7. Which rocket is the longest?

8. Which rocket is the shortest?

9. What is the difference in length between the longest and the shortest rockets?

10. If the 3 rockets were put end to end on the ground, how long would they stretch?

11. How much longer is the Atlas rocket than the Jupiter rocket?

★ 12. How much longer is the Saturn rocket than the Jupiter and Atlas rockets put end to end?

═══ SOMETHING EXTRA ═══

You Find Out.

Each problem below is missing a fact needed to solve it. First find out what fact is missing. Then find the fact in a reference book. Solve the problem using the fact you have discovered.

1. Neil Armstrong was the first American to walk on the moon. About how many miles did he travel from the earth to the moon?

2. On August 22, 1975, the Viking I mission left Earth. It landed on Mars on July 20, 1976. How far did Viking I travel from Earth to Mars?

Multiply. pages 76–85

1. $\begin{array}{r}3\\ \times 5\end{array}$	2. $\begin{array}{r}2\\ \times 8\end{array}$	3. $\begin{array}{r}4\\ \times 4\end{array}$	4. $\begin{array}{r}1\\ \times 9\end{array}$	5. $\begin{array}{r}3\\ \times 6\end{array}$	6. $\begin{array}{r}8\\ \times 8\end{array}$	7. $\begin{array}{r}6\\ \times 7\end{array}$
8. $\begin{array}{r}3\\ \times 9\end{array}$	9. $\begin{array}{r}2\\ \times 5\end{array}$	10. $\begin{array}{r}7\\ \times 2\end{array}$	11. $\begin{array}{r}6\\ \times 0\end{array}$	12. $\begin{array}{r}8\\ \times 1\end{array}$	13. $\begin{array}{r}7\\ \times 5\end{array}$	14. $\begin{array}{r}0\\ \times 7\end{array}$

15. $6 \times 2 = \square$ 16. $0 \times 2 = \square$ 17. $6 \times 5 = \square$ 18. $3 \times 4 = \square$

19. $4 \times 9 = \square$ 20. $7 \times 4 = \square$ 21. $3 \times 8 = \square$ 22. $9 \times 7 = \square$

23. $5 \times 9 = \square$ 24. $8 \times 6 = \square$ 25. $4 \times 8 = \square$ 26. $8 \times 9 = \square$

Find each missing factor. pages 86–87

27. $3 \times \square = 18$ 28. $\square \times 7 = 28$ 29. $8 \times \square = 40$ 30. $\square \times 9 = 18$

31. $9 \times \square = 54$ 32. $\square \times 9 = 9$ 33. $\square \times 8 = 56$ 34. $5 \times \square = 20$

35. $6 \times \square = 54$ 36. $\square \times 5 = 5$ 37. $\square \times 5 = 35$ 38. $4 \times \square = 24$

Divide. pages 90–99

39. $3\overline{)18}$ 40. $5\overline{)10}$ 41. $8\overline{)32}$ 42. $6\overline{)30}$ 43. $1\overline{)8}$ 44. $4\overline{)16}$

45. $2\overline{)6}$ 46. $7\overline{)49}$ 47. $4\overline{)20}$ 48. $8\overline{)0}$ 49. $4\overline{)36}$ 50. $9\overline{)81}$

51. $35 \div 5 = \square$ 52. $18 \div 2 = \square$ 53. $12 \div 3 = \square$

54. $28 \div 7 = \square$ 55. $54 \div 9 = \square$ 56. $5 \div 1 = \square$

57. $42 \div 6 = \square$ 58. $54 \div 6 = \square$ 59. $27 \div 9 = \square$

Solve. If there is not enough information, tell what is missing. pages 88–89, 102–103

60. In Fred's coin collection there are 3 rows of 8 Lincoln pennies. How many Lincoln pennies are there in all?

61. Nancy arranged her space photos in groups of 5. How many groups of space photos did she have?

Find each product.

1. $\begin{array}{r} 2 \\ \times 7 \\ \hline \end{array}$

2. $\begin{array}{r} 5 \\ \times 5 \\ \hline \end{array}$

3. $\begin{array}{r} 3 \\ \times 4 \\ \hline \end{array}$

4. $\begin{array}{r} 5 \\ \times 1 \\ \hline \end{array}$

5. $\begin{array}{r} 6 \\ \times 2 \\ \hline \end{array}$

6. $\begin{array}{r} 7 \\ \times 4 \\ \hline \end{array}$

7. $\begin{array}{r} 5 \\ \times 8 \\ \hline \end{array}$

8. $\begin{array}{r} 4 \\ \times 4 \\ \hline \end{array}$

9. $\begin{array}{r} 8 \\ \times 6 \\ \hline \end{array}$

10. $\begin{array}{r} 3 \\ \times 7 \\ \hline \end{array}$

11. $\begin{array}{r} 4 \\ \times 9 \\ \hline \end{array}$

12. $\begin{array}{r} 5 \\ \times 7 \\ \hline \end{array}$

13. $8 \times 7 = \square$

14. $9 \times 9 = \square$

15. $0 \times 1 = \square$

16. $3 \times 3 = \square$

17. $2 \times 8 = \square$

18. $6 \times 9 = \square$

Find each missing factor.

19. $6 \times \square = 36$

20. $\square \times 9 = 45$

21. $9 \times \square = 72$

22. $5 \times \square = 30$

23. $\square \times 4 = 20$

24. $8 \times \square = 24$

Find each quotient.

25. $4\overline{)32}$

26. $5\overline{)25}$

27. $1\overline{)3}$

28. $9\overline{)27}$

29. $0 \div 6 = \square$

30. $63 \div 7 = \square$

31. $5 \div 1 = \square$

Solve. If there is not enough information, tell what is missing.

32. Magda has 48 baseball cards. She has the same number of cards for each of 6 teams. How many cards does she have for each team?

33. The students gave 4 reports a day on famous American writers. How many days did it take to give all the reports?

The school library has 40 books about famous Americans. There are 7 each about Presidents, inventors, scientists, writers, and artists. The rest are about folk heroes. How many books are about folk heroes?

FACTOR FUN

These three pairs of factors have a product of 16. The factors of 16 are 1, 2, 4, 8, and 16.

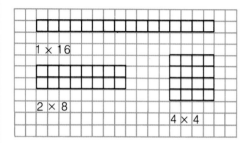

This flagpole is made of drawings for the product 20.

What are the factors of 20?
1, 2, 4, 5, 10, 20

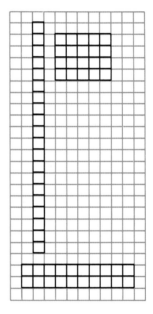

To make drawings for other products, you will need:

- graph paper (large grid)
- scissors
- paste
- construction paper

Use graph paper to show the pairs of factors for each product.

1. 9   2. 12   3. 15

4. 18   5. 8   6. 10

Cut out the rectangles for one of the products. Arrange them to make a picture. Paste the picture on colored construction paper, and label it with the product you chose.

COMBINATIONS

Mr. and Mrs. Wayne want to buy a swimming pool. They can buy a round or rectangular pool. Each pool comes in white, blue, or brown. How many choices do the Waynes have?

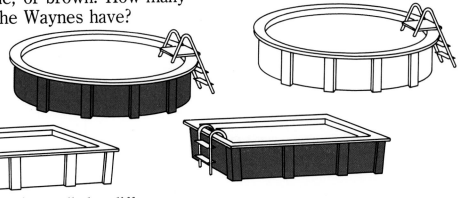

The pictures show all the different pools the Waynes can choose from. There are 6 different pools.

You can multiply to find how many choices in all.

There are 2 shape choices: round or rectangle.
There are 3 color choices: white, blue, or brown.
There are 2 × 3 choices in all.   2 × 3 = 6

Draw a picture to show all the choices. Check by multiplying.

1. The children have snacks in the afternoon. They can have either juice or milk. With their drink the children can choose either an apple or a pretzel. How many different snacks can they choose?

2. Larry made sandwiches for the trip. There was a choice of cheese, roast beef, turkey, or tuna. Each could be on either white or whole wheat bread. How many different sandwiches could be made?

3. Polly bought a red sweater, a green sweater, and a yellow sweater. She can wear any of the sweaters with her blue slacks, black slacks, or brown slacks. How many different outfits can she make?

4. Ben made badges for the club members. Each badge had one letter from A–E. Then there was a number from 1–3. How many different badges could be made?

FLOWCHARTS

Sometimes we break down a complicated problem into small steps that are easy to solve.

A **flowchart** can be used to show the steps.

This flowchart shows the steps for the subtraction 486 − 273.

The ⬭ shape is used for **START** or **STOP.**

The ▭ shape is used for giving instructions.

The arrow ↓ is used to show which instruction to follow next.

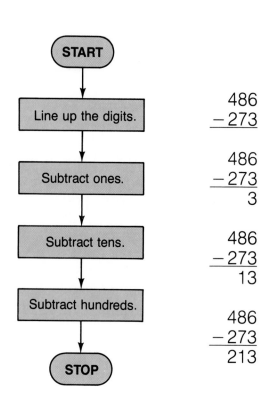

$$486$$
$$-273$$

$$\begin{array}{r}486\\-273\\\hline 3\end{array}$$

$$\begin{array}{r}486\\-273\\\hline 13\end{array}$$

$$\begin{array}{r}486\\-273\\\hline 213\end{array}$$

Use the flowchart to find each difference.

1. 698 − 501 = □
2. 750 − 50 = □
3. 129 − 17 = □

4. 914 − 603 = □
5. 224 − 221 = □
6. 888 − 333 = □

7. Draw a flowchart to show how to add 325 + 462.

★8. Draw a flowchart to show how to add 136 + 45.

Add this step to your flowchart: | Regroup ones. |

A flowchart can help us prepare instructions
for the computer in an orderly way. It helps
to organize our ideas.

This flowchart tells us to multiply a number by 3,
and then to add 3.

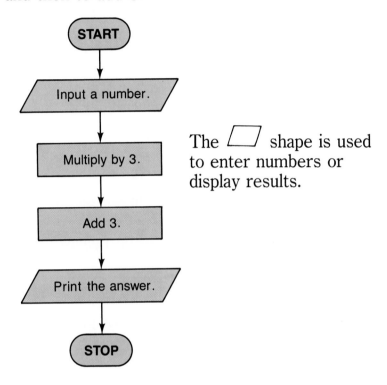

The ⟋ ⟋ shape is used
to enter numbers or
display results.

**Use the flowchart. Tell what the output will be for
each input.**

9. 5   **10.** 8   **11.** 6   **12.** 9   ★**13.** 10

14. Arrange the steps of this flowchart in the correct order.

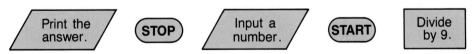

15. Complete this flowchart for $4 \times 9 \div 6 \times 8 \div 2 = \square$

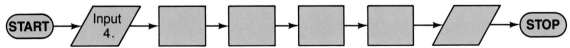

Choose the correct answer. Write A, B, C, or D.

1. $7 + 5 = \square$

A 11   C 14

B 12   D not given

2. $7 + \square = 2 + 7$

A 3   C 0

B 4   D not given

3. $10 - 8 = \square$

A 2   C 4

B 3   D not given

4. $9 - \square = 0$

A 9   C 0

B 1   D not given

5. What fact is related to $17 - 8 = 9$?

A $8 + 8 = 16$ C $18 - 9 = 9$

B $9 + 6 = 15$ D not given

6. What is the value of 3 in 3,906?

A 300   C 3,000

B 30,000   D not given

7. What is the value of 5 in 156,972?

A 5,000   C 500,000

B 50,000   D not given

8. What is the value of 7 in 17,233,159?

A 7,000,000   C 700,000

B 70,000,000   D not given

9. Compare. 156 ● 165

A >   C =

B <   D not given

10. Compare. 2,375 ● 275

A <   C >

B =   D not given

11. Round 3,594 to the nearest hundred.

A 3,600   C 4,000

B 3,500   D not given

12. $192 + 31 + 206 = \square$

A 329   C 429

B 439   D not given

13. $314 + 299 = \square$

A 603   C 614

B 613   D not given

14.   674
       $+498$

A 1,072   C 1,174

B 1,162   D not given

CUMULATIVE REVIEW

Choose the correct answer. Write A, B, C, or D.

15. Estimate. $465 + 290 = \square$

   A 700   **C** 800

   B 600   **D** not given

22. $6 \times 7 = \square$

   A 36   **C** 42

   B 13   **D** not given

16. Estimate. $362 - 206 = \square$

   A 200   **C** 300

   B 100   **D** not given

23. $6 \times 0 = \square$

   A 1   **C** 6

   B 0   **D** not given

17. $671 - 212 = \square$

   A 359   **C** 469

   B 459   **D** not given

24. $9 \times 1 = \square$

   A 10   **C** 8

   B 9   **D** not given

18.
$$\begin{array}{r} 1{,}009 \\ -\ \ 263 \\ \hline \end{array}$$

   A 846   **C** 736

   B 735   **D** not given

25. $8 \times \square = 56$

   A 3   **C** 4

   B 7   **D** not given

19.
$$\begin{array}{r} 4{,}326 \\ -2{,}437 \\ \hline \end{array}$$

   A 1,898   **C** 1,880

   B 1,889   **D** not given

26. $32 \div 4 = \square$

   A 6   **C** 8

   B 7   **D** not given

20. $200 - 78 = \square$

   A 122   **C** 132

   B 232   **D** not given

27. $6\overline{)12}$

   A 2   **C** 4

   B 3   **D** not given

21. $6{,}241 - 5{,}986 = \square$

   A 1,255   **C** 1,256

   B 256   **D** not given

28. $81 \div 9 = \square$

   A 8   **C** 7

   B 9   **D** not given

Choose the correct answer. Write A, B, C, or D.

Use the picture for 29 and 30.

29. How many fish did Pat catch?

A 6 fish   C 2 fish

B 4 fish   D not given

30. If Pat's mother cooks 2 fish for dinner, how many fish will be left?

A 1 fish   C 3 fish

B 2 fish   D not given

Choose the correct operation to solve each problem.

31. Manuel took 3 books home from the library. His brother took 4 books. How many books did they take in all?

A multiply   C add

B subtract   D not given

32. Jack's bowling score was 103. Sally's was 92. How many more points did Jack score than Sally?

A add   C subtract

B multiply   D not given

What fact do you need to solve 33?

33. Kim bought 6 copies of a book. How much did each cost?

A cost of the books   C the title of each book

B the sales tax   D not given

Use the picture for 34 and 35.

34. How many basketballs and softballs are there?

A 12   C 10

B 8   D not given

Choose the correct operation to solve the problem.

35. Frank bought a basketball and a football. How much did he spend?

A add   C subtract

B multiply   D not given

Theme: The States

Telling Time

The Gleasons are leaving in the morning for a trip across the United States.

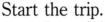

Start the trip.
- read   eight o'clock
- write   8 o'clock or 8:00

Stop for lunch.
- read   twelve thirty or half past twelve
- write   12:30

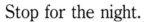

Stop for the night.
- read   five forty-five or quarter to six
- write   5:45

To show time between midnight and noon, write A.M. The Gleasons started their trip at 8:00 A.M.

To show time between noon and midnight, write P.M. The Gleasons stopped for the night at 5:45 P.M.

| 60 minutes = 1 hour |
| 24 hours = 1 day |

CLASSWORK

Read each time. Write the time using numbers.

1.

2.

3.

4.

Choose A.M. or P.M.

5. Sunrise at 5:20   6. Lunch at 1:15   7. Sunset at 6:12   8. Breakfast at 7:40

114

Read each time. Write the time using numbers.

1.
2.
3.
4.

5.
6.
7.
8.

9. 4 minutes after 9

10. half past 3

11. quarter to 5

12. quarter past 1

Write these times in order from earliest to latest.

★13. 11:15 P.M., noon, eight forty-five P.M., 12:01 P.M., 12:30 P.M., seven thirty A.M.

APPLICATION

Write the time using numbers. Include A.M. or P.M.

14. The Gleasons stopped for gas at ten forty in the morning.

15. The Gleasons finished their lunch at one o'clock.

16. The family stopped to enjoy the view at three thirty-five.

★17. The Gleasons slept from nine forty-five until seven thirty the next morning.

=== LOGICAL THINKING ===

What time is it?

There are four digits.
The sum of the first two digits is greater than 2.
The sum of the last two digits is 9.
The last digit is odd.
The difference between the last two digits is 1.

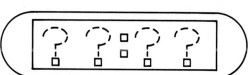

Elapsed Time

In how many minutes will the bus leave for Orlando?

TIME	BUS TO	LEAVES AT
	Yellowstone Park, Wyo.	8:00
	Orlando, Fla.	8:05
	Williamsburg, Va.	8:10
Now	New York City, N.Y.	8:15

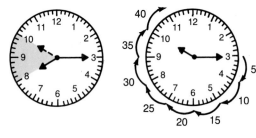

Count by fives to find the number of minutes from 7:50 to 8:05.

The bus will leave in 15 minutes.

The bus to New York City stops 2 hours and 40 minutes after it leaves. What time will it be then?

Count 8:15 + 1 hour + 1 hour to 10:15.
Then count 40 minutes.
The time will be 10:55.

CLASSWORK

Find each time.

1. 5 minutes after

2. 2 hours after

3. 10 minutes before

Tell how much time has passed.

4. start

end

5. start

end

Find each time.

1. 4 hours after

2. 15 minutes after

3. 1 hour before

4. 20 minutes after 7:50

5. 35 minutes before 2:40

6. 1 hour and 10 minutes after 6:25

Tell how much time has passed.

7. start   end

8. start   end

9. start   8:25 A.M.
   end   9:10 A.M.

10. start   3:10 P.M.
   end   5:00 P.M.

Use the rule to find each missing time.

Rule: Subtract 10 minutes.

	Input	Output
11.	2:10	
12.	1:15	
13.	6:30	

Rule: Add 1 hour and 34 minutes.

	Input	Output
★ 14.	3:00	
★ 15.	4:15	
★ 16.	9:19	

APPLICATION

Use the table to answer these questions.

17. The Frank family arrived at the Metropolitan Museum 25 minutes before it opened. What time was it?

18. The Franks left the Natural History Museum at 2:15 P.M. How much time did they have to get to the United Nations before it closed?

	Visitor Hours
American Museum of Natural History	10:00 A.M.–5:45 P.M
United Nations	9:15 A.M.–4:45 P.M.
Metropolitan Museum of Art	9:30 A.M.–5:15 P.M.

★19. At 3:10 P.M. Mrs. Frank put money in the parking meter. It was enough for 1 hour and 25 minutes of parking. Will that last until closing time at the United Nations?

117

Calendar

Every March, horned larks nest outside the Valdezes' cabin in Kansas. They fly away 7 months later. In what month do the birds leave?

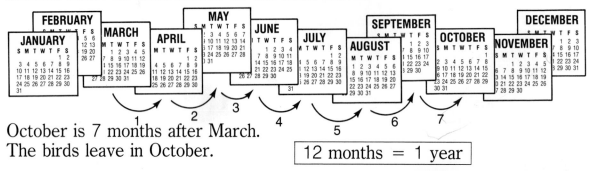

October is 7 months after March.
The birds leave in October.

12 months = 1 year

Look at this calendar for March.

MARCH						
Sun.	Mon.	Tues.	Wed.	Thurs.	Fri.	Sat.
		1	2	3	4	5
6	7	8	9	10	11	12
13	14	15	16	17	18	19
20	21	22	23	24	25	26
27	28	29	30	31		

This year, the larks arrived on the third Thursday in March. The date was March 17.

7 days = 1 week

April, June, September, and November each have 30 days. February has 28 days. All other months have 31 days. In Leap Year, February has 29 days.

365 days = 1 year
366 days = Leap Year

CLASSWORK

Use the calendars on this page to answer these questions.

1. Which month is 4 months before July?

2. Which month is 9 months after November?

3. What is the date of the second Wednesday in March?

4. What is the date of the fourth Monday in March?

118

PRACTICE

Give the month that is 6 months before each month.

1. September
2. October
3. April
4. January

Give the month that is 7 months after each month.

5. March
6. May
7. August
8. December

What day and date is it? Use the calendar on page 118.

9. 1 day before March 5

10. 5 days before March 20

11. 5 days after March 9

12. 7 days after March 13

★13. 5 days before March 4

★14. 2 days after March 30

APPLICATION

Use the calendars on page 118.

15. Mr. Valdez took a trip to Wichita on the first Friday in March. He returned home 5 days later. What day and date was his return?

16. Mrs. Valdez had a meeting on the third Tuesday of March. She prepared slides 3 days before. What day and date was that?

★17. The Valdez family went away for vacation for 8 weeks. They left on June 15. In what month will they return?

★18. Jimmy Valdez went to Topeka on Wednesday, June 30. He returned 2 days later. What day and date was his return?

CALCULATOR

APRIL						
S	M	T	W	T	F	S
					1	2
3	4	5	6	7	8	9
10	11	12	13	14	15	16
17	18	19	20	21	22	23
24	25	26	27	28	29	30

Look at the square shaded area on the calendar. Multiply the middle number by 9. Then subtract all 9 numbers in the square from the product.

$(9 \times 12) - 4 - 5 - 6 - 11 - 12 - 13 - 18 - 19 - 20 = \square$

What is the answer?

Choose another 3-by-3 square. Try it again.

Money Values

Which coin will Suzy use in the telescope?

penny
$.01 or 1¢

nickel
$.05 or 5¢

dime
$.10 or 10¢

quarter
$.25 or 25¢

half-dollar
$.50 or 50¢

Suzy will use a quarter in the telescope.

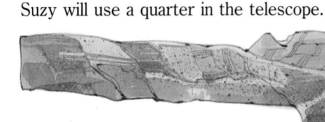

Suzy paid $6.36 for a book about the Badlands in South Dakota.

six dollars and thirty-six cents

To count money, start with the bill or coin of greatest value. End with the bill or coin of least value.

CLASSWORK

Write the value.

1.

2.

3.

4.

Write the value.

1.  2.  3.

4. 1 five-dollar bill, 1 one-dollar bill, 2 quarters, 1 nickel

5. 1 five-dollar bill, 2 one-dollar bills, 3 quarters, 1 dime

6. 3 ten-dollar bills, 2 one-dollar bills, 3 nickels

Compare. Use >, <, or = for ●.

7. $1.98 ● $1.89   8. $.09 ● $.59   9. 1 quarter, 2 dimes ● $.45

★10. 7 dimes, 16 pennies ● 3 quarters, 1 dime, 1 penny

★11. 3 quarters, 3 dimes, 13 pennies ● 1 dollar, 8 pennies

★12. 5 dollars, 7 nickels, 4 pennies ● 4 dollars, 6 quarters, 9 pennies

APPLICATION

13. Suzy has a quarter, a dime, and 3 pennies. Can she buy a $.45 postcard?

★14. Suzy has 4 coins. Their value is 86¢. What coins does she have?

MENTAL ARITHMETIC

If postcards are 29¢ each, how much will 3 cost?

Think
30¢ + 30¢ + 30¢ − 3¢ = 87¢

Do these without using a pencil or a calculator.

1. 4 postcards at 49¢ each = ☐   2. 6 postcards at 26¢ each = ☐

3. 3 postcards at 38¢ each = ☐   4. 8 postcards at 22¢ each = ☐

Using Money

Jason is collecting bumper stickers from every state. What bills and coins does he need to buy this one?

NEW MEXICO
LAND OF ENCHANTMENT
$ 1.32

Start with the bill or coin of greatest value.

Stop counting when you reach the amount you need.

one dollar,   twenty-five,   thirty,   thirty-one, thirty-two

Jason needs a one-dollar bill, a quarter, a nickel, and two pennies.

He could pay with a one-dollar bill and thirty-two pennies. He tries to use the fewest possible bills and coins.

CLASSWORK

**Name the bills and coins needed for each amount.
Use the fewest possible bills and coins.**

1. $.35   2. $.28   3. $.42   4. $1.80

5. $3.05   6. $4.25   7. $7.25   8. $10.50

9. Name the bills and coins needed to make $1.12 using exactly 1 bill and 8 coins.

10. Name the bills and coins needed to make $1.26 using exactly 1 bill and 4 coins.

Name the bills and coins needed for each amount.
Use the fewest possible bills and coins.

1. $.30
2. $.40
3. $.14
4. $.85
5. $.45
6. $.97
7. $1.65
8. $1.92
9. $1.79
10. $3.15
11. $5.12
12. $4.11
13. $6.39
14. $7.49
15. $9.75
16. $15.25

Name the bills and coins needed to make each amount.

17. $1.00, with 10 coins
18. $.87, with 6 coins
19. $.28, with 6 coins
20. $1.25, with 11 coins
21. $.41, with 4 coins
22. $.76, with 6 coins

APPLICATION

23. Fred paid a $.40 toll with 4 coins. He did not use any dimes. What coins did he use?

24. Jason's father has 3 quarters. The toll is $.90. Write a number sentence that can be used to find out how much more he needs to pay the toll.

★ 25. How many different ways can Ann pay the exact amount for a $.25 toll? She may not use pennies.

═ MATH HISTORY ═

Euclid was a famous mathematician. He wrote the *Thirteen Books of Elements,* a collection of the mathematics of his time. Euclid made general statements about mathematics. One of the statements was: Things which are equal to the same thing are also equal to one another.

Here is an example of Euclid's statement, using money.

10 pennies = 1 dime
2 nickels = 1 dime
so 10 pennies = 2 nickels

Think of other examples of Euclid's statement.

Counting Change

Sharon bought a metal dinosaur for $.76. She paid for it with a one-dollar bill. What change should she get?

▶To count change, start with the cost of the item. Use coins of least value first. End with the amount used to pay for the item.

| $.76 | $.77 | $.78 | $.79 | $.80 | $.90 | $1.00 |

Sharon should get $.24 in change.

▶Another way to find change is to subtract.

$$\begin{array}{r} \overset{9\ 10}{\$\cancel{1}.\cancel{0}\cancel{0}} \\ -\quad .76 \\ \hline \$\ .24 \end{array}$$

CLASSWORK

Count the change. Write the total amount of change.

1. A dinosaur eraser costs $.49.
   Sharon pays $1.00.
   Count pennies.
   Count half-dollars.
   Total change

2. A dinosaur model costs $5.79.
   Sharon pays $10.00.
   Count pennies.
   Count dimes.
   Count dollars.
   Total change

Subtract to find the change.
List the bills and coins given.

3. Dinosaur buttons cost $.59.
   Amount paid $1.00

4. A dinosaur book costs $3.35.
   Amount paid $5.00

PRACTICE

Count the change. Write the total amount of change.

1.

Amount paid $2.00
Count pennies.
Count dimes.
Count quarters.
Total change

2.

Amount paid $5.00
Count nickels.
Count quarters.
Count dollars.
Total change

Subtract to find the change.
List the bills and coins.

	3.	4.	5.	6.
Cost	$ .65	$1.55	$ 8.29	$ 3.70
Amount Paid	$1.00	$5.00	$10.00	$10.00

APPLICATION

7. Darlene bought a dinosaur model that was on sale for $4.55. She gave the sales clerk $5.00. What change should she get?

★ 8. Allen bought 4 pencils for $.25 each. His change was $9.00. How much did he give the sales clerk?

★ 9. Andy bought stickers for $1.69. His change was 1 penny, 1 nickel, 1 quarter, and 3 one-dollar bills. How much did he give the clerk?

=== VISUAL THINKING ===

Complete the pattern.

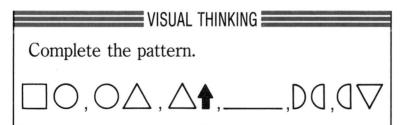

1. $217 - 56 = \square$

2. $403 - 89 = \square$

3. $\square \times 6 = 24$

4. $25 \div 5 = \square$

5. $789 + 45 = \square$

6. $538 - 126 = \square$

7. $9 \times 1 = \square$

8. $45 \div 9 = \square$

9. $1,054 - 743 = \square$

10. $276 + 95 = \square$

11. $0 \times 8 = \square$

12. $45 \div 5 = \square$

13. $\$5.34 + \$.95 = \square$

14. $\$7.52 - \$.84 = \square$

15. $\square \times 7 = 42$

16. $54 \div 6 = \square$

17. $\$7.50 + 0 = \square$

18. $\$7.00 - \$.68 = \square$

19. $(9 + 8) + 4 = \square$

20. $5 \times (2 \times 3) = \square$

Problem Solving

TOO MUCH INFORMATION

Many times there are extra facts in a problem. You have to decide which facts are needed.

There is a meeting at school to talk about the trip to Sacramento. It takes Donald 35 minutes to walk to school. It takes him 15 minutes if he rides his bicycle. He left his house at 8:15 A.M. and walked. What time did he get to school?

THINK   **What is the question?**

What time did Donald get to school?

What facts are needed?

He left home at 8:15 A.M. He walked.

It takes 35 minutes to walk to school.

What facts are extra?

It takes Donald 15 minutes to ride his bicycle to school.

PLAN   **How can you find the answer?**

Look at the time Donald left his house. Then count 35 minutes more.

SOLVE   **Carry out the plan. Do the work and find the answer.**

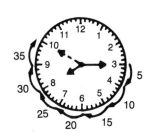

Donald arrived at school at 8:50 A.M.

LOOK   **Did you use the correct facts?**
BACK   **Does your answer make sense?**

Yes, 35 minutes after 8:15 A.M is 8:50 A.M.

Read each problem. Tell what facts are extra.

1. The children stopped for breakfast at 8:00 A.M. Louis spent $1.50 and Jan spent $1.70. Louis gave the cashier a $5 bill to pay for his food. How much change did he get?

2. The class learned that California is about 770 miles long and 360 miles wide. It has about 2,100 square miles of lakes. How much longer is California than it is wide?

3. Picture postcards of the state capitol cost 20¢ each. Bob bought 4 postcards and gave the clerk $1.00. How much did Bob spend for the postcards?

4. Tour tapes of the capitol rent for $3.00. John rented a tour tape. He used it for 2 hours. How much did John pay to rent the tape?

5. Marcia sells souvenirs at the capitol on weekends. She sold 75 souvenirs on Saturday and 80 on Sunday. She makes 20¢ for each souvenir she sells. How many souvenirs did she sell last week?

6. Lenny is paid $7.00 per hour to trim bushes around the capitol. He started at 1:00 P.M., and by 4:00 P.M. he was finished. How long did it take Lenny to trim the bushes?

Tell which fact is extra in each problem. Then solve each.

7. There were 180 children from 6 schools visiting the capitol. Of these, 120 children went to visit the State Assembly. The rest of the children went to visit the Senate. How many children went to the Senate?

★ 8. To help keep the grounds at the capitol clean, the refreshment stand owner will pay 5¢ for each can returned. Tom and Mary picked up the cans. Tom collected 45 cans. Together they collected 80 cans. How much did they earn in all?

=== CREATE YOUR OWN PROBLEM ===

The children finished lunch at 2:30 P.M. They will meet the governor at 4:00 P.M. There is a 45-minute tour that leaves on the hour. The tour guide is 23 years old.

Make up two different problems. Each problem should use some, but not all, of the facts.

Pictographs

The Pulaski family kept a record of
the money they spent on a trip from
Arizona to Colorado.

This **pictograph** shows what the Pulaskis spent.

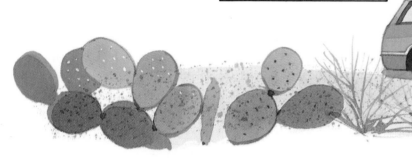

	DOLLARS SPENT
Food	$ $ $ $ $ $ $ $ $ $
Gas for Car	$ $ $ $ $ $ $ $ $
Souvenirs	$ $ $
Camping	$ $ $ $ $ $ $
Entertainment	$ $ $ $ $

Each $ stands for $10.

Count by tens to find the amount spent
for each item. Each $ stands for $5.

The pictograph shows that the Pulaskis
spent $100 for food.

CLASSWORK

Use the pictograph to answer each question.

1. On what item did the Pulaskis spend the least money?

2. On what item did they spend the most money?

3. How much money did they spend for gas?

4. How much more did they spend for camping
   than for souvenirs?

5. How much did they spend on entertainment?

128

This pictograph shows the number of cars Juan saw from different states.

	CARS
Idaho	🚗 🚗 🚗 🚗 🚗 🚗 🚗
Washington	🚗 🚗 🚗
Oregon	🚗 🚗
Montana	🚗 🚗 🚗 🚗 🚗
Other	🚗 🚗 🚗 🚗

Each 🚗 stands for 20 cars.

Use the pictograph to answer each question.

1. What does this symbol stand for: 🚗 ?

2. How many cars from Oregon did Juan see?

3. Did Juan see more cars from Idaho or from Oregon?

4. Did Juan see more cars from Montana or Washington?

5. How many cars did he see from "other" states?

6. How many more cars did Juan see from Idaho than from Washington?

★7. How many cars did Juan see from both Montana and Idaho?

APPLICATION

Laura counted these vehicles in one afternoon: 30 buses, 45 campers, 15 tractors, 5 trailers, 10 vans.

8. How many tractors and trailers were there?

★9. Complete the pictograph to show the facts.

★10. How many vehicles were there in all?

	KINDS OF VEHICLES				
Buses	⊕	⊕	⊕		
Campers	⊕	⊕	⊕	⊕	◖
Tractors					
Trailers					
Vans					

Each ⊕ stands for 10 vehicles.

Bar Graphs

Kate made a table and a bar graph to show how many miles her family traveled in each state.

Follow Kate's steps to draw this bar graph.

Step 1 Draw a horizontal line (→) on graph paper. Write the names of the states under the line.

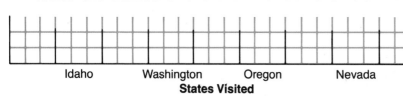

Idaho   Washington   Oregon   Nevada
States Visited

Step 2 Draw a vertical line (↑) on the left. Let each box equal 50 miles.

Step 3 For each state, draw a bar to show the number of miles traveled there. Give the graph a title.

State	Miles
Idaho	150
Washington	400
Oregon	500
Nevada	250

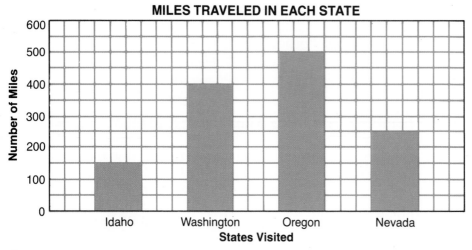

MILES TRAVELED IN EACH STATE

CLASSWORK

Use the bar graph to answer each question.

1. In which states did the family travel more than 300 miles?

2. In which states did they travel less than 300 miles?

3. Were more miles traveled in Washington or Oregon?

On a camping trip the Smiths visited several western states.

Use the graph to answer each question.

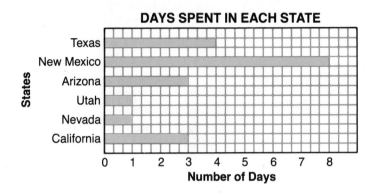

DAYS SPENT IN EACH STATE

1. How many states did the Smiths visit?

2. In which state did the Smiths spend the most time?

3. In which states did the Smiths spend the least time?

4. How many days did the Smiths spend in New Mexico? Utah? California?

5. Did the Smiths spend less time in Texas or California?

6. Did the Smiths spend more time in Nevada or Texas?

7. In which states did the Smiths spend fewer than 4 days?

8. In which states did the Smiths spend more than 3 days?

9. How much more time did the Smiths spend in California than in Utah?

★ 10. In which state did the Smiths spend half the amount of time spent in New Mexico?

APPLICATION

The table shows how long Ed lived in each of 3 states.

11. Use the facts to make a bar graph.

State	Number of Years
Alabama	3
Georgia	2
Florida	4

Use the graph to answer these questions.

12. Where has Ed lived the longest?

★ 13. How old is Ed?

Line Graphs

Mr. Rafael has an inn with 24 guest rooms near Crescent City, California. This line graph shows how many rooms were occupied one week.

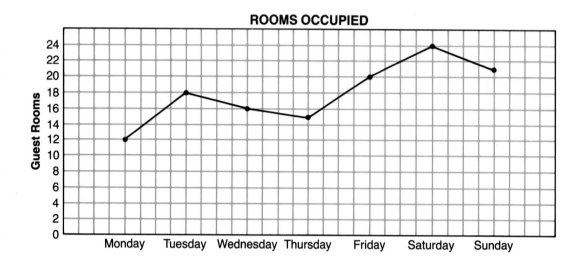

A **line graph** is a good way to show changes over time.

Look at the point for Tuesday on the graph. Look across to the number of guest rooms used on that day.

The graph shows that there were 18 rooms occupied on Tuesday.

CLASSWORK

Use the line graph to answer each question.

1. How many rooms were occupied on Friday?

2. How many rooms were occupied on Thursday?

3. On what day were the most rooms occupied?

4. On what day were the fewest rooms occupied?

Use the line graph to answer each question.

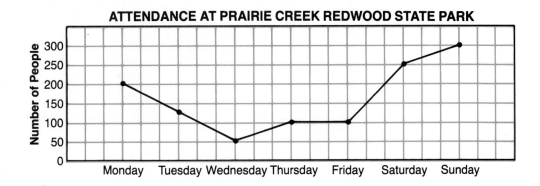

ATTENDANCE AT PRAIRIE CREEK REDWOOD STATE PARK

1. How many people visited the park on Monday?

2. How many people visited the park on Saturday?

3. On which day did the fewest people visit the park?

4. On which day did the most people visit the park?

5. Did more people visit the park on Monday or Friday?

6. On which two days was attendance the same?

7. Which days show attendance at fewer than 150?

★ 8. How many people visited the park on Tuesday?

Tell whether attendance increased or decreased.

9. from Monday to Wednesday

10. from Wednesday to Thursday

11. from Tuesday to Wednesday

12. from Friday to Sunday

APPLICATION

13. The park needs extra help when attendance is over 200. On which days does the park need extra help?

14. What was the total attendance at the park from Friday until Sunday?

★ 15. Find out the daily attendance in your class for a week. Make a line graph. Write 3 questions about the graph.

Circle Graphs

Certain states are famous for different foods. Wisconsin is famous for cheese.

A **circle graph** shows how a whole is divided into parts.

Cheese Production in the United States

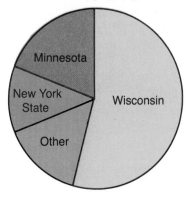

The circle stands for all of the cheese produced in the United States. More than half of all the cheese produced in the United States comes from Wisconsin. So, more than half of the graph is used for Wisconsin cheese.

Minnesota produces the second greatest amount of cheese. Next in order is New York State.

CLASSWORK

Use the circle graph below to answer each question.

Apple Production in the United States

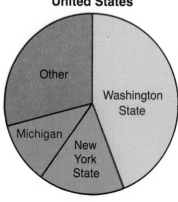

1. Which state produces the greatest amount of apples?

2. Which state produces the least amount of apples?

3. Does Washington State produce half, more than half, or less than half of all United States apples?

Use the circle graphs to answer each question.

Potato Production in the United States

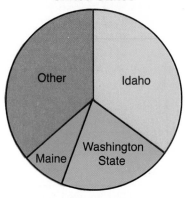

Cherry Production in the United States

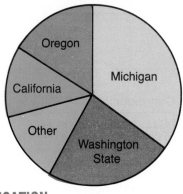

1. Do more potatoes come from Idaho or from Washington State?

2. Does Idaho grow more than half or less than half of all the potatoes in the United States?

★ 3. If you eat a potato, is it more likely to come from Idaho or Maine?

4. Which state grows the greatest amount of cherries?

5. Does Washington State or California grow more cherries?

6. Does Michigan grow half or less than half of all the cherries grown in the United States?

★ 7. If you eat United States cherries, are they more likely to come from Michigan or Oregon?

APPLICATION

Marla is doing a report on her home state.
She makes a circle graph to help plan her report.

Use her graph to answer the questions.

Report on Home State

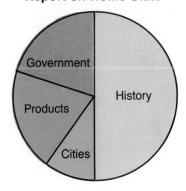

8. Will more of the report be on products or on cities?

9. What topic will make up half of the report?

★ 10. If Marla's report is 10 pages long, how many pages will be on history? on government? on products? on cities?

Problem Solving

SKILLS AND STRATEGIES REVIEW The States

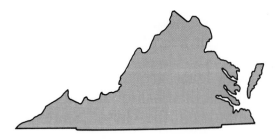

Virginia

Size: 40,815 square miles
Population: 5,135,000

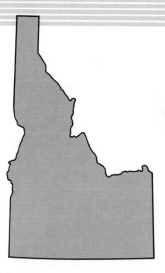

Idaho

Size: 83,557 square miles
Population: 857,000

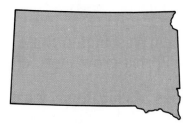

South Dakota

Size: 77,047 square miles
Population: 689,000

Connecticut

Size: 5,009 square miles
Population: 3,108,000

I am one of the states shown!

1. I am the largest state. Which state am I?

2. I have the least number of people. Which state am I?

3. I have more than 2,000,000 people. I have less than 10,000 square miles. Which state am I?

4. I have fewer than 1,000,000 people. I have more than 80,000 square miles. Which state am I?

5. I have fewer people than Virginia. I have less than 6,000 square miles. Which state am I?

6. I have more people than Idaho and South Dakota. I have more than 10,000 square miles. Which state am I?

7. I have more than 4,000,000 people. The cardinal is my state bird. Which state am I?

★8. Texas is a large state. It contains 267,338 square miles. Is Texas bigger than all four of us put together?

Use the graph to answer each question.

APPLES PICKED	
Golden Delicious	🍎 🍎 🍎 🍎 🍎 🍎 🍎
Red Delicious	🍎 🍎 🍎 🍎 🍎
McIntosh	🍎 🍎
Pippin	🍎 🍎
Rome Beauty	

🍎 = 400 pounds

9. Which kind of apple was picked the most?

10. Which kind of apple was picked the least?

11. Were more McIntosh or more Red Delicious apples picked?

12. How many pounds of McIntosh apples were picked?

13. Which two kinds of apples had the same number of pounds picked?

14. How many more pounds of Golden Delicious than Red Delicious apples were picked?

15. How many more pounds of Pippin apples are needed to equal the amount of Red Delicious picked?

★ 16. If 400 more pounds of Rome Beauty apples are picked, how many pounds of Rome Beauties will there be?

VACATION EXPENSES			
	New York	**Philadelphia**	**Washington, D.C.**
Hotel and food	$485.00	$375.00	$415.00
Car rental	$ 70.00	$ 65.00	$ 82.00

Use the table to answer each question.

17. How much less does it cost to rent a car in New York than in Washington, D.C.?

18. Does it cost less to spend a vacation in New York without renting a car or in Philadelphia with a rental car?

CHAPTER REVIEW

Use the clock face at the right to answer. pages 114–117

1. What time does the clock show?

2. What time will it be in 45 minutes?

3. By 5:30, how much time will have passed?

Write the value. Use a dollar sign and decimal point. pages 120–121

4. 1 quarter, 3 dimes, 4 nickels

5. 1 dollar, 5 dimes, 2 pennies

List the coins and bills needed to make change. pages 122–125

6. A stamp costs $.22. You pay $1.00.

7. A bus ticket costs $2.60. You pay $5.00.

Use the graphs to answer the questions. pages 128–129, 132–133

VISITORS AT ISLAND PARK	
Mon.	♀ ♀
Tues.	♀ ♀ ♀ ♀
Wed.	♀ ♀ ♀
Thurs.	♀ ♀ ♀ ♀ ♀
♀ stands for 100 visitors	

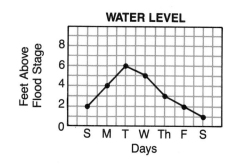

8. On what day were there the most visitors at the park?

10. Was the water level rising or falling between Monday and Tuesday?

9. How many visitors were there on Tuesday?

11. What was the water level on Friday?

Solve. Tell whether any information is not needed. pages 126–127, 136–137

12. Pat got up at 7:15 A.M. She studied for 2 hours. Her breakfast cost $1.50. How much change did she get from $5.00?

13. Warren left the house at 10:20 A.M. He was out for 2 hours and 50 minutes. What time was it then?

Use the clock face at the right to answer.

1. What time does the clock show?

2. What time will it be in 35 minutes?

3. How much time has passed since 12:30?

Write the value. Use a dollar sign and decimal point.

4. 1 dime, 3 nickels, 2 pennies   5. 2 dollars, 2 quarters, 7 pennies

6. 1 ten-dollar bill, 4 quarters, 5 nickels, 3 pennies

List the coins and bills needed to make change.

	7.	8.	9.
Cost	$.89	$1.65	$4.85
Amount Paid	$1.00	$5.00	$10.00

Use the graphs to answer the questions.

RAINY DAYS

(bar graph: Number of Days vs. months May, June, July)

BURTON FAMILY'S EXPENSES

10. What month had the most rain?

11. Did it rain more in May or July?

12. What did the Burtons spend the most for?

13. What did they spend the least for?

Solve. Tell whether any information is not needed.

14. Roger had a tuna sandwich, milk, and fruit for lunch. His bill was $3.45. What was his change from $10.00?

15. Pamela was in school at 8:30 A.M. She spent 3 hours and 15 minutes in class. What time was it then?

Susan bought three items costing $1.75, $2.50, and $8.75. She paid for the items with a ten-dollar bill and a five-dollar bill. How much change should she get?

MAKING A SUNDIAL

People need to measure time. Today, we measure time with clocks that use springs, or electricity, or even atoms.

The oldest known clock is the sundial. Babylonians used sundials 4,000 years ago. A sundial uses the sun and shadows to measure time.

Make your own sundial. See how it works!

These are the supplies you need:

- a sheet of white paper
- a stick about the length of a pencil
- a lump of clay
- masking tape

This is what you do.

1. Place the sheet of paper in the sunlight. Tape it down firmly.

2. Use the lump of clay to stand the stick in the middle of the paper.

3. Trace the shadow the stick makes. Write down what time it is when you do this.

Observe how many hours it takes for the shadow to line up again with the line you traced.

The amount of time it takes for the shadow to line up again is called a *solar day*. It is 24 hours long.

TIME ZONES

This map shows times in different parts of the United States. The United States is divided into 6 time zones. If you travel from east to west, each time zone is one hour earlier. If you travel from west to east, each time zone is one hour later.

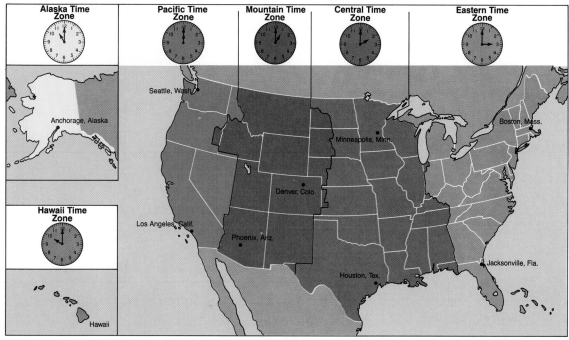

Use the map to answer these questions.

1. What time is it on the Mountain Time clock? Pacific Time clock?

2. If it is 3:00 P.M. in Boston, what time is it in Anchorage?

Complete the chart.

Zones	Hawaii	Alaska	Pacific	Mountain	Central	Eastern
Times		6:00 P.M.				
					noon	
				3:00 A.M.		

Solve. Find the time difference between your town and Frankfurt, Germany. What time would you place a telephone call to talk to a friend when it is 5:00 P.M. in Frankfurt?

Choose the correct answer. Write A, B, C, or D.

1. 563 + 172 = □

   A 735   C 391

   B 381   D not given

2. 308 − 199 = □

   A 119   C 108

   B 109   D not given

3. 8 × 9 = □

   A 63   C 17

   B 72   D not given

4. 7 × 0 = □

   A 0   C 1

   B 7   D not given

5. 4 × □ = 20

   A 4   C 16

   B 5   D not given

6. 25 ÷ 5 = □

   A 4   C 20

   B 3   D not given

7. 8 ÷ 8 = □

   A 0   C 1

   B 64   D not given

8. What time is it?

   A 7:10   C 7:40

   B 2:40   D not given

9. What time will it be in 18 minutes?

   A 12:46   C 1:25

   B 12:35   D not given

10. What is the value?

    A $2.53   C $2.75

    B $2.78   D not given

What fact do you need to solve each problem?

11. Sam bought 5 postcards. How much did they cost?

    A the cost of   C Sam's
      postage   hometown

    B cost of each   D not given
      postcard

12. Kim bought a gift for her sister. She gave the clerk $10.00. How much change did she receive?

    A her sister's   C the cost of
      name   the gift

    B what the gift   D not given
      was

Theme: Sports

Multiplication Patterns

Many items that you buy are packaged in multiples of 10 such as 10, 20, 30, or 40. Other items are packaged in multiples of 100 such as 100, 200, 300, or 400. In this lesson you will use multiples of 10 and multiples of 100 to explore patterns.

WORKING TOGETHER

Work in teams of four. Each team needs 30 small cups and several hundred counters such as corn kernels or dried beans. Put 10 counters in each cup to make "tens cups."

Experiment. Decide how to record what you do. Use drawings, number sentences, a description with words, or some other way to record your work.

- Choose any multiple of 10 less than 80. Stack tens cups to show this number.

- Make another stack to show the number. Put the stacks together. Record your work and the final result.

- Keep making equal stacks of tens cups until you have made as many stacks as you can. Record your work and the result each time you make another equal stack.

- Choose other multiples of 10 and repeat the experiment several times.

Now make some "hundreds cups." Fill 3 large cups with 100 counters in each. Place your hundreds cups with those that other teams filled. These new cups will be used for a class experiment.

Work with the whole class. Watch while one student experiments as before, using hundreds cups instead of tens cups.

- As a class, agree on a multiple of 100 that is less than 600.

- Choose a way to make your own record to show what happens when the hundreds cups are stacked.
- Make a new record each time the demonstrator experiments with a different multiple of 100.

SHARING YOUR THINKING

1. Discuss the methods that were used to record the results of the experiments.

2. Look at your work with multiples of 10. Discuss patterns that you notice when you multiply with these numbers. Then discuss patterns and examples for multiples of 100.

3. Compare your work for multiples of 10 and multiples of 100. How is it the same? How is it different?

THINKING IT THROUGH

A Calculator Game for Two Players

Use what you have learned about multiplying with multiples of 10 and multiples of 100 to play this game. Play this game several times. Take turns being Player A or Player B.

Player A 1. Think of a multiplication example. Let one factor be a multiple of 10, 100, or 1,000. Choose a one-digit number for the other factor. Record the numbers on paper but do not show your partner.

2. Use your calculator. Multiply the numbers. Do not let your partner see what you enter. Show the product in the display to your partner.

Player B Use another calculator. Experiment to find factors for this product. Record each pair of factors you find.

Player A Check your partner's work until you see the factors that you used.

Using Multiplication Patterns

Work with a partner.
Use counters, tens cups, and hundreds cups.

1. Think of a two-digit number.
   * Build this number several times.
   * Make a drawing to show your work.

2 × 56

   * Combine the counters using the fewest possible cups. There can not be more than 9 counters left outside the cups.

   * Draw and record your final result.

112

2. Choose different two-digit numbers and repeat the activity several times.

Discuss these questions with your group.

1. What are some numbers that can be multiplied by 2 to get final results less than 100?

   • What is the greatest two-digit number you can multiply by 2 to get a result less than 100? Explain how you know.

2. What are some numbers you can multiply by 3 to get results less than 100?

   • What is the greatest result you can get when you multiply a two-digit number by 3? Explain why.

3. Can you ever get a result greater than 1,000 when you multiply a two-digit number by a one-digit number? Why or why not?

═══ THINKING IT THROUGH ═══

Some products you buy show how many items there are in the package.

• For each drawing choose any number of packages from 1 to 10. Record your choices.

• Figure out how many items there are in each set of packages. Show your work.

• Discuss how you can use multiplication to help you in everyday life. Share several examples.

Using Multiplication

Some of the products you buy do not tell how many items are in the package. How could you estimate the number of items?

WORKING TOGETHER

Work in a group of 4. You will need a clear plastic bag and some type of counters to fill the bag.

1. Take an empty bag. Decide how to fill it so that you can estimate the number of counters you use. You may want to keep repeating an amount such as a handful, a cupful, or a spoonful.

   • Record your procedure and your estimate.

   • Empty the bag. Count and record the total.

   • Put all the counters back into the bag.

2. Trade bags with another group that used a different type of counter.

   • Choose and carry out a plan for using multiplication to make an estimate without opening the bag.

   • Record your procedure and your result.

3. Share your result with the other group. Compare your estimate with the other group's estimate. Compare each of your estimates to the total that you counted earlier.

Work as a class.

1. Discuss how you used multiplication to help you make your estimates.

2. Was your estimate closer when you filled a bag or when you examined a bag that someone else filled?

3. If you were to fill your bag again, what would you do to help you make a closer estimate?

4. If you were to estimate the contents of a closed container again, how would you improve your procedure?

==== THINKING IT THROUGH ====

1. Choose some consumer products that are not marked to show how many are in the package. Describe how you would use multiplication to help you estimate the number of items in each package.

   • if you could not open the package.

   • if you could open the package.

2. List and discuss other situations in everyday life where you can multiply to help you estimate.

3. Work as a class. Fill a large container with counters. Pretend that these are peanuts.

   • Decide how to share the counters so that each person in the class can get about the same amount.

   • Test your plan by distributing the counters.

   • Discuss what happens.

   • If you like, make a new plan and try again.

   • What plan would you use if you could spread out the items in the bottom of a box? Test this plan and discuss what happens.

Multiplying Two-Digit Numbers

Marie plays on a women's basketball team. She scored 14 points in each of the last 3 games. How many points did she score in all?

$3 \times 14 = \square$

Step 1
Multiply ones.
Regroup.

$$\begin{array}{r} 1 \\ 14 \\ \times\ 3 \\ \hline 2 \end{array}$$

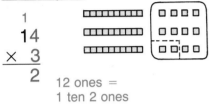

12 ones =
1 ten 2 ones

Step 2
Multiply tens.
Add 1 ten.

$$\begin{array}{r} 1 \\ 14 \\ \times\ 3 \\ \hline 42 \end{array}$$

3 tens + 1 ten =
4 tens

Marie scored 42 points in all.

Another Example

Multiply ones.
Regroup.

$$\begin{array}{r} 3 \\ 39 \\ \times\ 4 \\ \hline 6 \end{array}$$

36 ones =
3 tens 6 ones

Multiply tens.
Add 3 tens.
Regroup.

$$\begin{array}{r} 3 \\ 39 \\ \times\ 4 \\ \hline 156 \end{array}$$

12 tens + 3 tens = 15 tens,
or 1 hundred 5 tens

CLASSWORK

Find each product.

1. $\begin{array}{r} 72 \\ \times\ 3 \end{array}$
2. $\begin{array}{r} 81 \\ \times\ 2 \end{array}$
3. $\begin{array}{r} 16 \\ \times\ 3 \end{array}$
4. $\begin{array}{r} 17 \\ \times\ 2 \end{array}$
5. $\begin{array}{r} 67 \\ \times\ 5 \end{array}$
6. $\begin{array}{r} 63 \\ \times\ 8 \end{array}$

7. $\begin{array}{r} 43 \\ \times\ 7 \end{array}$
8. $\begin{array}{r} 26 \\ \times\ 8 \end{array}$
9. $\begin{array}{r} 65 \\ \times\ 6 \end{array}$
10. $\begin{array}{r} 82 \\ \times\ 5 \end{array}$
11. $\begin{array}{r} 76 \\ \times\ 2 \end{array}$
12. $\begin{array}{r} 92 \\ \times\ 9 \end{array}$

13. $6 \times 15 = \square$
14. $4 \times 24 = \square$
15. $9 \times 36 = \square$
16. $8 \times 58 = \square$

Find each product.

1. 63 × 3	2. 54 × 2	3. 11 × 5	4. 49 × 5
5. 89 × 9	6. 90 × 7	7. 41 × 9	8. 35 × 7
9. 72 × 4	10. 12 × 8	11. 48 × 6	12. 93 × 6

13. $7 \times 31 = \square$ 14. $3 \times 32 = \square$

15. $9 \times 35 = \square$ 16. $4 \times 56 = \square$

Follow the rule to find each missing number.

Rule: Multiply by 3.

	Input	Output
17.	10	
18.	23	
19.	50	
20.	18	
21.	46	

Rule: Multiply by 6.

	Input	Output
22.	31	
23.	15	
24.	87	
25.	54	
26.	77	

Compare. Use >, <, or = for ●.

★27. 8×21 ● 4×42 ★28. 3×67 ● 5×33

APPLICATION

29. Jeff runs for 25 minutes each day. How many minutes of running does Jeff do in 5 days?

★30. The Adams School sent 27 students to the track meet. Jefferson and Roosevelt schools each sent 59 students to the track meet. How many students came from all 3 schools?

Mixed Practice

1. 63 − 27		2. 8 × 6	
3. 47 + 23		4. 43 − 22	
5. 7 × 5		6. 60 − 35	
7. 58 + 43		8. 86 + 77	

9. $431 + 298 = \square$

10. $627 - 49 = \square$

11. $56 \div 7 = \square$

12. $658 + 517 = \square$

13. $36 \div 4 = \square$

14. $302 - 138 = \square$

15. $56 \div 8 = \square$

16. $9 \times 8 = \square$

Round to the underlined place.

17. 4̲75   18. 2̲9

19. 3̲,163   20. 82̲4

21. 1̲12   22. 39̲9

23. 7,0̲93   24. 2̲,692

Multiplying Three-Digit Numbers

A gymnastics team from Columbus, Georgia went to Atlanta, Georgia for a meet. How many miles did the team travel round trip?

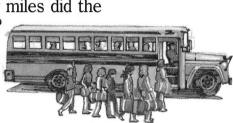

Georgia Mileage Chart

Multiply to find the number of miles round trip.

```
  1
117
×   2
    4
```
14 ones =
1 ten 4 ones

```
  1
117
×   2
   34
```
2 tens + 1 ten =
3 tens

```
  1
117
×   2
  234
```

The team traveled 234 miles round trip.

Find 3 × 268.

Multiply ones.
Regroup if necessary.

```
  2
268
×   3
    4
```

Multiply tens.
Add any extra tens.
Regroup if necessary.

```
 22
268
×   3
   04
```

Multiply hundreds.
Add any extra hundreds.

```
 22
268
×   3
  804
```

CLASSWORK

Find each product.

1. 243
    × 2

2. 315
    × 3

3. 152
    × 5

4. 237
    × 4

5. 106
    × 8

6. 3 × 123 = □

7. 6 × 128 = □

8. 5 × 167 = □

Find each product.

1.	198 × 4	2.	317 × 2	3.	264 × 3	4.	183 × 5	5.	124 × 6
6.	102 × 9	7.	308 × 3	8.	235 × 4	9.	257 × 3	10.	458 × 2
11.	234 × 2	12.	103 × 8	13.	279 × 3	14.	396 × 2	15.	135 × 6

16. 2 × 295 = ☐   17. 6 × 116 = ☐   18. 3 × 316 = ☐

19. 4 × 184 = ☐   20. 7 × 129 = ☐   21. 5 × 149 = ☐

Find each missing digit.

★22.	3∎4 × ∎ 668	★23.	∎21 × ∎ 9∎3	★24.	∎04 × ∎ 816	★25.	∎35 × ∎ 810	★26.	25∎ × 2 ∎06

APPLICATION

Use the map on page 152.

27. How many miles round trip must the Augusta team travel to a meet in Tifton?

28. Cindy scored 112 points and Ann scored 115 points at the Tifton meet. At the Augusta meet, Cindy scored 97 points. How many more points did Cindy score in Tifton than in Augusta?

★ 29. On one tour, the Columbus team traveled to Tifton and Waycross. How many miles did the team travel round trip?

Problem Solving

MAKING AND USING TABLES

A *table* is a way to organize facts. A table is sometimes used to help solve problems.

1. Here is the scoreboard for the baseball game. The game was 7 innings long. Who won, and what was the final score?

What is the question?

Who won, and what was the final score?

What are the facts?

The game was 7 innings long. The scoreboard shows the number of runs scored for each team.

How can the answer be found?

Look at the scoreboard. Add up the runs scored for each team.

Tigers: 3 + 1 + 1 = 5 runs
Bears: 2 + 2 = 4 runs
The Tigers won by a score of 5 to 4.

Did you read the table correctly?
Is your arithmetic correct?

Yes. 3 + 1 + 1 = 5 runs
    2 + 2 = 4 runs

2. Parking costs $2.00 for the first hour and $1.00 an hour after that. The Burts parked their car for 5 hours. How much did it cost?

Copy and complete to solve the problem.

Parking Fees				
Hours	1	2	3	
Cost	$2.00	$3.00	$4.00	

154

The table shows the points scored by boys on the basketball team.

Player	Points
John	5
Luis	8
Scott	3
Willie	2
Mike	5

1. Who scored the most points?

2. How many points did Willie score?

3. Who scored 3 points?

4. What two players scored the same number of points?

5. How many more points did Luis score than Scott?

6. What was the total number of points scored?

The girls' basketball team played a game. Mary scored 5 points, Alice scored 3 points, Janet scored 7 points, Louise scored 1 point, and Karen scored 2 points.

7. Make a table for this game.

8. Who scored the most points?

9. How many points did Karen score?

10. How many points were scored in all?

Copy and complete to solve the problem.

11. Sara can swim 2 lengths of the pool in 3 minutes. If she swims at the same pace, how long will it take her to swim 8 lengths of the pool?

Lengths of pool	2	4	6	
Minutes	3	6	9	

12. Warren made lemonade. He used 8 cups of water for every 4 lemons. How much water is needed for 16 lemons?

Lemons	4	8			
Cups of water	8	16			

=CREATE YOUR OWN PROBLEM=

The table shows the price of tickets to the school track meet. Make up 2 problems using the table.

Number of tickets	1	2	3	4	5	6 or more
Cost per ticket	$2.00	$1.75	$1.50	$1.25	$1.10	$1.00

Greater Products

A public swimming pool is 164 feet long. Jonathan swam the length of the pool 8 times. How many feet did he swim?

$8 \times 164 = \square$

Step 1 Multiply ones. Regroup if necessary.	**Step 2** Multiply tens. Add any extra tens. Regroup if necessary.	**Step 3** Multiply hundreds. Add any extra hundreds. Regroup if necessary.

$$\begin{array}{r} 3 \\ 164 \\ \times\ \ 8 \\ \hline 2 \end{array}$$
32 ones = 3 tens 2 ones

$$\begin{array}{r} 53 \\ 164 \\ \times\ \ 8 \\ \hline 12 \end{array}$$
48 tens + 3 tens = 51 tens, or 5 hundreds 1 ten

$$\begin{array}{r} 53 \\ 164 \\ \times\ \ 8 \\ \hline 1{,}312 \end{array}$$
8 hundreds + 5 hundreds = 13 hundreds, or 1 thousand 3 hundreds

Jonathan swam 1,312 feet.

CLASSWORK

Find each product.

1. $\begin{array}{r} 208 \\ \times\ \ 9 \\ \hline \end{array}$
2. $\begin{array}{r} 425 \\ \times\ \ 3 \\ \hline \end{array}$
3. $\begin{array}{r} 524 \\ \times\ \ 4 \\ \hline \end{array}$
4. $\begin{array}{r} 679 \\ \times\ \ 5 \\ \hline \end{array}$
5. $\begin{array}{r} 896 \\ \times\ \ 6 \\ \hline \end{array}$

6. $7 \times 218 = \square$
7. $2 \times 856 = \square$
8. $8 \times 906 = \square$

Find each product.

1. 564×2	2. 605×9	3. 731×8	4. 269×3	5. 250×5
6. 128×3	7. 853×6	8. 416×6	9. 804×8	10. 317×2
11. 723×3	12. 518×5	13. 159×7	14. 673×4	15. 178×6

16. $9 \times 401 = \square$

17. $8 \times 352 = \square$

18. $6 \times 129 = \square$

19. $5 \times 384 = \square$

20. $2 \times 592 = \square$

21. $4 \times 810 = \square$

★ 22. **Find the first three products. Look for the pattern. Use the pattern to find the next six products.**

a. $9 \times 111 = \square$ b. $9 \times 222 = \square$ c. $9 \times 333 = \square$

d. $9 \times 444 = \square$ e. $9 \times 555 = \square$ f. $9 \times 666 = \square$

g. $9 \times 777 = \square$ h. $9 \times 888 = \square$ i. $9 \times 999 = \square$

APPLICATION

23. The gallery at the pool has 175 seats. It was filled for the 3 days of the swimming meet. How many people watched the 3-day meet from the gallery?

★ 24. The 4 members of a relay team each swam the 164-foot length of the pool twice. What is the total number of feet they swam?

CALCULATOR

Use only the digits 1, 2, 3, and 4.
Use a different digit in each place.
How many different products can you make?
What is the least product you can make?
What is the greatest product you can make?

Estimating Products

At the U.S. National Hot Air Balloon Championship, one balloon stayed up 48 minutes. A second balloon stayed up 3 times as long. About how long was the second balloon in the air?

▶To estimate a product, round each factor to its greatest place. Then multiply.

$$
\begin{array}{r} 48 \\ \times\ 3 \end{array}
\quad \text{rounds to} \quad
\begin{array}{r} 50 \\ \times\ 3 \\ \hline 150 \end{array}
\ \text{estimated product}
$$

The second balloon was in the air about 150 minutes.

Estimate to be sure a product makes sense.

$$
\begin{array}{r} 536 \\ \times\ 7 \\ \hline 3{,}752 \end{array}
\quad \text{rounds to} \quad
\begin{array}{r} 500 \\ \times\ 7 \\ \hline 3{,}500 \end{array}
$$

Exact product and estimate are close.
The answer makes sense.

CLASSWORK

Estimate each product.

1. $\begin{array}{r} 32 \\ \times\ 4 \end{array}$

2. $\begin{array}{r} 44 \\ \times\ 2 \end{array}$

3. $\begin{array}{r} 27 \\ \times\ 8 \end{array}$

4. $\begin{array}{r} 213 \\ \times\ 3 \end{array}$

5. $\begin{array}{r} 682 \\ \times\ 5 \end{array}$

6. $6 \times 709 = \square$

7. $5 \times 169 = \square$

8. $7 \times 850 = \square$

PRACTICE

Estimate each product.

1.   17
   × 4
	2. 38
	   × 6
		3. 91
		   × 3
			4. 75
			   × 5
				5. 63
				   × 8

6.   65
   × 9
	7. 33
	   × 7
		8. 58
		   × 2
			9. 41
			   × 5
				10. 86
				   × 8

11.   164
    × 2
	12. 318
	    × 5
		13. 725
		    × 7
			14. 881
			    × 8
				15. 346
				    × 3

16. $4 \times 53 = \square$

17. $8 \times 97 = \square$

18. $6 \times 126 = \square$

19. $2 \times 359 = \square$

20. $7 \times 375 = \square$

21. $4 \times 934 = \square$

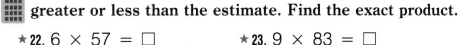

Estimate. Tell whether each product should be greater or less than the estimate. Find the exact product.

★ 22. $6 \times 57 = \square$

★ 23. $9 \times 83 = \square$

★ 24. $4 \times 435 = \square$

★ 25. $5 \times 185 = \square$

★ 26. $8 \times 665 = \square$

★ 27. $7 \times 649 = \square$

APPLICATION

28. In a distance race, a balloon traveled 219 feet. The winning balloon traveled 3 times as far. Estimate the distance traveled by the winner.

★ 29. Nine buses arrived at the balloon area. Each bus held 48 people. Estimate how many people will not have seats in a stand that seats 400 people.

LOGICAL THINKING

Sara arranged some balloon stickers for an art project this way:

Then she rearranged them so that they looked like this:

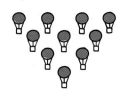

Sara moved only 3 stickers in the first arrangement to get the second. Can you figure out the moves?

Multiplying Greater Numbers

On Saturday there were 3 times as many people at the tennis matches as there were on Wednesday. How many people came to the matches on Saturday?

Day	Number of People at the Tennis Matches
Wednesday	1,975
Thursday	2,609
Friday	3,860
Saturday	

Multiply to find the answer.

Step 1 Multiply ones. Regroup if necessary.	**Step 2** Multiply tens. Add any extra tens. Regroup if necessary.	**Step 3** Multiply hundreds. Add any extra hundreds. Regroup if necessary.	**Step 4** Multiply thousands. Add any extra thousands.
¹ 1,975 × 3 = 5	²¹ 1,975 × 3 = 25	²²¹ 1,975 × 3 = 925	²²¹ 1,975 × 3 = 5,925

There were 5,925 people at the tennis matches on Saturday.

Estimate to be sure the answer makes sense.

$$\begin{array}{r} 1,975 \\ \times \quad 3 \end{array}$$ rounds to $$\begin{array}{r} 2,000 \\ \times \quad\quad 3 \\ \hline 6,000 \end{array}$$ Exact product and estimate are close. The answer makes sense.

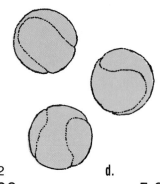

More Examples

a.
$$\begin{array}{r} ^{2\,4} \\ 7,138 \\ \times \quad 6 \\ \hline 42,828 \end{array}$$

b.
$$\begin{array}{r} ^{6\,\,4\,7} \\ 4,759 \\ \times \quad 8 \\ \hline 38,072 \end{array}$$

c.
$$\begin{array}{r} ^{1\,\,\,2} \\ 1,306 \\ \times \quad 4 \\ \hline 5,224 \end{array}$$

d.
$$\begin{array}{r} ^{5} \\ 5,008 \\ \times \quad 7 \\ \hline 35,056 \end{array}$$

CLASSWORK

Multiply. Estimate to be sure each answer makes sense.

1.
$$\begin{array}{r} 2,276 \\ \times \quad 2 \end{array}$$

2.
$$\begin{array}{r} 1,196 \\ \times \quad 3 \end{array}$$

3.
$$\begin{array}{r} 1,820 \\ \times \quad 4 \end{array}$$

4.
$$\begin{array}{r} 4,089 \\ \times \quad 7 \end{array}$$

5.
$$\begin{array}{r} 6,974 \\ \times \quad 8 \end{array}$$

6. $5 \times 4,576 = \square$

7. $9 \times 1,293 = \square$

8. $6 \times 8,917 = \square$

Multiply. Estimate to be sure each answer makes sense.

1.	2,773 × 3	2.	2,479 × 2	3.	1,643 × 5	4.	1,497 × 4	5.	3,855 × 2
6.	6,812 × 7	7.	2,345 × 6	8.	4,821 × 5	9.	1,465 × 9	10.	7,081 × 8
11.	8,910 × 6	12.	5,769 × 5	13.	6,153 × 4	14.	7,008 × 9	15.	6,345 × 8

16. $2 \times 6,318 = \square$

17. $3 \times 8,547 = \square$

18. $4 \times 5,284 = \square$

19. $6 \times 7,603 = \square$

20. $2 \times 1,997 = \square$

21. $5 \times 4,359 = \square$

★22. $4 \times 15,982 = \square$

★23. $8 \times 29,194 = \square$

★24. $7 \times 40,753 = \square$

APPLICATION

25. Each of the 4 refreshment stands stocked 1,575 cans of orange juice. How many cans of orange juice were stocked in all?

26. Look at the table on page 160. On Sunday they expect about 2 times as many people as there were on Thursday. Estimate the number of people they expect on Sunday.

★27. At Tuesday's tennis matches 1,500 paper sun visors were given away free. During the next three days 4 times as many visors were given away. How many visors were given away in all?

Look at the table on page 160.

CALCULATOR

Multiply $9 \times 3,402$.

What should the ones digit be?

The ones digit in the product should be 8 because $9 \times 2 = 18$.

$$\begin{array}{r} {}^{3}\ {}^{1} \\ 3,402 \\ \times\quad 9 \\ \hline 30,618 \end{array}$$

Tell what the ones digit in each product should be. Then use your calculator to find each product. Check that the ones digit is correct.

1. $3 \times 2,007$ 2. $8 \times 4,879$

3. $6 \times 3,557$ 4. $4 \times 1,054$

Multiplying Money

Item	Cost
Horn	$ 4.75
Mirror	$ 5.99
Ankle wrap	$ 8.50
Lock	$24.95

What is the cost of 3 mirrors?

Multiply money the same way you multiply other numbers.

Step 1

```
  2
$5.99
×   3
    7
```

Step 2

```
 2 2
$5.99
×   3
   97
```

Step 3

```
 2 2
$5.99
×   3
$17.97
```
Write the dollar sign and decimal point in the product.

The cost of 3 mirrors is $17.97.

Find 2 × $24.95. Estimate to be sure the product makes sense.

```
  1 1
$24.95    rounds to    $20
×    2                 ×  2
$49.90                 $40
```
Exact product and estimate are close. The answer makes sense.

CLASSWORK

Multiply.

1. $.74
   × 4

2. $.32
   × 9

3. $3.95
   × 3

4. $10.28
   × 7

5. $69.15
   × 8

Estimate each product.

6. 5 × $10.88 = ☐

7. 6 × $17.35 = ☐

8. 9 × $71.45 = ☐

Multiply.

1. $.31
    × 2

2. $.14
    × 3

3. $.62
    × 6

4. $2.73
    × 3

5. $4.87
    × 8

6. $6.90
    × 8

7. $6.29
    × 9

8. $70.80
    × 6

9. $36.57
    × 7

10. $19.86
    × 3

11. 3 × $.44 = ☐

12. 8 × $.68 = ☐

13. 5 × $1.90 = ☐

14. 7 × $4.89 = ☐

15. 6 × $43.19 = ☐

16. 9 × $58.85 = ☐

Multiply. Estimate to be sure each answer makes sense.

17. $12.50
    × 4

18. $17.89
    × 5

19. $26.12
    × 6

20. $38.96
    × 4

21. $82.35
    × 8

Which number sentence is false?

22. a. 5 × $.89 = $4.45

    b. 4 × $6.58 = $26.32

    c. 7 × $3.25 = $24.45

    d. 3 × $73.56 = $220.68

23. a. 8 × $.49 = $3.92

    b. 2 × $7.18 = $14.36

    c. 9 × $37.25 = $335.25

    d. 6 × $49.64 = $296.84

Solve.

★24. $20 − (3 × $2.75) = ☐

★25. $50 + (2 × $17.50) = ☐

APPLICATION

Use the price list at the top of page 162.

26. Alice bought 4 horns for the members of her bicycle club. How much did they cost in all?

27. Ms. Corey sold 6 locks during the weekend. How much money was she paid for them in all?

28. Jerry bought a horn and a lock. How much did they cost in all?

★29. Mr. Berg bought 7 mirrors and 5 ankle wraps for his Boy Scouts. What was his change from $100?

Problem Solving

SKILLS AND STRATEGIES REVIEW At Play

TICKETS

BASKETBALL GAME ADMISSION
ADULTS: $1.95
STUDENTS: $1.25

Solve each problem. If a fact is missing, make up a fact. Then solve the problem.

1. The county basketball league has 6 teams. Each team in the league has 22 players. How many players are there in all?

2. The coach bought 22 basketball jerseys. He also bought 3 basketballs at $18.95 each. How much were all the basketballs?

3. The basketball league's leading scorer scored 117 points. The runner-up scored 19 points less. How many points did the runner-up score?

4. Every seat was filled at the high school basketball game. There were 3 times as many fans at the state college basketball game. How many people were at the state college game?

5. There are 24 boys and 16 girls in the band. There are 12 cheerleaders. How many students are in the school band?

6. Mark scored 4 times as many points as Chris. Chris scored 5 points. How many points did Mark score?

7. A group of 7 students went to the game. How much did they pay for their tickets in all?

8. The basketball game started at 7:00 P.M. and lasted 2 hours. What time did the game end?

★ 9. A glass of orange juice at the refreshment stand cost $.75. Mr. Pérez bought 3 glasses of juice. He paid with a $5.00 bill. How much change did he get?

★ 10. Seven members of the Lee family went to the basketball game. Five members of the family were adults and two were students. What was the total cost of the tickets?

164

Use the table to solve the following problems.

COUNTY BASKETBALL LEAGUE STANDINGS		
Team	Won	Lost
Sharks	8	3
Blue Hens	8	3
Tigers	7	
Devils	6	5
Beavers	3	8
Owls	1	10

11. How many games have the Beavers won?

12. How many games have the Blue Hens lost?

13. Each team plays 15 games in a season. How many games do the Devils still have to play?

14. Each team has played the same number of games. How many games have the Tigers lost?

15. How many more games have the Owls lost than the Sharks?

16. How many more games have the Tigers won than the Beavers?

★17. The score at halftime was Tigers 34, Devils 29. If both teams score an equal number of points in the second half, by how many points will the Tigers win the game?

★18. At halftime the score was Sharks 28, Blue Hens 22. If the Sharks score 5 points in the second half, how many points must the Blue Hens score to win the game?

═══════ SOMETHING EXTRA ═══════

You Find Out ·

Ask the people in your class to name their favorite sport. Make a bar graph to show the answers.

What sport was chosen by the most students?

Find each product. pages 144–153, 156–157

1. 32
× 2

2. 15
× 3

3. 16
× 6

4. 94
× 8

5. 62
× 9

6. 126
× 4

7. 115
× 7

8. 600
× 9

9. 300
× 4

10. 835
× 8

11. 635
× 2

12. 436
× 7

13. 865
× 6

14. 549
× 3

15. 674
× 5

16. 6 × 718 = ☐

17. 9 × 991 = ☐

18. 7 × 742 = ☐

Estimate each product. pages 158–159

19. 35
× 5

20. 62
× 3

21. 127
× 9

22. 475
× 7

23. 785
× 8

Multiply. Estimate to be sure each answer makes sense. pages 160–163

24. 1,300
× 4

25. 4,806
× 2

26. 3,671
× 3

27. 5,486
× 6

28. 1,075
× 8

29. $.72
× 7

30. $1.15
× 5

31. $8.76
× 7

32. $9.14
× 4

33. $5.87
× 3

34. 5,400
× 2

35. $28.63
× 5

36. $10.73
× 9

37. 4,563
× 7

38. 1,500
× 6

39. 9 × $.92 = ☐

40. 8 × $3.25 = ☐

41. 3 × $19.85 = ☐

42. 6 × 4,384 = ☐

43. 7 × $65.83 = ☐

44. 4 × 9,980 = ☐

Solve. pages 154–155, 164–165

45. A book about famous American athletes costs $9.89. How much would 9 books cost?

46. The price of one paperback book is $5.00. The price of each additional book, up to 10 books, goes down 25¢. Lee bought 6 books. Make a table. How much did the sixth book cost?

Multiply.

1. $\begin{array}{r} 21 \\ \times\ 4 \\ \hline \end{array}$ 2. $\begin{array}{r} 39 \\ \times\ 2 \\ \hline \end{array}$ 3. $\begin{array}{r} 84 \\ \times\ 3 \\ \hline \end{array}$ 4. $\begin{array}{r} 216 \\ \times\ 4 \\ \hline \end{array}$ 5. $\begin{array}{r} 338 \\ \times\ 5 \\ \hline \end{array}$

6. $9 \times 80 = \square$ 7. $9 \times 800 = \square$

8. $7 \times 804 = \square$ 9. $6 \times 830 = \square$

Estimate each product.

10. $\begin{array}{r} 26 \\ \times\ 8 \\ \hline \end{array}$ 11. $\begin{array}{r} 51 \\ \times\ 2 \\ \hline \end{array}$ 12. $\begin{array}{r} 375 \\ \times\ 6 \\ \hline \end{array}$ 13. $\begin{array}{r} 929 \\ \times\ 9 \\ \hline \end{array}$ 14. $\begin{array}{r} 755 \\ \times\ 4 \\ \hline \end{array}$

Find each product.

15. $\begin{array}{r} \$.45 \\ \times\ 3 \\ \hline \end{array}$ 16. $\begin{array}{r} \$2.98 \\ \times\ 8 \\ \hline \end{array}$ 17. $\begin{array}{r} 4,863 \\ \times\ 7 \\ \hline \end{array}$ 18. $\begin{array}{r} 9,305 \\ \times\ 6 \\ \hline \end{array}$ 19. $\begin{array}{r} \$67.28 \\ \times\ 5 \\ \hline \end{array}$

20. $2 \times \$3.86 = \square$ 21. $6 \times \$12.39 = \square$

22. $7 \times \$83.25 = \square$ 23. $8 \times 2,945 = \square$

Solve.

24. There are 465 seats in the Edison School gym. Every seat was filled for the 9 home games of the basketball season. How many people watched the home games from the seats?

25. A season's ticket to Edison School's soccer matches costs $11.50. You pay $11.00 a ticket if you buy a pair. Sonya bought 7 tickets. Make a table. How much did she pay?

Soccer shoes cost $14.75 a pair. Jerseys cost $6.49 each. Ms. Jackson wants to buy each of her 2 children soccer shoes and a jersey. If she has $50 to spend, can she also buy a soccer ball that costs $8.00?

THE MULTIPLICATION GAME

To play the multiplication game, you will need:

- number cards marked 0–9
- a paper bag
- paper and pencils

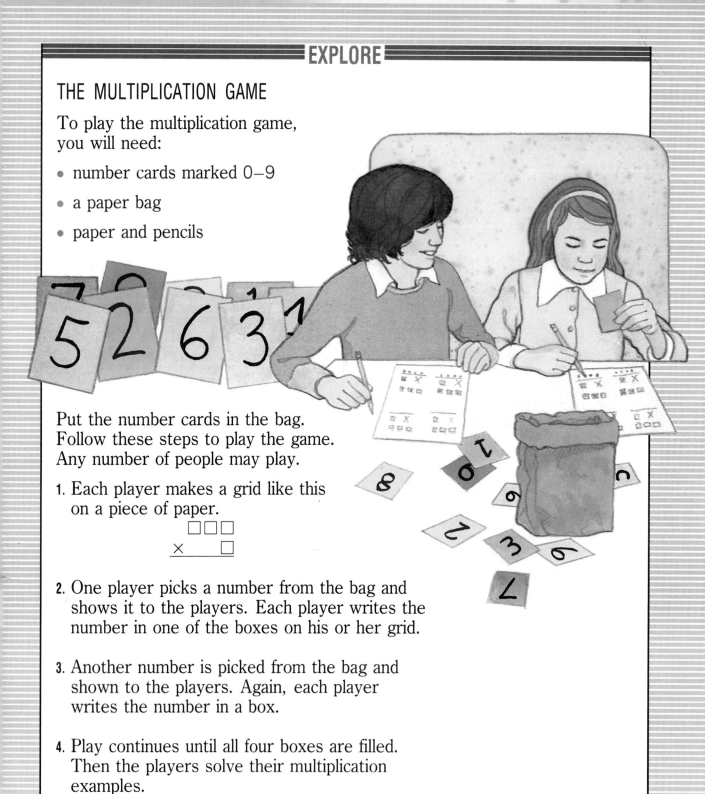

Put the number cards in the bag. Follow these steps to play the game. Any number of people may play.

1. Each player makes a grid like this on a piece of paper.

$$\frac{\square\square\square}{\times\ \ \ \square}$$

2. One player picks a number from the bag and shows it to the players. Each player writes the number in one of the boxes on his or her grid.

3. Another number is picked from the bag and shown to the players. Again, each player writes the number in a box.

4. Play continues until all four boxes are filled. Then the players solve their multiplication examples.

5. The player with the greatest product is the winner. That player may pick the cards for the next game.

A SHORTCUT FOR ADDITION

Karl Friedrich Gauss (1777–1855) was a famous German mathematician and astronomer. One day in school his teacher gave him this problem.

Find the sum of the first 100 numbers.

1 + 2 + 3 + 4 + . . . + 99 + 100

Gauss surprised his teacher by solving the problem very quickly.

This drawing shows a method Gauss could have used. See how you can find the sum of all the numbers from 1 to 10.

The sum of each pair is 11. There are 5 pairs.

$$5 \times 11 = \square$$

The answer is 55.

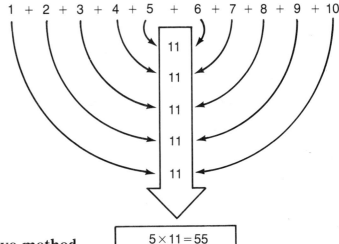

Find each sum, using the above method.

1. 6 + 7 + 8 + 9 + 10 + 11

2. 21 + 22 + 23 + 24 + 25 + 26 + 27 + 28 + 29 + 30

3. 2 + 4 + 6 + 8 + 10 + 12 + 14 + 16

4. 3 + 6 + 9 + 12 + 15 + 18 + 21 + 24 + 27 + 30

5. What answer did young Gauss give to his teacher?

USING BASIC IN PROGRAMS

A **program** is a list of instructions for the computer. A program is often written in the computer language BASIC.

In BASIC, * means multiplication and / means division.

Lines are usually numbered by 10's. Then we can add lines in between without renumbering.

```
10 PRINT 4 * 22
20 PRINT 18/3
30 PRINT 7 * 200
40 END

RUN
88
6
1400
```

The last instruction should be END.

When we type RUN, the computer follows the instructions in order by line number.

Suppose we want to add a line to this program.

To add a line to print 7, type 35 PRINT 7.

```
10 PRINT 1
20 PRINT 3
30 PRINT 5
40 PRINT 9
50 END
35 PRINT 7

RUN
1
3
5
7
9
```

The computer does line 35 after line 30.

For each program, tell what the output will be.

```
1. 10 PRINT 463 + 721
   20 PRINT 902 - 527
   30 END
```

```
2. 10 PRINT 2 * 76
   20 PRINT 21/3
   30 END
```

```
3. 10 PRINT 2
   30 PRINT 6
   20 PRINT 4
   40 END
```

```
4. 10 PRINT 25 + 35 + 45
   20 PRINT 3 * 105
   30 PRINT 5 * 567
   40 END
   25 PRINT 700 + 245
```

In BASIC, quotation marks can be used in PRINT statements. The computer will display *exactly* what is typed inside the quotation marks.

These lines tell the computer to print what is inside the quotation marks.

The computer will compute 6 × 132.

```
10 PRINT "HELLO"
20 PRINT "LET'S MULTIPLY"
30 PRINT "6 TIMES 132"
40 PRINT 6 * 132
50 END
RUN
HELLO
LET'S MULTIPLY
6 TIMES 132
792
```

For each program, tell what the output will be.

5.
```
10 PRINT "START WITH 15"
20 PRINT "DIVIDE BY 3"
30 PRINT "ADD 2"
40 PRINT 15/3 + 2
50 END
```

6.
```
10 PRINT "LET'S MULTIPLY"
20 PRINT "5 TIMES 243 ="
30 PRINT 5 * 243
40 PRINT "3 * 265 ="
50 PRINT 3 * 265
60 END
```

=== AT THE COMPUTER ===

1. Enter and RUN each program in 1-4, page 170, and 5 and 6 above.

2. Compare each output with your answer.

★ 3. On Your Own: Write a program to print this output. RUN your program to test it.
```
HELLO
LET'S COMPUTE
426 + 87 =
513
8 * 901 =
7208
14/7 =
2
382 - 75 =
307
```

Choose the correct answer. Write A, B, C, or D.

1. What is the value of 7 in
1,746,291?

   A 7,000,000   **C** 70,000

   B 700,000   **D** not given

2. Estimate. 746 − 374 = □

   A 1,100   **C** 300

   B 200   **D** not given

3. 8 × 6 = □

   A 48   **C** 14

   B 40   **D** not given

4. 45 ÷ 9 = □

   A 5   **C** 6

   B 36   **D** not given

5. What time is it?

   A 6:17   **C** 6:19

   B 5:19   **D** not given

6. What time will it be in
3 hours 21 minutes?

   A 7:45   **C** 6:37

   B 8:37   **D** not given

7. What is the value?

   A $14.56   **C** $15.46

   B $15.56   **D** not given

8. How many pets are owned by
the students in Grade 2?

PETS OWNED	
Grade 1	🐾🐾🐾🐾🐾
Grade 2	🐾🐾🐾🐾🐾🐾🐾
Grade 3	🐾🐾🐾🐾

Each 🐾 stands for 2 pets.

   A 14   **C** 10

   B 8   **D** not given

Answer each question.

Terry bought tennis balls for $1.19
and a shoehorn for $.45. A tennis
racket costs $98.95. How much did
he spend?

9. Which fact is not needed?

   A Tennis balls   **C** A shoehorn
       cost $1.19.   costs $.45.

   B A racket   **D** not given
       costs $98.95.

10. How much did Terry spend in all?

   A $1.64   **C** $1.54

   B $.74   **D** not given

Theme: Exploring Space

Understanding Division

You will need one-dollar bills and ten-dollar bills
in play money. Work in groups of four to share
different amounts of money. If there are more than
four students in a group, take turns sharing the bills.
Other students can act as banker and recorder.

1. Take a stack of one-dollar bills about $\frac{1}{8}$ inch thick.

   - Have each person in your group take a dollar
     as the stack passes from person to person.

   - Stop when there are not enough bills left for each
     person to have the same amount of money.
     Place any remaining bills in the center of the table.

   - Use the results of your activity to find the
     number of bills in the original stack.

   - Decide how to record your work to show what
     happened when you did this activity.

   - Repeat this activity several times with different
     stacks of dollar bills. Record your work.

2. Now use ten-dollar bills and one-dollar bills. Choose
   any amount less than $100. Take the least possible
   number of bills for that amount.

   - Share the bills until each person has the same amount of
     money. Exchange a ten-dollar bill for 10 ones, as needed.

   - Place any remaining bills in the center of the table.

   - Record your work to show what happened.

   - Repeat this activity several times.

1. When did you need to exchange ten-dollar bills for one-dollar bills in order to share equally? Discuss several examples.

2. Use your records.

   * Describe what happened when you did the activities.

   * What do you notice about the possible remainders when 4 people share?

THINKING IT THROUGH

Work in a group of 4 students to test your predictions.

1. Predict the possible remainders when 2 people share; when 3 people share. Explain your reasoning.

   * Share amounts of money less than $100. Record your work. Show all the possible remainders when 2 people share.

   * Share amounts of money less than $100 again. Record your work. Show all the possible remainders when 3 people share.

2. Predict all possible remainders when 8 people share. Test your prediction. Record an example to show each possible remainder.

3. Sometimes the remainder is zero when you share. How can you tell that the remainder will be zero without doing an experiment? Discuss several examples.

Exploring Division

Work with a partner. You will need play money and a number cube that shows 1 through 6. Use what you know about making equal groups of dollar bills to play this game.

Place a stack of 30 one-dollar bills between you. Take turns.

- Count out 10 or more bills from the stack. Place the bills in front of you.

- Roll the number cube to find out how many groups to make.

- Make equal groups of bills. Stop when there are not enough bills left for each group to have the same number of bills. Score 1 point for each remaining bill.

- Return all bills to the original stack.

After 3 turns, the player with the fewest points wins.

5
2
4
3
1
6

1. What is a good strategy to use when playing this game? Discuss.

   • Are there amounts of money that are better to choose than others? Give several examples.

   • Explain the reasons for your choices.

2. Is there a best number to get when you roll the number cube? Explain your answer.

THINKING IT THROUGH

1. Play the game several more times to try the strategies that you discussed.

2. Which four numbers would you choose if you had four turns during a game and you had to choose a different number of bills for each turn?

   • Make a table. Use Workmat 1 if you wish. List your choices in order.

   • For each choice, list the numbers on the cube that would give you zero as a remainder.

3. Share your data with others. Compare your results. Explain why there is or is not one way to select the four best numbers.

Exploring Division Patterns

Understanding some number patterns will help you divide greater numbers.

Work with a partner. Use play money. Make equal groups of bills to show each of these divisions. Decide how to record your results.

1. $12 \div 6$
   $120 \div 6$
   $1{,}200 \div 6$

2. $10 \div 5$
   $100 \div 5$
   $1{,}000 \div 5$

3. $60 \div 2$
   $600 \div 2$
   $6{,}000 \div 2$

4. $80 \div 4$
   $800 \div 4$
   $8{,}000 \div 4$

SHARING YOUR THINKING

1. How are the division problems in each group alike? How are they different?

2. What patterns do you notice in the quotients for each group of divisions?

3. Discuss how using patterns can help you find each of these quotients. Find each quotient.

   $140 \div 7$ $1{,}400 \div 7$ $1{,}500 \div 3$

THINKING IT THROUGH

1. Use play money to show your work.

   - Find the quotient for each of these divisions:
     $6{,}000 \div 2$, $800 \div 2$, and $40 \div 2$. Now find $6{,}840 \div 2$.

   - Use patterns to find each quotient: $1{,}530 \div 3$, $1{,}536 \div 3$, and $1{,}509 \div 3$.

   - Make up some other divisions that are like this.

2. Work with a partner. Take turns completing the division patterns. Find each quotient.

   - $3\overline{)30}$, $3\overline{)60}$, $3\overline{)90}$, ..., $3\overline{)270}$

   - $4\overline{)400}$, $4\overline{)800}$, $4\overline{)1{,}200}$, ..., $4\overline{)3{,}600}$

   - $6\overline{)600}$, $6\overline{)1{,}200}$, $6\overline{)1{,}800}$, ..., $6\overline{)5{,}400}$

- Make up other division patterns like these.

3. Suppose you want to divide each number by 3: 175, 145, 165, 192, 139, and 129. For each division, tell whether the quotient would be closer to the quotient for $3\overline{)120}$, $3\overline{)150}$, or $3\overline{)180}$. Explain your answers.

4. Look at each division below.
   - What division pattern is it close to?
   - Use the division pattern to estimate the quotient.

   $4\overline{)827}$ $4\overline{)119}$ $2\overline{)6,319}$ $5\overline{)1,486}$

   - Discuss your patterns and your estimates.

5. Display the bills shown at the right. How can you make 2 equal shares? 3 equal shares? 4 equal shares? 5 equal shares?

6. Use play money. Choose any amount between 500 and 800. Make 4 equal groups. Record your results. Repeat this investigation several times. You may want to use Workmat 1 to record your work.

EXPLORING DIVISION							
Total Amount			Number of Equal Groups	Amount in Each Group			
hundreds	tens	ones		hundreds	tens	ones	Remainder
6	3	8	4	1	5	9	2

   - Discuss when you needed to exchange hundreds or tens to be able to share.

7. How can you divide without using models?
   - Decide on a plan. Use your plan to show several divisions. Record your work.
   - Share your division records with others. Discuss how they are alike and how they are different.

Dividing Two-Digit Numbers

A space shuttle takes 7 people on each full flight. How many full flights are needed for 89 people? How many people would not get on a full flight?

$89 \div 7 = \square$

Step 1
Decide where to place the first digit in the quotient.

$7\overline{)89}$ **Think**
There are enough tens to divide.

Step 2
Divide.
Then multiply.

$\begin{array}{r} 1 \\ 7\overline{)89} \\ 7 \end{array}$ **Think** $7\overline{)8}$
$\leftarrow 1 \times 7$

Step 3
Subtract and compare.

$\begin{array}{r} 1 \\ 7\overline{)89} \\ -7 \\ \hline 1 \end{array}$
This must be less than the divisor. $1 < 7$

Step 4
Bring down ones.
Divide. Then multiply.

$\begin{array}{r} 12 \\ 7\overline{)89} \\ -7\downarrow \\ \hline 19 \\ 14 \end{array}$ **Think**
1 ten 9 ones = 19 ones
$7\overline{)19}$

Step 5
Subtract and compare.

$\begin{array}{r} 12 \text{ R}5 \\ 7\overline{)89} \\ -7\downarrow \\ \hline 19 \\ -14 \\ \hline 5 \end{array}$
$5 < 7$
Write the remainder in the quotient.

Check

$\begin{array}{r} 1 \\ 12 \\ \times\ 7 \\ \hline 84 \\ +\ 5 \\ \hline 89 \end{array}$
quotient
divisor

remainder
dividend

There would be 12 full flights. Five people would not get on a full flight.

CLASSWORK

Divide. Check by multiplying.

1. $2\overline{)77}$ 2. $3\overline{)95}$ 3. $4\overline{)92}$ 4. $2\overline{)90}$ 5. $5\overline{)64}$

6. $90 \div 8 = \square$ 7. $84 \div 6 = \square$ 8. $92 \div 7 = \square$

180

Divide. Check by multiplying.

1. 4)$\overline{47}$ 2. 7)$\overline{99}$ 3. 6)$\overline{83}$

4. 6)$\overline{98}$ 5. 5)$\overline{75}$ 6. 2)$\overline{35}$

7. 5)$\overline{70}$ 8. 4)$\overline{71}$ 9. 7)$\overline{95}$

10. 3)$\overline{55}$ 11. 4)$\overline{97}$ 12. 3)$\overline{66}$

13. 9)$\overline{56}$ 14. 1)$\overline{47}$ 15. 3)$\overline{74}$

16. $59 \div 2 = \square$ 17. $71 \div 6 = \square$

18. $88 \div 5 = \square$ 19. $65 \div 9 = \square$

What remainders are possible when you divide by each number?

★ 20. 3 ★ 21. 4 ★ 22. 7

APPLICATION

23. A space traffic plan calls for 90 flights in 6 months. There will be the same number of flights each month. How many flights will there be each month?

★ 24. A space shuttle orbited the earth 129 times in 8 days. It made the same number of orbits for each of 7 days. The last day it made 17 orbits. How many orbits did the shuttle make on the other days?

LOGICAL THINKING

Use the digits 3, 4, and 5 exactly once to get each quotient.

1. $\dfrac{6 \ R4}{\square)\square\square}$ 2. $\dfrac{1\ 8}{\square)\square\square}$ 3. $\dfrac{1\ 3\ R1}{\square)\square\square}$

1. 68
   $\times\ 8$

2. 964
   $+378$

3. 397
   $\times\ \ 7$

4. 8,642
   $-4,991$

5. 524
   365
   $+249$

6. 4,860
   $-2,538$

7. 408
   $\times\ \ 5$

8. $5,684 + 362 = \square$

9. $295 \times 6 = \square$

10. $1,482 - 508 = \square$

11. $784 \times 8 = \square$

12. $327 + 48 = \square$

13. $302 - 69 = \square$

14. $516 \times 3 = \square$

15. $416 \times 4 = \square$

Dividing Three-Digit Numbers

Viking 1 traveled 334 days to reach Mars. How many full weeks did it travel? How many extra days did it travel to reach Mars?

Find 334 ÷ 7.

Step 1
Decide where to place the first digit in the quotient.

7)334   **Think**
Not enough hundreds. There are enough tens to divide.

Step 2
Divide. Then multiply.

```
   4
7)334   Think 7)33
  28
```

Step 3
Subtract and compare.

```
   4
7)334
 -28
   5    5 < 7
```

Step 4
Bring down ones. Divide. Then multiply.

```
  47
7)334      Think
 -28|      5 tens 4 ones =
  54       54 ones
  49       7)54
```

Step 5
Subtract and compare.

```
  47 R5
7)334
 -28
  54
 -49
   5    5 < 7
```
Write the remainder in the quotient.

Check
```
   4
  47
 × 7
 329
 + 5
 334
```

Viking 1 traveled 47 weeks and 5 days to reach Mars.

CLASSWORK

Divide. Check by multiplying.

1. 2)147
2. 3)367
3. 3)104
4. 2)425
5. 5)125

6. 110 ÷ 4 = □
7. 930 ÷ 8 = □
8. 407 ÷ 6 = □

PRACTICE

Divide. Check by multiplying.

1. 3)157   2. 2)864   3. 4)136   4. 3)413   5. 2)125

6. 5)324   7. 4)527   8. 5)159   9. 2)169   10. 3)726

11. 5)393   12. 6)136   13. 4)599   14. 6)557   15. 3)146

16. 6)205   17. 7)880   18. 5)382   19. 8)907   20. 7)400

21. 8)938   22. 9)210   23. 7)301   24. 6)350   25. 9)105

26. $522 \div 7 = \square$ 27. $603 \div 9 = \square$ 28. $730 \div 6 = \square$

29. $568 \div 9 = \square$ 30. $939 \div 7 = \square$ 31. $328 \div 9 = \square$

★ 32. What number begins this chain?

APPLICATION

33. Viking 2 took 359 days to reach Mars. How many full weeks did Viking 2 take to travel toward Mars? How many extra days did it travel to reach Mars?

★ 34. Four satellites took a total of 114 pictures of Earth. Star Satellite took as many pictures as the other 3 satellites combined. How many pictures did Star Satellite take?

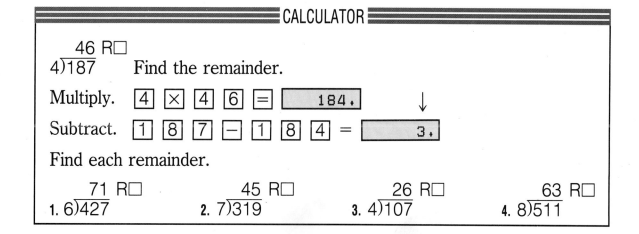

183

Problem Solving

MAKING A LIST

Sometimes the answer to a problem has many parts. A *list* can be used to show all the choices.

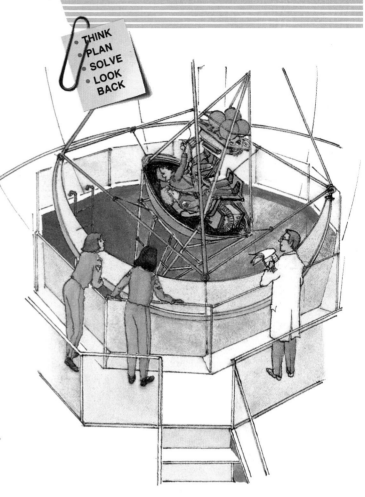

1. Ann, Betty, Carla, and David are student pilots. They work in pairs. How many different pairs are possible?

Make a list to show all the pairs.

Ann—Betty	Betty—Carla
Ann—Carla	Betty—David
Ann—David	Carla—David

There are 6 possible pairs.

Check to see if you listed all the pairs. Did each pilot work with every other pilot? Each pilot is listed three times. Your answer is correct.

2. Each student pilot is going to take a solo flight. Ann is the first to fly. How many different ways can the other 3 pilots take their turns?

Make a list to show all the ways the 3 pilots could take their turns after Ann.

Ann goes first.

First	Second	Third	Fourth
Ann	Betty	Carla	David
Ann	Betty	David	Carla
Ann	Carla	Betty	David

Copy and complete the list. Be careful not to show the same way more than once.

184

Solve each problem by making a list.

1. Lionel has 1 red and 1 blue shirt. He wears them with either his tan or gray pants. How many different ways can Lionel dress?

2. Larry, Marla, and Nancy had a flying contest. How many different ways could they have finished?

3. Pam has a flying lesson at 3:00 P.M. She has a test at 10:00 A.M. At 12:30 P.M. Pam is meeting her sister for lunch. Order the things Pam has to do today.

4. A row of seats is numbered 1–20. The students are told to sit in every other seat during a test. The first person sits in seat number 1. What number seat will the fifth person sit in?

Use the table to solve each question. Make a list to help you.

5. Tanya got a score of 4 on the quiz. What questions could she have gotten right?

QUIZ	
Question	Points
A	4
B	2
C	3
D	1

6. What questions would you have to answer correctly to get a score of 5?

★7. Wayne answered 2 questions correctly. What scores could he have gotten on the quiz?

★8. Cindy answered 3 questions correctly. What scores could she have gotten on the quiz?

CREATE YOUR OWN PROBLEM

1. Here is a recipe for fruit salad. Write a shopping list of what you need to buy to make this salad. You want to feed 8 people.

2. Look up the recipe for your favorite dish. Write a shopping list of what you would need to make it.

STARBURST FRUIT SALAD
1 medium apple, chopped
1 cup fresh seedless green grapes
1 can (11 ounces) mandarin orange segments
2 bananas, sliced

Mix fruit together. Cover and refrigerate. Makes 4 or 5 servings.

Zeros in the Quotient

Apollo 16 astronauts brought 215 pounds of rocks back from the moon. If 2 scientists shared the rocks equally, how many full pounds could each study? How many extra pounds would there be to study?

$215 \div 2 = \square$

Step 1
Decide where to place the first digit in the quotient.

$$2)\overline{215}$$
Think
There are enough hundreds to divide.

Step 2
Divide. Then multiply.

$$\begin{array}{r} 1 \\ 2)\overline{215} \\ 2 \end{array}$$
Think $2)\overline{2}$

Step 3
Subtract and compare.

$$\begin{array}{r} 1 \\ 2)\overline{215} \\ -2 \\ \hline 0 \end{array}$$
$0 < 2$

Step 4
Bring down tens. Divide.

$$\begin{array}{r} 10 \\ 2)\overline{215} \\ -2\downarrow \\ \hline 01 \end{array}$$
Think $2)\overline{1}$
Not enough tens to divide. Write 0 in the quotient.

Step 5
Bring down ones. Divide. Then multiply.

$$\begin{array}{r} 107 \\ 2)\overline{215} \\ -2\downarrow \\ \hline 015 \\ 14 \end{array}$$
Think
1 ten 5 ones = 15 ones
$2)\overline{15}$

Step 6
Subtract and compare.

$$\begin{array}{r} 107 \text{ R1} \\ 2)\overline{215} \\ -2 \\ \hline 015 \\ -14 \\ \hline 1 \end{array}$$
$1 < 2$
Write the remainder in the quotient.

Each scientist could study 107 full pounds of rocks. There would be 1 extra pound.

CLASSWORK

Divide. Check by multiplying.

1. $4)\overline{83}$ 2. $3)\overline{905}$ 3. $6)\overline{840}$ 4. $8)\overline{805}$ 5. $7)\overline{562}$

PRACTICE

Divide. Check by multiplying.

1. $2\overline{)416}$
2. $4\overline{)406}$
3. $3\overline{)326}$
4. $9\overline{)985}$
5. $6\overline{)645}$

6. $7\overline{)73}$
7. $8\overline{)806}$
8. $5\overline{)545}$
9. $2\overline{)81}$
10. $2\overline{)661}$

11. $6\overline{)605}$
12. $5\overline{)54}$
13. $4\overline{)723}$
14. $3\overline{)782}$
15. $3\overline{)32}$

16. $9\overline{)972}$
17. $7\overline{)846}$
18. $5\overline{)550}$
19. $8\overline{)964}$
20. $6\overline{)609}$

21. $5\overline{)700}$
22. $2\overline{)817}$
23. $3\overline{)908}$
24. $4\overline{)92}$
25. $9\overline{)946}$

26. $941 \div 2 = \square$
27. $841 \div 3 = \square$
28. $562 \div 4 = \square$

29. $600 \div 6 = \square$
30. $720 \div 6 = \square$
31. $917 \div 9 = \square$

Find each missing number.

	★ 32.	★ 33.	★ 34.	★ 35.	★ 36.
Divisor	3	8	4	6	$\square$
Quotient	112	124	244	$\square$	209
Remainder	2	$\square$	3	$\square$	2
Dividend	$\square$	997	$\square$	643	629

APPLICATION

On Earth an object weighs 6 times its weight on the moon.

Find the weight of each on the moon.

37. An astronaut who weighs 180 pounds on Earth

38. A baby hippopotamus that weighs 654 pounds on Earth

★ 39. A lunar rover that weighs 456 pounds on Earth and a 168-pound astronaut

Dividing Greater Numbers

The camp cook wants to order 2,325 packages of freeze-dried strawberries. There are 6 packages to a box. How many boxes should she order?

$2{,}325 \div 6 = \square$

Step 1
Decide where to place the first digit in the quotient.

$$6\overline{)2{,}325}$$ **Think**
Not enough thousands.
Divide hundreds.

Step 2
Divide. Then multiply. Subtract and compare. Bring down. Continue dividing.

```
       387 R3
   6)2,325
     -18
       52
      -48
       45
      -42
        3
```

3 extra packages are needed.
The cook should buy another box.

Check
```
    5 4
    387
  ×   6
  2,322
 +    3
  2,325
```

The cook should order 388 boxes.

More Examples

```
a.    1,591
   3)4,773
     -3
      17
     -15
       27
      -27
        03
       - 3
         0
```

```
b.     408 R7
    9)3,679
     -36
      079
     - 72
        7
```

```
c.    2,076 R2
    4)8,306
     -8
      030
     -28
       26
      -24
        2
```

CLASSWORK

Divide. Check by multiplying.

1. $3\overline{)7{,}488}$ 2. $5\overline{)7{,}018}$ 3. $4\overline{)1{,}928}$ 4. $7\overline{)6{,}523}$

188

PRACTICE

Divide. Check by multiplying.

1. 3)3,180
2. 5)2,615
3. 6)1,937
4. 4)4,366

5. 9)8,349
6. 2)8,417
7. 7)4,949
8. 8)9,004

9. 5)4,152
10. 3)6,300
11. 4)6,592
12. 2)1,763

13. 7)5,832
14. 9)5,006
15. 8)8,536
16. 6)5,025

17. 8)1,600
18. 6)5,505
19. 9)9,828
20. 7)7,023

21. 7,476 ÷ 4 = □
22. 2,369 ÷ 3 = □
23. 2,847 ÷ 9 = □

24. 1,154 ÷ 9 = □
25. 4,136 ÷ 2 = □
26. 7,851 ÷ 7 = □

27. 4,282 ÷ 6 = □
28. 6,005 ÷ 5 = □
29. 7,650 ÷ 8 = □

★30. Divide 72,590 by 3.
★31. Divide 10,368 by 9.

APPLICATION

32. The space camp needs 5,780 instant breakfast drinks. There are 7 breakfast drinks in each box. How many boxes should the camp buy?

★33. A group of 4 children was chosen for a special project. The group must work 1,368 hours. Each child works on the project 3 hours a day. How many days will the project last?

═══ ESTIMATION ═══

Without finding the quotient, tell how many digits each quotient would have.

1. 3)48
2. 4)39

3. 2)105
4. 5)942

5. 6)7,258
6. 7)6,235

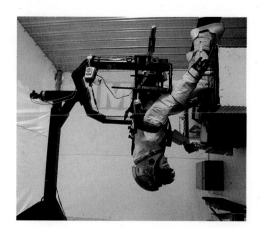

189

Dividing Money

Mr. Stone bought 3 model rocket ship kits for his science class. He paid $59.85 in all. Each kit was the same price. Find the cost of each kit.

$59.85 ÷ 3 = □

Divide money the same way you divide other numbers.

```
      $19.95
  3)$59.85
     −3↓
      29
     −27↓
       28
      −27↓
        15
       −15
         0
```
Remember to write the dollar sign and the decimal point in the quotient.

Check
```
   22 1
  $19.95
 ×      3
  $59.85
```

Each kit costs $19.95.

More Examples

```
a.     $ .65
    7)$4.55
     −4 2↓
        35
       −35
         0
```

```
b.      $ 3.40
     6)$20.40
      −18 ↓↓
         2 4↓
        −2 4↓
          00
         − 0
           0
```

```
c.      $ 7.05
     8)$56.40
      −56 ↓↓
         040
        −40
          0
```

CLASSWORK

Divide. Check by multiplying.

1. 2)$5.76

2. 4)$15.04

3. 5)$.75

4. 3)$75.21

5. $3.84 ÷ 6 = □

6. $53.10 ÷ 9 = □

7. $56.42 ÷ 7 = □

Divide. Check by multiplying.

1. $2\overline{)\$.46}$ 2. $3\overline{)\$1.35}$ 3. $3\overline{)\$.96}$ 4. $4\overline{)\$2.40}$

5. $3\overline{)\$3.27}$ 6. $2\overline{)\$16.90}$ 7. $5\overline{)\$40.25}$ 8. $7\overline{)\$84.00}$

9. $8\overline{)\$40.72}$ 10. $9\overline{)\$6.84}$ 11. $8\overline{)\$93.76}$ 12. $9\overline{)\$34.65}$

13. $4\overline{)\$15.56}$ 14. $7\overline{)\$.70}$ 15. $5\overline{)\$20.00}$ 16. $3\overline{)\$15.51}$

17. $\$.48 \div 4 = \square$ 18. $\$20.88 \div 6 = \square$ 19. $\$94.15 \div 7 = \square$

20. $\$6.50 \div 5 = \square$ 21. $\$38.88 \div 8 = \square$ 22. $\$90.81 \div 9 = \square$

Choose the correct number sentence and solve.

23. Five space stickers cost $3.75. What is the cost of 1 space sticker?

a. $5 \times \$3.75 = \square$

b. $\$3.75 \div 5 = \square$

c. $\$3.75 - 5 = \square$

d. $\$3.75 + 5 = \square$

24. A model kit costs $18.75. How much would 4 kits cost?

a. $\$18.75 \div 4 = \square$

b. $\$18.75 + \$18.75 = \square$

c. $4 + \square = \$18.75$

d. $4 \times \$18.75 = \square$

Compare. Use >, <, or = for ●.

★ 25. $\$18.51 \div 3$ ● $\$24.68 \div 4$ ★ 26. $\$528.25 \div 5$ ● $\$639.30 \div 6$

APPLICATION

SPACE MODELS IN STOCK			
Model	Apollo	Viking	Challenger
Number in stock	4	6	7
Total value	$47.80	$58.50	$48.65

27. Find the cost of 1 Apollo model.

★ 28. Find the cost of 2 Viking models.

★ 29. Find the cost of 3 Challenger models.

Averages

For good health, astronauts exercise while in space. What is the average number of minutes the astronaut exercised each day?

Astronaut Exercise Log

Day	Minutes Exercised
Monday	32
Tuesday	26
Wednesday	32
Thursday	38

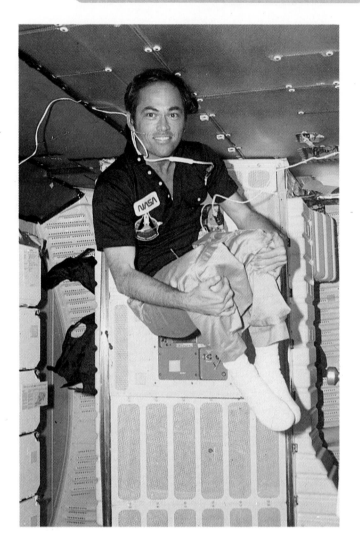

▶To find an average, add to find the sum. Then divide the sum by the number of addends.

$$32 + 26 + 32 + 38 = 128$$

$$
\begin{array}{r}
32 \leftarrow \text{average} \\
\text{number of days} \rightarrow 4)\overline{128} \leftarrow \text{total minutes} \\
-12 \\
\hline
08 \\
-8 \\
\hline
0
\end{array}
$$

The astronaut exercised an average of 32 minutes each day.

CLASSWORK

Find each average.

1. 37, 46, 31

2. 62, 48, 52

3. 95, 89

4. 71, 85, 81

5. 105, 115

6. 276, 250, 284

7. 93, 113, 118

8. $7.39, $8.43, $3.83

9. $10.32, $8.98

10. 29, 55, 37, 63

11. 94, 78, 88, 72

12. 119, 92, 103, 86

Find each average.

1. 5, 6, 10

2. 16, 8, 9

3. 76, 82

4. 51, 66, 42

5. 432, 330

6. 717, 864, 606

7. $.15, $.25, $.32

8. $5.76, $8.43, $6.78

9. $28.64, $30.28

10. 78, 53, 79, 42

11. 116, 136, 129, 143

 ★12. 86, 56, 73, 92, 107, 126

★13. 1,342; 2,656; 1,714; 1,960

Find each total.

★14. Average: 30 minutes per day
Number of days: 5
Total minutes: ☐

★15. Average: 38 minutes per day
Number of days: 6
Total minutes: ☐

APPLICATION

16. What was the average number of minutes Lamont exercised?

17. What was the average number of minutes everyone exercised on Monday?

NUMBER OF MINUTES EXERCISED			
	Andy	**Lamont**	**Keisha**
Monday	26	34	39
Tuesday	35	32	29
Wednesday	30	44	41
Thursday	37	38	31

18. Who spent the most time exercising in one day?

★19. On what day did the people average the most exercise time?

═ MENTAL ARITHMETIC ═

What is the average of 36, 45, 23, and 28? ___~~48~~___
You can tell this answer is wrong without doing the work.
What is the greatest number given? 45
What is the least number given? 23
The average should be between 23 and 45.   48 > 45
Find between what two numbers the average will be.

1. 65, 74, 80, 61, 77

2. 244, 250, 279, 263, 272

Problem Solving

SKILLS AND STRATEGIES REVIEW   Space City

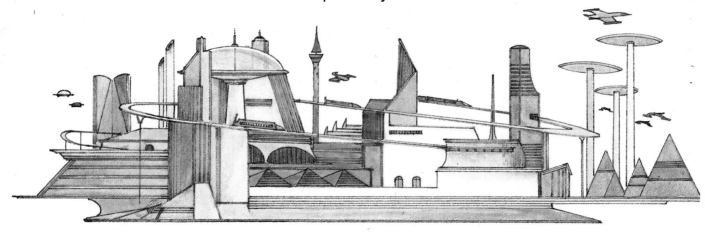

Read and solve each problem.

MAGAZINE ORDER FORM	
ONE-YEAR SUBSCRIPTION	PRICE
AIR AND SPACE (12 issues)	$14.50
SPACE HOME (6 issues)	$10.80
SPACE CARS (12 issues)	$ 9.60
SPECIAL OFFER: All 3 for $33.00	

1. The Space City Publishing Company mailed this order form. Stuart ordered *Air and Space* and *Space Cars*. How much did it cost him?

2. How much does each issue of *Space Home* cost?

3. How much is saved by ordering all 3 magazines on the special offer?

4. The newsstand price of *Space Cars* is $1.00 per copy. Adam bought a one-year subscription. How much did he save over the newsstand price?

5. The newsstand price of *Space Home* is $2.00 per issue. Julia bought the 6-issue subscription. How much did she save over the newsstand price?

6. The Space City firefighters had 52 ladders to stack. They put 6 ladders in each stack. How many ladders were left?

7. The firefighters arrived at a fire at 6:15 A.M. They put out the fire and left at 7:30 A.M. How long were they at the fire?

8. There are 5 members on the Space City police force—Molly, Burt, Carol, Linda, and Jack. They take turns riding in pairs in a patrol car. Make a list to show all the possible pairs.

★9. The Space City fire chief has 6 robots. The mayor has 3 more than the fire chief. The police chief has twice as many as the mayor. How many robots does the police chief have?

Problem Solving

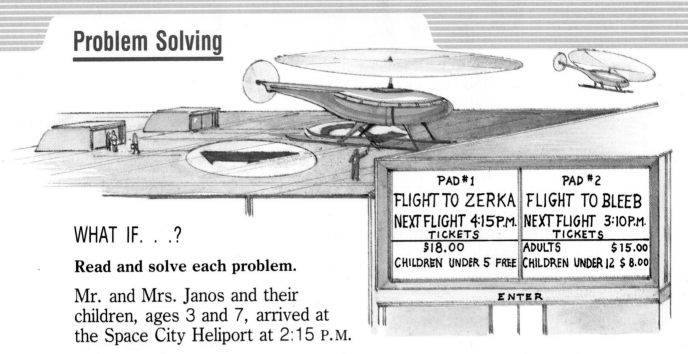

PAD #1	PAD #2
FLIGHT TO ZERKA	FLIGHT TO BLEEB
NEXT FLIGHT 4:15 P.M.	NEXT FLIGHT 3:10 P.M.
TICKETS	TICKETS
$18.00	ADULTS $15.00
CHILDREN UNDER 5 FREE	CHILDREN UNDER 12 $8.00

ENTER

WHAT IF. . .?

Read and solve each problem.

Mr. and Mrs. Janos and their children, ages 3 and 7, arrived at the Space City Heliport at 2:15 P.M.

1. How long must they wait for a trip to Zerka?

2. How much will the total cost of the trip be?

3. If Mr. Janos gives the ticket clerk $60, how much change will he receive?

4. If the trip to Zerka takes 2 hours and 15 minutes, when will they arrive at Zerka?

What if the helicopter takes off 45 minutes late?

5. How long will they have to wait for the trip?

6. What will the total cost of the trip be?

7. What time will they leave for Zerka?

8. If the trip takes 2 hours and 15 minutes, what time will they arrive at Zerka?

Mrs. Cooper and her children, ages 6, 11, and 13, want to go to Bleeb. They arrive at the heliport at 1:00 P.M. There are 24 people in line ahead of the Cooper family.

9. How long must they wait for their trip to Bleeb?

★10. What will the total cost of the trip be?

What if the sign reads   Children Under 16: $8.00?

11. How much will the tickets for the trip cost?

12. If Mrs. Cooper pays with a $50 bill, how much will her change be?

Divide. Check by multiplying. pages 174–181

1. $2\overline{)17}$ 2. $6\overline{)27}$ 3. $5\overline{)32}$ 4. $7\overline{)56}$ 5. $3\overline{)39}$

6. $9\overline{)87}$ 7. $4\overline{)88}$ 8. $3\overline{)37}$ 9. $4\overline{)49}$ 10. $5\overline{)75}$

11. $96 \div 8 = \square$ 12. $64 \div 2 = \square$ 13. $67 \div 4 = \square$

Find each quotient. Check by multiplying. pages 182–183

14. $2\overline{)358}$ 15. $3\overline{)846}$ 16. $7\overline{)778}$ 17. $6\overline{)348}$ 18. $4\overline{)553}$

19. $8\overline{)417}$ 20. $9\overline{)657}$ 21. $2\overline{)108}$ 22. $9\overline{)820}$ 23. $8\overline{)500}$

24. $176 \div 3 = \square$ 25. $507 \div 5 = \square$ 26. $490 \div 7 = \square$

27. $309 \div 9 = \square$ 28. $209 \div 7 = \square$ 29. $486 \div 6 = \square$

Divide. Check by multiplying. pages 186–191

30. $7\overline{)\$8.40}$ 31. $4\overline{)\$2.44}$ 32. $5\overline{)5,100}$ 33. $9\overline{)7,364}$

34. $2\overline{)1,185}$ 35. $3\overline{)\$15.18}$ 36. $6\overline{)4,958}$ 37. $8\overline{)\$17.04}$

38. $\$.88 \div 8 = \square$ 39. $\$26.95 \div 5 = \square$ 40. $5,718 \div 7 = \square$

41. $\$32.16 \div 8 = \square$ 42. $\$70.35 \div 7 = \square$ 43. $\$12.36 \div 6 = \square$

Find each average. pages 192–193

44. 436, 400, 433 45. $.98, $.80, $.85, $.81

46. 112, 123, 115, 130 47. 18, 15, 19, 104

Solve. pages 184–185, 194–195

48. Mrs. Lee bought 4 model space shuttle kits for her children. She paid $87.80 altogether. Each kit was the same price. What was the cost of each kit?

49. Jerry, Kathy, Linda, Mark, and Nancy want to write their science reports about NASA. Only two of them can write the report on NASA. Make a list to show all the pairs the teacher can choose.

Find each quotient. Check by multiplying.

1. $3\overline{)29}$

2. $9\overline{)90}$

3. $8\overline{)99}$

4. $7\overline{)91}$

5. $5\overline{)175}$

6. $4\overline{)607}$

7. $6\overline{)649}$

8. $8\overline{)765}$

9. $50 \div 6 = \square$

10. $379 \div 4 = \square$

11. $763 \div 7 = \square$

12. $785 \div 9 = \square$

13. $426 \div 6 = \square$

14. $900 \div 7 = \square$

Divide. Check by multiplying.

15. $3\overline{)\$2.67}$

16. $8\overline{)\$9.52}$

17. $7\overline{)\$.98}$

18. $6\overline{)7,200}$

19. $5\overline{)3,162}$

20. $8\overline{)\$21.36}$

21. $4\overline{)5,728}$

22. $6\overline{)4,829}$

23. $\$74.25 \div 3 = \square$

24. $\$40.05 \div 5 = \square$

25. $\$54.63 \div 9 = \square$

26. $\$84.77 \div 7 = \square$

27. $130 \div 5 = \square$

28. $659 \div 8 = \square$

Find each average.

29. 34, 53, 27

30. $4.12, $3.68, $5.88

31. 28, 41, 22, 37

Solve.

32. Steve bought 3 posters with pictures of space shuttles. Each poster was the same price. The total cost was $19.65. How much did each poster cost?

33. The toy shop has space helmets in 3 colors: red, white, and blue. They also have 3 colors in space suits: red, white, and blue. Make a list to show all the different space outfits you could make.

Five astronauts have spent a total of 3,530 hours in space. Four of them have spent the same amount of time. The fifth astronaut has spent 650 hours. How many hours did each of the other astronauts spend in space?

FINDING UNIT PRICES

What is the price of one box of
Star Apple Juice?

Divide to find the price of one box
of juice. This is the **unit price**.

```
    $.33
3)$.99
  − 9
    09    The price of
  − 9    one box of Star
    0    Apple Juice is $.33.
```

Walter is comparing prices to
find the better buy. The table
shows the price of the same
items at two different stores.

Which store has the better
buy on peas?

Item	Store A	Store B
Peas	4 cans for $1.96	$.50 a can
Apples	$.25 each	6 for $1.38
Tuna	$.59 a can	2 cans for $1.20
Beans	4 cans for $1.00	$.24 a can
Muffins	6 for $.96	2 for $.30

Find the price of one
can at Store A.

```
     $ .49
4)$1.96
   − 1 6        $.49 a can at Store A
     36
   − 36
      0
```

Compare the prices for one can.
$.49 < $.50

Store A has the better buy on peas.

Find each unit price.

1. 5 ears of corn for $1.00

2. 2 cans of cat food for $.56

3. 3 rolls of paper towels for $1.59

4. 4 containers of yogurt for $1.28

Use the table above.

Which store has the better buy on each item?

5. apples

6. tuna

7. beans

8. muffins

9. Look in the newspaper to find ads from different
supermarkets. Compare prices of the same items.
Which store has the better buy?

THE SPACE MYSTERY

Three astronauts brought some moon rocks back to their starship. They wanted to divide the rocks into three equal parts and put them in separate bags. But they were too tired so they left the rocks on the floor and went to sleep.

That night one astronaut woke up and started to pack the rocks. He divided them into three equal piles. There was one extra rock, which he put into a storage bin. Then he packed one of the equal piles into a rock bag and decided to finish in the morning. He went back to sleep.

Later that night a second astronaut woke up. He divided the remaining rocks into three equal piles. Again there was one extra rock, which he put into a storage bin. Then he put one of the equal piles into a rock bag. He decided to finish in the morning and went back to sleep.

In the morning the third astronaut woke up first. He was surprised to see how few rocks were on the floor. He divided the rocks into three equal piles as the others had done. Again there was an extra rock, which he put into a storage bin. After he put one of the piles into a rock bag, there were six rocks left on the floor. How many rocks did the astronauts collect that day? (Work backwards.)

Choose the correct answer. Write A, B, C, or D.

1. $5 + 9 = \square$

  A 13   **C** 14

  B 15   **D** not given

8. $5 \times 5 = \square$

  A 25   **C** 20

  B 10   **D** not given

2. $7 + 8 + 6 = \square$

  A 21   **C** 22

  B 20   **D** not given

9. $7 \times 0 = \square$

  A 7   **C** 8

  B 1   **D** not given

3. $6 - \square = 6$

  A 6   **C** 0

  B 12   **D** not given

10. $9 \times \square = 9$

  A 0   **C** 81

  B 1   **D** not given

4. Estimate. $330 + 187 = \square$

  A 600   **C** 400

  B 500   **D** not given

11. $35 \div 5 = \square$

  A 6   **C** 7

  B 30   **D** not given

5. $5{,}219 + 3{,}457 = \square$

  A 8,666   **C** 8,876

  B 1,762   **D** not given

12. $6\overline{)42}$

  A 7   **C** 9

  B 6   **D** not given

6. $1{,}006 - 728 = \square$

  A 288   **C** 278

  B 378   **D** not given

13. Name the fewest number of coins needed to make $.84.

  A 3 quarters,   **C** 2 quarters,
       1 nickel   3 dimes,
                       4 pennies

7. Estimate. $749 - 162 = \square$

  A 700   **C** 500

  B 600   **D** not given

  B 1 half–dollar,   **D** not given
       1 quarter,
       1 nickel,
       4 pennies

Choose the correct answer. Write A, B, C, or D.

14. How much time has passed?

A 41 min   **C** 45 min

B 51 min   **D** not given

Money Spent on School Supplies

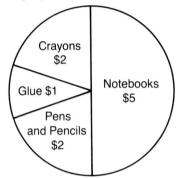

15. On what was the most money spent?

A crayons   **C** pens and pencils

B glue   **D** not given

16. $9 \times 60 = \square$

A 54   **C** 5,400

B 540   **D** not given

17. $7 \times 26 = \square$

A 182   **C** 185

B 142   **D** not given

18. $\begin{array}{r} 324 \\ \times\ \ \ 9 \\ \hline \end{array}$

A 2,886   **C** 2,916

B 2,716   **D** not given

19. Estimate. $3 \times 5,972 = \square$

A 15,000   **C** 18,000

B 2,716   **D** not given

20. $\begin{array}{r} 5,364 \\ \times\ \ \ \ \ 5 \\ \hline \end{array}$

A 26,520   **C** 26,800

B 26,820   **D** not given

21. $4\overline{)69}$

A 16 R3   **C** 18

B 17 R1   **D** not given

22. $57 \div 9 = \square$

A 6 R3   **C** 6 R8

B 6 R7   **D** not given

23. $254 \div 5 = \square$

A 5 R4   **C** 50 R4

B 5 R54   **D** not given

24. $3\overline{)7,420}$

A 247 R31   **C** 2,407 R1

B 2,473 R1   **D** not given

25. What is the average?
$16.20, $13.70, $15.40

A $15.00   **C** $15.10

B $14.90   **D** not given

Choose the correct answer. Write A, B, C, or D.

Use the picture for 26–27.

26. How many fish are in the tank?

A 12   C 10

B 8   D not given

27. How many more yellow fish than red fish are there?

A 1   C 3

B 2   D not given

Choose the correct operation to solve the problem.

28. Fernando bought 6 ties for $6.28 each. How much did he spend in all?

A add   C multiply

B subtract   D not given

Which fact do you need to solve the problem?

29. Pat shared some stamps equally with 5 friends. How many stamps did each friend get?

A the cost of   C the number of
each stamp   stamps Pat had

B his friends'   D not given
names

Which fact is not needed to solve the problem?

30. Tim arrived at the pool at 12:00 P.M. He had tuna fish for lunch. He left at 3:15 P.M. How long did Tim stay at the pool?

A He had   C Tim left at
tuna fish.   3:15 P.M.

B Tim arrived   D not given
at 12:00 P.M.

Use the table for 31–33.

NEWSPAPER DRIVE RESULT	
Student	Pounds of Paper
Janet	15
Ryan	22
Alan	9
Randy	31

31. Which student brought in the most pounds during the drive?

A Alan   C Randy

B Ryan   D not given

32. How many more pounds did Ryan bring in than Janet?

A 5 pounds   C 7 pounds

B 6 pounds   D not given

33. How many pounds of paper did Alan and Janet bring in?

A 27 pounds   C 41 pounds

B 40 pounds   D not given

Theme: Washington D.C.

Exploring Decimals

You can spend only part of a dollar to buy a souvenir in Washington, D.C.

Work with a partner.

1. List some items that you can buy for less than a dollar.

2. Use grid paper. For each item on your list, cut out a rectangular shape containing 100 squares to represent a one-dollar bill.

3. Write the name of one item on the back of each rectangle. Decide how to shade the front to show what part of a dollar you need to pay for the item.

WORKING TOGETHER

Exchange rectangles with another pair of students.

1. Make a list of each item you receive. Use a dollar sign and a decimal point to record how much each item costs.

2. Share your list with the students whose rectangles you have. Discuss whether the prices on your list match the prices they used for each item.

3. Discuss what the unshaded part of each rectangle can show. Share your ideas.

1. Look at the rectangles that different people made. Identify different patterns your classmates used to shade parts of a dollar. Which patterns make it easy to find the cost of an item without counting all the shaded squares?

2. Discuss how patterns can make it easier to name part of a whole.

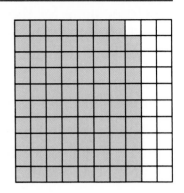

THINKING IT THROUGH

Work in a group of four.

1. Make a money line for a dollar like the one shown below. Divide and label your money line to show parts of a dollar.

0 $1.00

2. Have each person select one of the shaded rectangles you made for page 204. Draw vertical arrows on the money line to show what part of a dollar is used to pay for each item. Show the name but not the cost for each of your items.

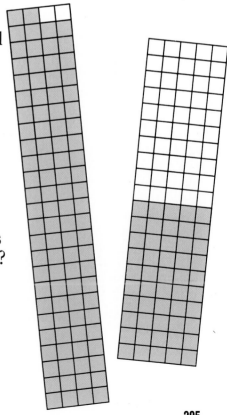

- Exchange your money line with that of another group. Read their money line and decide about how much each of their items costs. Check with them to see if your answers are reasonable.

- Look at the money lines that different groups made. Were some easier to read than others? If so, why? Discuss different things you can do to make it easier to read a money line.

3. How is shading a rectangle the same as using a money line to show part of a dollar? How is it different?

Working With Decimals

Experiment with beans on 10 × 10 grids to create designs for the initial letter of your first and last names. Shade other 10 × 10 grids to record your designs.

1. Estimate how many parts out of the 100 parts in each grid are shaded.

2. Rearrange the beans you used on each grid to make them easier to count. How many parts out of 100 are used for each initial?

3. The decimal 0.46 means 46 parts out of 100. Read this decimal as forty-six **hundredths** of a whole.

   • Write a decimal to show the shaded part for each of your initials.
   • Share and read your decimals with your classmates.

Explore with a calculator.

1. Use the numbers 3 and 100 with one of the operations +, −, ×, or ÷. Experiment until you see 0.03 in the display.

2. Now enter two numbers to show how many parts out of 100 you used for one of your initials. Display a decimal to match the decimal you wrote for this initial. Repeat this activity for your second initial.

Experiment again with beans.

1. Count out a pile of 100 beans.

2. Pick a handful from the pile. Estimate what part out of 100 you took.

3. Arrange the beans on a 10 × 10 grid to make them easier to count. Use a calculator. Enter two numbers to show how many parts out of 100 you have. Record the decimal that shows what part of the pile is in your handful.

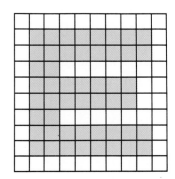

SHARING YOUR THINKING

Work with a partner.

1. How is writing a decimal for part of a whole like writing an amount of money? How is it different?

2. Use your initials and the initials of your partner, done on page 206. Arrange the drawings from least to greatest amount of shading.

   • Order the decimals for the four initials from the least to greatest.

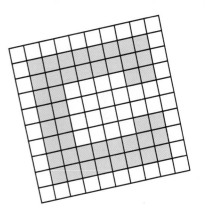

   • How is comparing decimals like comparing whole numbers? How is it different?

3. Write a decimal that shows the shaded part for one of your initials. Discuss how you can use this decimal to find a decimal for the unshaded part of your grid. Experiment with a calculator to try your ideas.

THINKING IT THROUGH

1. Think about what the word *hundredths* means. Figure out and discuss what the word *tenths* means.

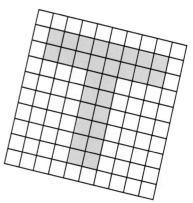

   • Find a way to divide a 10 × 10 grid into tenths.
   • Shade any number of tenths in your grid. Record a decimal for the shaded part of your grid. Use a calculator to display your decimal.
   • Explain why 20 hundredths, or 0.20, is the same as 2 tenths, or 0.2.
   • Use the decimals for the shaded and the unshaded parts of your grid. What happens when you add these two decimals?

2. Show how you would enter whole numbers to display the decimals 0.02 and 0.2 in your calculator. Use grids or a calculator to explain why these two decimals are different. Discuss how you can identify the greater decimal.

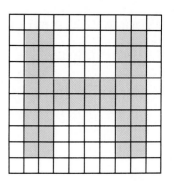

207

Adding And Subtracting Decimals

Cut grid paper into the pieces shown on this page. Then cut a 10 × 10 grid. Label it ONE WHOLE.

Find the pieces you could combine to fill the whole grid in the center.

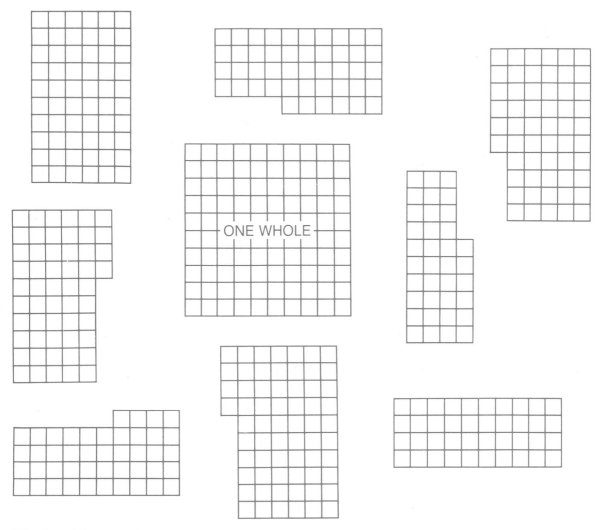

Work with a partner.

1. Write decimals to show how you made each whole.

2. Scramble the grid pieces. Choose any grid piece. Record the decimal needed to complete the whole. Check by finding the piece needed to make the whole. Repeat this activity for every grid piece.

1. Discuss strategies that you used to complete a whole.

2. Discuss several examples that you did in **2** on page 208. Use a calculator to help you find or check a number sentence for each example. Record your work.

THINKING IT THROUGH

1. Scramble the grid pieces and arrange them in a stack.

   • Draw two pieces at a time from the stack.

   • Place them on your whole grid.

   • Decide how to record what happens each time.

   • Repeat this activity several times.

2. Explain how you can tell whether the sum of two decimals will be more than one, less than one, or equal to one.

Using Decimals

Work with a partner.

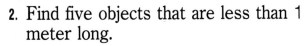

1. Use centimeter grid paper to make a measuring tape with 100 centimeters. Your whole tape will be 1 meter long.

   - Cut out 10 sections with 10 squares in each row.

   - Lightly shade five of the sections.

   - Tape the sections end to end in a strip, alternating shaded and unshaded sections.

2. Find five objects that are less than 1 meter long.

   - Measure the length of each object.

   - Use a decimal to record what part of a meter shows the measure of each object.

   - Use five pieces of paper. On one side of each piece, describe one of the objects that you measured. On the other side, write a decimal to show what part of a meter you used to measure the object.

WORKING TOGETHER

Exchange your five pieces of paper with another pair of students.

- Display the names of the objects.

- Decide how to rearrange the items in order from shortest to longest.

- Check the other side of the paper to see if the decimals are in order.

Decide which objects placed end to end would be closest in length to a whole meter.

1. Discuss when it might not be possible to place the actual objects end to end to complete the last activity on page 210.

2. Discuss ways to find out the combined length of the objects without moving them.

3. Discuss how a calculator can help you to figure this out. Experiment with a calculator to try your ideas.

Use what you have learned about decimals and place value.

1. Make a list of the patterns that you notice in the diagram below.

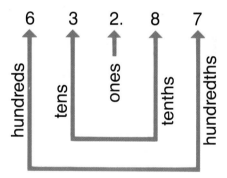

2. What value do you think is given to the third place to the right of the decimal point? Share and explain your ideas. Use a calculator to try your ideas.

3. Write a number less than 1 with three digits to the right of the decimal point. How can you use a meter tape to show what your number means?

Working with Tenths and Hundredths

Ann is a Senate page. She spent 1.5 hours opening mail. She spent 2.8 hours doing errands. How many hours did Ann spend on these tasks?

$1.5 + 2.8 = \square$

Step 1
Line up the decimal points.

$$\begin{array}{r} \downarrow \\ 1.5 \\ +2.8 \\ \hline \end{array}$$

Step 2
Add tenths.
Regroup.

$$\begin{array}{r} 1 \\ 1.5 \\ +2.8 \\ \hline 3 \end{array}$$
13 tenths = 1 one 3 tenths

Step 3
Add ones.
Place the decimal point in the answer.

$$\begin{array}{r} 1 \\ 1.5 \\ +2.8 \\ \hline 4.3 \end{array}$$

Check by adding up.

$$\begin{array}{r} 1 \\ 1.5 \uparrow \\ +2.8 \\ \hline 4.3 \end{array}$$

Ann spent 4.3 hours on these tasks.

Another Example Find $17.24 - 15.36$.

Step 1
Line up the decimal points.

$$\begin{array}{r} \downarrow \\ 17.24 \\ -15.36 \\ \hline \end{array}$$

Step 2
Not enough hundredths.
Regroup tenths.
Subtract hundredths.

$$\begin{array}{r} 1\ 14 \\ 1\ 7.2\!\!\!/\ 4\!\!\!/ \\ -1\ 5.3\ 6 \\ \hline 8 \end{array}$$
2 tenths 4 hundredths = 1 tenth 14 hundredths

Step 3
Not enough tenths.
Regroup ones.
Subtract tenths.

$$\begin{array}{r} 11 \\ 6\ \not7\ 14 \\ 1\ 7.2\!\!\!/\ 4\!\!\!/ \\ -1\ 5.3\ 6 \\ \hline 8\ 8 \end{array}$$
7 ones 1 tenth = 6 ones 11 tenths

Step 4
Continue to subtract and regroup.
Place the decimal point.

$$\begin{array}{r} 11 \\ 6\ \not7\ 14 \\ 1\ 7.2\!\!\!/\ 4\!\!\!/ \\ -1\ 5.3\ 6 \\ \hline 1.8\ 8 \end{array}$$

CLASSWORK

Add or subtract.

1. $\begin{array}{r} 3.4 \\ +2.4 \\ \hline \end{array}$

2. $\begin{array}{r} 2.6 \\ -1.9 \\ \hline \end{array}$

3. $\begin{array}{r} 99.2 \\ -\ 0.5 \\ \hline \end{array}$

4. $\begin{array}{r} 4.56 \\ +2.62 \\ \hline \end{array}$

5. $\begin{array}{r} 8.91 \\ -1.34 \\ \hline \end{array}$

6. $56.6 - 8.7 = \square$

7. $92.13 + 9.22 = \square$

8. $5.33 - 3.66 = \square$

PRACTICE

Add or subtract.

1.	0.4	**2.**	1.3	**3.**	8.4	**4.**	8.9	**5.**	44.3
	+0.3		+2.6		−5.6		+4.7		−12.4

6.	4.01	**7.**	3.45	**8.**	6.78	**9.**	6.69	**10.**	44.44
	+2.09		−2.16		−3.92		+0.53		−25.55

11.	6.5	**12.**	3.88	**13.**	12.0	**14.**	4.51	**15.**	89.13
	+2.5		−1.96		− 9.8		+2.91		−88.47

16. $3.2 - 1.9 = \square$ **17.** $34.25 - 10.99 = \square$ **18.** $0.94 + 0.07 = \square$

19. $1.07 + 9.16 = \square$ **20.** $8.92 - 3.45 = \square$ **21.** $12.23 + 4.91 = \square$

Find each missing digit.

22.	8.■	**23.**	9.3	**24.**	■4.6	★**25.**	■■.41	★**26.**	12.3■
	−■.3		+ ■.■		− ■.9		− 4.■3		− 1.■3
	1.2		15.1		14.		84.6		.11

APPLICATION

27. The Secret Service man put 12.7 liters of gas in his car one week. The next week he put in 10.8 liters. How many liters of gas was that in all?

★**28.** Ann had 100 envelopes to write. She did 0.25 of them before lunch, 0.12 after lunch, and 0.41 at home. How many envelopes had she done? How many were left?

VISUAL THINKING

Which path is the shortest? Longest?

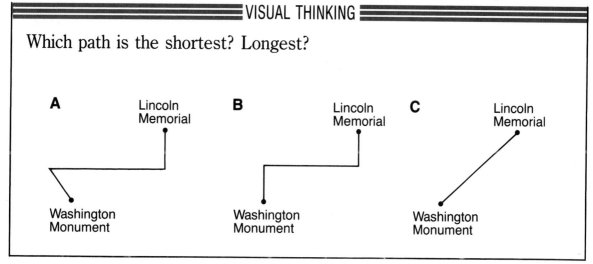

Using Tenths and Hundredths

Tony copied a quilting pattern at the Smithsonian. He used 0.9 of one piece of graph paper and 0.78 of another. What part of the graph paper did the pattern cover?

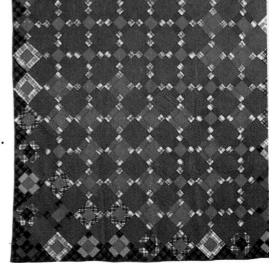

$$0.9 + 0.78 = \square$$

Step 1
Line up the decimal points. Use zeros to hold places.

$$\begin{array}{r} 0.9\,0 \\ +\,0.78 \end{array}$$

Step 2
Add. Regroup, if necessary. Place the decimal point.

$$\begin{array}{r} {}^{1} \\ 0.90 \\ +\,0.78 \\ \hline 1.68 \end{array}$$

Check by adding up.

$$\begin{array}{r} {}^{1} \\ 0.90 \\ +\,0.78 \\ \hline 1.68 \end{array}$$

The pattern covered 1.68 of the graph paper.

Find $9 - 8.47$.

Step 1
Line up the decimal points. Use zeros to hold places.

$$\begin{array}{r} 9.0\,0 \\ -\,8.4\,7 \end{array}$$

Step 2
Subtract. Regroup, if necessary. Place the decimal point.

$$\begin{array}{r} {}^{9} \\ {}^{8\ \cancel{10}\ 10} \\ 9.\cancel{0}\,\cancel{0} \\ -\,8.4\,7 \\ \hline 0.5\,3 \end{array}$$

Check by adding.

$$\begin{array}{r} {}^{1\ 1} \\ 0.5\,3 \\ +\,8.4\,7 \\ \hline 9.0\,0 \end{array}$$

CLASSWORK

Add or subtract.

1. $\begin{array}{r} 5.3 \\ +\,3.66 \end{array}$

2. $\begin{array}{r} 7.1 \\ -\,4.92 \end{array}$

3. $\begin{array}{r} 0.8 \\ -\,0.05 \end{array}$

4. $\begin{array}{r} 0.19 \\ -\,0.15 \end{array}$

5. $\begin{array}{r} 5.34 \\ +\,4.5 \end{array}$

6. $8 + 4.63 = \square$

7. $6 - 5.5 = \square$

8. $16 - 8.27 = \square$

PRACTICE

Add or subtract.

1. $\begin{array}{r} 6.81 \\ +3.4 \\ \hline \end{array}$

2. $\begin{array}{r} 9.84 \\ -4.3 \\ \hline \end{array}$

3. $\begin{array}{r} 0.16 \\ -0.09 \\ \hline \end{array}$

4. $\begin{array}{r} 9.2 \\ -4.86 \\ \hline \end{array}$

5. $\begin{array}{r} 0.6 \\ +7.58 \\ \hline \end{array}$

6. $\begin{array}{r} 7.8 \\ -5.46 \\ \hline \end{array}$

7. $\begin{array}{r} 1.4 \\ -0.9 \\ \hline \end{array}$

8. $\begin{array}{r} 0.13 \\ -0.07 \\ \hline \end{array}$

9. $\begin{array}{r} 7 \\ +3.86 \\ \hline \end{array}$

10. $\begin{array}{r} 1.83 \\ -1.79 \\ \hline \end{array}$

11. $\begin{array}{r} 25.8 \\ -13.62 \\ \hline \end{array}$

12. $\begin{array}{r} 44 \\ -35.9 \\ \hline \end{array}$

13. $\begin{array}{r} 0.09 \\ +0.09 \\ \hline \end{array}$

14. $\begin{array}{r} 54.3 \\ -9.83 \\ \hline \end{array}$

15. $\begin{array}{r} 9 \\ -1.09 \\ \hline \end{array}$

16. $6.23 + 5.2 = \square$

17. $7.5 + 3.67 = \square$

18. $1.2 - 0.95 = \square$

19. $134 - 3.65 = \square$

20. $28.9 + 0.02 = \square$

21. $0.9 - 0.06 = \square$

22. $35.8 + 73.09 = \square$

23. $0.3 - 0.08 = \square$

24. $6.9 + 10.12 = \square$

25. $99.01 - 0.3 = \square$

26. $1 - 0.56 = \square$

27. $62 - 9.99 = \square$

Compare. Use >, <, or = for ●.

★ 28. 2×12 ● $25.5 - 1.8$

★ 29. $810 \div 9$ ● $89 + 1.03$

APPLICATION

30. The museum manager has small displays set 3.75 meters apart. She has larger displays set 8.5 meters apart. What is the difference in meters?

★ 31. Michael has $5.20 to spend for gifts. He wants gifts that cost $.25, $.85, $2.10, $.95, and $3. Does he have enough money? How much more money does he need?

CALCULATOR

Use a calculator to complete the magic square. The sums of the numbers in all rows, columns, and diagonals should be the same.

		7.6
		3.3
	6.9	6.5

215

Problem Solving

TWO-STEP PROBLEMS

Sometimes it takes two steps to solve a problem.

Frank works at the botanic gardens at the foot of Capitol Hill. He mixed 4.5 kilograms of sand with 5.5 kilograms of soil. Then he used 2.4 kilograms of the mixture to pot some cactus plants. How much of the mixture was left?

THINK   **What is the question?**

How much of the mixture was left?

What are the facts?

The mixture was 4.5 kilograms of sand and 5.5 kilograms of soil. Frank used 2.4 kilograms of the mixture.

PLAN   **How can you find the answer?**

Find the total amount of kilograms in the mixture. Subtract the amount Frank used from that total.

SOLVE   **Carry out the plan.**

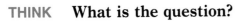

Step 1
```
    1
   4.5
 + 5.5
  10.0
```

Step 2
```
   9
  10 10
  1Ø.Ø
 - 2.4
   7.6
```

There were 7.6 kilograms of the mixture left.

LOOK BACK   **Is your arithmetic correct?**

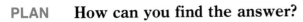

Check Step 1
```
   1
  5.5
 + 4.5
  10.0
```

Check Step 2
```
   1
  2.4
 + 7.6
  10.0
```
The answer is correct.

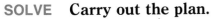

Read each problem. Choose the correct steps, then solve.

1. In one week, Frank earns $105.00. He worked for 3 weeks this month. He spent $85.95 and saved the rest. How much money did he save?

   a. add, divide

   b. multiply, add

   c. divide, add

   d. multiply, subtract

2. Frank opened a box of tulip bulbs. There were 6 bags of 12 red tulips each. There was a bag of 50 yellow tulips. How many bulbs were in the box?

   a. add, subtract

   b. multiply, add

   c. add, divide

   d. multiply, subtract

Solve.

3. Frank lives in Suitland, Maryland. He travels 9.5 kilometers to work each day. How many kilometers does he travel in 5 days if he goes to work and comes home again each day?

4. The mums needed to be potted. Frank potted 175 white mums and 125 pink mums. It took him 6 hours. What is the average number of mums Frank potted in one hour?

5. Frank needs 8 pots. Clay pots cost $7.50 each. Ceramic pots cost $12.85 each. How much more money will Frank spend if he buys ceramic pots?

★ 6. Frank ordered some fertilizer. He ordered 6 bags of orchid fertilizer for $12.69 each and 2 bags of rose fertilizer for $9.25 each. How much did the order total?

━━━━━ CREATE YOUR OWN PROBLEM ━━━━━

Frank orders bulbs from this catalog.

1. How much does it cost to buy 1 bag of crocus bulbs and 1 bag of hyacinth bulbs?

2. Write a problem that needs two steps to solve.

Bag of 100 Bulbs
Tulips $24.25 Hyacinths $48.65
Crocus $7.20 Daffodils $33.59

217

Millimeter and Centimeter

The Treasury Department prints stamps. These stamps are about 3 centimeters long.

A measurement consists of a number and a unit of measure.

▶The **centimeter (cm)** is a unit of length in the **metric system of measurement.**

A finger is about 1 cm wide.

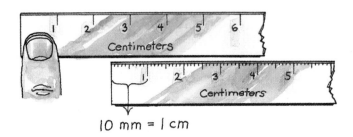

▶The **millimeter (mm)** is another unit of length.

1 centimeter = 10 millimeters

10 mm = 1 cm

Measured to the nearest centimeter, this pencil is about 8 cm long.

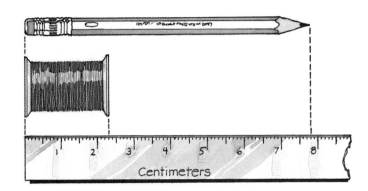

Measured to the nearest millimeter, this spool of thread is about 23 mm long.

CLASSWORK

Measure each length to the nearest centimeter.

1.

2.

Measure each length to the nearest millimeter.

3.

4.

5.

Measure each length to the nearest centimeter.

1.    2.    3.

4.    5.    6.

Measure each length to the nearest millimeter.

7.    8.    9.

Estimate each length in centimeters.
Then measure to the nearest centimeter.

10. _____   11. _____

12. _____   13. _____

Write *true* or *false* for each. Correct
any false sentences.

★14. A millimeter is 0.1 of the length
of a centimeter.

★15. A centimeter is 100 times the length
of a millimeter.

APPLICATION

Trace your hand and take these
measurements to the nearest
centimeter.

16. longest and shortest finger

17. width of hand

Use a string to take these
measurements to the nearest
millimeter.

★18. around your thumb

★19. around your wrist

Meter and Kilometer

The doorknob of the door to the Oval Office is about 1 meter from the floor.

▶The **meter (m)** is a unit of length in the metric system.

1 meter = 100 centimeters

▶The **kilometer (km)** is a unit used to measure longer lengths.

1 kilometer = 1,000 meters

A fast walker can walk 1 kilometer in about 10 minutes.

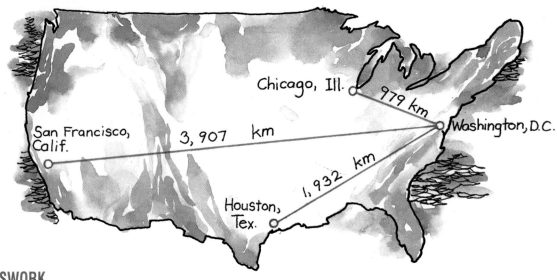

CLASSWORK

Choose centimeters, meters, or kilometers to measure each.

1. height of a bicycle

2. distance to the moon

3. length of your pencil

4. length of a river

5. distance between 2 airports

6. length of a car

Complete.

7. 2 km = _____ m

8. 3 m = _____ cm

9. _____ km = 9,000 m

Complete the chart. First, estimate each length.
Then measure to the nearest meter.

	Distance	Estimate	Actual Measurement
1.	Length of classroom		
2.	Width of classroom		
3.	Height of door		
4.	Width of door		
5.	Length of hallway		

Choose centimeters, meters, or kilometers
to measure each.

6. length of Potomac River

7. depth of Potomac River

8. height of Lincoln Memorial

9. length of President's signature

10. distance from Washington to London

11. height of dome on the Capitol

Complete.

12. 1 km = ____ m

13. 5 km = ____ m

14. ____ m = 600 cm

15. ____ km = 7,000 m

16. 10 m = ____ cm

17. 12 km = ____ m

18. 4,000 m = ____ km

19. 2,000 m = ____ km

20. 8,000 m = ____ km

★ 21. 1.5 m = ____ cm

★ 22. 2.5 m = ____ cm

★ 23. 3.5 m = ____ cm

APPLICATION

24. Juan walked 2 kilometers along the canal between Georgetown and Cumberland. Sam walked 1,750 meters. Who walked farther? How much farther?

★ 25. Jane walked 1 kilometer to the Capitol. Then she walked 500 meters farther. Pat walked 2 kilometers to the Capitol. Who walked farther? How many meters farther?

Gram and Kilogram

The National Zoological Park has young rain frogs. The frog on the left weighs about 1 gram.

▶The **gram (g)** is a unit of mass in the metric system.

It is common outside the field of science to use the word weight to mean the same as mass.

The gram is used to measure the weight of very light objects.

▶The **kilogram (kg)** is a unit used to measure the weight of heavier objects.

1 kilogram = 1,000 grams

A paper clip weighs about 1 gram.

Your book weighs about 1 kg.

about 20 g

about 20 kg

CLASSWORK

Choose grams or kilograms to measure each.

1.    2.    3.

4.    5.    6.

Complete.

7. 2 kg = _____ g   8. 8,000 g = _____ kg   9. 4 kg = _____ g

10. 3,000 g = _____ kg   11. 19 kg = _____ g   12. 10,000 g = _____ kg

Choose grams or kilograms to measure each.

1.

2.

3.

4.

5.

6.

Choose the best answer.

7. An egg weighs ___.
   a. 5 g
   b. 50 g
   c. 500 g

8. A man weighs ___.
   a. 77 g
   b. 7 g
   c. 77 kg

9. A bicycle weighs ___.
   a. 14 kg
   b. 14 g
   c. 140 g

Complete.

10. 5 kg = ___ g

11. ___ g = 6 kg

12. ___ g = 7 kg

13. 2,000 g = ___ kg

14. 9,000 ___ = 9 kg

15. 4,000 g = 4 ___

Name 3 objects that fit each description.

★16. weigh less than 1 kilogram

★17. weigh more than 10 kilograms

APPLICATION

18. At the zoo, a Savannah Monitor lizard weighed 2 kilograms. A Tegu lizard weighed 500 grams. Which lizard weighed more?

★19. Sam saw 100 adult rain frogs. Each weighed 20 grams. Did the adult rain frogs weigh more, less, or the same as the 2-kilogram lizard?

ESTIMATION

Choose 5 items in the classroom. Estimate and measure the weight of each. List the items in a chart. Let your classmates estimate each weight.

Milliliter and Liter

The lambs at the National Zoological Park are fed 2 liters of milk a day.

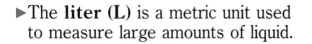

▶ The **liter (L)** is a metric unit used to measure large amounts of liquid.

about 1 liter   about 4 liters   about 10 liters

▶ The **milliliter (mL)** is used to measure small amounts of liquids.

An eyedropper holds about 1 mL. A teaspoon holds about 5 mL.

1 liter = 1,000 milliliters

CLASSWORK

Choose liters or milliliters to measure each.

1. water in a swimming pool
2. soup in a cup
3. milk in a glass
4. cough syrup in a spoon
5. water in a bathtub
6. glue in a jar

Complete.

10. 3 L = _____ mL   11. 2,000 mL = _____ L   12. 10 L = _____ mL

PRACTICE

Choose liters or milliliters to measure each.

1. water in a sink
2. oil in a drum
3. juice in a glass
4. tea in a cup
5. tea in a kettle
6. perfume in a bottle

Choose liters or milliliters for each sentence.

7. Rose used 5 _____ of suntan lotion.

8. Mr. Alvarez put 50 _____ of gas in his car.

9. The tank truck held 20,000 _____ of milk.

Choose the best answer.

10. A tablespoon contains
    a. 15 mL b. 150 mL c. 1,500 mL

11. A glass of milk contains
    a. 25 mL b. 250 mL c. 500 mL

12. A water pitcher contains
    a. 12 mL b. 120 mL c. 1,200 mL

Complete.

13. 2 L = _____ mL
14. 6,000 mL = _____ L

★ 15. 2.5 L = _____ mL
★ 16. 6.5 L = _____ mL

APPLICATION

17. A monkey drank 250 milliliters of milk in the morning and 500 milliliters at night. How much milk did the monkey drink?

★ 18. Two liters of mashed bananas were divided evenly among 4 monkeys. How many milliliters did each monkey get?

Mixed Practice

1. $\begin{array}{r} 3,512 \\ \times \quad 6 \\ \hline \end{array}$

2. $\begin{array}{r} 5,294 \\ + \quad 385 \\ \hline \end{array}$

3. $4 \times 1,078 = \square$

4. $692 \div 8 = \square$

5. $\begin{array}{r} 6,079 \\ +7,365 \\ \hline \end{array}$

6. $7\overline{)3,528}$

7. $\begin{array}{r} 3,016 \\ - \quad 937 \\ \hline \end{array}$

8. $4,219 \div 3 = \square$

9. $\$.76 + \$.54 = \square$

10. $\$3.25 + \$.98 = \square$

11. $6 \times \$.87 = \square$

12. $\begin{array}{r} 16,000 \\ - \quad 9,352 \\ \hline \end{array}$

13. $5,000 - 261 = \square$

14. $4,070 + 395 = \square$

15. $7 \times 803 = \square$

16. $216 \div 9 = \square$

17. $7 \times \$4.95 = \square$

18. $\$18.20 \div 4 = \square$

225

Degree Celsius

In January the temperature in Washington, D.C. is usually between −8°C and 1°C.

In June the temperature is often between 22°C and 32°C.

▶The **degree Celsius** (°C) is a metric unit used to measure temperature.

To read the temperature, look at the number or mark beside the top of the red column.

- read   twenty-two degrees Celsius
- write   22°C

The Celsius temperature on a cold day may be −5°C.

- read   minus five degrees Celsius, or five degrees below zero Celsius
- write   −5°C

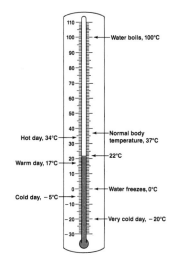

CLASSWORK

Use the thermometer above.

1. What is the boiling point of water?

2. What is the freezing point of water?

3. What is normal body temperature?

4. How many degrees are there between the freezing and boiling points of water?

Read and write each Celsius temperature shown.

5.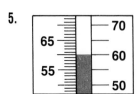

6.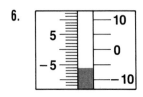

7.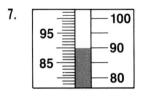

Read and write each Celsius temperature shown.

1. 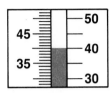 2. 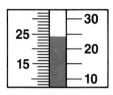 3. 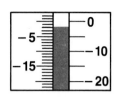 4.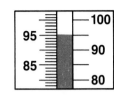

Choose the most reasonable temperature.

5. hot soup

   a. 40°C   b. 80°C   c. 108°C

6. snowball

   a. 20°C   b. 5°C   c. −10°C

7. swimming pool

   a. 29°C   b. 19°C   c. 9°C

8. drinking water

   a. 10°C   b. −10°C   c. 25°C

Complete. Follow each rule, if given.

Rule: Add 9°.

	Input	Output
9.	4°C	
10.	25°C	
11.	17°C	

Rule: Subtract 8°.

	Input	Output
12.	40°C	
13.	13°C	
14.	10°C	

Find the rule.

★15.	Input	Output
	−10°C	5°C
	0°C	15°C
	42°C	57°C

APPLICATION

Steve graphed the temperature at 9 A.M. every day.

16. What was the highest temperature?

17. What day had the lowest temperature?

18. What was the average temperature?

Keep a record of the outside temperature for 5 days. Take the reading at the same time each day.

★19. Make a line graph to show the data.

★20. Make up three questions about your graph.

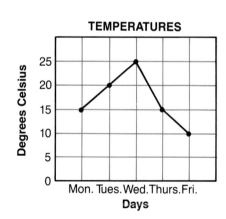

TEMPERATURES

Problem Solving

SKILLS AND STRATEGIES REVIEW On the Road

Read and solve each problem.

1. The Snyders plan to take 3 days to drive 1,560 kilometers to Washington, D.C. They plan to drive the same distance each day. How many kilometers do they plan to drive each day?

2. The drive to Harrisonburg took 3 hours. Buddy said they had driven about 2,000 meters. Sandy said they had driven about 200 kilometers. Who was correct?

3. The first night, their motel room cost $42.85. The tax was $2.14 and breakfast was $8.50. How much change did Mr. Snyder receive from $60.00?

4. The Snyders stopped for gas three times. They bought 59.7 liters, 56.2 liters, and 46.7 liters. How many liters of gas did they buy in all?

5. Sandy packed a yellow blouse, a brown blouse, and 3 skirts—red, blue, and striped. Make a list to see whether Sandy will have more than 5 different outfits for the trip.

6. All four members of the Snyder family ordered a turkey dinner. The price of each dinner was $12.95 including tax. How much did the Snyders spend in all if they left a tip of $8.00?

★7. Mrs. Snyder bought film for her camera. Each of 4 rolls contains 24 pictures and each of 2 rolls contains 36 pictures. How many pictures can she take?

★8. Buddy counted 10 telephone poles in one minute. Mr. Snyder told him there were about 40 meters between poles. About how far had they gone in that minute?

Sandy and Buddy kept a tally of the states on the license plates they saw.

LICENSE PLATES	
Virginia	~~||||~~ ~~||||~~ ~~||||~~ ||||
Pennsylvania	~~||||~~ |||
District of Columbia	~~||||~~ ~~||||~~ ||
Maryland	~~||||~~
North Carolina	~~||||~~ ~~||||~~ |||
New York	|||

9. How many license plates did they tally?

10. For how many states were more than 12 license plates tallied? What were they?

11. Buddy thinks they saw more cars from Virginia and Pennsylvania than from all the others combined. Was he right?

12. Make a bar graph to show the data.

SOMETHING EXTRA

You can play a game with license plates. Suppose you saw these plates.

13. On which license plate is the sum of the digits 25?

14. On which license plates is the sum of the digits less than 20?

15. Which license plates show numbers that are divisible by 4?

16. Which license plates show a number you can read when turned upside down?

17. Which license plates show the same number when they are turned upside down?

★18. How many different license plates can you make using the digits 5, 9, 2, and 6? You can use each digit only once in a license plate.

229

DECIMALS

Write each decimal. pages 204–207

1. 3 tenths
2. 5 hundredths
3. 1 and 6 hundredths

4. 24 hundredths
5. nine and two tenths
6. thirteen hundredths

Compare. Use >, <, or = for ●. pages 206–211

7. 0.15 ● 0.19
8. 8.1 ● 0.81
9. 10.16 ● 10.06

10. 17.9 ● 17.90
11. 21.3 ● 21.2
12. 0.40 ● 4.00

Use < to order the decimals from least to greatest. pages 206–211

13. 1.41   1.04   1.40
14. 0.32   0.3   0.29

15. 2.6   2.9   2.39
16. 0.09   0.02   0.18

Add or subtract. pages 208–215

17. $\begin{array}{r} 9.6 \\ +7.6 \\ \hline \end{array}$
18. $\begin{array}{r} 0.7 \\ +2.4 \\ \hline \end{array}$
19. $\begin{array}{r} 6.2 \\ -5.7 \\ \hline \end{array}$
20. $\begin{array}{r} 0.43 \\ -0.33 \\ \hline \end{array}$
21. $\begin{array}{r} 0.5 \\ 2.3 \\ +0.7 \\ \hline \end{array}$

22. $0.6 + 3 = \square$
23. $6.49 + 5.82 = \square$
24. $3.63 - 2.7 = \square$

25. $8.13 - 7.96 = \square$
26. $0.66 + 4.35 = \square$
27. $9 - 6.54 = \square$

28. $2.72 + 9.28 = \square$
29. $3.8 - 0.12 = \square$
30. $7.64 + 6.9 = \square$

Solve. pages 216–217; 228–229

31. Aurora has 4 reports due on Friday. She finished 0.5 of a report on Monday and 2.75 reports on Wednesday. How much does she have left to do?

32. Harry swam 2 lengths of the pool in 62.4 seconds. He improved his time by 0.01 second each day for 3 days. What was his time then?

DECIMALS

Write each decimal.

1. four tenths

2. three hundredths

3. two and six tenths

4. 9 and 9 tenths

5. 6 hundredths

6. 36 hundredths

Compare. Use >, <, or = for ●.

7. 4.9 ● 4.98

8. 9.80 ● 9.08

9. 13.4 ● 13.40

10. 28.5 ● 28.49

Use < to order the decimals from least to greatest.

11. 0.3   0.13   0.31

12. 6.06   6.60   6.04

Add or subtract.

13.
$$\begin{array}{r} 8.7 \\ +9.8 \\ \hline \end{array}$$

14.
$$\begin{array}{r} 0.6 \\ +2.2 \\ \hline \end{array}$$

15.
$$\begin{array}{r} 5 \\ -1.8 \\ \hline \end{array}$$

16.
$$\begin{array}{r} 3 \\ -1.2 \\ \hline \end{array}$$

17.
$$\begin{array}{r} 0.6 \\ 3.9 \\ +4.2 \\ \hline \end{array}$$

18. $0.4 + 0.7 + 0.2 = \square$

19. $3.58 + 4.32 = \square$

20. $9.45 + 0.55 = \square$

21. $9.54 - 8.4 = \square$

22. $3.12 - 2.2 = \square$

23. $6 - 4.85 = \square$

Solve.

24. Elly scored 3.7 on her first dive. She scored 4.5 on her second dive. How much higher was the score on the second dive than on the first?

25. Luis averaged 7.3 points per basketball game. Dan's average was 1.5 points higher than Luis's. What was Dan's average per basketball game?

Each week, the pet store manager increases food for the baby hamsters by the same amount. How much will she feed them during weeks 4 and 5?

Week	1	2	3	4	5
Grams of food	18.5	25	31.5		

METRIC MEASUREMENT

Measure each length to the nearest centimeter. pages 218–219

1. [   ]   2. [   ] 3. [   ]

Measure each length to the nearest millimeter. pages 218–219

4. [   ]   5. [   ]   6. [   ]

Choose the best answer. pages 218–226

7. A crayon is _____ long.

  a. 6 cm   **b.** 6 m   **c.** 60 cm

8. Two towns are _____ apart.

  a. 60 cm   **b.** 6 m   **c.** 6 km

9. A dog weighs _____.

  a. 40 g   **b.** 200 kg   **c.** 20 kg

10. A juice glass contains _____.

  a. 100 mL   **b.** 1 L   **c.** 10 mL

Complete. pages 218–226

11. 2 m = _____ cm   12. 3 km = _____ m   13. 400 cm = _____ m

14. 7 kg = _____ g   15. 12,000 g = _____ kg   16. 10 kg = _____ g

17. 4 L = _____ mL   18. 2,000 mL = _____ L   19. 17 L = _____ mL

Write each Celsius temperature shown. pages 226–227

20. 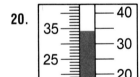   21.    22. 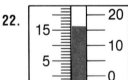   23.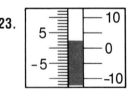

Solve. pages 216–217, 228–229

24. Janet swam 400 centimeters using a breaststroke and 600 centimeters using a butterfly stroke. Then she swam 300 centimeters underwater. How many meters is this?

25. Stan bought 1 liter of milk. He used 500 milliliters of milk to bake bread. He used 200 milliliters in soup. How many milliliters did he have left?

METRIC MEASUREMENT

Measure each length to the nearest centimeter.

1. _____   2. ____   3. _____

Measure each length to the nearest millimeter.

4. ____   5. _____   6. _____

Choose the best answer.

7. A doorway is ____ high.

    a. 20 cm   **b.** 2 m   **c.** 2 km

8. A kitten is ____ long.

    a. 30 cm   **b.** 3 m   **c.** 30 m

9. A notebook weighs ____.

    a. 500 g   **b.** 5 g   **c.** 5 kg

10. A teaspoon contains ____.

    a. 70 mL   **b.** 100 mL   **c.** 5 mL

Complete.

11. 600 cm = ____ m   12. 5 km = ____ m   13. 8 m = ____ cm

14. 9 kg = ____ g   15. 3,000 g = ____ kg   16. 4 kg = ____ g

17. 7,000 mL = ____ L   18. 2 L = ____ mL   19. 3,000 mL = ____ L

Write each Celsius temperature shown.

20. 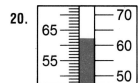   21. 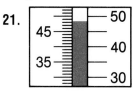   22. 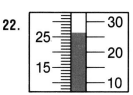   23.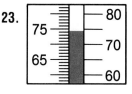

Solve.

24. Ed mixed a liter of orange juice and 500 milliliters of pineapple juice. How many milliliters of juice did he have?

25. A boat can hold 240 kilograms. Susan weighs 38.2 kilograms. Bob weighs 44.5 kilograms. If Susan and Bob are in the boat, how many more kilograms can it hold?

Lila hiked 3.5 kilometers. How many meters did she hike?

COMPASS COURSE

A compass is an instrument for showing directions.

Hold a compass level and turn it until the needle points to N. Point to an object that is north of you. Point to the south, the east, and the west.

Set up a compass course on the school grounds that looks like the drawing.

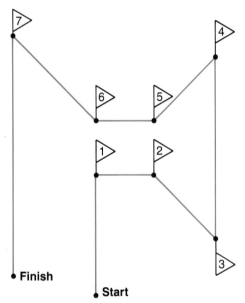

From Start, go 40 steps north. Then continue: 20 steps east, 30 steps southeast, 60 steps north, 30 steps southwest, 20 steps west, 40 steps northwest, and 80 steps south.

Now set up your own compass course. Use places such as the school door, a flagpole, the swings, or a large tree. Put a card at each place to tell the distance and direction to the next place. Have your friends follow the course. Have them tell you all the places they found.

MAP READING

Pretend that you and your family are on a visit to Washington, D.C. Use this map to answer the questions.

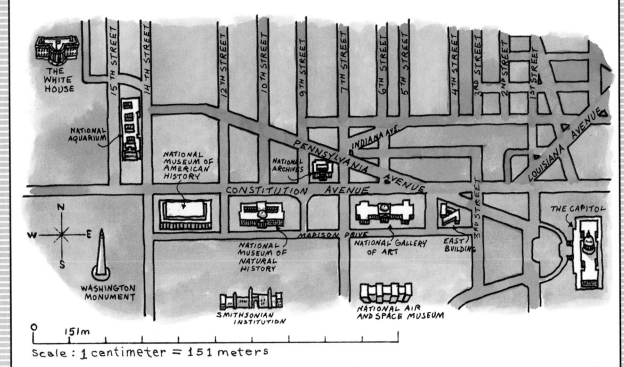

Scale : 1 centimeter = 151 meters

1. What street would you take to go from the National Gallery of Art to the National Museum of American History?

2. In what direction would you be going?

3. What museum would you pass along the way?

4. On the scale of meters, what does 1 centimeter equal?

5. About how many meters is it from the National Museum of American History to the Washington Monument? This distance measures about 3 centimeters on the map.

6. Measure the distance from 3rd Street to 12th Street along Pennsylvania Avenue. How many centimeters did you measure? Would this be greater or less than 1 kilometer?

USING BASIC: LET STATEMENTS

The LET statement is
one way of entering
and storing information
in the computer.

LET A = 3.5

This tells the computer
to store the value 3.5 in
a memory location named A.
The names, called **variables,**
might be 1 or 2 letters or a
letter followed by a number.

A is given the value 3.5.
B is given the value 4.9.
To find the value of S, the
computer adds A + B.
The semicolon tells the computer to
print the value of S right after the
previous output.

```
10  LET A = 3.5
20  LET B = 4.9
30  LET S = A + B
40  PRINT "THE SUM IS ";S
50  END
RUN
THE SUM IS 8.4
```

For each program, tell what the output will be.

```
1. 10  LET A = 13.07
   20  LET B = 10.65
   30  LET D = A - B
   40  PRINT "THE DIFFERENCE
   IS ";D
   50  END
```

```
2. 10  LET X = 12.31
   20  LET Y = 6.8
   30  LET Z = 497.32
   40  LET S = X + Y + Z
   50  PRINT "THE SUM IS ";S
   60  END
```

```
3. 10  LET KG = 15
   20  LET G = KG * 1000
   30  PRINT "NUMBER OF GRAMS
   = ";G
   40  END
```

```
4. 10  LET MM = 400
   20  LET CM = MM/10
   30  PRINT "NUMBER OF
   CENTIMETERS IS ";CM
   40  END
```

This program to find an average of test grades uses LET statements. The test grades are named T1, T2, and T3.

A flowchart helps to show the steps.

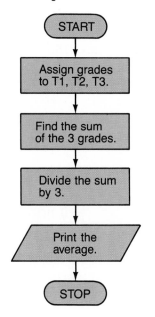

```
10  PRINT "AN AVERAGE PROGRAM"
20  LET T1 = 94
30  LET T2 = 78
40  LET T3 = 89
50  LET S = T1 + T2 + T3
60  LET A = S/3
70  PRINT "YOUR AVERAGE IS ";A
80  END


RUN
AN AVERAGE PROGRAM
YOUR AVERAGE IS 87
```

Complete each program. Then tell what the output will be.

```
5. 10  LET T1 = 70
   20  LET T2 = 80
   30  LET T3 = 95
   40  LET T4 = 83
   50  LET S = T1 + T2 + T3 + T4
   60
   70
   80  END
```

```
6. 10  LET A = 134.31
   20  LET B = 10.5
   30
   40  PRINT "THE DIFFERENCE
   IS ";D
   50  END
```

═══════════════ AT THE COMPUTER ═══════════════

1. Enter and RUN 1–4 on page 236 and 5 and 6 above.

2. Compare the computer output with your answers.

★3. On Your Own: Write a program to change 20,000 grams to kilograms. RUN your program to test it.

MAINTAINING SKILLS

Choose the correct answer. Write A, B, C, or D.

1. What is the value of 3 in 23,547?

   A 30,000   C 300

   B 3,000   D not given

2. $425 - 231 = \square$

   A 194   C 656

   B 214   D not given

3. $72 \div 8 = \square$

   A 9   C 7

   B 8   D not given

4. How much money is 2 dimes and 1 nickel?

   A $.15   C $.25

   B $.20   D not given

5. Estimate. $6 \times 239 = \square$

   A 120   C 12,000

   B 1,800   D not given

6. $5 \times 4,083 = \square$

   A 20,005   C 20,415

   B 20,405   D not given

7. $43 \div 6 = \square$

   A 7 R3   C 6 R1

   B 7 R1   D not given

8. $7,219 \div 3 = \square$

   A 246 R1   C 2,406 R1

   B 2,403   D not given

9. $\$24.48 \div 8 = \square$

   A $3.06   C $4.06

   B $.36   D not given

10. What is the decimal for 17 hundredths?

    A 1.7   C 0.17

    B 0.017   D not given

11. $5.04 + 6.27 = \square$

    A 11.21   C 11.32

    B 11.31   D not given

12. $15 - 6.37 = \square$

    A 8.63   C 8.73

    B 11.37   D not given

13. How many milliliters in a liter?

    A 10   C 1,000

    B 100   D not given

Make a list to help solve.

14. Paula, Gina, and Alex had a race. How many different ways could they have finished?

    A 4   C 8

    B 6   D not given

15. If Paula was always first, how many ways could they have finished?

    A 4   C 2

    B 6   D not given

Theme: Forests

Multiplying by Ten

Students in an art class are cutting out triangles to make trees. Find the number of triangles needed for 10 trees of each type.

$$10 \times 5 = 50 \qquad \begin{array}{r} 5 \\ \times\,10 \\ \hline 50 \end{array}$$

They need 50 triangles for these trees.

$$10 \times 10 = 100 \qquad \begin{array}{r} 10 \\ \times\,10 \\ \hline 100 \end{array}$$

They need 100 triangles for these trees.

$$10 \times 17 = 170 \qquad \begin{array}{r} 17 \\ \times\,10 \\ \hline 170 \end{array}$$

They need 170 triangles for these trees.

▶When multiplying by 10, write 0 in ones place. Then multiply by 1.

More Examples

$$\begin{array}{r} 395 \\ \times\ 10 \\ \hline 3{,}950 \end{array} \qquad \begin{array}{r} 450 \\ \times\ 10 \\ \hline 4{,}500 \end{array} \qquad \begin{array}{r} 700 \\ \times\ 10 \\ \hline 7{,}000 \end{array} \qquad \begin{array}{r} 806 \\ \times\ 10 \\ \hline 8{,}060 \end{array}$$

CLASSWORK

Multiply.

1. $\begin{array}{r} 4 \\ \times 10 \\ \hline \end{array}$
2. $\begin{array}{r} 12 \\ \times 10 \\ \hline \end{array}$
3. $\begin{array}{r} 36 \\ \times 10 \\ \hline \end{array}$
4. $\begin{array}{r} 850 \\ \times\ 10 \\ \hline \end{array}$
5. $\begin{array}{r} 702 \\ \times\ 10 \\ \hline \end{array}$
6. $\begin{array}{r} 300 \\ \times\ 10 \\ \hline \end{array}$

7. $10 \times 9 = \square$

8. $10 \times 40 = \square$

9. $10 \times 600 = \square$

Multiply.

1. 33×10	2. 6×10	3. 10×10	4. 24×10	5. 50×10	6. 19×10
7. 7×10	8. 83×10	9. 140×10	10. 685×10	11. 308×10	12. 96×10
13. 290×10	14. 47×10	15. 541×10	16. 78×10	17. 200×10	18. 903×10

19. $10 \times 0 = \square$

20. $10 \times 62 = \square$

21. $10 \times 97 = \square$

22. $10 \times 510 = \square$

23. $10 \times 45 = \square$

24. $10 \times 100 = \square$

Find each missing number.

★25. $(10 \times \square) + 4 = 254$

★26. $(10 \times \square) + 37 = 867$

★27. $(10 \times 35) + \square = 362$

★28. $(10 \times 72) + \square = 748$

APPLICATION

29. Mrs. Philip's class counted 78 rows of oak trees in the forest preserve. Each row had 10 trees. How many oak trees were there in all?

30. At the preserve, 29 students were each given a bag of 10 acorns. What was the total number of acorns given out?

★31. Seedlings were planted in rows of 10. There were 46 rows of spruce, 52 rows of pine, and 38 rows of ash seedlings. How many seedlings were planted in all?

★32. Section A had 10 pine and 10 fir seedlings in each of 34 rows. Section B had 20 spruce and 20 juniper seedlings in each of 17 rows. Which section had more?

LOGICAL THINKING

Jim will make 11 cuts in this board. He is making 10-inch pieces. How long is the board?

Multiplying by Tens

Imagine 20 giraffes each 16 feet tall standing on top of one another! They would reach the top of this redwood tree. How tall is the tree?

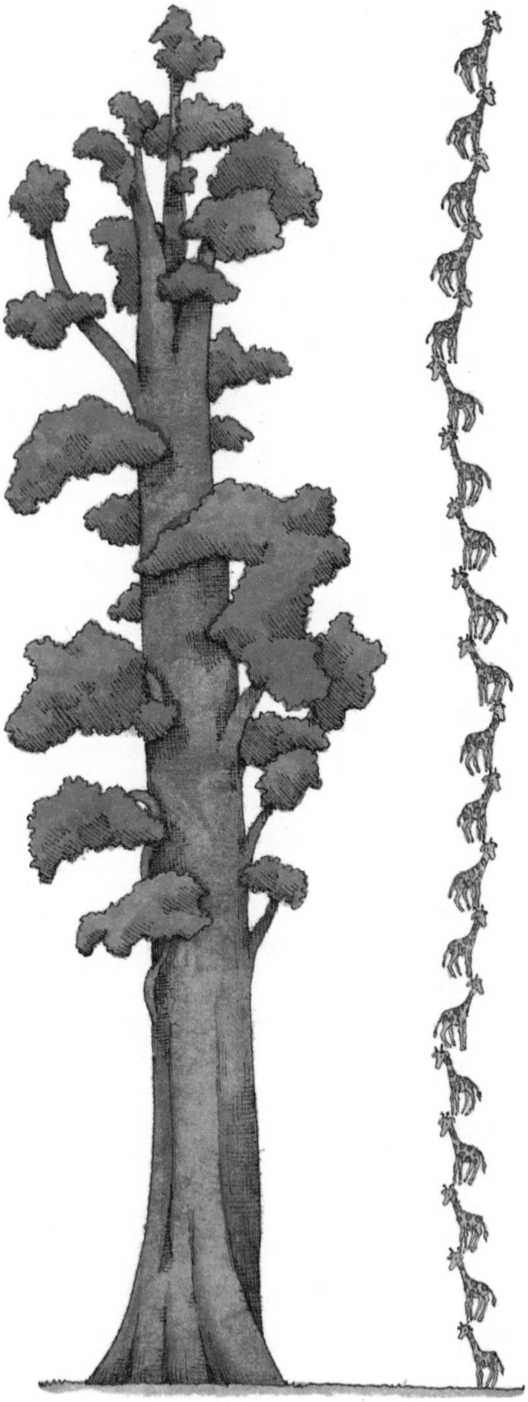

$$20 \times 16 = \square$$

Step 1
Write 0 in ones place.

```
   16
 × 20
    0
```

Step 2
Multiply by tens.

```
   1
   16
 × 20
  320
```

The tree is 320 feet tall.

Another Example

Write 0 in ones place.

```
  325
 × 60
    0
```

Multiply by tens.

```
   1 3
  325
 × 60
19,500
```

CLASSWORK

Find each product.

1.	2.	3.	4.	5.	6.
67 × 30	52 × 90	316 × 60	190 × 70	427 × 50	293 × 80

7. $20 \times 84 = \square$

8. $40 \times 792 = \square$

9. $30 \times 536 = \square$

Find each product.

1. 37 ×50	2. 10 ×20	3. 58 ×30	4. 45 ×40	5. 80 ×10	6. 64 ×60
7. 279 × 80	8. 386 × 50	9. 99 ×70	10. 92 ×40	11. 260 × 10	12. 497 × 90
13. 500 × 90	14. 206 × 30	15. 458 × 10	16. 300 × 70	17. 209 × 80	18. 449 × 50
19. 180 × 40	20. 617 × 20	21. 522 × 60	22. 435 × 70	23. 902 × 10	24. 241 × 30

25. $30 \times 9 = \square$

26. $90 \times 90 = \square$

27. $50 \times 0 = \square$

28. $60 \times 20 = \square$

29. $40 \times 21 = \square$

30. $20 \times 50 = \square$

Follow the rule to find each missing number.

Rule: Multiply by 30.

	Input	Output
31.	50	
32.	183	
33.	200	

Rule: Multiply by 50.

	Input	Output
34.	36	
35.	102	
36.	345	

Rule: Multiply by 40; then add 55.

	Input	Output
★ 37.	8	
★ 38.	281	
★ 39.	520	

APPLICATION

40. As a seedling, an oak tree can be 3 feet tall. Fully grown it is sometimes 50 times as tall. How tall can an oak tree grow?

41. An orange tree is 18 feet tall. A redwood tree is 30 times taller. What is the height of the redwood tree?

42. A forest contains 430 spruce trees. There are 60 more pine than spruce trees in this same forest. What is the total number of trees in this forest?

★ 43. To finish building a garage, Mr. Jacobs needs 250 feet of pine. He has 14 boards that are each 10 feet long. How many more 10-foot boards must he buy?

Multiplying by Tens and Ones

Each ring shows the tree growth for 12 months. Count the rings in the diagram. Find the age of this tree in months.

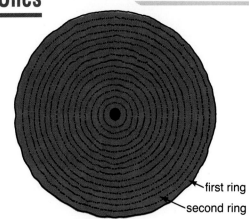

first ring

second ring

Find 16 × 12.

Step 1 Multiply by ones.	**Step 2** Multiply by tens.	**Step 3** Add.

1	1	1
12	12	12
×16	×16	×16
72 ← 6 × 12	72	72
	120 ← 10 × 12	+120
		192

The age of the tree is 192 months.

Find 25 × 79.

Multiply by ones.	Multiply by tens.	Add.
	1	1
4	~~4~~	~~4~~
79	79	79
×25	×25	×25
395 ← 5 × 79	395	395
	1580 ← 20 × 79	+1 580
		1,975

CLASSWORK

Find each product.

1. 13
   ×23

2. 30
   ×81

3. 46
   ×45

4. 52
   ×67

5. 18
   ×96

6. 89
   ×28

7. 43 × 74 = □

8. 82 × 63 = □

9. 39 × 95 = □

Find each product.

1.	59 ×11	2.	12 ×24	3.	60 ×38	4.	82 ×17	5.	30 ×40	6.	79 ×36
7.	25 ×90	8.	46 ×78	9.	80 ×57	10.	34 ×60	11.	27 ×83	12.	80 ×91
13.	65 ×26	14.	98 ×73	15.	90 ×50	16.	47 ×81	17.	38 ×49	18.	33 ×65

19. $14 \times 46 = \square$ 20. $17 \times 10 = \square$ 21. $39 \times 11 = \square$

22. $86 \times 68 = \square$ 23. $44 \times 70 = \square$ 24. $26 \times 29 = \square$

25. $65 \times 99 = \square$ 26. $16 \times 57 = \square$ 27. $92 \times 89 = \square$

Choose the correct number sentence and solve.

28. A tree has 23 rings. Each ring means the tree grew 12 months. Find the age of the tree.

 a. $23 + 12 = \square$ b. $23 \times 1 = \square$
 c. $23 \times 12 = \square$ d. $23 - 12 = \square$

Find each missing number.

★29. $23 \times 19 = 486 - \square$ ★30. $94 \times 60 = 5,400 + \square$

APPLICATION

31. Brian counted 21 boxes of park maps. Each box contains 75 maps. How many park maps are there?

★32. Nan and Steve entered a canoe race. They can do about 15 paddle strokes in 30 seconds. How many strokes can they do in one hour?

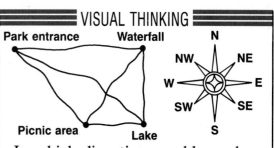

VISUAL THINKING

In which direction would you be traveling if you went from:
1. waterfall to lake?
2. lake to picnic area?
3. entrance to picnic area?

Problem Solving

MAKING AND USING DRAWINGS

Sometimes making a drawing can
help you solve a problem.

1. There are four friends taking a hike in the
   forest. They walk one behind the other.
   Marsha is ahead of Jerry. Elena is behind
   Jerry. Marsha is behind Brad.
   Who is leading the hike?

Make a drawing. Use the facts in the problem.

Step 1	Step 2	Step 3
Show Marsha ahead of Jerry.	Show Elena behind Jerry.	Show Marsha behind Brad.
Jerry Marsha	Elena Jerry Marsha	Elena Jerry Marsha Brad

Brad is leading the hike.

Do the facts in the problem match the drawing?
Yes. Your answer is correct.

2. The drawing shows a part of the forest. There
   are four groves in this part. Each grove has
   the same number of trees. How many trees
   are in this part of the forest?

   Use the drawing. Count the number of trees in
   1 grove. Then multiply that number by the
   number of groves.

   Solve the problem.

PRACTICE

Which drawing at the right shows the facts in each problem?

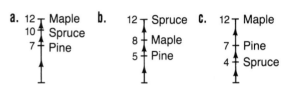

1. The ranger walks 30 meters east. Then he walks 40 meters south. Then he walks 2 meters west and 1 meter north.

2. The pine tree is 7 meters tall. The maple is 5 meters taller than the pine. The spruce is 3 meters shorter than the pine.

Which problem at the right can be solved by using the drawing at the left?

3.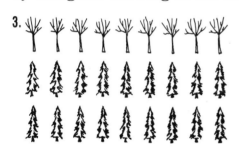

a. There are 9 oak trees. There are 2 times as many fir trees. How many fir trees are there?

b. There are 18 oak trees. There are 2 times as many fir trees. How many fir trees are there?

Make a drawing to help you solve each problem.

4. The pine tree is younger than the oak. The maple tree is older than the oak. The age of the spruce is between the oak and the maple. Which tree is the youngest?

★5. Jan and Stu leave camp and go 300 meters east. They turn and go 65 meters south, then 385 meters west. Then they go 42 meters north and 85 meters east. How far are they from camp?

=== CREATE YOUR OWN PROBLEM ===

1. Write the facts that you see in the drawing of fence posts and rails.

2. Write one problem that can be answered by using the facts.

3. Write one problem that can be answered by adding on to the drawing.

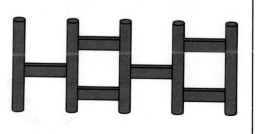

Estimating Products

In Kenneth Grahame's *The Wind in the Willows,* Mr. Badger prepares for winter. About 35 hazelnuts fit in a basket. About how many hazelnuts would he store in 12 baskets?

▶To estimate a product, round each factor to its greatest place. Then multiply.

$$
\begin{array}{r}
35 \quad \text{rounds to} \quad 40 \\
\times 12 \quad \text{rounds to} \quad \times 10 \\
\hline
400
\end{array}
$$

Mr. Badger would store about 400 hazelnuts.

More Examples

$$
\begin{array}{r}
176 \quad \text{rounds to} \quad 200 \\
\times \ 34 \quad \text{rounds to} \quad \times \ 30 \\
\hline
6{,}000
\end{array}
\qquad
\begin{array}{r}
641 \quad \text{rounds to} \quad 600 \\
\times \ 26 \quad \text{rounds to} \quad \times \ 30 \\
\hline
18{,}000
\end{array}
$$

CLASSWORK

Estimate each product.

1. $\begin{array}{r} 32 \\ \times 48 \\ \hline \end{array}$
2. $\begin{array}{r} 235 \\ \times \ 59 \\ \hline \end{array}$
3. $\begin{array}{r} 84 \\ \times 16 \\ \hline \end{array}$
4. $\begin{array}{r} 934 \\ \times \ 30 \\ \hline \end{array}$
5. $\begin{array}{r} 552 \\ \times \ 70 \\ \hline \end{array}$
6. $\begin{array}{r} 875 \\ \times \ 43 \\ \hline \end{array}$

7. $75 \times 18 = \square$
8. $54 \times 789 = \square$
9. $20 \times 655 = \square$

PRACTICE

Estimate each product.

1. $\begin{array}{r}23\\\times 57\end{array}$	2. $\begin{array}{r}49\\\times 65\end{array}$	3. $\begin{array}{r}37\\\times 18\end{array}$	4. $\begin{array}{r}62\\\times 40\end{array}$
5. $\begin{array}{r}74\\\times 29\end{array}$	6. $\begin{array}{r}827\\\times\ \ 50\end{array}$	7. $\begin{array}{r}95\\\times 40\end{array}$	8. $\begin{array}{r}910\\\times\ \ 17\end{array}$
9. $\begin{array}{r}472\\\times\ \ 10\end{array}$	10. $\begin{array}{r}128\\\times\ \ 71\end{array}$	11. $\begin{array}{r}394\\\times\ \ 83\end{array}$	12. $\begin{array}{r}681\\\times\ \ 68\end{array}$

13. $43 \times 24 = \square$ 14. $25 \times 79 = \square$

15. $86 \times 391 = \square$ 16. $60 \times 739 = \square$

 Estimate each product. Tell whether each product should be greater or less than the estimate. Use a calculator to find the exact product.

★ 17. $\begin{array}{r}38\\\times 45\end{array}$	★ 18. $\begin{array}{r}83\\\times 64\end{array}$	★ 19. $\begin{array}{r}333\\\times\ \ 14\end{array}$	★ 20. $\begin{array}{r}450\\\times\ \ 66\end{array}$

APPLICATION

21. About how many potatoes would Mr. Badger have in 16 baskets of potatoes?

22. About how many apples are there in 28 baskets of apples?

★ 23. A farmer sells 18 baskets of turnips. He also sells 12 baskets each of apples and potatoes. About how many baskets of food does the farmer sell in all?

Mixed Practice

1. $136 + 589 = \square$

2. $4,189 - 757 = \square$

3. $26 + 98 + 6 = \square$

4. $5 \times 17 = \square$

5. $216 \div 9 = \square$

6. $\$.61 + \$.74 = \square$

7. $8 \times 3,624 = \square$

8. $5,480 - 694 = \square$

9. $2,085 \div 5 = \square$

10. $\$3.84 - \$.52 = \square$

11. $6,145 \div 6 = \square$

12. $343 + 83 = \square$

13. $4 \times 3,295 = \square$

14. $1,280 - 882 = \square$

15. $7 \times \$12.55 = \square$

16. $5,035 \div 5 = \square$

17. $3,265 + 498 = \square$

18. $6 \times 563 = \square$

19. $2,000 - 476 = \square$

20. $2,339 \div 6 = \square$

249

Multiplying Three-Digit Numbers

Pat makes wooden nutcrackers to sell to gift shops. She plans to make the same number of nutcrackers each month. Find the number of nutcrackers that Pat can sell in one year.

12 × 175 = ☐

Step 1 Multiply by ones.	**Step 2** Multiply by tens.	**Step 3** Add.
1 1 175 × 12 350 ← 2 × 175	1 1 175 × 12 350 1750 ← 10 × 175	1 1 175 × 12 350 + 1 750 2,100

Pat can sell 2,100 nutcrackers in one year.

Estimate to be sure the answer makes sense.

$$175 \text{ rounds to } 200$$
$$\times 12 \text{ rounds to } \times 10$$
$$2,000$$

Exact product and estimate are close. The answer makes sense.

CLASSWORK

Multiply. Estimate to be sure each answer makes sense.

1. 272
    × 32

2. 380
    × 41

3. 603
    × 65

4. 795
    × 12

5. 864
    × 73

6. 14 × 279 = ☐

7. 58 × 175 = ☐

8. 91 × 450 = ☐

9. 50 × 832 = ☐

10. 46 × 941 = ☐

11. 35 × 704 = ☐

Multiply. Estimate to be sure each answer makes sense.

1. $\begin{array}{r} 191 \\ \times\ 12 \\ \hline \end{array}$	2. $\begin{array}{r} 305 \\ \times\ 19 \\ \hline \end{array}$	3. $\begin{array}{r} 215 \\ \times\ 38 \\ \hline \end{array}$	4. $\begin{array}{r} 202 \\ \times\ 78 \\ \hline \end{array}$	5. $\begin{array}{r} 579 \\ \times\ 49 \\ \hline \end{array}$
6. $\begin{array}{r} 693 \\ \times\ 36 \\ \hline \end{array}$	7. $\begin{array}{r} 439 \\ \times\ 75 \\ \hline \end{array}$	8. $\begin{array}{r} 500 \\ \times\ 58 \\ \hline \end{array}$	9. $\begin{array}{r} 971 \\ \times\ 84 \\ \hline \end{array}$	10. $\begin{array}{r} 495 \\ \times\ 90 \\ \hline \end{array}$
11. $\begin{array}{r} 408 \\ \times\ 62 \\ \hline \end{array}$	12. $\begin{array}{r} 646 \\ \times\ 88 \\ \hline \end{array}$	13. $\begin{array}{r} 758 \\ \times\ 76 \\ \hline \end{array}$	14. $\begin{array}{r} 880 \\ \times\ 19 \\ \hline \end{array}$	15. $\begin{array}{r} 307 \\ \times\ 98 \\ \hline \end{array}$

16. $20 \times 655 = \square$ 17. $72 \times 996 = \square$ 18. $55 \times 517 = \square$

19. $90 \times 289 = \square$ 20. $67 \times 700 = \square$ 21. $32 \times 478 = \square$

★22. $80 \times 5,300 = \square$ ★23. $35 \times 1,684 = \square$ ★24. $58 \times 2,175 = \square$

APPLICATION

25. Wendy owns a gift shop. She ordered 25 boxes of greeting cards. Each box contains 150 cards. How many cards did Wendy order?

26. Wendy orders 13 nutcrackers a month from Pat. How many nutcrackers would Wendy order in 12 months?

★27. Pat gives 1 free nutcracker for each 20 nutcrackers ordered. How many free nutcrackers would you receive if you ordered 150 nutcrackers?

CALCULATOR

If there are no parentheses, use this rule to calculate.
Do all the multiplications or divisions first.
Then do all the additions or subtractions.

1. $438 + 217 \times 42 = \square$ 2. $512 \times 38 - 109 = \square$

3. $85 \times 429 - 700 = \square$ 4. $329 + 175 \times 20 = \square$

Multiplying Money

It costs $2.50 to buy a newspaper for 1 week. What does it cost to buy a newspaper for 52 weeks?

$52 \times \$2.50 = \square$

Multiply money the same way you multiply other numbers.

Step 1	Step 2	Step 3
1 $2.50 × 52 500	2 $2.50 × 52 500 12500	2 $2.50 × 52 5 00 +125 00 $130.00

Write the dollar sign and decimal point in the product.

It costs $130 for 52 weeks.

Find 23 × $176.

Estimate to be sure the answer makes sense.

```
  1 1
  2 1
 $176   rounds to      $200
×   23   rounds to   ×    20
  528                 $4,000
+3 520
 $4,048
```

Exact product and estimate are close. The answer makes sense.

CLASSWORK

Multiply.

1. $.23 × 24	2. $.30 × 15	3. $.27 × 50	4. $6.45 × 28	5. $4.55 × 70

Multiply. Estimate to be sure each answer makes sense.

6. 43 × $54 = □   7. 37 × $689 = □   8. 71 × $912 = □

Multiply.

1. $.71 × 23	2. $.68 × 13	3. $.76 × 40	4. $8.90 × 82	5. $2.84 × 75
6. $4.89 × 66	7. $3.09 × 70	8. $2.17 × 96	9. $6.15 × 56	10. $2.07 × 87

11. 93 × $.30 = ☐   12. 69 × $.95 = ☐   13. 40 × $.90 = ☐

14. 48 × $1.14 = ☐   15. 13 × $7.09 = ☐   16. 60 × $3.00 = ☐

Multiply. Estimate to be sure each answer makes sense.

17. $115 × 19	18. $368 × 12	19. $190 × 35	20. $278 × 29	21. $421 × 54

Find each missing number.

★ 22. 38 × $4.72 = (30 × $4.72) + (☐ × $4.72)

★ 23. 75 × $3.94 = (☐ × $3.94) + (5 × $3.94)

APPLICATION

24. Mr. Holmes ordered daily newspapers for 27 students. If it costs $1.35 for each student, how much did the newspapers cost?

★ 25. John sells a daily newspaper for $.25. It costs him $.17 for a newspaper. What profit does he make if he sells 85 newspapers?

MENTAL ARITHMETIC

How much greater is the second product than the first?

1. $2.25 × 30	$2.25 × 31	2. $1.20 × 40	$1.20 × 42	
3. $1.25 × 60	$1.25 × 64	4. $2.10 × 80	$2.10 × 83	

Problem Solving

SKILLS AND STRATEGIES REVIEW

The fantasy Kingdom of Emong is deep in the forest. Emongs are hardworking people.

Read and solve each problem.

1. There are 872 people in Emong. Of these, 342 are men, 367 are women, and the rest are children. How many are children?

2. The Emong children go to school 6 days a week. They spend 5 hours a day in school. How many hours a week are the children in school?

The Emongs use unicorns and tricorns as work animals.

3. How many horns do Jade's animals have?

4. How many horns do Plib's unicorns have?

5. How many horns do Burg's tricorns have?

6. How many more tricorns does Plib have than Glos?

★8. The Emongs have a field which is divided as shown. They want to plant oats, corn, barley, and hay. How can these crops be planted so that no crop is next to itself in a row, column, or at corners?

ANIMALS OWNED				
Owner's Name	Unicorns	Number of Horns	Tricorns	Number of Horns
Jem	3	3	2	6
Jade	2	2	6	18
Glos	5	5	4	
Burg	7	7	3	
Plib	6			27

7. Kolo counted 7 horns in his flock. How many unicorns and how many tricorns might he have in his flock?

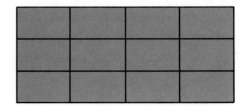

Problem Solving

WHAT WOULD YOU DO . . . ?

Recycled newspapers can be used instead of trees to make newsprint. Each ton of newspapers can save 18 trees. As a project, the fourth graders at Wilson School decide to collect old newspapers. Their goal is to save 90 trees before June 30. You are in charge of the project.

Answer each question and explain.

1. One ton is 2,000 pounds. The students must collect 5 tons of newspapers. How many pounds is that?

2. You would like to begin on March 1. How many months do you have to reach your goal?

3. What will you do to collect enough newspapers by June 30? Describe your plan.

With your teacher's help, you decide on a plan. You will set a monthly goal for each student.

4. The newspapers are tied into 20-pound bundles. Each ton contains 100 of these bundles. How many bundles are there in 5 tons?

5. If the class collects 125 bundles each month, will they reach their goal?

6. Each of the 40 fourth graders must collect about 4 bundles each month. How many total bundles is that each month? Can they reach their goal if they collect this amount each month?

```
NEWSPAPER DRIVE
Bundles
Collected
                          625
         June 30         500
            May          375
          April          250
          March          125
```

What would you do?

7. Some fifth graders offer to help with your project. Because there are now 50 students, you change the plan. Could each student collect 3 bundles a month? How many bundles would you have in 4 months? About how many trees could you save with the new plan?

Find each product. pages 240–245

1. $\quad 7$ $\times 10$	2. $\quad 24$ $\times 10$	3. $\quad 60$ $\times 10$	4. $\quad 786$ $\times\ 10$	5. $\quad 950$ $\times\ 10$
6. $\quad 47$ $\times 20$	7. $\quad 68$ $\times 50$	8. $\quad 70$ $\times 90$	9. $\quad 458$ $\times\ 70$	10. $\quad 850$ $\times\ 80$
11. $\quad 76$ $\times 11$	12. $\quad 28$ $\times 35$	13. $\quad 70$ $\times 64$	14. $\quad 55$ $\times 27$	15. $\quad 46$ $\times 89$

16. $10 \times 19 = \square$ 17. $10 \times 840 = \square$ 18. $40 \times 32 = \square$

19. $60 \times 925 = \square$ 20. $53 \times 75 = \square$ 21. $94 \times 38 = \square$

Estimate each product. pages 248–249

22. $\quad 43$ $\times 28$	23. $\quad 67$ $\times 39$	24. $\quad 721$ $\times\ 63$	25. $\quad 450$ $\times\ 73$	26. $\quad 325$ $\times\ 57$

27. $35 \times 51 = \square$ 28. $76 \times 19 = \square$ 29. $68 \times 489 = \square$

Multiply. Estimate to be sure each answer makes sense. pages 250–251

30. $\quad 176$ $\times\ 18$	31. $\quad 257$ $\times\ 23$	32. $\quad 426$ $\times\ 69$	33. $\quad 887$ $\times\ 54$	34. $\quad 919$ $\times\ 38$

Find each product. pages 252–253

35. $\quad \$.38$ $\times\ 16$	36. $\quad \$.95$ $\times\ 40$	37. $\quad \$.74$ $\times\ 28$	38. $\quad \$1.26$ $\times\ 50$	39. $\quad \$3.55$ $\times\ 78$

40. $84 \times \$75 = \square$ 41. $92 \times \$.60 = \square$ 42. $33 \times \$1.98 = \square$

Solve. pages 246–247, 254–255

43. Dave stands just behind Alan, and Carl stands just in front of Alan. Sal stands just behind Dave. Who stands in front? Make a drawing.

44. Ed bought 22 seedlings for his nursery. Each seedling costs $7.85. Estimate the total cost.

Multiply.

1. $\begin{array}{r} 29 \\ \times 10 \\ \hline \end{array}$
2. $\begin{array}{r} 375 \\ \times\ 10 \\ \hline \end{array}$
3. $\begin{array}{r} 76 \\ \times 40 \\ \hline \end{array}$
4. $\begin{array}{r} 630 \\ \times\ 70 \\ \hline \end{array}$

5. $\begin{array}{r} 47 \\ \times 16 \\ \hline \end{array}$
6. $\begin{array}{r} 56 \\ \times 28 \\ \hline \end{array}$
7. $\begin{array}{r} 34 \\ \times 68 \\ \hline \end{array}$
8. $\begin{array}{r} 67 \\ \times 45 \\ \hline \end{array}$

9. $50 \times 729 = \square$
10. $37 \times 89 = \square$
11. $32 \times 58 = \square$

12. $27 \times 94 = \square$
13. $60 \times 481 = \square$
14. $70 \times 564 = \square$

Estimate each product.

15. $68 \times 33 = \square$
16. $44 \times 793 = \square$
17. $92 \times 546 = \square$

Multiply. Estimate to be sure each answer makes sense.

18. $\begin{array}{r} 235 \\ \times\ 24 \\ \hline \end{array}$
19. $\begin{array}{r} 843 \\ \times\ 76 \\ \hline \end{array}$
20. $\begin{array}{r} 415 \\ \times\ 87 \\ \hline \end{array}$
21. $\begin{array}{r} 903 \\ \times\ 58 \\ \hline \end{array}$

22. $\begin{array}{r} 677 \\ \times\ 31 \\ \hline \end{array}$
23. $\begin{array}{r} 209 \\ \times\ 54 \\ \hline \end{array}$
24. $\begin{array}{r} 181 \\ \times\ 63 \\ \hline \end{array}$
25. $\begin{array}{r} \$47 \\ \times\ 92 \\ \hline \end{array}$

26. $43 \times 726 = \square$
27. $88 \times \$291 = \square$

Find each product.

28. $\begin{array}{r} \$.82 \\ \times\ 40 \\ \hline \end{array}$
29. $\begin{array}{r} \$.75 \\ \times\ 63 \\ \hline \end{array}$
30. $\begin{array}{r} \$1.99 \\ \times\ 50 \\ \hline \end{array}$
31. $\begin{array}{r} \$6.07 \\ \times\ 24 \\ \hline \end{array}$

Solve. Make a drawing for 33.

32. Ned's Nursery has 60 pine trees for sale at $8.75 each. How much money would Ned get if he sold them all?

33. The pine tree is 6 meters tall. The maple tree is 3 meters taller than the pine tree. The oak tree is 2 meters taller than the maple tree. How tall is the oak tree?

Mr. Garcia bought 35 maps of Redwood National Park for his students. Each map cost $1.25. He paid with 5 ten-dollar bills. What was his change?

ESTIMATION

The question About how many? is a question of estimation. It can be fun to look for the answer.

Try this example of estimation: Guess how many peanuts fill the jar.

This is what you need:
- a small unopened jar of peanuts

This is what you do:

1. Look at the side of the jar. Count the number of layers that fill the jar from top to bottom.

2. Look at the bottom of the jar. Count the number of peanuts that fill the bottom.

3. Multiply the number of peanuts in one layer by the number of layers of peanuts in the jar.

Have everyone in your class make an estimate. Then open the jar. Count the peanuts to see who made the closest estimate.

Try another one! Take an empty jar. Fill it with pieces of breakfast cereal. Follow the steps above to find out how many pieces fill the jar. Ask someone in your class to guess the number. Compare results!

USING A FORMULA

The Crane family drove 3 hours to get to the campground. Mr. Crane drove at a rate of 55 miles per hour. How far did the Cranes travel?

You can use this formula to help you solve the problem.

Distance = rate × time

A formula is a way of giving a rule.

To find the distance traveled, multiply the rate times the time. You know the rate and time for this problem. Multiply to find the distance.

Distance = 55 × 3
Distance = 165

$$\begin{array}{r} 1 \\ 55 \\ \times\ 3 \\ \hline 165 \end{array}$$

The Cranes traveled 165 miles.

Use the distance formula to solve each problem.

1. Sara went on a bicycle trip. She rode her bicycle for 4 hours. Sara rode at a rate of 8 miles per hour. How far did she ride?

2. It took Peter 5 hours to drive from home to San Francisco, California. Peter drove at a rate of 48 miles per hour. What is the distance from Peter's home to San Francisco?

3. An express train travels at a rate of 90 miles per hour. How far does it travel in 6 hours?

4. A jet plane flew at a rate of 575 miles per hour. How far did it fly in 13 hours?

Choose the correct answer. Write A, B, C, or D.

1. Round 4,842 to the nearest thousand.

A 4,000   C 4,800

B 5,000   D not given

2. $3,064 - 1,346 = \square$

A 1,718   C 4,410

B 2,322   D not given

3. $2,109 \div 3 = \square$

A 61   C 73

B 703   D not given

4. What is the average of 16, 45, and 5?

A 93   C 31

B 21   D not given

5. $6.5 + 0.38 = \square$

A 6.88   C 6.12

B 1.03   D not given

6. $4,000 \text{ m} = \underline{\quad} \text{ km}$

A 40   C 4

B 400   D not given

7. $10 \times 905 = \square$

A 95   C 90,500

B 9,050   D not given

8. $60 \times 463 = \square$

A 46,300   C 27,680

B 2,778   D not given

9. $28 \times 275 = \square$

A 7,600   C 7,700

B 770   D not given

10. $31 \times \$7.40 = \square$

A $29.60   C $296.00

B $229.40   D not given

Solve.

Carol bought 3 oranges at the fruit stand for $.45. She also bought 2 apples for $.12 each and 4 bananas for $.15 each.

11. What was the total cost of the apples?

A $.12   C $.36

B $.24   D not given

12. What was the total cost of the oranges and bananas?

A $.30   C $1.05

B $.45   D not given

13. What was her change after paying for the fruit with $2.00?

A $.71   C $.29

B $.81   D not given

Theme: People at Work

Dividing by Tens

Max is drawing 80 frames for his newspaper comic strip. The same number of frames will appear each day for 20 days. How many frames are in Max's daily comic strip?

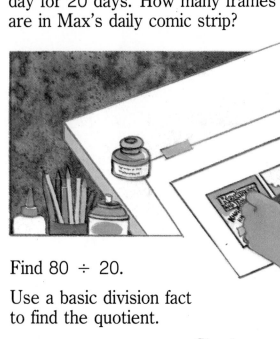

Find 80 ÷ 20.

Use a basic division fact to find the quotient.

$8 \div 2 = 4$ Check
$80 \div 20 = 4$ $20 \times 4 = 80$

Max's daily comic strip has 4 frames.

More Examples

$$40\overline{)80} = 2$$ $$50\overline{)250} = 5$$ $$70\overline{)210} = 3$$ $$90\overline{)360} = 4$$

CLASSWORK

Find each quotient. Check by multiplying.

1. $6 \div 2 = \square$
   $60 \div 20 = \square$

2. $12 \div 3 = \square$
   $120 \div 30 = \square$

3. $32 \div 8 = \square$
   $320 \div 80 = \square$

4. $90\overline{)630}$ 5. $70\overline{)420}$ 6. $50\overline{)400}$ 7. $40\overline{)240}$ 8. $70\overline{)490}$

9. $60\overline{)480}$ 10. $90\overline{)540}$ 11. $20\overline{)140}$ 12. $70\overline{)280}$ 13. $40\overline{)320}$

Find each quotient. Check by multiplying.

1. $15 \div 3 = \square$
   $150 \div 30 = \square$

2. $18 \div 2 = \square$
   $180 \div 20 = \square$

3. $16 \div 4 = \square$
   $160 \div 40 = \square$

4. $30\overline{)90}$

5. $60\overline{)480}$

6. $90\overline{)360}$

7. $90\overline{)810}$

8. $80\overline{)240}$

9. $40\overline{)320}$

10. $20\overline{)160}$

11. $50\overline{)350}$

12. $70\overline{)350}$

13. $30\overline{)180}$

14. $80\overline{)480}$

15. $70\overline{)210}$

16. $70\overline{)560}$

17. $90\overline{)540}$

18. $70\overline{)490}$

19. $70\overline{)630}$

20. $90\overline{)720}$

21. $80\overline{)640}$

22. $30\overline{)240}$

23. $90\overline{)450}$

Follow the rule, if given, to complete.

Rule: Divide by 60.

	Input	Output
24.	360	
25.	180	
26.	540	
27.	420	

Rule: Divide by 80.

	Input	Output
28.	160	
29.	400	
30.	720	
31.	560	

Find the rule.

★ 32.	Input	Output
	200	4
	100	2
	450	9
	300	6

APPLICATION

33. Last week Max did 120 drawings for his book of cartoons. He worked a total of 40 hours. What was the average number of drawings per hour?

★ 34. A book has 200 drawings. Each of 30 pages has the same number of drawings. The rest of the pages have a total of 80 drawings. How many drawings are on each of the 30 pages?

=== LOGICAL THINKING ===

Use the clues to answer each question.

1. The divisor is a multiple of 10. The dividend has 2 digits. The quotient is 2. The remainder is 0. What are the possible division examples?

2. The divisor is a multiple of 10. The dividend has 3 digits. The quotient is 3. The remainder is 0. What are the possible division examples?

Dividing with Remainders

The school librarian has 85 computer books to divide equally among 20 teachers. What is the greatest number of books she can give each teacher? How many computer books will be left?

$85 \div 20 = \square$

Step 1
Decide where to place the first digit in the quotient.

$20\overline{)85}$ **Think** Not enough tens. Divide ones.

Step 2
Divide. Then multiply.

$\begin{array}{r} 4 \\ 20\overline{)85} \\ 80 \end{array}$ **Think** $2\overline{)8}$

Step 3
Subtract and compare.

$\begin{array}{r} 4 \text{ R5} \\ 20\overline{)85} \\ -80 \\ \hline 5 \end{array}$ $5 < 20$
Write the remainder in the quotient.

Check
$\begin{array}{r} 20 \\ \times\ 4 \\ \hline 80 \\ +\ 5 \\ \hline 85 \end{array}$

Each teacher can get 4 books.
There will be 5 computer books left.

Find $557 \div 90$.

Step 1
Decide where to place the first digit in the quotient.

$90\overline{)557}$ **Think** Not enough hundreds or tens. Divide ones.

Step 2
Divide. Then multiply.

$\begin{array}{r} 6 \\ 90\overline{)557} \\ 540 \end{array}$ **Think** $9\overline{)55}$

Step 3
Subtract and compare.

$\begin{array}{r} 6 \text{ R17} \\ 90\overline{)557} \\ -540 \\ \hline 17 \end{array}$ $17 < 90$
Write the remainder in the quotient.

CLASSWORK

Divide. Check by multiplying.

1. $30\overline{)97}$
2. $40\overline{)168}$
3. $60\overline{)200}$
4. $80\overline{)520}$
5. $90\overline{)755}$

264

PRACTICE

Divide. Check by multiplying.

1. 20)̄43
2. 30)̄72
3. 10)̄69
4. 20)̄78
5. 40)̄98

6. 60)̄248
7. 40)̄139
8. 70)̄456
9. 80)̄390
10. 60)̄165

11. 50)̄480
12. 90)̄270
13. 60)̄350
14. 30)̄131
15. 70)̄170

16. 80)̄600
17. 20)̄105
18. 40)̄237
19. 50)̄200
20. 60)̄410

21. 40)̄279
22. 50)̄330
23. 60)̄475
24. 20)̄130
25. 70)̄270

26. 30)̄253
27. 60)̄599
28. 90)̄776
29. 30)̄295
30. 60)̄540

31. 340 ÷ 70 = ☐
32. 155 ÷ 20 = ☐
33. 360 ÷ 90 = ☐

34. 406 ÷ 50 = ☐
35. 385 ÷ 40 = ☐
36. 300 ÷ 40 = ☐

Find each missing digit.

★37. ▮0)̄300   4 R▮▮

★38. ▮0)̄402   5 R▮▮

★39. ▮0)̄340   3 R▮▮

★40. ▮0)̄505   5 R▮▮

APPLICATION

41. The City Board of Education received 450 computer books. Tracy was asked to deliver an order of 60 books to each school. What is the greatest number of schools that can get a delivery? How many books will not be delivered?

42. The City Board of Education has computer disks in stock. It can send 50 disks to each of 9 schools. If it does this there will be 35 disks left. How many disks does the Board of Education have in stock?

★43. Six schools received a total of 870 math books. The high school received as many books as the other 5 schools combined. How many books did the high school receive?

Estimating Quotients

Dan types 55 words per minute. About how long will it take him to type a report with 545 words?

▶ To estimate the quotient, round the divisor to its greatest place. Find the first digit of the quotient.

$55\overline{)545}$ rounds to $60\overline{)545}$

Think

$60\overline{)545}$
$6\overline{)54}$

$55\overline{)\overset{9}{545}}$ estimated quotient

It will take Dan about 9 minutes to type the report.

Estimate 74 ÷ 23.

$23\overline{)74}$ rounds to $20\overline{)74}$

Think

$20\overline{)74}$
$2\overline{)7}$

$23\overline{)\overset{3}{74}}$ estimated quotient

CLASSWORK

Estimate each quotient.

1. $23\overline{)58}$ 2. $51\overline{)85}$ 3. $28\overline{)273}$ 4. $63\overline{)227}$ 5. $37\overline{)178}$

6. 357 ÷ 68 = ☐   7. 296 ÷ 82 = ☐   8. 876 ÷ 92 = ☐

9. 604 ÷ 77 = ☐   10. 64 ÷ 31 = ☐   11. 523 ÷ 58 = ☐

PRACTICE

Estimate each quotient.

1. $27\overline{)76}$ 2. $19\overline{)65}$ 3. $44\overline{)68}$

4. $39\overline{)332}$ 5. $34\overline{)178}$ 6. $68\overline{)130}$

7. $53\overline{)399}$ 8. $71\overline{)340}$ 9. $26\overline{)181}$

10. $75\overline{)145}$ 11. $57\overline{)501}$ 12. $72\overline{)400}$

13. $28\overline{)220}$ 14. $91\overline{)382}$ 15. $79\overline{)589}$

16. $258 \div 94 = \square$ 17. $410 \div 76 = \square$

18. $540 \div 65 = \square$ 19. $545 \div 93 = \square$

Each quotient is an estimate. Give all the possible missing digits.

★20. $4\blacksquare\overline{)167}$ (quotient 3) ★21. $8\blacksquare\overline{)349}$ (quotient 4) ★22. $6\blacksquare\overline{)570}$ (quotient 9)

APPLICATION

23. Anna types 55 words per minute. About how long will it take her to type a letter with 425 words?

24. Irene is transferring 252 files to computer disks. She can get about 45 files on each disk. About how many disks will she use?

★25. Dan uses 21 sheets of paper for each report. He has 3 piles of paper with 45 sheets in each pile. How many full reports can Dan make?

Mixed Practice

1. $$\begin{array}{r} \$465.38 \\ + 594.82 \end{array}$$

2. $$\begin{array}{r} 236 \\ \times \quad 7 \end{array}$$

3. $$\begin{array}{r} 5,446 \\ - \quad 985 \end{array}$$

4. $$\begin{array}{r} 3,964 \\ + \quad 832 \end{array}$$

5. $$\begin{array}{r} 125 \\ \times \quad 92 \end{array}$$

6. $$\begin{array}{r} \$45.00 \\ - \quad 9.06 \end{array}$$

7. $24 \times 37 = \square$

8. $651 + 79 = \square$

9. $509 \div 6 = \square$

10. $7,010 - 469 = \square$

11. $793 \div 5 = \square$

Compare. Use >, <, or =.

12. $347 \bullet 350$

13. $6,202 \bullet 6,199$

14. $0.6 \bullet 0.5$

15. $17.7 \bullet 17.8$

16. $2.3 \bullet 2.30$

One-Digit Quotients

A photographer took 85 pictures of the sunset. Each roll of film had 36 frames. How many full rolls of film did she use? How many frames of another roll did she use?

Divide 85 by 36.

Step 1
Decide where to place the first digit in the quotient.

$$36\overline{)85}$$

Think Not enough tens. Divide ones.

Step 2
Round the divisor and estimate.

$$40$$
$$36\overline{)85}$$

Think
$$40\overline{)85}$$
$$4\overline{)8}$$
Try 2.

Step 3
Divide. Then multiply. Subtract and compare.

$$\begin{array}{r} 2 \text{ R13} \\ 36\overline{)85} \\ -72 \\ \hline 13 \end{array}$$ $13 < 36$

The photographer used 2 rolls of film and 13 more frames.

More Examples

a. $142 \div 29 = \square$

$$\begin{array}{r} 4 \text{ R26} \\ 29\overline{)142} \\ -116 \\ \hline 26 \end{array}$$

Check
$$\begin{array}{r} 3 \\ 29 \\ \times\ 4 \\ \hline 116 \\ +\ 26 \\ \hline 142 \end{array}$$

b. $256 \div 32 = \square$

$$\begin{array}{r} 8 \\ 32\overline{)256} \\ -256 \\ \hline 0 \end{array}$$

Check
$$\begin{array}{r} 1 \\ 32 \\ \times\ 8 \\ \hline 256 \end{array}$$

CLASSWORK

Divide. Check by multiplying.

1. $42\overline{)76}$ 2. $27\overline{)80}$ 3. $48\overline{)225}$ 4. $71\overline{)300}$ 5. $18\overline{)125}$

6. $95 \div 51 = \square$ 7. $475 \div 62 = \square$ 8. $821 \div 88 = \square$

Divide. Check by multiplying.

1. $12\overline{)39}$ 2. $17\overline{)42}$ 3. $11\overline{)78}$ 4. $19\overline{)68}$ 5. $21\overline{)96}$

6. $34\overline{)149}$ 7. $53\overline{)106}$ 8. $57\overline{)200}$ 9. $39\overline{)225}$ 10. $45\overline{)311}$

11. $64\overline{)320}$ 12. $78\overline{)734}$ 13. $33\overline{)198}$ 14. $75\overline{)425}$ 15. $69\overline{)180}$

16. $38\overline{)298}$ 17. $73\overline{)624}$ 18. $52\overline{)416}$ 19. $94\overline{)355}$ 20. $29\overline{)287}$

21. $49\overline{)165}$ 22. $18\overline{)141}$ 23. $32\overline{)316}$ 24. $58\overline{)442}$ 25. $71\overline{)486}$

26. $92\overline{)846}$ 27. $63\overline{)394}$ 28. $29\overline{)214}$ 29. $69\overline{)634}$ 30. $48\overline{)436}$

31. $116 \div 61 = \square$ 32. $387 \div 43 = \square$ 33. $817 \div 92 = \square$

Find each missing divisor or dividend.

★34. $81\overline{)\rule{1.5em}{0pt}}$ with quotient 5   ★35. $\rule{1.5em}{0pt}\overline{)168}$ with quotient 7   ★36. $46\overline{)\rule{1.5em}{0pt}}$ with quotient 8   ★37. $\rule{1.5em}{0pt}\overline{)572}$ with quotient 6 R2

APPLICATION

38. Pat works the same number of hours each day. She worked 138 hours in 23 days. How many hours does Pat work each day?

★39. A photographer ordered 100 rolls of film. She ordered 12 full packages of film and 4 extra rolls. How many rolls of film are in a full package?

CALCULATOR

To find $115 \div 36$, keep subtracting 36 from 115 until you have less than 36 left. Count the number of times you subtracted 36. This is your quotient. What is left is the remainder.

$115 - 36 - 36 - 36 = 7$ $115 \div 36 = 3 \text{ R7}$

Find each quotient by subtracting.

1. $36\overline{)183}$ 2. $36\overline{)247}$ 3. $42\overline{)145}$ 4. $42\overline{)168}$

Problem Solving

GUESS AND TEST

Sometimes a problem can be solved by making a guess at the answer. If you guess correctly, the problem is solved. If not correct, you try another guess and test again.

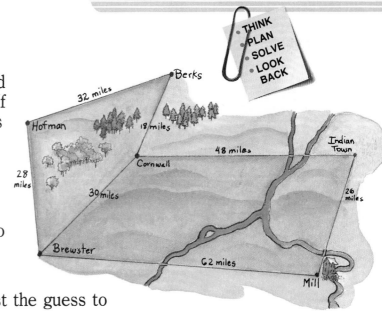

Mr. and Mrs. Cole are antique dealers. They drove a truckload of furniture 106 miles from Hofman to Indian Town. What route did they take?

Use the map to guess a route. Test the guess to see if the number of miles is correct. If it is not correct, make another guess and test it.

First Guess

Hofman → Berks → Cornwall → Indian Town
32 + 18 + 48 = 98 miles
This guess is too small. Look for a longer route.

Second Guess

Hofman → Brewster → Mill → Indian Town
28 + 62 + 26 = 116 miles
This guess is too large. Look for a shorter route.

Third Guess

Hofman → Brewster → Cornwall → Indian Town
28 + 30 + 48 = 106 miles
This guess is correct.
Mr. and Mrs. Cole drove from Hofman to Brewster to Cornwall to Indian Town.

Check your answer by adding the other way.

48 + 30 + 28 = 106 miles

Your answer is correct.

PRACTICE

Use the map on page 270 for 1 and 2.

1. What route is 92 miles from Berks to Mill?

2. What route is 104 miles from Mill to Brewster?

Use the chart for 3 and 4.

3. Mr. Jaffe bought a magazine and a photo from the library collection. He spent $4.80. What did he buy?

4. Alice bought a magazine, a photo, and a postcard. She spent $6.20. What did she buy?

LIBRARY COLLECTION	
Magazines	
Set A	$4.10
Set B	$4.85
Photos	
Set A	$.75
Set B	$.70
Postcards	
Set A	$.60
Set B	$.35

Solve.

5. Mr. Cole sold $92 worth of glass pieces. Saucers sold for $14 each, bowls for $22 each, and vases for $20 each. How many of each type of glass piece did he sell?

6. Mrs. Cole sold 13 desks. Some were rolltop and some were Queen Anne style. She sold 5 more rolltops than Queen Anne style. How many of each kind of desk did she sell?

★7. The Coles sold furniture at 3 antique shows. They sold 4 chairs at the first show and 14 chairs at the second show. The average number of chairs sold for the 3 shows was 10. How many chairs were sold at the third show?

★8. Mrs. Cole sold 8 antique dolls last month. The 4-inch dolls were $35.50 each. The 12-inch dolls were $62 each. She collected $390, but lost the receipts. Find the number of each kind of doll she sold.

========= CREATE YOUR OWN PROBLEM =========

Mr. and Mrs. Cole sold 6 chairs. Write a problem for which the answer is "Mrs. Cole sold 2 chairs and Mr. Cole sold 4 chairs."

Changing Overestimates

Jorge has 185 tulips to make 21 flower arrangements. Every arrangement must be the same. What is the greatest number of tulips Jorge can use in each arrangement? How many extra tulips would he have?

$185 \div 21 = \square$

Step 1
Decide where to place the first digit in the quotient.

$$21\overline{)185}$$

Think
Not enough hundreds or tens. Divide ones.

Step 2
Round the divisor and estimate.

$$\overset{20}{21\overline{)185}}$$

Think
$20\overline{)185}$
$2\overline{)18}$
Try 9.

Step 3
Divide. Change the estimate.

$$\begin{array}{r} 9 \\ 21\overline{)185} \\ -189 \end{array}$$

$189 > 185$
9 is too much.
Try 8.

Step 4
Divide. Then multiply. Subtract and compare.

$$\begin{array}{r} 8\ \text{R17} \\ 21\overline{)185} \\ -168 \\ \hline 17 \end{array}$$

$17 < 21$

Jorge can use 8 tulips in each arrangement.
He would have 17 extra tulips.

CLASSWORK

Divide.

1. $23\overline{)45}$
2. $24\overline{)86}$
3. $32\overline{)190}$
4. $83\overline{)493}$
5. $71\overline{)495}$

6. $95 \div 24 = \square$
7. $262 \div 34 = \square$
8. $725 \div 91 = \square$

Divide.

1. $42\overline{)83}$ 2. $22\overline{)64}$ 3. $33\overline{)96}$ 4. $74\overline{)146}$ 5. $24\overline{)148}$

6. $94\overline{)455}$ 7. $31\overline{)240}$ 8. $93\overline{)642}$ 9. $52\overline{)252}$ 10. $91\overline{)541}$

11. $23\overline{)185}$ 12. $63\overline{)557}$ 13. $43\overline{)295}$ 14. $73\overline{)659}$ 15. $92\overline{)726}$

16. $44\overline{)208}$ 17. $84\overline{)190}$ 18. $54\overline{)158}$ 19. $32\overline{)247}$ 20. $72\overline{)430}$

21. $83\overline{)482}$ 22. $82\overline{)485}$ 23. $21\overline{)189}$ 24. $62\overline{)300}$ 25. $24\overline{)116}$

26. $330 \div 84 = \square$ 27. $78 \div 12 = \square$ 28. $134 \div 34 = \square$

29. $274 \div 93 = \square$ 30. $132 \div 22 = \square$ 31. $472 \div 54 = \square$

★32. $90 \div 12 = \square$ ★33. $181 \div 24 = \square$ ★34. $270 \div 34 = \square$

Choose the correct number sentence and solve.

35. Lucia has 130 mums. What is the greatest number she can use in each of 14 arrangements?

   a. $14 \times 130 = \square$

   b. $130 - 14 = \square$

   c. $130 \div 14 = \square$

   d. $\square + 14 = 130$

36. Flora had 150 roses. She sold 8 dozen roses. How many roses did she sell?

   a. $150 \div 8 = \square$

   b. $8 \times 150 = \square$

   c. $150 \div 12 = \square$

   d. $8 \times 12 = \square$

APPLICATION

37. Jorge has 462 wildflowers. How many can he put in each of 54 of the same corsages? How many extra flowers will he have?

★38. Diego is making 16 arrangements. He needs 8 yellow daisies and 15 white daisies for each one. How many more white daisies than yellow daisies should he order?

273

Changing Underestimates

How many batches of sauce can chef Louisa make with 90 tomatoes? How many tomatoes will she have left?

Find 90 ÷ 16.

Step 1
Decide where to place the first digit in the quotient.

```
   □
16)90   Think
        Not enough tens.
        Divide ones.
```

Step 2
Round the divisor and estimate.

```
20  □
16)90   Think
        20)90
         2)9
        Try 4.
```

Step 3
Divide. Change the estimate.

```
    4
16)90
  -64
   26   26 > 16
        4 is not enough.
        Try 5.
```

Step 4
Divide. Then multiply. Subtract and compare.

```
    5 R10
16)90
  -80
   10   10 < 16
```

Chef Louisa can make 5 batches of sauce.
She will have 10 tomatoes left.

CLASSWORK

Find each quotient.

1. 16)49 2. 38)156 3. 18)75 4. 49)294 5. 28)56

6. 338 ÷ 55 = □ 7. 189 ÷ 36 = □ 8. 79 ÷ 18 = □

Find each answer.

1. $67 \overline{)412}$
2. $85 \overline{)260}$
3. $29 \overline{)116}$
4. $27 \overline{)119}$
5. $59 \overline{)475}$

6. $38 \overline{)229}$
7. $35 \overline{)346}$
8. $68 \overline{)345}$
9. $76 \overline{)319}$
10. $18 \overline{)144}$

11. $49 \overline{)295}$
12. $57 \overline{)416}$
13. $78 \overline{)392}$
14. $87 \overline{)176}$
15. $77 \overline{)392}$

16. $75 \overline{)630}$
17. $69 \overline{)347}$
18. $63 \overline{)582}$
19. $36 \overline{)152}$
20. $46 \overline{)142}$

21. $60 \overline{)300}$
22. $43 \overline{)205}$
23. $26 \overline{)252}$
24. $28 \overline{)173}$
25. $16 \overline{)140}$

26. $345 \div 65 = \square$
27. $186 \div 23 = \square$
28. $443 \div 47 = \square$

29. $340 \div 48 = \square$
30. $625 \div 87 = \square$
31. $291 \div 58 = \square$

★ 32. $(239 + 86) \div (15 \times 5) = \square$ ★ 33. $55 \times (333 \div 37) - 100 = \square$

APPLICATION

Use the recipe on page 274.

How many batches of sauce can chef Louisa make with each amount of tomatoes? How many extra tomatoes will she have?

34. 50
35. 65
36. 120
37. 150

Solve.

38. Ms. Julia bought 118 mussels. How many servings of 12 mussels each can she make? How many mussels will be left?

★ 39. Chef Louisa made 3 batches of the sauce recipe on page 274. How many more teaspoons of cinnamon than cloves did she use?

MENTAL ARITHMETIC

One correct quotient is given for each division.
Find it by looking only at the remainder.

1. $21 \overline{)140}$ a. 6 R14   b. 7 R34   c. 6 R24

2. $37 \overline{)320}$ a. 8 R44   b. 8 R42   c. 8 R24

Two-Digit Quotients

Pablo writes 15 pages each week for his book about baseball players. How many weeks will he take to write 210 pages?

$210 \div 15 = \square$

Step 1
Decide where to place the first digit in the quotient.

$$15\overline{)210}$$

Think
Not enough hundreds.
Divide tens.

Step 2
Round the divisor and estimate.

$$\overset{20}{15}\overline{)210}$$

Think
$20\overline{)21}$
$2\overline{)2}$
Try 1.

Step 3
Divide. Then multiply. Subtract and compare.

$$\begin{array}{r} 1 \\ 15\overline{)210} \\ -15 \\ \hline 6 \end{array}$$ 6 < 15

Step 4
Bring down. Divide. Then multiply. Subtract and compare.

$$\begin{array}{r} 14 \\ 15\overline{)210} \\ -15\downarrow \\ \hline 60 \\ -60 \\ \hline 0 \end{array}$$ 0 < 15

Check

$$\begin{array}{r} 15 \\ \times 14 \\ \hline 60 \\ +150 \\ \hline 210 \end{array}$$

Pablo will take 14 weeks to write 210 pages.

CLASSWORK

Divide and check.

1. $89\overline{)985}$ 2. $12\overline{)552}$ 3. $40\overline{)926}$ 4. $18\overline{)486}$ 5. $28\overline{)599}$

6. $972 \div 36 = \square$ 7. $945 \div 45 = \square$ 8. $895 \div 67 = \square$

PRACTICE

Divide and check.

1. $30\overline{)840}$ 2. $28\overline{)598}$ 3. $20\overline{)946}$ 4. $19\overline{)969}$ 5. $32\overline{)945}$

6. $56\overline{)952}$ 7. $13\overline{)572}$ 8. $21\overline{)965}$ 9. $34\overline{)701}$ 10. $29\overline{)744}$

11. $36\overline{)827}$ 12. $75\overline{)900}$ 13. $15\overline{)496}$ 14. $23\overline{)989}$ 15. $35\overline{)979}$

16. $38\overline{)722}$ 17. $15\overline{)402}$ 18. $24\overline{)738}$ 19. $78\overline{)936}$ 20. $29\overline{)870}$

21. $618 \div 19 = \square$ 22. $594 \div 17 = \square$ 23. $889 \div 37 = \square$

24. $858 \div 26 = \square$ 25. $864 \div 27 = \square$ 26. $800 \div 43 = \square$

★27. $1,000 \div 25 = \square$ ★28. $1,168 \div 37 = \square$ ★29. $1,998 \div 57 = \square$

In each example, the divisor and the quotient are the same. Guess and test to find the number.

30. $\square\overline{)529}$ 31. $\square\overline{)196}$ 32. $\square\overline{)676}$ 33. $\square\overline{)961}$ 34. $\square\overline{)289}$

APPLICATION

35. Carla packs 48 books in each carton. She must fill an order of 900 books. How many cartons of 48 will she fill? How many books must she send in the last carton?

36. In 2 weeks, Pablo worked a total of 62 hours on his book. During the second week, he worked 12 fewer hours than the first week. How many hours did he work the second week?

★37. A printer prepares 4,950 baseball programs. He packs them in bundles of 50 each. How many full bundles can he pack?

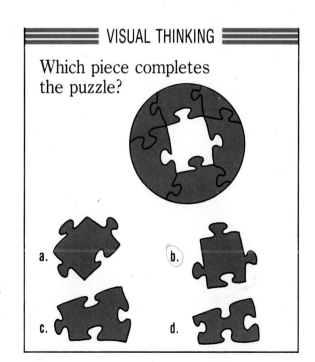

VISUAL THINKING

Which piece completes the puzzle?

a.   b.

c.   d.

277

Dividing Money

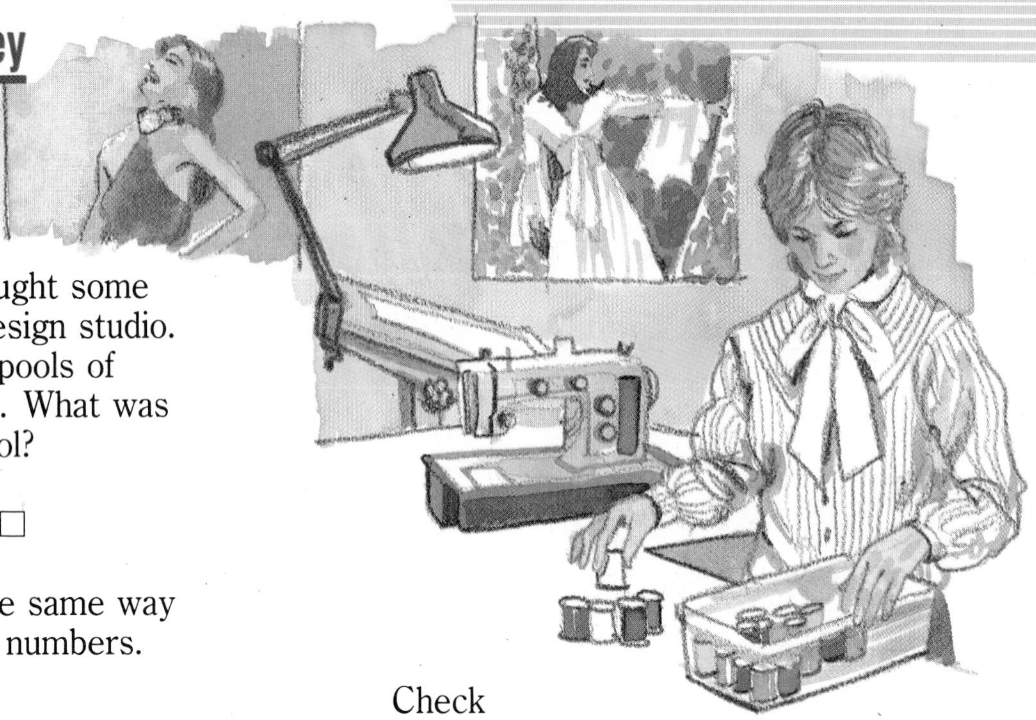

Mrs. Gordon bought some thread for her design studio. She bought 24 spools of thread for $5.52. What was the cost per spool?

$\$5.52 \div 24 = \square$

Divide money the same way you divide other numbers.

$$\begin{array}{r} \$.23 \\ 24\overline{)\$5.52} \\ -4\,8\downarrow \\ \hline 72 \\ -72 \\ \hline 0 \end{array}$$

Remember to write the dollar sign and decimal point in the quotient.

Check

$$\begin{array}{r} {}^{1} \\ \$.23 \\ \times\ \ 24 \\ \hline 92 \\ +4\,60 \\ \hline \$5.52 \end{array}$$

Each spool costs $.23.

More Examples

a. $\$7.80 \div 26 = \square$

$$\begin{array}{r} \$.30 \\ 26\overline{)\$7.80} \\ -7\,8\downarrow \\ \hline 00 \\ -0 \\ \hline \end{array}$$

b. $\$3.44 \div 86 = \square$

$$\begin{array}{r} \$.04 \\ 86\overline{)\$3.44} \\ -3\,44 \\ \hline 0 \end{array}$$

CLASSWORK

Divide and check.

1. $21\overline{)\$2.73}$ **2.** $43\overline{)\$8.60}$ **3.** $18\overline{)\$7.38}$ **4.** $41\overline{)\$9.43}$ **5.** $75\overline{)\$1.50}$

6. $\$3.20 \div 64 = \square$ **7.** $\$8.80 \div 22 = \square$ **8.** $\$5.76 \div 16 = \square$

Divide and check.

1. 15)$5.10
2. 37)$7.40
3. 40)$9.60
4. 80)$6.40
5. 17)$5.95

6. 15)$4.80
7. 58)$9.28
8. 67)$8.04
9. 42)$9.66
10. 24)$4.56

11. 18)$5.40
12. 19)$7.60
13. 94)$7.52
14. 35)$7.00
15. 33)$9.24

16. 39)$3.90
17. 26)$5.20
18. 89)$6.23
19. 12)$7.80
20. 53)$6.89

21. 87)$5.22
22. 36)$9.72
23. 92)$9.20
24. 43)$9.46
25. 66)$8.58

26. $4.80 ÷ 80 = ☐
27. $8.41 ÷ 29 = ☐
28. $8.47 ÷ 11 = ☐

29. $6.60 ÷ 12 = ☐
30. $6.48 ÷ 72 = ☐
31. $7.98 ÷ 38 = ☐

Compare. Use >, <, or = for ●.

★ 32. $5.22 ÷ 58 ● $4.62 ÷ 42
★ 33. $4.30 ÷ 86 ● $2.44 ÷ 61

APPLICATION

Find the price of 1 button.

	Kind of Button	Price per Dozen (12)	Price of 1 (Unit price)
34.	Plastic	$1.44	
35.	Glass	$4.08	
36.	Ceramic	$6.60	
37.	Brass	$9.60	

38. Mrs. Gordon bought 35 yards of lace for $7.35. How much did it cost per yard?

39. A fabric costs $3.85 a yard. How much would 15 yards cost?

★ 40. Marla bought 15 inches of ribbon for $1.80. On sale it would cost $1.65 for 15 inches. What is the difference in the cost per inch?

★ 41. Carol bought 5 buttons at $.23 a button. She also bought a zipper for $1.89. How much change did she receive from a five-dollar bill?

Problem Solving

Read the sign. Then solve 1–4.

1. The Anderson family arrived at the store 20 minutes before it opened on Tuesday. What time was it?

2. On Saturday, Danny works from 11:30 A.M. until closing. How many hours does he work?

3. Jason starts work when the store opens on Monday. He works for 4 hours and 30 minutes. What time is it then?

★4. At 6:20 P.M. Amy put money in the parking meter. It was enough for 2 hours and 35 minutes. Will that last until closing time if it is Tuesday?

Solve.

5. The hostess in the coffee shop can seat 4 people at each table. A group of 15 people came in. How many tables were needed to seat the group?

6. Mr. Cimino ordered a sandwich and juice for lunch. He spent $2.90. What did he order?

★7. James ordered a sandwich, juice, and dessert. He received $2.70 in change from $5.00. What did James order?

Wayne's Coffee Shop
MENU

·Sandwiches·	
Chicken	$1.25
Roast beef	$2.35
Tuna	$1.10

·Desserts·	
Yogurt	$ .65
Granola bar	$ .25
Fruit cup	$1.75

·Juices·	
Apple	$ .55
Orange	$ .45

Yuri is selling out the store's supply of greeting cards. The sale sign is shown below.

Number of Greeting Cards	1–3	4–6	7–9	10–12	13 or more
Price for Each Card	$1.00	90¢	85¢	80¢	75¢

8. Marcia bought 8 cards. How much did she spend?

9. Linda bought 10 cards. How much did she spend?

10. Jonathan bought 9 greeting cards. How much change did he get from $10.00?

11. Greeting cards usually sell for $1.25 each. How much money did Paula save by buying 5 cards on sale?

★12. Mr. Lewis and Mrs. Neu each want to buy 6 cards. How much will they save if they buy 12 cards and share them equally?

★13. Mrs. Craster wants to buy 12 cards. Yuri tells her to buy 13 cards because the extra card will only cost 15¢. Is he correct?

SOMETHING EXTRA

Then

Now

Mr. Brown bought a coat for $25, a hat for $3.50, shoes for $6.00, and an umbrella for $3.75; what did he pay for all?[†]

Mr. Smith bought a coat for $100, a hat for $17.50, shoes for $50.00, and an umbrella for $12.95. What did he pay for all?

[†]*An Intermediate Arithmetic,*
New York: Silver Burdett and Co., 1902, p. 110, #1.

CHAPTER REVIEW

Find each quotient. Check. pages 262–265

1. $20\overline{)60}$
2. $50\overline{)300}$
3. $70\overline{)280}$
4. $30\overline{)180}$
5. $40\overline{)290}$

6. $80\overline{)406}$
7. $90\overline{)360}$
8. $60\overline{)500}$
9. $50\overline{)450}$
10. $20\overline{)115}$

11. $590 \div 70 = \square$
12. $540 \div 60 = \square$
13. $440 \div 60 = \square$

Estimate each quotient. pages 266–267

14. $18\overline{)52}$
15. $42\overline{)89}$
16. $57\overline{)92}$
17. $65\overline{)156}$
18. $33\overline{)269}$

19. $611 \div 94 = \square$
20. $735 \div 77 = \square$
21. $260 \div 45 = \square$

Divide and check. pages 268–269, 272–275

22. $21\overline{)46}$
23. $19\overline{)62}$
24. $12\overline{)34}$
25. $46\overline{)238}$
26. $33\overline{)250}$

27. $64\overline{)318}$
28. $87\overline{)371}$
29. $57\overline{)289}$
30. $75\overline{)390}$
31. $63\overline{)421}$

32. $299 \div 36 = \square$
33. $177 \div 84 = \square$
34. $198 \div 28 = \square$

Find each quotient. Check by multiplying. pages 276–279

35. $21\overline{)882}$
36. $30\overline{)450}$
37. $13\overline{)660}$
38. $21\overline{)\$2.52}$
39. $16\overline{)375}$

40. $76\overline{)988}$
41. $94\overline{)\$7.52}$
42. $37\overline{)779}$
43. $54\overline{)\$8.10}$
44. $71\overline{)\$4.97}$

45. $\$5.20 \div 26 = \square$
46. $\$6.66 \div 18 = \square$
47. $959 \div 19 = \square$

Solve. pages 270–271, 280–281

48. Selena spent 24 days last month writing her book. She worked the same number of hours each day. She worked a total of 120 hours. How many hours did she write each day?

49. Herman sold 45 calculators in June and July. He sold 7 fewer calculators in July than in June. How many calculators did he sell in June?

Divide. Check by multiplying.

1. $40\overline{)80}$ 2. $70\overline{)630}$ 3. $60\overline{)450}$ 4. $30\overline{)195}$

5. $450 \div 50 = \square$ 6. $505 \div 80 = \square$

Estimate each quotient.

7. $46\overline{)90}$ 8. $22\overline{)67}$ 9. $75\overline{)590}$ 10. $88\overline{)703}$ 11. $34\overline{)149}$

Find each quotient. Check by multiplying.

12. $18\overline{)100}$ 13. $64\overline{)192}$ 14. $48\overline{)291}$ 15. $74\overline{)571}$

16. $32\overline{)250}$ 17. $45\overline{)189}$ 18. $84\overline{)485}$ 19. $73\overline{)288}$

20. $261 \div 29 = \square$ 21. $450 \div 55 = \square$

Divide. Check by multiplying.

22. $34\overline{)782}$ 23. $18\overline{)\$5.76}$ 24. $38\overline{)479}$ 25. $42\overline{)\$2.52}$

26. $24\overline{)607}$ 27. $35\overline{)\$5.25}$ 28. $14\overline{)\$4.20}$ 29. $60\overline{)726}$

30. $768 \div 17 = \square$ 31. $\$3.95 \div 79 = \square$

Solve.

32. Pablo buys lined paper for writing his book. He bought 15 pads for $8.25. How much did each pad cost?

33. Mr. O'Boyle is an artist. He used 24 cutouts for 2 mobiles. One mobile had 8 more cutouts than the other. How many cutouts were on the smaller mobile?

Chris works in a gift shop. He collected $79.80 for selling 32 key chains and 68 butterfly magnets. Each magnet cost $.75. What was the price of each key chain?

USING THE SIGNS

To play Using the Signs you will need:

- 2 sets of number cards marked 1–12
- 2 sets of operation cards marked +, −, ×, ÷, =

Lay out the following cards in this order.

| 7 | 5 | 1 | = | 3 |

What operation cards can you use to make a true number sentence?

| 7 | − | 5 | + | 1 | = | 3 |

Now lay out these cards.

| 3 | 2 | 1 | = | 6 |

There are 3 different ways to use the signs to make a true sentence. Experiment with the cards. What are the 3 ways?

Try these cards.

| 6 | 2 | 2 | = | 6 |

How many different ways of using the signs will make the number sentence true? What are they?

Play with a partner. See who can use the most division signs in making these sentences true.

1. 7 ☐ 8 ☐ 8 = 7

2. 3 ☐ 3 ☐ 3 = 3

3. 6 ☐ 2 ☐ 1 = 3

4. 9 ☐ 2 ☐ 3 = 6

5. 3 ☐ 9 ☐ 3 = 9

6. 8 ☐ 5 ☐ 10 = 4

7. 6 ☐ 10 ☐ 12 = 5

8. 5 ☐ 10 ☐ 10 = 5

DIVISIBILITY

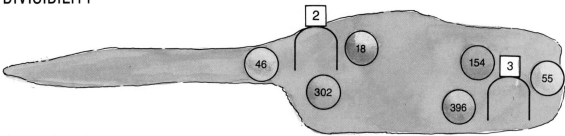

A number is **divisible** by another number when the remainder is 0.

$$\begin{array}{r} 9 \\ 2\overline{)18} \\ -18 \\ \hline 0 \end{array}$$ 18 is divisible by 2.

$$\begin{array}{r} 9 \\ 2\overline{)19} \\ -18 \\ \hline 1 \end{array}$$ 19 is not divisible by 2.

There are rules for finding whether a number is divisible by another number.

▶A number is divisible by 2 if its last digit is 0, 2, 4, 6, or 8.

32<u>6</u> is divisible by 2.
1,59<u>0</u> is divisible by 2.

▶A number is divisible by 5 if its last digit is 0 or 5.

86<u>5</u> is divisible by 5.
43<u>0</u> is divisible by 5.

▶To find whether a number is divisible by 3, find the sum of its digits. Continue to add until there is only one digit in the sum. If the sum is divisible by 3, the number is divisible by 3.

Is 537 divisible by 3?
$5 + 3 + 7 = 15$
$1 + 5 = 6$
6 is divisible by 3, so 537 is divisible by 3.

Solve.

1. I am a three-digit number. All my digits are the same. I am divisible by 3 and 5. What number am I?

2. I am a two-digit number. I am divisible by 2, 3, and 5. What number am I?

3. Write a rule for divisibility by 10. Use the rule for divisibility by 5 as a model. Show that the rule works.

4. I am a three-digit number. I am divisible by 2, 3, 5, and 10. My tens digit is one less than my hundreds digit. What number am I?

INPUT STATEMENTS

In BASIC, we can use an INPUT statement to enter information while a program is running.

The computer will display a question mark and wait for you to enter a number.

```
10  PRINT "FIND FACTORS OF 144"
20  PRINT "ENTER A POSSIBLE FACTOR"
30  INPUT F
40  LET Q = 144/F
50  PRINT F; "INTO 144 = ";Q
60  PRINT "DOES F DIVIDE 144 EVENLY?"
70  PRINT "IF IT DOES, THEN F IS A FACTOR"
80  PRINT "IF NOT, THEN F IS NOT A FACTOR"
90  END
```

When the program is RUN, a question mark is displayed, waiting for F.

If we enter 9, the computer computes the quotient and displays the output.

```
RUN
FIND FACTORS OF 144
ENTER A POSSIBLE FACTOR
? 9
9 INTO 144 = 16
DOES F DIVIDE 144 EVENLY?
IF IT DOES, THEN F IS A FACTOR
IF NOT, THEN F IS NOT A FACTOR
```

Use the program above. Tell what the output will be after each number is entered.

1. 12	**2.** 2	**3.** 4	**4.** 5	**5.** 24
6. 36	**7.** 144	**8.** 7	**9.** 1	**10.** 48

In order to find all the factors of 144, we must RUN the program again and again. An easy way to do this is to use a GOTO statement in the program.

```
10  PRINT "FIND FACTORS OF 144"
20  PRINT "ENTER A POSSIBLE FACTOR"
30  INPUT F
40  LET Q = 144/F
50  PRINT F; "INTO 144 = ";Q
60  PRINT "DOES F DIVIDE 144 EVENLY?"
70  PRINT "IF IT DOES, THEN F IS A FACTOR"
80  PRINT "IF NOT, THEN F IS NOT A FACTOR"
90  GOTO 20
100 END
```

GOTO 20 tells the computer to go to line 20 and continue on from there.

When the program is RUN, the computer does lines 10–80.

```
RUN
FIND FACTORS OF 144
ENTER A POSSIBLE FACTOR
? 3
3 INTO 144 = 48
DOES 3 DIVIDE 144 EVENLY?
IF IT DOES, THEN F IS A FACTOR
IF NOT, THEN F IS NOT A FACTOR
ENTER A POSSIBLE FACTOR
?
```

Then line 90 tells it to go back to line 20 and repeat the lines.

Programs are stopped in different ways on different computers.

AT THE COMPUTER

1. Enter and RUN the program on this page. Enter the numbers in 1–10 on page 286.

2. Compare the computer output with your answers.

3. On Your Own: Write a program using INPUT and GOTO to find the average of test grades. Use the program on page 237 to help you.

CUMULATIVE REVIEW

Choose the correct answer. Write A, B, C, or D.

1. $7 + 5 + 6 = \square$

   A 12   C 11

   B 18   D not given

2. What is the value of 6 in 3,467?

   A 60   C 6,000

   B 600   D not given

3. Estimate. $712 + 586 = \square$

   A 100   C 1,200

   B 1,300   D not given

4. $736 - 241 = \square$

   A 515   C 495

   B 595   D not given

5. $7 \times \square = 42$

   A 6   C 4

   B 7   D not given

6. $0 \div 9 = \square$

   A 1   C 9

   B 0   D not given

7. What time will it be 30 minutes after 11:45 A.M.?

   A 12:15 A.M.   C 12:30 P.M.

   B 12:15 P.M.   D not given

8. How much money is 3 quarters and 4 pennies?

   A $.79   C $.54

   B $.75   D not given

9. $6 \times 262 = \square$

   A 1,562   C 1,572

   B 1,322   D not given

10. $7 \times 6,035 = \square$

    A 42,245   C 4,645

    B 4,215   D not given

11. $855 \div 6 = \square$

    A 142 R3   C 140 R5

    B 152 R3   D not given

12. $1,211 \div 4 = \square$

    A 32 R3   C 312 R3

    B 3,002 R3   D not given

13. What decimal is 7 and 32 hundredths?

    A 7.32   C 73.2

    B 7.032   D not given

14. Compare. 36.5 ● 36.07

    A >   C =

    B <   D not given

CUMULATIVE REVIEW

Choose the correct answer. Write A, B, C, or D.

15. $4.6 + 3.17 = \square$

   A 7.77   **C** 1.43

   B 3.63   **D** not given

16. $12.03 - 4.52 = \square$

   A 12.51   **C** 7.51

   B 8.51   **D** not given

17. ___ g = 6 kg

   A 60   **C** 0.06

   B 6,000   **D** not given

18. $30 \times 97 = \square$

   A 291   **C** 127

   B 2,910   **D** not given

19. $35 \times 32 = \square$

   A 175   **C** 1,120

   B 1,110   **D** not given

20. Estimate. $36 \times 821 = \square$

   A 32,000   **C** 2,400

   B 24,000   **D** not given

21. $37 \times 864 = \square$

   A 8,640   **C** 31,968

   B 21,968   **D** not given

22. $12 \times \$4.75 = \square$

   A $14.25   **C** $5,700

   B $57.00   **D** not given

23. $60\overline{)420}$

   A 7   **C** 8

   B 70   **D** not given

24. $285 \div 30 = \square$

   A 90 R15   **C** 9 R15

   B 7 R15   **D** not given

25. Estimate. $51\overline{)463}$

   A 8   **C** 10

   B 9   **D** not given

26. $254 \div 38 = \square$

   A 6 R26   **C** 6 R34

   B 7 R12   **D** not given

27. $22\overline{)887}$

   A 4 R7   **C** 40 R9

   B 47   **D** not given

28. $\$8.10 \div 45 = \square$

   A $.20   **C** $.18

   B $.19   **D** not given

Choose the correct answer. Write A, B, C, or D.

Which fact is not needed to solve the problem?

29. Bryan lives 2 miles from school. It takes him 40 minutes to walk to school. How far does he walk to and from school in one week?

    A 2 miles from school   C one week

    B 40 minutes to school   D not given

Use the table for 30–31.

FISHING CONTEST RESULTS	
Students	Fish Caught
Barry	13
Tyrone	16
Kim	13

30. What was the total number of fish caught by the three students?

    A 42   C 41

    B 31   D not given

31. What was the average number of fish caught by the three students?

    A 13   C 15

    B 14   D not given

Solve.

32. A computer prints Alicia's name 10 times across a line. If there is a space between each name, what is in space 23?

    A C   C A

    B L   D not given

33. Ralph collected $.50 from each student for a gift. There are 22 students in class. How much more does he need for a $15.00 gift?

    A $11.00   C $5.00

    B $4.00   D not given

Use the drawing for 34–35.

Tallest

Jack
Leslie
Bob
Andrea

Shortest

34. Who is the tallest person?

    A Andrea   C Jack

    B Leslie   D not given

35. Who is taller than Andrea and shorter than Leslie?

    A Bob   C Andrea

    B Jack   D not given

Fractions **10**

Theme: Countries of the World

Parts of Regions

Italy's flag has 3 equal parts.
There is 1 green part.

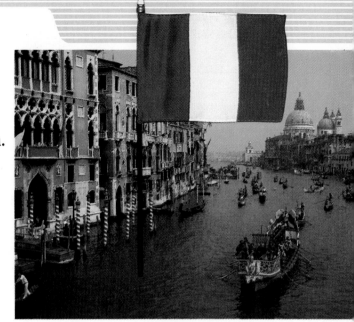

▶A **fraction** may name part of a region.

1 green part ⟶ **1** ⟵ numerator
3 parts in all ⟶ **3** ⟵ denominator

Read $\frac{1}{3}$ as one third.

The fraction $\frac{1}{3}$ tells what part
of the flag is green.

More Examples

a.

$\frac{3}{4}$, or three fourths,
is blue.

b.
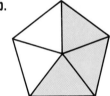

$\frac{2}{5}$, or two fifths,
is *not* blue.

c.
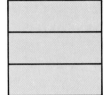

$\frac{3}{3}$, or three thirds,
is blue.
$\frac{3}{3}$ = 1, or one whole.

CLASSWORK

Write the fraction that tells what part is blue.

1.

2.

3.

4.

5.

6.

7.

8.
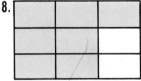

PRACTICE

Write the fraction that tells what part is blue.

1.

2.

3.

4.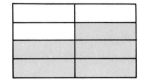

5.

6.

7.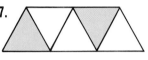

8.

Write a fraction for each answer.

9.

10.

11.

_____ is blue.

_____ is not blue.

_____ is blue.

_____ is not blue.

_____ is blue.

_____ is not blue.

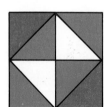

12. _____ is not green.

★13. _____ is white or red.

★14. _____ is green or white.

★15. _____ is green or red.

APPLICATION

Use the flag on page 292.

16. What part is red?

17. What part is not white?

★18. What part is red or green?

═══ LOGICAL THINKING ═══

Look at the flag of Italy on page 292.

Rearrange the three parts in a different order.

How many other flags can you make by doing this?

Parts of Groups

Jane Goodall is a zoologist who studies chimpanzees in Africa. There are 5 chimps in this group. Write a fraction to tell what part of the group is sitting.

▶A fraction may name part of a group.

$\dfrac{2}{5}$ ← 2 are sitting
← 5 are in the group

$\dfrac{2}{5}$ of the group is sitting.

Another Example

What part of the bunch of bananas is green?

$\dfrac{3}{8}$ ← 3 green bananas
← 8 bananas in all

$\dfrac{3}{8}$ of the bunch is green.

CLASSWORK

Write the fraction that tells what part is blue.

1.

2.

3.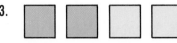

Write a fraction that tells what part is blue.

1.

2.

3.

4.

5.

6.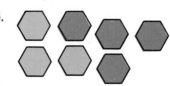

What part of the set of calculator keys has

7. square keys?

8. round keys?

9. keys with a number?

★ 10. keys with a number or a decimal point?

★ 11. keys with an odd number or an equal sign?

APPLICATION

12. There are 3 boys and 2 girls watching the chimps. What part of the group is girls?

13. A zoologist spent 5 days in one week studying chimps. What part of the week did she spend studying chimps?

★ 14. A chimp was given 10 bananas for lunch. The chimp ate 6. What part of the bananas was left?

VISUAL THINKING

$\frac{5}{9}$ of the dots are blue in every group except one. What part is blue in the different group?

295

Equivalent Fractions

Kevin and Kathleen saw this cheese wheel in Cheddar, England. Kevin bought $\frac{1}{4}$ of it. Kathleen bought $\frac{2}{8}$ of it. Did Kevin and Kathleen buy the same amount of cheese?

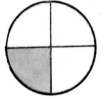 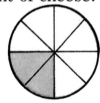

$$\frac{1}{4} = \frac{2}{8}$$

$\frac{1}{4}$ and $\frac{2}{8}$ name the same amount.

Yes, Kevin and Kathleen bought the same amount.

▶**Equivalent fractions** name the same amount. $\frac{1}{4}$ and $\frac{2}{8}$ are equivalent fractions.

More Examples

a.
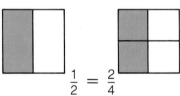

$$\frac{1}{2} = \frac{2}{4}$$

$\frac{1}{2}$ and $\frac{2}{4}$ are equivalent fractions.

b.
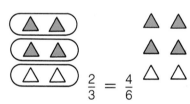

$$\frac{2}{3} = \frac{4}{6}$$

$\frac{2}{3}$ and $\frac{4}{6}$ are equivalent fractions.

CLASSWORK

Complete.

1.
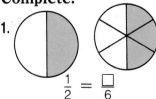

$$\frac{1}{2} = \frac{\square}{6}$$

2.

$$\frac{\square}{5} = \frac{2}{10}$$

3.

$$\frac{1}{4} = \frac{\square}{12}$$

PRACTICE

Complete.

1.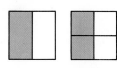

$$\frac{1}{2} = \frac{\square}{4}$$

2.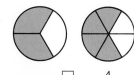

$$\frac{\square}{3} = \frac{4}{6}$$

3.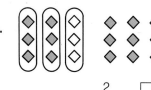

$$\frac{2}{3} = \frac{\square}{9}$$

4.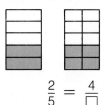

$$\frac{2}{5} = \frac{4}{\square}$$

5.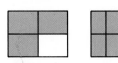

$$\frac{3}{\square} = \frac{6}{8}$$

6.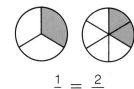

$$\frac{1}{3} = \frac{2}{\square}$$

Write an equivalent fraction for each.

7.

$$\frac{2}{3}$$

8.

$$\frac{1}{3}$$

9.

$$\frac{4}{4}$$

In the picture on the right, $\frac{1}{2}$ of the squares are blue. Show this by writing

10. an equivalent fraction in twelfths.

★11. an equivalent fraction in fourths.

★12. an equivalent fraction in sixths.

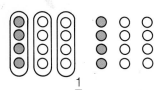

APPLICATION

Solve. Make a drawing to find the answer.

13. A cheese pie is cut into 4 equal parts. The cheese pie must be shared by 8 people. How can it be divided equally?

14. Beth bought $\frac{1}{4}$ of a cheese wheel. Then Joan bought $\frac{1}{2}$ of it. Did they buy the same amount?

15. The baker used $\frac{1}{2}$ dozen eggs. How many twelfths are equivalent to $\frac{1}{2}$?

★16. Rhoda filled $\frac{3}{4}$ cup with flour. Write 2 equivalent fractions to show the part of the cup she did not use.

297

Finding Equivalent Fractions

Mrs. O'Boyle baked 2 loaves of Irish soda bread. She divided one into 2 equal parts. She divided the other into 4 equal parts. Brian took $\frac{1}{2}$ of a loaf. Deirdre took the same amount of the other loaf. How many fourths did Deirdre take?

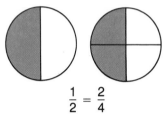

$$\frac{1}{2} = \frac{2}{4}$$

$\frac{1}{2}$ and $\frac{2}{4}$ are equivalent fractions.

Deirdre took two fourths.

▶ To find an equivalent fraction multiply the numerator and denominator by the same number.

$$\frac{1}{2} = \frac{1 \times 2}{2 \times 2} = \frac{2}{4}$$

Remember that $\frac{2}{2}$ is another name for 1.

More Examples

a. $\frac{2}{3} = \frac{2 \times 2}{3 \times 2} = \frac{4}{6}$ **b.** $\frac{2}{3} = \frac{2 \times 4}{3 \times 4} = \frac{8}{12}$ **c.** $\frac{1}{2} = \frac{1 \times 5}{2 \times 5} = \frac{5}{10}$

CLASSWORK

Complete. Write the equivalent fraction for each.

1.
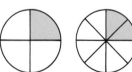

$$\frac{1}{4} = \frac{1 \times 2}{4 \times 2} = \frac{\square}{8}$$

2.

$$\frac{1}{2} = \frac{1 \times 3}{2 \times 3} = \frac{\square}{6}$$

3.
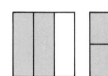

$$\frac{2}{3} = \frac{2 \times 2}{3 \times 2} = \frac{\square}{6}$$

4. $\frac{1}{3} = \frac{1 \times 4}{3 \times 4} = \frac{4}{\square}$

5. $\frac{1}{8} = \frac{1 \times \square}{8 \times \square} = \frac{3}{24}$

6. $\frac{1}{7} = \frac{1 \times \square}{7 \times \square} = \frac{4}{28}$

298

PRACTICE

Complete. Write the equivalent fraction for each.

1. $\dfrac{1}{2} = \dfrac{1 \times 3}{2 \times 3} = \dfrac{\square}{6}$

2. $\dfrac{1}{3} = \dfrac{1 \times 3}{3 \times 3} = \dfrac{\square}{9}$

3. $\dfrac{3}{4} = \dfrac{3 \times 2}{4 \times 2} = \dfrac{\square}{8}$

4. $\dfrac{1}{4} = \dfrac{1 \times 3}{4 \times 3} = \dfrac{3}{\square}$

5. $\dfrac{2}{5} = \dfrac{2 \times 2}{5 \times 2} = \dfrac{4}{\square}$

6. $\dfrac{1}{2} = \dfrac{1 \times 4}{2 \times 4} = \dfrac{4}{\square}$

7. $\dfrac{2}{3} = \dfrac{2 \times 2}{3 \times 2} = \dfrac{4}{\square}$

8. $\dfrac{7}{8} = \dfrac{7 \times 2}{8 \times 2} = \dfrac{\square}{16}$

9. $\dfrac{3}{4} = \dfrac{3 \times 3}{4 \times 3} = \dfrac{9}{\square}$

10. $\dfrac{4}{5} = \dfrac{4 \times \square}{5 \times \square} = \dfrac{16}{20}$

11. $\dfrac{1}{6} = \dfrac{1 \times \square}{6 \times \square} = \dfrac{5}{30}$

12. $\dfrac{5}{8} = \dfrac{5 \times \square}{8 \times \square} = \dfrac{20}{32}$

Multiply each numerator and denominator by 2 to find an equivalent fraction.

13. $\dfrac{1}{2}$

14. $\dfrac{2}{3}$

15. $\dfrac{4}{5}$

16. $\dfrac{1}{6}$

17. $\dfrac{5}{8}$

18. $\dfrac{7}{10}$

Multiply each numerator and denominator by 3 to find an equivalent fraction.

19. $\dfrac{1}{3}$

20. $\dfrac{2}{5}$

21. $\dfrac{1}{4}$

22. $\dfrac{5}{6}$

23. $\dfrac{3}{4}$

24. $\dfrac{1}{10}$

Write an equivalent fraction for each.

★ 25. $\dfrac{1}{8}$

★ 26. $\dfrac{1}{5}$

★ 27. $\dfrac{1}{7}$

★ 28. $\dfrac{3}{6}$

★ 29. $\dfrac{7}{8}$

★ 30. $\dfrac{9}{10}$

APPLICATION

31. Maura ate $\dfrac{2}{3}$ of a shepherd's pie. Her brother Sean ate $\dfrac{5}{6}$ of a shepherd's pie. Did they both eat the same amount?

32. Una drank $\dfrac{1}{2}$ of a glass of milk. Write an equivalent fraction to show the amount of milk Una drank.

★ 33. Seamus ate $\dfrac{1}{3}$ of a loaf of soda bread. Find 2 equivalent fractions for the amount of soda bread left.

Lowest Terms

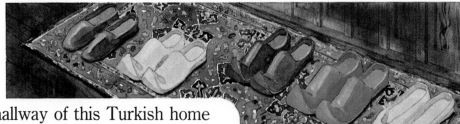

In the hallway of this Turkish home there are 10 slippers. The family keeps 6 of the 10 slippers for guests. What fraction of the slippers are for guests?

$\frac{6}{10}$ of the slippers are for guests.

There are 5 pairs of slippers. $\frac{3}{5}$ of the pairs are for guests.

$\frac{6}{10}$ and $\frac{3}{5}$ are equivalent fractions.

▶To find an equivalent fraction divide the numerator and the denominator by the same number.

$$\frac{6}{10} = \frac{6 \div 2}{10 \div 2} = \frac{3}{5}$$

$\frac{3}{5}$ is a fraction in lowest terms.

▶A fraction is in **lowest terms** when 1 is the only number that will divide both the numerator and the denominator.

Write $\frac{6}{12}$ as a fraction in lowest terms.

$$\frac{6}{12} = \frac{6 \div 2}{12 \div 2} = \frac{3}{6} \qquad \frac{3}{6} = \frac{3 \div 3}{6 \div 3} = \frac{1}{2} \quad \text{lowest terms}$$

CLASSWORK

Complete. Write each fraction in lowest terms.

1.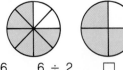
$$\frac{6}{8} = \frac{6 \div 2}{8 \div 2} = \frac{\square}{4}$$

2.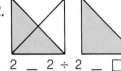
$$\frac{2}{4} = \frac{2 \div 2}{4 \div 2} = \frac{\square}{2}$$

3.
$$\frac{3}{6} = \frac{3 \div 3}{6 \div 3} = \frac{1}{\square}$$

4. $\frac{2}{6}$

5. $\frac{3}{9}$

6. $\frac{5}{10}$

7. $\frac{3}{12}$

8. $\frac{10}{15}$

9. $\frac{4}{10}$

Complete. Write each fraction in lowest terms.

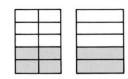
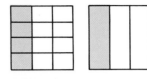

1. $\frac{4}{10} = \frac{4 \div 2}{10 \div 2} = \frac{\square}{5}$

2. $\frac{4}{12} = \frac{4 \div 4}{12 \div 4} = \frac{\square}{3}$

3. $\frac{7}{14} = \frac{7 \div 7}{14 \div 7} = \frac{1}{\square}$

4. $\frac{5}{15} = \frac{5 \div 5}{15 \div 5} = \frac{1}{\square}$

5. $\frac{2}{12}$

6. $\frac{5}{20}$

7. $\frac{9}{12}$

8. $\frac{6}{9}$

9. $\frac{3}{15}$

10. $\frac{3}{24}$

11. $\frac{14}{21}$

12. $\frac{15}{20}$

13. $\frac{5}{30}$

14. $\frac{7}{28}$

15. $\frac{2}{16}$

16. $\frac{9}{18}$

17. $\frac{20}{32}$

18. $\frac{18}{27}$

19. $\frac{8}{24}$

20. $\frac{4}{24}$

★21. $\frac{10}{100}$

★22. $\frac{25}{100}$

★23. $\frac{50}{100}$

★24. $\frac{75}{100}$

APPLICATION

25. Celine has 6 mittens. Four of them are blue. What fraction of her pairs of mittens are blue?

26. Lee and Tim together have 8 belts. Lee has 4 more than Tim. What fraction of the belts belong to Lee? Guess and test.

★27. Aileen used 4 shoelaces. This was $\frac{2}{3}$ of a package. How many shoelaces were in the package?

1. $\begin{array}{r} 364 \\ 14 \\ +932 \\ \hline \end{array}$

2. $\begin{array}{r} 6{,}415 \\ -3{,}999 \\ \hline \end{array}$

3. $\begin{array}{r} 514 \\ \times\ 67 \\ \hline \end{array}$

4. $5\overline{)586}$

5. $\begin{array}{r} 436.81 \\ +\ \ 7.52 \\ \hline \end{array}$

6. $\begin{array}{r} 600.52 \\ -\ \ 43.71 \\ \hline \end{array}$

7. $2.49 + 6.4 = \square$

8. $52.10 - 8.47 = \square$

9. $\$9.04 - \$.85 = \square$

10. $7.4 - 3.29 = \square$

11. $19.6 + 0.75 = \square$

Give the value of the digit 5.

12. 4,135

13. 26.05

14. 3,586.1

15. 0.52

16. 15,346

Problem Solving

EXPERIMENT

Sometimes the best way to solve a problem is to experiment. You can do the action to find the answer.

1. Monte Rosa, in Switzerland, is about $\frac{1}{2}$ as tall as Mount Everest, in Nepal. Are you more or less than $\frac{1}{2}$ as tall as the door to your classroom?

How can the answer be found?

Experiment.

Find $\frac{1}{2}$ the height of the door to your classroom. Then compare it with your height.

Carry out the plan.

Going from top to bottom, find the middle of the classroom door. That should be about $\frac{1}{2}$ the height of the door.

Mark the spot. (You can use a piece of tape.)

Then stand next to the door.

Compare your height with the mark. Is it more or less?

2. The Tigris River is about $\frac{1}{4}$ the length of the Nile River. What can you find in your classroom that is $\frac{1}{4}$ the length of your arm?

Experiment to solve each problem.

1. Your class wants to buy a Swiss cuckoo clock. The clock costs $150. If each class member gives $3, will you have enough money to buy the clock?

2. There are many cars in Rome. People have a hard time crossing the street. How many cars pass your window in 5 minutes?

3. The town of Alice Springs is about halfway between the east and west coasts of Australia. What is about halfway between the front and back of your classroom?

4. Mauna Loa, in Hawaii, is about twice as high as Mount Mitchell in North Carolina. What is about twice as high as your classroom desk?

5. Mount Olympus in Greece is about $\frac{1}{3}$ as tall as Mount Everest. What can you find in your classroom that is about $\frac{1}{3}$ as tall as the classroom door?

6. In Kenya, people watch ostrich races. An ostrich can cover 10 yards with 3 steps. How many steps do you take to cover 10 yards?

7. The flag of China has 5 stars. How many more stars does the flag in your classroom have?

8. The Rhine River is about $\frac{1}{2}$ the length of the Ural River. Is your arm more or less than $\frac{1}{2}$ the length of your leg?

CREATE YOUR OWN PROBLEM

Choose one of the facts. Write a problem that can be solved by doing an experiment.

Facts

The St. Lawrence River is about $\frac{1}{2}$ as long as the Amazon River.

The flag of Chad has 3 stripes.

Kenya has almost 2 times as many people as Belgium.

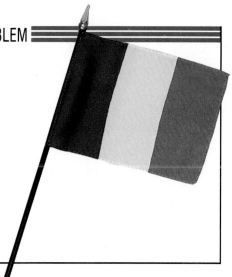

Comparing Fractions

Ron filled $\frac{4}{5}$ of a row with stamps. Dan filled $\frac{2}{5}$ of a row. Who has filled more space in his row?

Judy filled $\frac{1}{2}$ of a row with coins. Jill filled $\frac{2}{3}$ of a row. Who has filled less space in her row?

$\frac{4}{5}$

$\frac{2}{5}$

$\frac{1}{2}$

$\frac{2}{3}$

$\frac{4}{5}$ and $\frac{2}{5}$ are like fractions.

$\frac{1}{2}$ and $\frac{2}{3}$ are unlike fractions.

Like fractions have the same denominators.

Unlike fractions have different denominators.

▶To compare like fractions, compare the numerators.

$$4 > 2, \text{ so } \frac{4}{5} > \frac{2}{5}.$$

$\frac{4}{5}$ is greater than $\frac{2}{5}$.

Ron has filled more space in his row.

▶To compare unlike fractions, find equivalent fractions with the same denominators. Then compare the numerators.

$$\frac{1}{2} = \frac{1 \times 3}{2 \times 3} = \frac{3}{6}$$

$$\frac{2}{3} = \frac{2 \times 2}{3 \times 2} = \frac{4}{6}$$

$$3 < 4, \text{ so } \frac{3}{6} < \frac{4}{6}$$

$\frac{1}{2}$ is less than $\frac{2}{3}$.

Judy has filled less space in her row.

CLASSWORK

Compare. Use > or < for ●.

1. $\frac{3}{4}$ ● $\frac{1}{4}$

2. $\frac{4}{6}$ ● $\frac{5}{6}$

3. $\frac{1}{4}$ ● $\frac{1}{8}$

4. $\frac{2}{6}$ ● $\frac{1}{2}$

5. $\frac{3}{4}$ ● $\frac{1}{2}$

6. $\frac{3}{7}$ ● $\frac{6}{7}$

7. $\frac{1}{2}$ ● $\frac{1}{4}$

8. $\frac{2}{5}$ ● $\frac{3}{5}$

9. $\frac{1}{2}$ ● $\frac{2}{5}$

10. $\frac{1}{3}$ ● $\frac{2}{4}$

PRACTICE

Compare. Use > or < for ●.

1. $\frac{4}{5}$ ● $\frac{2}{5}$ 2. $\frac{3}{4}$ ● $\frac{5}{8}$ 3. $\frac{2}{6}$ ● $\frac{2}{3}$ 4. $\frac{1}{3}$ ● $\frac{1}{2}$ 5. $\frac{1}{5}$ ● $\frac{2}{3}$

6. $\frac{2}{8}$ ● $\frac{6}{8}$ 7. $\frac{2}{3}$ ● $\frac{3}{4}$ 8. $\frac{6}{10}$ ● $\frac{1}{2}$ 9. $\frac{4}{6}$ ● $\frac{5}{6}$ 10. $\frac{1}{3}$ ● $\frac{1}{6}$

11. $\frac{1}{2}$ ● $\frac{3}{8}$ 12. $\frac{1}{8}$ ● $\frac{1}{4}$ 13. $\frac{1}{2}$ ● $\frac{5}{6}$ 14. $\frac{3}{8}$ ● $\frac{1}{3}$ 15. $\frac{5}{9}$ ● $\frac{2}{3}$

16. $\frac{2}{3}$ ● $\frac{2}{5}$ 17. $\frac{7}{10}$ ● $\frac{3}{10}$ 18. $\frac{1}{3}$ ● $\frac{2}{9}$ 19. $\frac{2}{5}$ ● $\frac{2}{4}$ 20. $\frac{1}{3}$ ● $\frac{2}{7}$

21. $\frac{5}{7}$ ● $\frac{6}{7}$ 22. $\frac{1}{3}$ ● $\frac{1}{4}$ 23. $\frac{2}{3}$ ● $\frac{5}{8}$ 24. $\frac{7}{10}$ ● $\frac{4}{5}$ 25. $\frac{3}{4}$ ● $\frac{4}{5}$

Use < to write the fractions in order from least to greatest.

★26. $\frac{3}{7}$, $\frac{2}{7}$, $\frac{6}{7}$ ★27. $\frac{1}{6}$, $\frac{1}{4}$, $\frac{1}{5}$ ★28. $\frac{3}{4}$, $\frac{2}{3}$, $\frac{1}{2}$

APPLICATION

29. Jon's gas tank was $\frac{3}{4}$ full on Wednesday. It was $\frac{5}{8}$ full on Thursday. On which day did Jon have more gas in the tank?

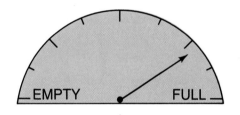

30. Estimate. Is the gas tank shown about $\frac{1}{2}$, $\frac{1}{3}$, or $\frac{3}{4}$ full?

★31. Estimate. Is the gas tank shown about $\frac{2}{3}$, $\frac{1}{4}$, or $\frac{1}{8}$ empty?

=== MENTAL ARITHMETIC ===

Compare the two fractions without finding equivalent fractions. Look at the denominators and the chart.

1. $\frac{1}{3}$ ● $\frac{1}{2}$ 2. $\frac{3}{4}$ ● $\frac{3}{5}$

3. $\frac{4}{5}$ ● $\frac{4}{6}$ 4. $\frac{2}{5}$ ● $\frac{2}{3}$

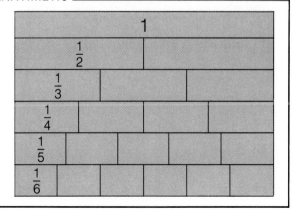

Fractional Parts

These 2 Alpine lilies have 12 petals. One lily has $\frac{1}{2}$ of these petals. How many petals does one lily have?

$\frac{1}{2}$ of 12 = ☐

Think 12 petals, 2 equal groups
Divide by 2. $12 \div 2 = 6$
           $\frac{1}{2}$ of 12 = 6

One lily has 6 petals.

$\frac{3}{4}$ of these daisies are yellow. How many daisies are yellow?
Find $\frac{3}{4}$ of 8.

Think 8 daisies, 4 equal groups
Divide by 4. $8 \div 4 = 2$
There are 2 daisies in each group.

3 groups are yellow.
Multiply by 3. $3 \times 2 = 6$

$\frac{3}{4}$ of 8 = 6
There are 6 yellow daisies.

CLASSWORK

Find each answer.

1. $\frac{1}{3}$ of 6 = ☐   2. $\frac{2}{3}$ of 6 = ☐

3. $\frac{1}{5}$ of 5 = ☐   4. $\frac{1}{4}$ of 8 = ☐   5. $\frac{2}{3}$ of 3 = ☐

Find each answer.

1. $\frac{1}{5}$ of 10 = ☐   2. $\frac{4}{5}$ of 10 = ☐

3. $\frac{1}{3}$ of 3 = ☐   4. $\frac{1}{4}$ of 12 = ☐   5. $\frac{1}{8}$ of 48 = ☐

6. $\frac{3}{8}$ of 8 = ☐   7. $\frac{4}{5}$ of 15 = ☐   8. $\frac{3}{10}$ of 20 = ☐

★9. $\frac{1}{100}$ of 100 = ☐   ★10. $\frac{10}{10}$ of 30 = ☐   ★11. $\frac{1}{10}$ of 1,000 = ☐

Find $\frac{2}{3}$ of each amount.

12. 3   13. 9   14. 27   15. 18   16. 30   17. 36

Choose the correct number sentence and solve.

18. Martha had 24 flowers. She gave $\frac{1}{8}$ of them to Sue. How many flowers did she give to Sue?

    a. 8 × 24 = ☐   b. 8 ÷ 24 = ☐

    c. 24 ÷ 8 = ☐   d. 24 − 8 = ☐

APPLICATION

19. Ben studied 12 wild roses in the Alps. $\frac{2}{3}$ of them were red roses. How many roses were red?

20. Experiment. Find $\frac{1}{2}$ the number of people in your class.

★21. A botanist studied some yellow lilies and some orange lilies in the Alps. There were 12 lilies and $\frac{5}{6}$ of them were yellow. How many were orange?

★22. Lydia has 18 flowers. Of these flowers $\frac{1}{2}$ are red and $\frac{1}{3}$ are yellow. The rest are pink. How many pink flowers does Lydia have?

Mixed Numbers

This Mexican potter divided balls of clay into fourths to form handles.

Five fourths is the same as one and one fourth.

$$\frac{5}{4} = 1\frac{1}{4} \longleftarrow \text{mixed number}$$

▶A **mixed number** has a whole number and a fraction.

Eight fourths is the same as two.

$$\frac{8}{4} = 2 \longleftarrow \text{whole number}$$

CLASSWORK

Write a mixed number or a whole number that tells what part is blue.

1.

2.

3.

4.

5.

6.

7.

8.

9.

PRACTICE

**Write a mixed number or a whole number
that tells what part is blue.**

1.

2.

3.

4.

5.

6.

7.

8.

9.

★10. How many halves
in 2 wholes?

★11. How many thirds
in 4 wholes?

★12. How many fifths
in 4 wholes?

APPLICATION

How many balls
of clay does the
potter have left?

13. $\frac{1}{4}$ of a ball was used.

14. $\frac{2}{4}$ of a ball was used.

★15. Steve needs $\frac{1}{2}$ a ball of clay to
make a lid. How many lids can
he make from 6 balls of clay?

═══ ESTIMATION ═══

Use the circles to help
you estimate which
number is closer to 2.

1. $1\frac{1}{2}$ or $1\frac{5}{8}$

2. $1\frac{3}{4}$ or $1\frac{5}{8}$

3. $2\frac{1}{2}$ or $2\frac{1}{4}$

Fractions and Mixed Numbers

Jerome used 7 Jaffa orange halves to make juice. How many oranges did he use?

If the numerator is greater than the denominator, you can divide to change a fraction to a mixed number.

Step 1
Divide the numerator by the denominator.

$$\frac{7}{2} = 2\overline{)7} \begin{array}{r} 3 \\ -6 \\ \hline 1 \end{array}$$

Step 2
Write the remainder as the numerator of the fraction. The denominator is the divisor.

$$2\overline{)7} \begin{array}{r} 3\frac{1}{2} \\ -6 \\ \hline 1 \end{array}$$

Jerome used $3\frac{1}{2}$ oranges.

Write $\frac{12}{4}$ as a whole number.

$$4\overline{)12} \begin{array}{r} 3 \\ -12 \\ \hline 0 \end{array} \longleftarrow \text{no extra fourths}$$

$$\frac{12}{4} = 3$$

CLASSWORK

Write a mixed number or a whole number for each fraction.

1. $\frac{8}{2}$

2. $\frac{20}{4}$

3. $\frac{7}{3}$

4. $\frac{12}{5}$

5. $\frac{13}{10}$

6. $\frac{13}{6}$

7. $\frac{9}{2}$

8. $\frac{5}{3}$

9. $\frac{19}{8}$

10. $\frac{11}{9}$

11. $\frac{12}{3}$

12. $\frac{21}{7}$

Write a mixed number or a whole number for each fraction.

1. $\frac{12}{2}$ 2. $\frac{9}{3}$ 3. $\frac{7}{5}$ 4. $\frac{9}{4}$ 5. $\frac{16}{8}$ 6. $\frac{11}{6}$

7. $\frac{13}{4}$ 8. $\frac{10}{10}$ 9. $\frac{15}{2}$ 10. $\frac{13}{8}$ 11. $\frac{10}{3}$ 12. $\frac{15}{5}$

13. $\frac{17}{3}$ 14. $\frac{18}{2}$ 15. $\frac{29}{5}$ 16. $\frac{27}{4}$ 17. $\frac{12}{6}$ 18. $\frac{30}{3}$

19. $\frac{20}{5}$ 20. $\frac{6}{6}$ 21. $\frac{14}{3}$ 22. $\frac{24}{2}$ 23. $\frac{37}{4}$ 24. $\frac{27}{8}$

Follow the rule to complete.

Rule: Write a whole number.

	Input	Output
25.	$\frac{16}{2}$	
26.	$\frac{18}{3}$	
27.	$\frac{24}{4}$	
28.	$\frac{20}{5}$	

Rule: Write a mixed number.

	Input	Output
29.	$\frac{13}{2}$	
30.	$\frac{17}{3}$	
31.	$\frac{27}{4}$	
32.	$\frac{43}{5}$	

Rule: Write a fraction to show thirds.

	Input	Output
★ 33.	2	
★ 34.	5	
★ 35.	$3\frac{1}{3}$	
★ 36.	$4\frac{2}{3}$	

APPLICATION

37. Mrs. Nuñez used $\frac{5}{2}$ teaspoons of red pepper to flavor chili. Write a mixed number to show the amount of pepper she used.

38. A chef used $\frac{10}{3}$ cups of flour to make bread. Write a mixed number to show how many cups of flour he used.

39. A chef uses $\frac{1}{2}$ of a strawberry to decorate each dessert. How many strawberries does she use for 25 desserts?

★ 40. A waitress put $\frac{1}{2}$ of a hard boiled egg on each salad. She used $7\frac{1}{2}$ eggs. How many salads did she serve?

Fractions and Decimals

Look at the 10 equal sections in this African necklace.

- read   Four tenths is blue.
- write $\frac{4}{10}$, or 0.4, is blue.

$$\frac{4}{10} = 0.4$$

fraction   decimal

Look at the 100 beads in the necklace.

- read   Forty hundredths is blue.
- write $\frac{40}{100}$, or 0.40, is blue.

$$\frac{40}{100} = 0.40$$

More Examples

fraction		decimal
$\frac{7}{10}$	=	0.7
$\frac{6}{100}$	=	0.06
$\frac{14}{100}$	=	0.14

mixed number		decimal
$3\frac{2}{10}$	=	3.2
$1\frac{4}{100}$	=	1.04
$2\frac{75}{100}$	=	2.75

CLASSWORK

Write a fraction and a decimal for the part that is blue.

1.

2.

3.

Write a decimal for each fraction or mixed number.

4. $\frac{8}{10}$

5. $\frac{12}{100}$

6. $3\frac{1}{10}$

7. $4\frac{9}{100}$

8. $\frac{76}{100}$

312

PRACTICE

Write a fraction and a decimal
for the part that is blue.

1.

2.

3.

Write a decimal for each fraction or mixed number.

4. $\frac{1}{10}$

5. $\frac{48}{100}$

6. $\frac{8}{100}$

7. $1\frac{3}{10}$

8. $2\frac{15}{100}$

9. $5\frac{6}{10}$

10. $\frac{94}{100}$

11. $3\frac{8}{10}$

12. $6\frac{5}{100}$

13. $2\frac{59}{100}$

Write a fraction or mixed number for each decimal.

14. 0.23

15. 0.8

16. 0.01

17. 6.1

18. 7.45

19. 0.02

20. 4.6

21. 1.05

22. 3.1

23. 0.9

Compare. Use > or < for ●.

★24. $\frac{8}{10}$ ● 0.09

★25. 0.34 ● $\frac{9}{10}$

★26. 1.06 ● $1\frac{60}{100}$

★27. 0.5 ● 0.39

APPLICATION

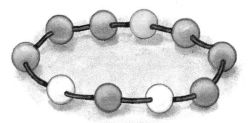

Write each answer as a fraction and a decimal.

28. What part of the bracelet is red?

★29. How much more of the bracelet
is blue than red?

★30. How much of the bracelet is
white or yellow?

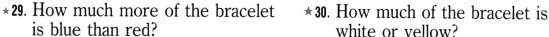

CALCULATOR

A calculator shows fractions as decimals.

To find $\frac{1}{2}$, press 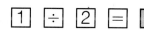  . $\frac{1}{2} = 0.5$

Use your calculator to find a decimal for each fraction.

1. $\frac{3}{10}$

2. $\frac{1}{5}$

3. $\frac{2}{10}$

4. $\frac{4}{5}$

5. $\frac{1}{4}$

6. $\frac{17}{10}$

313

Problem Solving

SKILLS AND STRATEGIES REVIEW Other Countries

1. In Thailand, elephants are used to pull heavy teak logs. The first elephant pulled $\frac{1}{3}$ of the load. The second elephant pulled $\frac{1}{4}$ of the load. Which elephant pulled more of the load?

2. In Venice, canals are used like streets. A gondola is a boat that is used as a taxi. There are 12 people. One gondola can take $\frac{1}{3}$ of the people. How many people can ride in one gondola?

3. Twenty-six people needed a ride from the train station in Venice to the hotel. Only $\frac{1}{2}$ these people got on the water bus. How many people still needed a ride?

4. The water bus leaves at 10 minutes past the hour and at 20 minutes to the hour. Ray's family arrives on the dock at 3:45 P.M. How long must they wait for the next water bus?

5. In Israel, Jaffa oranges are packed into crates to be sent to other countries. The workers packed a shipment in crates as shown on the right. They must repack the crates so that each has the same number of oranges. How many oranges will each crate have then?

6. There are 90 seats on the hydrofoil that goes from Dover, England to Calais, France. Today, twice as many seats are empty as are filled. How many seats are filled?

When you spell *PERU* on the telephone buttons, the numbers add up to 25.

P E R U
7 + 3 + 7 + 8 = 25

7. What country can you find whose name has the greatest sum?

8. What country can you find whose name has the least sum?

Problem Solving

WHAT WOULD YOU DO . . . ?

While traveling in Mexico, you want to buy gifts to take home. You decide to buy piñatas for 4 friends and 2 young cousins. A small piñata costs $3. A large piñata costs $4. You do not want to spend more than $20.

Answer each question and explain.

1. Could you spend exactly $20 if you bought 1 small piñata and some large piñatas?

2. Would you consider buying piñatas in different combinations? Describe your plan.

3. Could you buy yourself a piñata as part of your plan?

While visiting in Mexico City, you want to take a tour. The poster describes 2 different tours you could take. Each tour begins and ends at the bus station.

4. How much time does each tour take?

5. Tour II begins at 10:15 A.M. You must arrive $\frac{1}{2}$ hour before the bus leaves. You want to shower, dress, and eat breakfast before the tour. What time must you get up?

6. You'd like to have $12 to spend on souvenirs. You don't want to spend more than $25 for the day. Which tour would you take?

What would you do?

7. The desk clerk at the hotel tells you about another tour of Mexico City. It is an 8-hour tour that begins at 9:30 A.M. The cost is $10.75, which includes lunch. Could you take this tour and still spend no more than $25? Would you arrive back in time to visit the souvenir shop, which closes at 4:00 P.M.?

See Beautiful Mexico City	
TOUR I	**TOUR II**
Leave: 8:30 A.M.	Leave: 10:15 A.M.
Return: 3:30 P.M.	Return: 3:15 P.M.
Cost: $19.95 (includes lunch and 1 hour for shopping)	Cost: $12.50 (includes lunch and ½ hour for shopping)
All tours leave from the Bus Station.	

Write the fraction that tells what part is blue. pages 292–295

1.

2.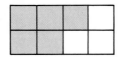

3.

4.

Complete. Write the equivalent fraction for each. pages 296–299

5.

$\frac{1}{2} = \frac{\square}{4}$

6.

$\frac{2}{3} = \frac{\square}{6}$

7.

$\frac{3}{4} = \frac{\square}{8}$

8. $\frac{1}{4} = \frac{1 \times \square}{4 \times \square} = \frac{2}{8}$

9. $\frac{4}{5} = \frac{4 \times \square}{5 \times \square} = \frac{12}{15}$

10. $\frac{2}{3} = \frac{2 \times \square}{3 \times \square} = \frac{6}{9}$

Complete. Write each fraction in lowest terms. pages 300–301

11. $\frac{3}{12} = \frac{3 \div 3}{12 \div 3} = \frac{\square}{4}$

12. $\frac{4}{8}$

13. $\frac{3}{9}$

Write > or < for ●. pages 304–305

14. $\frac{2}{5} ● \frac{1}{5}$

15. $\frac{1}{2} ● \frac{3}{4}$

16. $\frac{6}{7} ● \frac{4}{7}$

17. $\frac{2}{3} ● \frac{5}{9}$

Find each answer. pages 306–307

18. $\frac{1}{4}$ of 8 = $\square$

19. $\frac{3}{4}$ of 8 = $\square$

20. $\frac{2}{3}$ of 6 = $\square$

Write a mixed number or a whole number. pages 308–311

21.

22. $\frac{6}{6}$

23. $\frac{10}{3}$

24. $\frac{12}{7}$

Write a decimal. pages 312–313

25. $\frac{7}{10}$

26. $2\frac{4}{100}$

Write a fraction. pages 312–313

27. 0.9

28. 0.37

Solve. pages 302–303, 314–315

29. What can you find in your classroom that is $\frac{1}{2}$ the length of your math book?

30. Sandra used $\frac{9}{2}$ cups of flour while baking. Write a mixed number to show the amount of flour used.

Write the fraction that tells what part is blue.

1.

2.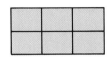

3.

Complete. Write the equivalent fraction.

4. $\frac{1}{5} = \frac{1 \times 2}{5 \times 2} = \frac{2}{\square}$

5. $\frac{2}{3} = \frac{2 \times 4}{3 \times 4} = \frac{\square}{12}$

6. $\frac{6}{7} = \frac{6 \times \square}{7 \times \square} = \frac{18}{21}$

Complete. Write each fraction in lowest terms.

7. $\frac{4}{12} = \frac{4 \div \square}{12 \div \square} = \frac{1}{3}$

8. $\frac{2}{6}$

9. $\frac{5}{10}$

Compare. Use > or < for ●.

10. $\frac{1}{8}$ ● $\frac{3}{8}$

11. $\frac{3}{4}$ ● $\frac{8}{12}$

12. $\frac{1}{6}$ ● $\frac{1}{5}$

13. $\frac{2}{3}$ ● $\frac{1}{2}$

Find each answer.

14. $\frac{1}{2}$ of 4 = $\square$

15. $\frac{1}{3}$ of 9 = $\square$

16. $\frac{2}{5}$ of 10 = $\square$

Write a mixed number or a whole number for each fraction.

17. $\frac{5}{5}$

18. $\frac{11}{6}$

19. $\frac{6}{3}$

20. $\frac{9}{4}$

Write a decimal for each fraction or mixed number.

21. $\frac{3}{10}$

22. $\frac{58}{100}$

23. $6\frac{4}{10}$

Solve.

24. There are $\frac{1}{2}$ as many letters in the word *Peru* as there are in the word *Thailand*. Are there more or less than $\frac{1}{2}$ as many letters in your first name as your last name?

25. A group of 15 children went to the zoo. There were 8 boys in the group. What part of the group was girls?

 A bus tour took 150 minutes. How many hours was the tour?

CLOCK FRACTIONS

A clock face is divided into 12 equal parts. At 9:00 the hands on the clock enclose 3 out of 12 spaces. Think of the 3 spaces as $\frac{1}{4}$ of the clock face.

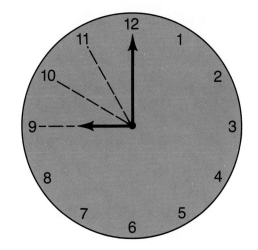

Make a clock of your own. Find the fractions at each hour.

These are the supplies you need:

- a large jar top
- 2 different-color sheets of paper
- scissors
- a marker

This is what you do.

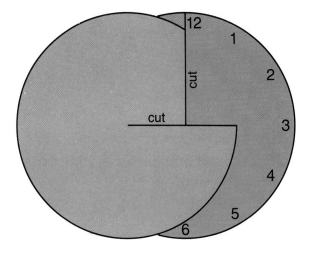

1. Trace a circle on each of the two sheets of paper. Use the jar top as a guide.

2. Cut out the two circles.

3. Make 1 cut from the edge to the center of each circle.

4. On one circle, write the numbers that appear on the face of a clock.

5. Slip one circle into the other through the cuts. Turn the circle without numbers. As you do this, different times will show on the circle with numbers.

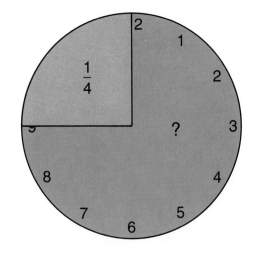

Find the fractions at 3:00, 8:00, and 2:00.

There is another fraction at 9:00. Can you name it?

MATH IN MUSIC

Numbers are an important part of music. They give order to the sounds we love to hear. People who write music use symbols to show these numbers.

A **meter signature** is a symbol that shows how beats are grouped in a measure.

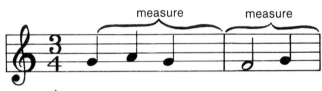

meter ⌐→ 3   Count this number of beats to a measure.
signature   4   This note (quarter note) gets one beat.

A **note** is a symbol that shows how long a sound should last.

Symbol	Name	Length of Sound
o	whole note	depends on the bottom number of the meter signature
♩	half note	half as long as a whole note
♩	quarter note	half as long as a half note
♪	eighth note	half as long as a quarter note

What do these meter signatures mean?

1. $\frac{4}{4}$

2. $\frac{2}{4}$

3. $\frac{3}{8}$

Tell how many beats the circled note gets.

4. $\frac{4}{4}$ ⓙ ♩ ♩ |

5. $\frac{2}{4}$ ⓙ ♪ ♩ |

6. $\frac{3}{8}$ ♩ ⓙ |

Choose the correct answer. Write A, B, C, or D.

1. $4,902 - 2,583 = \square$

   A 2,309   **C** 7,485

   B 2,319   **D** not given

2. $7,441 \div 7 = \square$

   A 1,063   **C** 163

   B 106   **D** not given

3. $5.6 + 42.03 = \square$

   A 42.59   **C** 425.9

   B 47.63   **D** not given

4. $47 \times 26 = \square$

   A 962   **C** 1,222

   B 73   **D** not given

5. $45 \times \$1.63 = \square$

   A \$49.25   **C** \$73.35

   B \$63.35   **D** not given

6. Estimate. $27\overline{)745}$

   A 30   **C** 45

   B 35   **D** not given

7. $782 \div 13 = \square$

   A 54   **C** 52 R6

   B 60 R2   **D** not given

8. What fraction is equivalent to $\frac{3}{7}$?

   A $\frac{1}{2}$ **C** $\frac{9}{21}$

   B $\frac{9}{14}$ **D** not given

9. What is $\frac{10}{15}$ in lowest terms?

   A $\frac{3}{5}$ **C** $\frac{2}{5}$

   B $\frac{2}{3}$ **D** not given

10. What is the mixed number for $\frac{13}{2}$?

   A $6\frac{1}{2}$ **C** $6\frac{1}{3}$

   B $7\frac{1}{2}$ **D** not given

Solve.

11. At a local market, apples cost $.35 and oranges cost $.32. Freda spent $2.01 for some apples and oranges. How many of each did she buy?

   A 3 apples,   **C** 2 apples,
      3 oranges   3 oranges

   B 4 apples,   **D** not given
      2 oranges

12. Lori has 2 stacks of paper. One is yellow, the other is blue. Together there are 72 sheets. There are 10 more sheets of blue than yellow. How many sheets of yellow paper are there?

   A 31   **C** 62

   B 41   **D** not given

Theme: Seasons

Exploring Fractions

Use six different-colored strips of construction paper of equal length.

1. Write the words ONE WHOLE on one of your strips.

ONE WHOLE

2. Fold and cut the remaining strips in the following ways:

   - two equal pieces
   - three equal pieces
   - four equal pieces
   - six equal pieces
   - twelve equal pieces

3. Label each piece you cut with a fraction.

$\frac{1}{2}$	$\frac{1}{2}$

$\frac{1}{3}$	$\frac{1}{3}$	$\frac{1}{3}$

4. Arrange some of your fraction pieces end to end. Place other fraction pieces end to end below these until you have an equal length. Display and discuss several examples. Record your work to show what you did with your fraction models.

SHARING YOUR THINKING

Share and compare different ways you used to fold a whole piece into twelfths. Discuss other possible ways to do this.

THINKING IT THROUGH

1. Use your set of fraction pieces. Choose any two pieces.

   • Lay them end to end along your ONE WHOLE piece.

   • Decide how you can use a single fraction to name the length of both pieces.

   • Repeat this activity several times. Write a number sentence to show what happens each time.

2. Trade your number sentences. Find some examples where you started with the same two fraction pieces, but gave the result in different ways. Discuss how this could happen.

3. In everyday life there are many situations in which people fold things into equal parts. Discuss situations in which you have seen things folded into equal parts. Show or describe how people do this.

Understanding Fractions

The Last Piece: A Fraction Strategy Game for 2–4 Players

Use your fraction pieces.

1. Display a ONE WHOLE piece.

2. Players take turns placing fraction pieces end to end to make a length equal to one whole.

3. Try not to be the person who places the last fraction piece to complete the whole.

WORKING TOGETHER

Play "The Last Piece" several times. Vary the game by changing the number of players each time. While others in your group are playing the game, compare the strategies they use with the strategies you would use.

1. Discuss different patterns that you noticed as you played "The Last Piece" game.

2. Discuss different strategies that players used to avoid placing the last piece.

3. Discuss how the number of players in the game affected your strategy.

4. Continue to play the game to test some of the strategies you have shared.

MATH CENTER

THINKING IT THROUGH

Start with all of your fraction pieces. Remove one of each kind of your fractions and set them aside. Use only the remaining pieces.

1. Display your ONE WHOLE strip. Find a way to use your remaining pieces to make a length that is the same as the whole strip. Write a number sentence to record your work.

2. Trade some fraction pieces for others to equal the whole strip in a different way. Record your work. Use Workmat 2 if you wish.

3. Exchange your number sentences with those of another group. Compare and discuss them. Lay your fraction pieces end to end to show each number sentence.

4. Explain to a partner how you used fractions in different ways to make a whole.

325

Adding And Subtracting Fractions

Build a Whole...or More: A Fraction Game for 2–4 Players

Use your fraction pieces.

1. Each player should display a ONE WHOLE piece.

2. Make a number cube. Label the faces with the following fractions. $\frac{1}{3}, \frac{1}{4}, \frac{1}{6}, \frac{1}{6}, \frac{1}{12}, \frac{1}{12}$

3. Toss the number cube to determine who will play first. The player who tosses the greatest fraction begins the game.

4. The first player tosses the number cube and chooses a fraction piece to match the fraction tossed. Place the fraction piece below the ONE WHOLE piece so that the ends line up on the left.

5. Take turns tossing the number cube. Continue placing fraction pieces end to end along the ONE WHOLE piece.

6. The game ends when a player builds a length greater than or equal to the ONE WHOLE piece.

7. When the game ends, record the total length that was built.

Play the "Build a Whole . . . or More" game several times.

Break Up a Whole: A Fraction Game for 2–4 Players

1. Each player should display two $\frac{1}{2}$ pieces to make a whole.

2. Use a number cube labeled $\frac{1}{3}, \frac{1}{4}, \frac{1}{6}, \frac{1}{6}, \frac{1}{12}, \frac{1}{12}$.

3. Toss the number cube to determine who will play first. The player who tosses the least fraction begins the game.

4. Take turns tossing the number cube. Find a way to remove an amount that matches the fraction tossed.

5. The game ends when a player tosses a fraction equal to or greater than the remaining fraction piece.

Play the "Break Up a Whole" game several times.

SHARING YOUR THINKING

1. Discuss the longest possible length that might be built when you play the "Build a Whole . . . or More" game.

2. Discuss strategies that helped you remove pieces in the "Break Up a Whole" game.

THINKING IT THROUGH

1. Display fraction pieces end to end to show a length greater than ONE WHOLE piece.

   • Decide how to use a fraction or a mixed number to name your length.

   • Write a number sentence to record your work.

   • Repeat this activity several times.

2. Make a list of the things you have learned about fractions by using fraction pieces.

Problem Solving

USING A MODEL

Sometimes you need to use a model to
help you plan the solution to a problem.

The owner of Rocky Ledge Resort is going to
plant bushes along 3 sides of a patio. Each side
measures 12 yards. A bush will be planted every
3 yards. How many bushes are needed?

How can the answer be found?

To help you plan the solution to this problem, use
paper and pencil to make a model of the patio.

Carry out the plan.

Draw a mark to show a bush every 3 yards.

Count the marks. There are 13 marks.

The owner needs 13 bushes.

Is your answer correct?

Did you use one bush every 3 yards? Check your
model. The answer is correct.

328

Use a model to help you plan the solution for each problem.

1. Rocky Ledge offers skiing in the winter. The cross-country trail is 16 miles long. There are 10 flags which can be used to mark the trail. Are there enough flags to place one at the beginning, one at the end, and one every 2 miles along the trail?

Selma started on a 12-mile ski trail. After skiing 6 miles, she was joined by Sandy. Selma stopped after skiing 3 miles more. Sandy continued to the end of the trail.

2. What fractional part of the trail did Selma ski?

3. What fractional part of the trail did Sandy ski?

4. What fractional part of the trail did they ski together?

5. What fractional part of the trail did Sandy ski alone?

6. A gardener wants to put plants along both sides of a path. The path is 7 feet long. How many plants are needed to put the plants 1 foot apart?

★7. Barry was riding along a straight 2-mile bicycle path. After $\frac{4}{5}$ mile, he was joined by Lisa. They rode together for $\frac{3}{5}$ mile. Then Barry stopped. Lisa went on for $\frac{2}{5}$ mile. How far did Lisa bicycle?

CREATE YOUR OWN PROBLEM

This model was used to find the number of posts needed to build a fence around the children's play area at Rocky Ledge. Write a problem for this model. Then solve the problem.

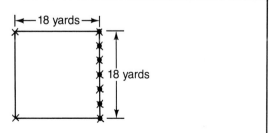

Adding and Subtracting Like Mixed Numbers

It takes $4\frac{5}{6}$ packages of yarn to knit a sweater. It takes $1\frac{2}{6}$ packages to knit a hat. How much yarn is needed for a sweater and a hat?

$$4\frac{5}{6} + 1\frac{2}{6} = \square$$

Step I
Add fractions.

$$\begin{array}{r} 4\frac{5}{6} \\ + 1\frac{2}{6} \\ \hline \frac{7}{6} \end{array}$$

Step 2
Add whole numbers.

$$\begin{array}{r} 4\frac{5}{6} \\ + 1\frac{2}{6} \\ \hline 5\frac{7}{6} \end{array}$$

Step 3
Rename fraction.

$$\begin{array}{r} 4\frac{5}{6} \\ + 1\frac{2}{6} \\ \hline 5\frac{7}{6} = 6\frac{1}{6} \end{array}$$

Think
$\frac{7}{6} = 1\frac{1}{6}$

$6\frac{1}{6}$ packages of yarn are needed.

Find $5\frac{7}{8} - 2\frac{3}{8}$.

Step 1
Subtract fractions.

$$\begin{array}{r} 5\frac{7}{8} \\ - 2\frac{3}{8} \\ \hline \frac{4}{8} \end{array}$$

Step 2
Subtract whole numbers.

$$\begin{array}{r} 5\frac{7}{8} \\ - 2\frac{3}{8} \\ \hline 3\frac{4}{8} \end{array}$$

Step 3
Write the answer in lowest terms.

$$\begin{array}{r} 5\frac{7}{8} \\ - 2\frac{3}{8} \\ \hline 3\frac{4}{8} = 3\frac{1}{2} \end{array}$$

Think
$\frac{4}{8} = \frac{4 \div 4}{8 \div 4} = \frac{1}{2}$

CLASSWORK

Add or subtract. Write each answer in lowest terms.

1. $\begin{array}{r} 5\frac{2}{4} \\ + 3\frac{1}{4} \\ \hline \end{array}$

2. $\begin{array}{r} 8\frac{4}{9} \\ + 1\frac{7}{9} \\ \hline \end{array}$

3. $\begin{array}{r} 4\frac{3}{5} \\ - 1\frac{1}{5} \\ \hline \end{array}$

4. $\begin{array}{r} 4\frac{1}{2} \\ - 3\frac{1}{2} \\ \hline \end{array}$

5. $\begin{array}{r} 7\frac{6}{10} \\ + \frac{3}{10} \\ \hline \end{array}$

6. $\begin{array}{r} 1\frac{5}{8} \\ - 1\frac{2}{8} \\ \hline \end{array}$

7. $6\frac{6}{7} - 2\frac{2}{7} = \square$

8. $5\frac{5}{6} - 3\frac{1}{6} = \square$

9. $2\frac{5}{12} + 3\frac{11}{12} = \square$

Add or subtract. Write each answer in lowest terms.

1. $\begin{array}{r} 3\frac{2}{5} \\ -2\frac{1}{5} \\ \hline \end{array}$

2. $\begin{array}{r} 6\frac{2}{6} \\ +3\frac{2}{6} \\ \hline \end{array}$

3. $\begin{array}{r} 5\frac{2}{3} \\ -1\frac{1}{3} \\ \hline \end{array}$

4. $\begin{array}{r} 6\frac{3}{4} \\ +2\frac{3}{4} \\ \hline \end{array}$

5. $\begin{array}{r} 8\frac{7}{8} \\ -\ \frac{2}{8} \\ \hline \end{array}$

6. $\begin{array}{r} 5\frac{1}{6} \\ +3\frac{1}{6} \\ \hline \end{array}$

7. $\begin{array}{r} 9\frac{3}{4} \\ -1\frac{3}{4} \\ \hline \end{array}$

8. $\begin{array}{r} 3\frac{7}{8} \\ +3\frac{5}{8} \\ \hline \end{array}$

9. $\begin{array}{r} 8\frac{5}{12} \\ +\ \frac{7}{12} \\ \hline \end{array}$

10. $\begin{array}{r} 3\frac{4}{9} \\ +1\frac{2}{9} \\ \hline \end{array}$

11. $\begin{array}{r} 6\frac{5}{7} \\ -\ \frac{2}{7} \\ \hline \end{array}$

12. $\begin{array}{r} 4\frac{2}{5} \\ -2\frac{1}{5} \\ \hline \end{array}$

13. $7\frac{5}{9} + 3\frac{2}{9} = \square$

14. $5\frac{1}{2} - 2\frac{1}{2} = \square$

★ 15. $(3 + 2\frac{1}{2}) - 1\frac{1}{2} = \square$

Follow the rule to complete.

Rule: Add $1\frac{2}{7}$.

	Input	Output
16.	$3\frac{4}{7}$	
17.	$1\frac{6}{7}$	
18.	$2\frac{3}{7}$	

Rule: Subtract $1\frac{1}{8}$.

	Input	Output
19.	$1\frac{2}{8}$	
20.	$2\frac{3}{8}$	
21.	$5\frac{5}{8}$	

APPLICATION

22. Ralph filled $7\frac{3}{4}$ bags with leaves. Rudy filled $5\frac{1}{4}$ bags with leaves. How many more bags of leaves did Ralph fill?

★ 23. Rosa wants to knit 2 scarves. She needs $4\frac{1}{2}$ packages of yarn for one, and $3\frac{1}{2}$ packages for the other. She has $9\frac{1}{2}$ packages. After making the scarves, how much yarn will she have left?

Mixed Practice

1. $5.1 + 6.5 = \square$

2. $4.64 + 3.81 = \square$

3. $82.1 - 49.6 = \square$

4. $3.6 - 2.9 = \square$

5. $\begin{array}{r} 99.62 \\ +48.43 \\ \hline \end{array}$

6. $\begin{array}{r} 137.72 \\ -\ 48.36 \\ \hline \end{array}$

7. $\begin{array}{r} 362 \\ \times\ \ 38 \\ \hline \end{array}$

8. $17 - 2.58 = \square$

9. $48 \times 97 = \square$

10. $386 \div 25 = \square$

11. $42\overline{)847}$

12. $\begin{array}{r} \$6.38 \\ \times\ \ \ 81 \\ \hline \end{array}$

13. $52.4 + 3.73 = \square$

14. $178.6 - 5.2 = \square$

15. $50 \times \$6.71 = \square$

16. $36\overline{)\$7.20}$

17. $32\overline{)946}$

18. $4.26 - 3.8 = \square$

Adding Unlike Fractions

One half of a flock of 8 geese is swimming. One eighth of the flock is standing on a rock. What part of the flock is swimming or on a rock?

$$\frac{1}{2} + \frac{1}{8} = \square$$

Something told the wild geese
It was time to go.
Though the fields lay golden
Something whispered, "Snow."

—Rachel Field

Step 1
Find equivalent fractions with the same denominator.

$$\frac{1}{2} = \frac{1 \times 4}{2 \times 4} = \frac{4}{8}$$
$$+\frac{1}{8} \qquad\quad = \frac{1}{8}$$

Step 2
Add.

$$\frac{1}{2} = \frac{4}{8}$$
$$+\frac{1}{8} = \frac{1}{8}$$
$$\overline{\frac{5}{8}}$$

Five eighths of the flock is swimming or standing on a rock.

Find $\frac{1}{3} + \frac{2}{8}$.

$$\frac{1}{3} = \frac{1 \times 8}{3 \times 8} = \frac{8}{24}$$
$$+\frac{2}{8} = \frac{2 \times 3}{8 \times 3} = \frac{6}{24}$$

$$\frac{1}{3} = \frac{8}{24}$$
$$+\frac{2}{8} = \frac{6}{24}$$
$$\overline{\frac{14}{24}}$$

Write the answer in lowest terms.

Think
$$\frac{14}{24} = \frac{14 \div 2}{24 \div 2} = \frac{7}{12} \qquad\qquad \frac{14}{24} = \frac{7}{12}$$

CLASSWORK

Complete. Write each sum in lowest terms.

1. $$\frac{1}{2} = \frac{1 \times 4}{2 \times 4} = \frac{4}{\square}$$
    $$+\frac{3}{8} \qquad\quad = \frac{3}{8}$$

2. $$\frac{1}{2} = \frac{1 \times 3}{2 \times 3} = \frac{\square}{6}$$
    $$+\frac{1}{3} = \frac{1 \times 2}{3 \times 2} = \frac{2}{\square}$$

3. $$\frac{3}{4}$$
    $$+\frac{1}{8}$$

4. $$\frac{1}{9}$$
    $$+\frac{1}{3}$$

5. $$\frac{2}{5}$$
    $$+\frac{1}{10}$$

6. $$\frac{1}{3}$$
    $$+\frac{1}{4}$$

7. $$\frac{7}{12}$$
    $$+\frac{1}{3}$$

8. $$\frac{2}{5}$$
    $$+\frac{1}{2}$$

332

Complete. Write each sum in lowest terms.

1. $\dfrac{1}{8} \qquad\qquad = \dfrac{1}{8}$

   $+\dfrac{1}{4} = \dfrac{1 \times 2}{4 \times 2} = \dfrac{\square}{8}$

2. $\dfrac{1}{4} = \dfrac{1 \times 3}{4 \times 3} = \dfrac{3}{\square}$

   $+\dfrac{2}{3} = \dfrac{2 \times 4}{3 \times 4} = \dfrac{8}{\square}$

3. $\dfrac{1}{2}$
   $+\dfrac{1}{8}$

4. $\dfrac{1}{6}$
   $+\dfrac{2}{3}$

5. $\dfrac{1}{4}$
   $+\dfrac{3}{8}$

6. $\dfrac{1}{12}$
   $+\dfrac{5}{6}$

7. $\dfrac{4}{9}$
   $+\dfrac{1}{3}$

8. $\dfrac{1}{4}$
   $+\dfrac{1}{12}$

9. $\dfrac{3}{4}$
   $+\dfrac{1}{6}$

10. $\dfrac{4}{12}$
    $+\dfrac{1}{2}$

11. $\dfrac{1}{4}$
    $+\dfrac{2}{5}$

12. $\dfrac{1}{2}$
    $+\dfrac{2}{8}$

13. $\dfrac{2}{3}$
    $+\dfrac{1}{5}$

14. $\dfrac{2}{3}$
    $+\dfrac{1}{12}$

★15. $\dfrac{3}{5} + \dfrac{1}{2} + \dfrac{1}{5} = \square$

★16. $\dfrac{1}{2} + \dfrac{2}{3} + \dfrac{2}{3} = \square$

★17. $\dfrac{1}{8} + \dfrac{1}{4} + \dfrac{1}{2} = \square$

APPLICATION

18. Lois wrote a poem about snow. She wrote for $\frac{1}{4}$ of an hour in the morning and $\frac{1}{2}$ of an hour in the afternoon. How much time did Lois spend in all writing her poem?

★19. Dan and Julius each spent $\frac{1}{2}$ of an hour raking leaves. Andy spent $\frac{1}{4}$ of an hour raking leaves. How much time did the boys spend raking leaves?

ESTIMATION

Use the drawings to help you estimate. Tell whether each sum would be more or less than 1. Do not find the exact answer. Just answer *more* or *less*.

1. $\dfrac{1}{2} + \dfrac{1}{3}$

2. $\dfrac{2}{3} + \dfrac{1}{2}$

3. $\dfrac{1}{4} + \dfrac{1}{2}$

4. $\dfrac{3}{4} + \dfrac{1}{8}$

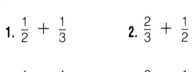

Subtracting Unlike Fractions

Marla is making costumes for the school's winter play. She uses $\frac{1}{2}$ of a roll of red ribbon and $\frac{1}{8}$ of a roll of blue ribbon. How much more red ribbon than blue ribbon does Marla use?

$$\frac{1}{2} - \frac{1}{8} = \square$$

Step 1
Find equivalent fractions with the same denominator.

$$\frac{1}{2} = \frac{1 \times 4}{2 \times 4} = \frac{4}{8}$$
$$-\frac{1}{8} = \quad\quad = \frac{1}{8}$$

Step 2
Subtract.

$$\frac{1}{2} = \frac{4}{8}$$
$$-\frac{1}{8} = \frac{1}{8}$$
$$\frac{3}{8}$$

Marla uses $\frac{3}{8}$ of a roll more red ribbon.

Find $\frac{4}{5} - \frac{2}{4}$.

$$\frac{4}{5} = \frac{4 \times 4}{5 \times 4} = \frac{16}{20}$$
$$-\frac{2}{4} = \frac{2 \times 5}{4 \times 5} = \frac{10}{20}$$

$$\frac{4}{5} = \frac{16}{20}$$
$$-\frac{2}{4} = \frac{10}{20}$$
$$\frac{6}{20}$$

Write the answer in lowest terms.

Think

$$\frac{6}{20} = \frac{6 \div 2}{20 \div 2} = \frac{3}{10} \qquad \frac{6}{20} = \frac{3}{10}$$

CLASSWORK

Complete. Write each difference in lowest terms.

1. $\frac{1}{2} = \frac{1 \times 2}{2 \times 2} = \frac{2}{\square}$
   $-\frac{1}{4} \qquad = \frac{1}{4}$

2. $\frac{2}{3} = \frac{2 \times 2}{3 \times 2} = \frac{4}{\square}$
   $-\frac{1}{2} = \frac{1 \times 3}{2 \times 3} = \frac{3}{\square}$

3. $\frac{1}{3}$
   $-\frac{1}{6}$

4. $\frac{5}{6}$
   $-\frac{1}{2}$

5. $\frac{7}{10}$
   $-\frac{1}{2}$

6. $\frac{3}{4}$
   $-\frac{1}{3}$

7. $\frac{7}{8}$
   $-\frac{3}{4}$

8. $\frac{4}{9}$
   $-\frac{1}{3}$

Complete. Write each difference in lowest terms.

1. $\dfrac{1}{3} = \dfrac{1 \times 2}{3 \times 2} = \dfrac{\square}{6}$

   $-\dfrac{1}{6} \qquad\quad = \dfrac{1}{6}$

2. $\dfrac{5}{8} \qquad\qquad = \dfrac{5}{8}$

   $-\dfrac{1}{2} = \dfrac{1 \times 4}{2 \times 4} = \dfrac{\square}{8}$

3. $\dfrac{1}{2}$
   $-\dfrac{3}{8}$

4. $\dfrac{2}{3}$
   $-\dfrac{1}{9}$

5. $\dfrac{11}{12}$
   $-\dfrac{1}{3}$

6. $\dfrac{6}{8}$
   $-\dfrac{3}{4}$

7. $\dfrac{5}{6}$
   $-\dfrac{1}{12}$

8. $\dfrac{6}{8}$
   $-\dfrac{1}{2}$

9. $\dfrac{9}{10}$
   $-\dfrac{1}{5}$

10. $\dfrac{6}{8}$
    $-\dfrac{1}{4}$

11. $\dfrac{7}{12}$
    $-\dfrac{1}{2}$

12. $\dfrac{5}{6}$
    $-\dfrac{1}{2}$

13. $\dfrac{2}{3}$
    $-\dfrac{3}{9}$

14. $\dfrac{2}{3}$
    $-\dfrac{5}{9}$

★ 15. $1 - \dfrac{1}{2} - \dfrac{1}{3} = \square$

★ 16. $1 - \dfrac{1}{4} - \dfrac{1}{3} = \square$

★ 17. $1 - \dfrac{1}{2} - \dfrac{2}{5} = \square$

APPLICATION

18. Joan used colored paper to make props for the play. She used $\dfrac{1}{3}$ of a package of green and $\dfrac{1}{6}$ of a package of blue. How much more green did she use?

19. Bob used $\dfrac{1}{8}$ of a package of red paper for props. Helen used $\dfrac{3}{4}$ of the same package. What part of the package of red paper was used?

20. The scenery includes a fireplace that is $2\dfrac{1}{2}$ yards wide. Roy put a light every $\dfrac{1}{2}$ yard across the top. How many lights did he use? Use a model.

★ 21. Rita, Jessica, and Ashawn are the only characters in the first scene. Rita has $\dfrac{1}{3}$ of the lines. Jessica has $\dfrac{1}{6}$ of the lines. What fractional part of the lines does Ashawn have?

LOGICAL THINKING

José, Pilar, and Marta practiced for the school play. José practiced for $\dfrac{1}{2}$ of an hour. Pilar practiced for $\dfrac{1}{4}$ of an hour less than José.

Marta practiced for $\dfrac{1}{2}$ of an hour more than Pilar.

How long did Marta practice?

Problem Solving

SKILLS AND STRATEGIES REVIEW A Parade

Every spring, Della, Stuart, and Richie work on the Hospital Day Parade. This spring they helped make the floats.

Use the chart to solve each problem.

Float	Time of Arrival	Performance Time
King Neptune	8:05	14 minutes
Jolly Roger	8:19	
Royal Court	8:31	16 minutes
Ragtime Band	8:47	11 minutes

1. At what time does the Royal Court arrive?

2. At what time does the Ragtime Band finish its performance?

3. How long does the Jolly Roger perform?

4. How long does it take all four floats to perform?

Solve.

5. Della and Stuart bought balloons. They spent a total of $12. Stuart spent $\frac{1}{2}$ as much as Della. How much money did each of them spend?

6. The three children tossed a football after they worked on the floats. Each one tossed the ball to the other two. How many times was the football tossed?

7. Richie worked on making the flowers for the Royal Court float for $3\frac{1}{4}$ hours. Then he worked on the leaves for $2\frac{1}{4}$ hours. How many hours did he work in all?

★ 8. Della used $\frac{3}{8}$ package of pink paper. Stuart used $\frac{1}{8}$ package of pink paper. What fractional part of the pink paper was not used?

A fact is missing in each problem. Choose the fact needed from the list at the right. Then solve the problem.

Problems

Facts

9. The parade started at 10:30 A.M. How long did it last?

a. He started at 4:00 P.M.

10. Stuart spent $3\frac{1}{2}$ hours making a costume for the Jolly Roger float. What time did he finish?

b. He spent $\frac{1}{4}$ of his time working on the stripes.

11. Richie made a crown of flowers. He started at 9:00 A.M. When did he finish?

c. The parade ended at 12:30 P.M.

12. Stuart worked on the stars of the flag on the King Neptune float for $\frac{1}{2}$ of the time. What fractional part of Stuart's time was spent working on the stars and stripes of the flag?

d. He worked for 4 hours.

===== SOMETHING EXTRA =====

Lucky L

This is a game for two players.

Here are the rules.

1. Decide who will go first.

2. Players take turns. At each turn, a player must decide to color 1, 2, or 3 spaces.

3. The player who gets the last space loses.

Make a copy of the game board. Decide on a plan and follow it. If your plan does not work, try again with another plan.

Start →

Last Space ↓

CHAPTER REVIEW

Add. Write each sum in lowest terms. pages 322–327

1. $\frac{1}{3} + \frac{1}{3} = \square$

2. $\frac{3}{7} + \frac{3}{7} = \square$

3. $\frac{3}{10} + \frac{2}{10} = \square$

4. $\begin{array}{r} \frac{5}{8} \\ +\frac{3}{8} \\ \hline \end{array}$

5. $\begin{array}{r} \frac{3}{6} \\ +\frac{4}{6} \\ \hline \end{array}$

6. $\begin{array}{r} \frac{2}{5} \\ +\frac{1}{5} \\ \hline \end{array}$

7. $\begin{array}{r} \frac{2}{7} \\ +\frac{6}{7} \\ \hline \end{array}$

8. $\begin{array}{r} \frac{1}{10} \\ +\frac{5}{10} \\ \hline \end{array}$

9. $\begin{array}{r} \frac{5}{6} \\ +\frac{1}{6} \\ \hline \end{array}$

Subtract. Write each difference in lowest terms. pages 322–327

10. $\frac{3}{8} - \frac{2}{8} = \square$

11. $\frac{4}{8} - \frac{2}{8} = \square$

12. $\frac{7}{10} - \frac{4}{10} = \square$

13. $\frac{7}{12} - \frac{6}{12} = \square$

14. $\frac{4}{9} - \frac{1}{9} = \square$

15. $\frac{11}{12} - \frac{5}{12} = \square$

Add or subtract. Write each answer in lowest terms. pages 330–331

16. $\begin{array}{r} 5\frac{2}{4} \\ +3\frac{1}{4} \\ \hline \end{array}$

17. $\begin{array}{r} 3\frac{1}{8} \\ +2\frac{5}{8} \\ \hline \end{array}$

18. $\begin{array}{r} 5\frac{5}{12} \\ -5\frac{4}{12} \\ \hline \end{array}$

19. $\begin{array}{r} 8\frac{5}{12} \\ -\frac{3}{12} \\ \hline \end{array}$

20. $\begin{array}{r} 3\frac{1}{2} \\ -1\frac{1}{2} \\ \hline \end{array}$

21. $\begin{array}{r} 6\frac{1}{4} \\ +3\frac{1}{4} \\ \hline \end{array}$

Add. Write each sum in lowest terms. pages 332–333

22. $\begin{array}{r} \frac{1}{2} \\ +\frac{1}{8} \\ \hline \end{array}$

23. $\begin{array}{r} \frac{1}{2} \\ +\frac{2}{8} \\ \hline \end{array}$

24. $\begin{array}{r} \frac{1}{2} \\ +\frac{1}{4} \\ \hline \end{array}$

25. $\begin{array}{r} \frac{2}{3} \\ +\frac{1}{9} \\ \hline \end{array}$

26. $\begin{array}{r} \frac{1}{4} \\ +\frac{1}{12} \\ \hline \end{array}$

27. $\begin{array}{r} \frac{1}{3} \\ +\frac{1}{2} \\ \hline \end{array}$

Subtract. Write each difference in lowest terms. pages 334–335

28. $\begin{array}{r} \frac{7}{12} \\ -\frac{2}{12} \\ \hline \end{array}$

29. $\begin{array}{r} \frac{6}{8} \\ -\frac{3}{4} \\ \hline \end{array}$

30. $\begin{array}{r} \frac{1}{2} \\ -\frac{1}{4} \\ \hline \end{array}$

31. $\begin{array}{r} \frac{2}{3} \\ -\frac{1}{9} \\ \hline \end{array}$

32. $\begin{array}{r} \frac{9}{10} \\ -\frac{1}{5} \\ \hline \end{array}$

33. $\begin{array}{r} \frac{5}{6} \\ -\frac{1}{12} \\ \hline \end{array}$

Solve. pages 328–329, 336–337

34. Joan planted $\frac{1}{3}$ of her garden with string beans and $\frac{1}{6}$ with cucumbers. What part of her garden was planted with string beans or cucumbers?

35. Terry put string along each row in his garden. Each row is 3 yards long. He put a stick every $\frac{1}{2}$ yard. How many sticks did he use for each row?

Add. Write each sum in lowest terms.

1. $\frac{3}{5} + \frac{1}{5} = \square$ 　　　　2. $\frac{1}{3} + \frac{1}{3} = \square$ 　　　　3. $\frac{1}{4} + \frac{1}{4} = \square$

4. $\frac{7}{10} + \frac{3}{10} = \square$ 　　　5. $\frac{3}{7} + \frac{5}{7} = \square$ 　　　6. $\frac{1}{3} + \frac{2}{9} = \square$

7. $\begin{array}{r} \frac{2}{7} \\ + \frac{3}{7} \\ \hline \end{array}$ 　　8. $\begin{array}{r} \frac{3}{8} \\ + \frac{5}{8} \\ \hline \end{array}$ 　　9. $\begin{array}{r} \frac{1}{6} \\ + \frac{1}{6} \\ \hline \end{array}$ 　　10. $\begin{array}{r} \frac{7}{9} \\ + \frac{7}{9} \\ \hline \end{array}$ 　　11. $\begin{array}{r} \frac{1}{2} \\ + \frac{1}{4} \\ \hline \end{array}$ 　　12. $\begin{array}{r} \frac{2}{3} \\ + \frac{1}{6} \\ \hline \end{array}$

Subtract. Write each difference in lowest terms.

13. $\frac{5}{7} - \frac{2}{7} = \square$ 　　　　14. $\frac{4}{10} - \frac{1}{10} = \square$ 　　　15. $\frac{5}{6} - \frac{1}{6} = \square$

16. $\frac{2}{3} - \frac{1}{3} = \square$ 　　　　17. $\frac{5}{9} - \frac{2}{9} = \square$ 　　　18. $\frac{1}{2} - \frac{1}{8} = \square$

19. $\begin{array}{r} \frac{4}{5} \\ - \frac{3}{5} \\ \hline \end{array}$ 　　20. $\begin{array}{r} \frac{7}{10} \\ - \frac{2}{10} \\ \hline \end{array}$ 　　21. $\begin{array}{r} \frac{3}{4} \\ - \frac{1}{4} \\ \hline \end{array}$ 　　22. $\begin{array}{r} \frac{2}{5} \\ - \frac{1}{10} \\ \hline \end{array}$ 　　23. $\begin{array}{r} \frac{1}{2} \\ - \frac{1}{4} \\ \hline \end{array}$ 　　24. $\begin{array}{r} \frac{5}{12} \\ - \frac{1}{3} \\ \hline \end{array}$

Add or subtract. Write each answer in lowest terms.

25. $\begin{array}{r} 5\frac{2}{3} \\ - 2\frac{1}{3} \\ \hline \end{array}$ 　　26. $\begin{array}{r} 6\frac{3}{8} \\ + 1\frac{2}{8} \\ \hline \end{array}$ 　　27. $\begin{array}{r} 4\frac{5}{7} \\ - 3\frac{4}{7} \\ \hline \end{array}$ 　　28. $\begin{array}{r} 2\frac{5}{9} \\ + 3\frac{1}{9} \\ \hline \end{array}$ 　　29. $\begin{array}{r} 5\frac{3}{4} \\ - 1\frac{2}{4} \\ \hline \end{array}$

30. $4\frac{5}{8} - 2\frac{1}{8} = \square$ 　　　　　31. $3\frac{1}{6} + 5\frac{3}{6} = \square$

Solve.

32. It took Joseph $\frac{3}{4}$ of an hour to rake the front yard. He spent $\frac{1}{2}$ of an hour raking the back yard. How much more time did he spend in the front yard?

33. The road to the beach had a sign every $\frac{1}{4}$ mile for a distance of 2 miles. How many signs were there? (Include both ends.)

Justin needs $\frac{1}{2}$ of a cup and $\frac{2}{3}$ of a cup of milk for cooking. There are $1\frac{1}{2}$ cups of milk left in a container. Is there enough milk for Justin?

STRING ART

The design you see on the right
was made by using thread to match
pairs of fractions. Each pair of
fractions has a sum of 1.

Create your own string art by
finding the design in the grid below.

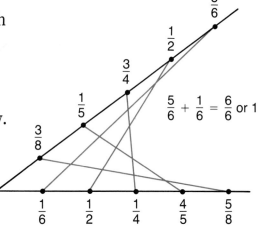

$$\frac{5}{6} + \frac{1}{6} = \frac{6}{6} \text{ or } 1$$

This is what you need:

- a piece of cardboard
- a piece of tracing paper
- transparent tape
- 1 pushpin or tack
- a strong needle and colored thread

This is what you do:

1. Trace the grid on tracing paper.

2. Tape the paper to cardboard.

3. Use the pushpin to make holes at
   each dot.

4. Stitch thread through the holes.
   Connect each pair of fractions that
   has a sum of 1.

Do you see a curve in the design?
That curve is called a **parabola.**

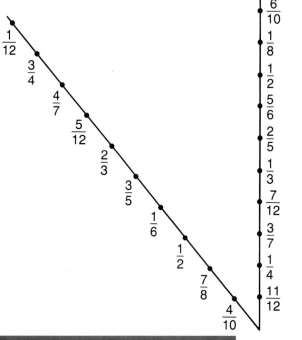

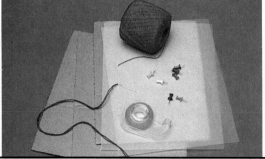

FRACTION PUZZLES

Each puzzle piece has a value. Add the value of the pieces to name the puzzle. Use a fraction or a mixed number.

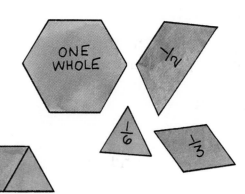

This puzzle has two pieces.

To find the sum, add the value of each of the pieces.

$$\frac{1}{3} \quad + \quad \frac{1}{6} \quad = \quad \frac{1}{6} \; \frac{1}{6} \; \frac{1}{6} \quad = \quad \frac{1}{2}$$

$$\frac{2}{6} + \frac{1}{6} \qquad\qquad \frac{3}{6}, \text{or } \frac{1}{2}$$

Solve each puzzle.

1.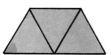

2.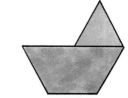

3.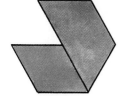

4.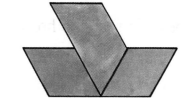

5.

6.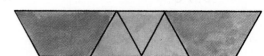

Try the following activities.

7. Make three different puzzles that show 1 whole.

8. Make other puzzles for a friend to solve.

COMPUTERS IN ART

Mrs. Smith needs to design a new painting. She uses a computer to help her. This way she does not make many sketches.

Today many artists use computers to help them with their work. Pictures made by a computer are called computer graphics. These are used in advertisements, exhibits, and films.

Movies can also use computers. Characters in the film may be designed and moved by the computer. The computer can do this much faster than a person can. The computer can also create special effects using color, lights, or sound.

Computers are also used by sculptors. The machines can help the sculptor design and change a shape. The computer can show pictures of the shape from different angles. All this helps the sculptor to create an original masterpiece.

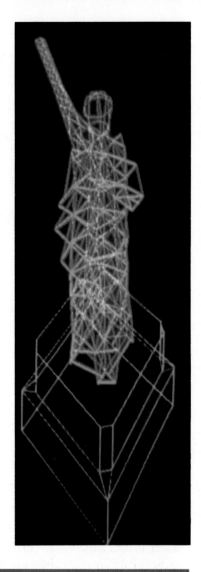

Computers are used by musicians. Electronic music is becoming very popular. Compositions are created using new pitch, tone, and volume. Sheet music can also be made by the computer.

Dancers use computers to form new dances. The computer can show the position and movement for each dancer.

PROJECTS

1. Make a list of movies that you think have used computer technology. Discuss your list in class.

2. Collect pictures from magazines and newspapers that show computer graphics. Make a bulletin board display for your collection.

3. Bring to class a record that uses electronic music. Listen to the record carefully. Compare that music with other records that do not use computers.

MAINTAINING SKILLS

Choose the correct answer. Write A, B, C, or D.

1. $9 \times \$4.53 = \square$

   A $40.77   C $36.27

   B $40.57   D not given

2. $411 \div 4 = \square$

   A 102 R3   C 102

   B 12 R3   D not given

3. $22 \times 324 = \square$

   A 1,296   C 7,088

   B 7,128   D not given

4. $325 \div 48 = \square$

   A 8 R5   C 6 R37

   B 7 R45   D not given

5. $\$9.28 \div 29 = \square$

   A $.30   C $32.00

   B $.32   D not given

6. What fraction is equivalent to $\frac{2}{3}$?

   A $\frac{6}{12}$ C $\frac{6}{9}$

   B $\frac{7}{21}$ D not given

7. Compare. $\frac{9}{10} \; \bullet \; \frac{1}{3}$

   A $<$ C $=$

   B $>$ D not given

8. What is the decimal for $3\frac{15}{100}$?

   A 0.315   C 3.15

   B 0.15   D not given

9. $\frac{2}{7} + \frac{3}{7} = \square$

   A $\frac{5}{7}$ C $\frac{6}{7}$

   B $\frac{5}{14}$ D not given

10. $5\frac{4}{10} - 2\frac{1}{10} = \square$

    A $3\frac{1}{2}$ C $3\frac{1}{10}$

    B $3\frac{1}{5}$ D not given

11. $\frac{2}{3} + \frac{1}{6} = \square$

    A $\frac{5}{6}$ C $\frac{1}{2}$

    B $\frac{1}{3}$ D not given

Solve.

12. Lisa used $\frac{7}{2}$ cups of flour while baking. What mixed number shows the amount of flour used?

    A $7\frac{1}{2}$ C $2\frac{1}{7}$

    B $3\frac{1}{2}$ D not given

13. Warren bought 12 apples. He used $\frac{1}{2}$ of them to make an apple pie. How many apples did Warren use to make the pie?

    A 2   C 6

    B 4   D not given

Theme: Pastimes

Fractions of an Inch

Rita made a spinner for a game.
How many inches long is the pointer?

The **inch (in.)** is a unit of length in
the **customary system of measurement.**
It is used to measure short lengths.

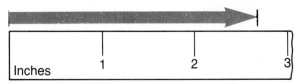

The pointer is between 2 inches
and 3 inches long. It is closer to
3 inches long. It is 3 inches long
to the nearest inch.

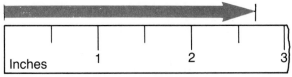

The pointer is $2\frac{1}{2}$ inches long to the
nearest $\frac{1}{2}$ inch.

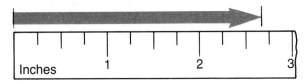

The pointer is $2\frac{3}{4}$ inches long to the
nearest $\frac{1}{4}$ inch.

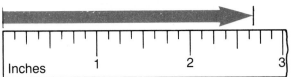

The pointer is $2\frac{5}{8}$ inches long to the
nearest $\frac{1}{8}$ inch.

CLASSWORK

Estimate the length of each. Then measure each.

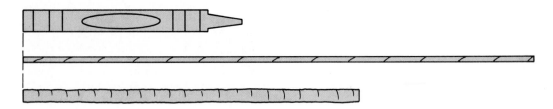

1. crayon to the nearest inch

2. crayon to the nearest $\frac{1}{2}$ inch

3. string to the nearest $\frac{1}{2}$ inch

4. pipe cleaner to the nearest inch

Measure each length to a smaller unit.

5. crayon in 1. to the nearest $\frac{1}{8}$ inch

6. pipe cleaner in 4. to the nearest $\frac{1}{4}$ inch

Estimate each length to the nearest inch.
Then measure each.

1.    2.

Estimate each length to the nearest $\frac{1}{2}$ inch.
Then measure each.

3.   4.

5.

Measure each length to the nearest $\frac{1}{4}$ inch.

6.   7.

Measure each length to the nearest $\frac{1}{8}$ inch.

8. your pencil   9. your pen   10. your math book

Draw a bar of each length.

11. $7\frac{1}{2}$ inches   12. $4\frac{3}{4}$ inches   13. $6\frac{7}{8}$ inches

Compare. Use >, <, or = for ●.

★ 14. $6\frac{3}{4}$ in. ● $6\frac{5}{8}$ in.   ★ 15. $4\frac{1}{2}$ in. ● $4\frac{2}{4}$ in.   ★ 16. $\frac{1}{16}$ in. ● $\frac{1}{8}$ in.

APPLICATION

VISUAL THINKING

Which pencil is longer?

Foot, Yard, and Mile

A football is about 12 inches long.
A football field is 100 yards long.

The **foot (ft), yard (yd),** and **mile (mi)** are units used to measure length.

12 inches	= 1 foot
36 inches	= 1 yard
3 feet	= 1 yard
5,280 feet	= 1 mile
1,760 yards	= 1 mile

A fast walker can walk 1 mile in about 20 minutes.

▶To change to a smaller unit, multiply.

3 ft = ___ in.

Think 1 ft = 12 in.

$$\begin{array}{r} 12 \\ \times\ 3 \\ \hline 36 \end{array}$$

3 ft = 36 in.

▶To change to a larger unit, divide.

72 in. = ___ yd

Think 36 in. = 1 yd

$$\begin{array}{r} 2 \\ 36\overline{)72} \\ -72 \\ \hline 0 \end{array}$$

72 in. = 2 yd

CLASSWORK

Choose foot, yard, or mile to measure each.

1. length of a room

2. height of a person

3. length of a sailboat

4. distance from Ohio to Utah

Estimate and measure each to the nearest foot.

5. height of a classmate

6. length of the chalkboard

Complete.

7. 12 in. = ___ ft

8. 24 in. = ___ ft

9. 1 yd = ___ ft

Choose foot, yard, or mile to measure each.

1. height of a door

2. length of your leg

3. distance across your state

4. length of a tennis court

Choose the best answer for each.

5. Jason's pogo stick is __ long.

 a. 8 ft   b. 1 yd   c. 10 in.

6. Sharon walked __ in 45 minutes.

 a. 2 mi   b. 200 yd   c. 6 ft

Complete.

7. 2 yd = __ ft

8. 36 in. = __ yd

9. 12 ft = __ yd

10. 108 in. = __ yd

11. 3 ft = __ in.

12. 3,520 yd = __ mi

Estimate and measure each to the nearest foot.

13. height of a door

14. height of your desk

Compare. Use >, <, or = for ●.

15. 1,760 yd ● 5,280 ft   ★16. 6 yd, 1 foot ● 20 ft   ★17. 2 ft, 5 in. ● 22 in.

APPLICATION

18. Susan needs a room 25 feet long to make a shuffleboard court. The garage is 9 yards long. Is the garage long enough?

19. Larry wants to plant bulbs along 1 yard of his garden. The bulbs are to be planted 9 inches apart. How many bulbs can Larry plant? Use a model to solve.

★20. Cora can ride a bicycle 6 miles an hour. How long will she take to go the 1,760 yards to school?

════ LOGICAL THINKING ════

Fred has one green, one red, and one blue crayon. The longest crayon is $4\frac{3}{4}$ inches long. The blue one is $\frac{3}{4}$ of an inch longer than the shortest crayon. The green one is $2\frac{3}{4}$ inches longer than the red one. How long is each crayon?

Ounce, Pound, and Ton

Jane likes to bake bread with her father. A loaf of baked bread weighs about 1 pound.

The **ounce (oz), pound (lb),** and **ton (T)** are customary units used to measure weight.

16 ounces = 1 pound
2,000 pounds = 1 ton

about 1 ounce

about 1 pound

about 2 tons

▶To change to a smaller unit, multiply.

2 lb = ___ oz

Think   1 lb = 16 oz
$$\begin{array}{r} 16 \\ \times\ 2 \\ \hline 32 \end{array}$$

2 lb = 32 oz

▶To change to a larger unit, divide.

48 oz = ___ lb

Think   16 oz = 1 lb
$$\begin{array}{r} 3 \\ 16)\overline{48} \\ -48 \\ \hline 0 \end{array}$$

48 oz = 3 lb

CLASSWORK

Choose ounce, pound, or ton to weigh each.

1.

2.

3.

Complete the table.

		4.	5.	6.	7.	8.	9.	10.	11.	12.
Pounds	1	2	3	4	5	6	7	8	9	10
Ounces	16									

Choose ounce, pound, or ton to weigh each.

1.  2.   3.

Choose the best answer for each.

4. An elephant weighs about ___.

   a. 75 lb   **b.** 2 T   **c.** 350 oz

5. A stick of butter weighs about ___.

   a. 4 oz   **b.** 2 lb   **c.** 1 T

Complete.

6. 3 lb = ___ oz

7. 64 oz = ___ lb

8. 4,000 lb = ___ T

9. ___ lb = 96 oz

10. 3 T = ___ lb

11. 8 lb = ___ oz

12. 32 oz = ___ lb

13. 5 lb = ___ oz

14. 144 oz = ___ lb

Compare. Write >, <, or = for ●.

15. 9,000 lb ● 4 T

16. 7 lb ● 128 oz

17. 160 oz ● 10 lb

★**18.** 1 lb 3 oz ● 21 oz

★**19.** 2 lb 6 oz ● 36 oz

★**20.** $\frac{1}{4}$ lb ● 4 oz

APPLICATION

21. José uses 4 ounces of butter for 1 pan of cornbread. How many pans of cornbread can he make with 2 pounds of butter?

★**22.** Edwina buys 5 pounds of chicken for $7.50. How many 8-ounce servings of chicken can she get from 5 pounds? What is the cost of each serving?

=== MENTAL ARITHMETIC ===

20 ounces equals how many pounds and ounces?

Think 16 oz = 1 lb
       20 − 16 = 4, so 20 oz = 1 lb 4 oz

How many pounds and ounces is each of these?

Think 32 oz = 2 lb   48 oz = 3 lb   64 oz = 4 lb

1. 33 oz   **2.** 50 oz   **3.** 24 oz   **4.** 67 oz

Cup, Pint, Quart, and Gallon

Mike was making a papier mâché piñata. He used 2 cups of water to make the paste.

The **cup (c)**, **pint (pt)**, **quart (qt)**, and **gallon (gal)** are units used to measure liquids.

2 cups = 1 pint   **2 pints = 1 quart**   **4 quarts = 1 gallon**

▶To change to a smaller unit, multiply.

2 pt = ___ c

Think 1 pt = 2 c
         2 × 2 = 4

2 pt = 4 c

▶To change to a larger unit, divide.

8 qt = ___ gal

Think 4 qt = 1 gal
         8 ÷ 4 = 2

8 qt = 2 gal

CLASSWORK

Choose cup, pint, quart, or gallon to measure each.

1.
2.
3.

Complete each table.

		4.	5.
Pints	1	2	3
Cups	2		

		6.	7.
Quarts	1		
Pints	2	4	6

Choose cup, pint, quart, or gallon to measure each.

1.

2.

3.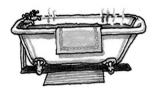

4. the amount of paint needed to paint your classroom

5. the amount of milk needed for a bowl of cereal

6. the amount of lemonade to serve your class

Complete the table.

		7.	8.	9.	10.	11.
Gallons	1	2	3	4	5	6
Quarts	4					

Complete.

12. 4 pt = ___ qt

13. 12 qt = ___ gal

14. 8 c = ___ pt

15. ___ qt = 6 gal

★16. ___ c = 3 qt

★17. ___ gal = 32 pt

APPLICATION

18. Melanie uses 1 cup of paint for ceramics every week. How many weeks will it take her to use 6 pints of paint?

★19. Each of 20 art students uses 2 cups of paint thinner a week. How many gallons of thinner should be ordered for 4 weeks?

CALCULATOR

A store owner pays $.84 for each quart of juice. He sells it for $1.29 per quart. Look at the sales table for 1 week.

	Mon.	Tues.	Wed.	Thurs.	Fri.	Sat.
Quarts of Juice Sold	63	52	48	73	60	84

1. How many gallons of juice were sold?

2. How much money did the store owner have left after paying for the juice?

Degree Fahrenheit

The temperature outside was 68°F, and there was a breeze. It was a good day to fly a kite.

The **degree Fahrenheit (°F)** is a customary unit used to measure temperature.

To read the temperature on a thermometer, look at the mark or number at the top of the red column.

- read   sixty-eight degrees Fahrenheit
- write   68°F

The Fahrenheit temperature on a very cold day might be −10°F.

- read   minus 10 degrees Fahrenheit, or 10 degrees Fahrenheit below zero
- write   −10°F

Each space on the thermometer shows 1°.

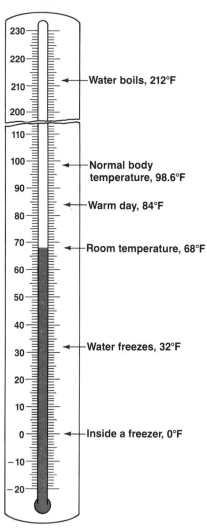

Water boils, 212°F

Normal body temperature, 98.6°F

Warm day, 84°F

Room temperature, 68°F

Water freezes, 32°F

Inside a freezer, 0°F

CLASSWORK

Use the thermometer above to answer these questions.

1. At what temperature does water boil?

2. At what temperature does water freeze?

3. What is normal body temperature?

4. Are you more likely to snow ski or go sailing if the temperature is 30°F?

Read and write each Fahrenheit temperature shown.

5.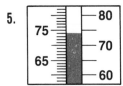

6.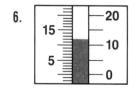

7.

PRACTICE

Read and write each Fahrenheit temperature shown.

1.

2.

Match the clothing with the most suitable temperature.

3. bathing suit   a. 75°F

4. T-shirt   b. 25°F

5. sweater   c. 85°F

6. winter jacket   d. 55°F

Find each missing number.

Rule: Subtract 6°.

	Input	Output
7.	70°F	
8.	108°F	
9.	6°F	

Find the rule.

★ 10.
Input	Output
56°F	65°F
−9°F	0°F
32°F	41°F

APPLICATION

11. The milk has to cool to 62°F before Kathy can make yogurt. If the temperature of the milk is 96°F, how many degrees does it have to fall?

★ 12. The temperature was 40°F when Jon went to sleep. In the morning there was ice in the birdbath. What is the least number of degrees the temperature could have fallen during the night?

Mixed Practice

1. $3.7 + 8.6 = \square$

2. $7.2 - 4.9 = \square$

3. $6.5 + 1.78 = \square$

4. $9.1 - 5.32 = \square$

5. $\frac{3}{5} + \frac{1}{5} = \square$

6. $\frac{7}{8} - \frac{3}{8} = \square$

7. $\begin{array}{r} 5\frac{3}{4} \\ -2\frac{2}{4} \\ \hline \end{array}$ 8. $\begin{array}{r} \frac{5}{7} \\ +\frac{4}{7} \\ \hline \end{array}$

9. $\begin{array}{r} 1\frac{1}{3} \\ +2\frac{1}{3} \\ \hline \end{array}$ 10. $\begin{array}{r} 4\frac{5}{6} \\ -1\frac{1}{6} \\ \hline \end{array}$

11. $\begin{array}{r} \frac{1}{4} \\ +\frac{1}{8} \\ \hline \end{array}$ 12. $\begin{array}{r} \frac{1}{2} \\ +\frac{1}{6} \\ \hline \end{array}$

13. $\begin{array}{r} \frac{2}{3} \\ -\frac{5}{9} \\ \hline \end{array}$ 14. $\begin{array}{r} \frac{5}{6} \\ -\frac{1}{3} \\ \hline \end{array}$

Compare. Use >, <, or = for ●.

15. $4.61 \, ● \, 4.08$

16. $3.79 \, ● \, 3.8$

17. $\frac{6}{7} \, ● \, \frac{5}{7}$

18. $\frac{3}{10} \, ● \, \frac{1}{2}$

19. $\frac{3}{4} \, ● \, \frac{6}{8}$

355

Problem Solving

PATTERNS

Carol uses 5 shells to make a game. She puts the number 1 on the first shell. The second shell has a 4, and the third has a 7. If Carol continues this pattern, what numbers will the last two shells have?

What is the question?

What numbers will the last two shells have?

What are the facts?

The numbers in the pattern are 1, 4, and 7.

How can the answer be found?

Find the rule for the pattern.
Find how you got from the first number in the pattern to the second number. See if this rule works for the rest of the pattern.

Carry out the plan to find the answer.

Each number is greater than the number before it.

$1 + \square = 4$ The rule could be Add 3.

$1 + 3 = 4$ and $4 + 3 = 7$.   The rule works.

So $7 + 3 = 10$ and $10 + 3 = 13$.

The last two shells will have the numbers 10 and 13 on them.

Check your answer. Did you follow the pattern?

The rule for the pattern is Add 3. The third shell had the number 7. The fourth shell would have $7 + 3$, or 10. The last shell would have $10 + 3$, or 13 on it. The answer is correct.

PRACTICE

Find the missing terms for each pattern.

1. 5, 10, 15, 20, _____, _____, 35

2. 12, 10, 8, 6, _____, _____

3. 3, 6, 12, 24, _____, _____

4. 37, 31, 25, 19, _____, _____

5. $\frac{1}{6}$, $\frac{2}{6}$, $\frac{3}{6}$, _____, _____

6. 3, 7, 12, 18, _____, _____

7. 50, 49, 47, 44, _____, _____

★8. A, C, F, J, _____, _____

Draw the next figure in each pattern.

9.

10.

Solve.

11. Bill used tiles to make a picture. He put 2 tiles in the first row and 4 tiles in the second. Then he put 6 tiles in the third row. If he continued this pattern, how many tiles were in the fifth row?

12. A scarf has 7 stripes. The first stripe is blue and the second is green. The pattern is repeated across the scarf. What color is the sixth stripe?

★13. In the game *Wizard* you get points for each star you collect. Jay collected 8 stars. Continue the table. Then find how many points Jay scored in all.

WIZARD SCORING	
Star Number	Point Value
1	1
2	3
3	6
4	10

CREATE YOUR OWN PROBLEM

Make up a pattern of numbers. Give it to a friend to find the next number in the pattern.

Experiments and Outcomes

In a game, players sometimes toss a coin to decide who goes first.

Tossing a coin is an **experiment**. There are 2 **possible outcomes**. The coin can land heads up or tails up.

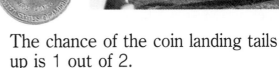

The **chance** of the coin landing heads up is 1 out of 2.

The chance of the coin landing tails up is 1 out of 2.

If you spin this spinner there are 4 possible outcomes. The spinner can stop on red, blue, green, or yellow.

The chance of the spinner stopping on one of these colors is 1 out of 4.

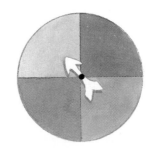

CLASSWORK

Use the box of marbles at the right to answer each question.

1. How many outcomes are possible if you pick one marble from the box?

2. What are the possible outcomes if you pick one marble from the box?

3. What is the chance of picking a blue marble?

4. What is the chance of picking a green marble?

5. Are the chances the same for each color marble in the box?

You spin each spinner once. How many possible outcomes are there for each? List the possible outcomes for each.

1.

2.

3.

The cards at the right are put in the paper bag. You pick one card out of the paper bag without looking.

4. How many possible outcomes are there?

5. List all the possible outcomes.

6. What is the chance of picking a green card?

7. What is the chance of picking a white card?

★ 8. What is the chance of picking a yellow card?

APPLICATION

9. The sides of a block are numbered 1, 2, 3, 4, 5, and 6. Tom tosses the block. What is the chance that the number 6 will land up?

10. Gina tosses the number block. Is the chance that the number 1 will land up the same as the chance that the number 4 will land up?

11. What pattern did Tyler use to put buttons in a box for an experiment? He chose 1 blue, 4 green, 8 red, and 13 white buttons. How many gold buttons did he choose next?

★ 12. Cindy picks a marble out of a jar. Her chances of picking a red marble are 2 out of 6. There are 6 marbles in the jar. How many red marbles are in the jar?

359

Exploring Outcomes

People who design games have to decide how to write rules to make the game fair. They examine all possible game outcomes when they write the rules.

Investigate what happens when you play this game five times.

Cup of Coins
A Game for 3 Players

RULES:

Decide who will be Player A, Player B, and Player C. Have one player keep score.

Place 2 pennies in a paper cup. Hold your hand over the cup. Shake the coins.

Remove your hand and look into the cup. Call out what you see.

Use the chart below to determine which player gets a point.

Take turns shaking the coins.

The first player to get 10 points wins the game. After each game, record whether Player A, Player B, or Player C is the winner.

"Cup of Coins" Game	
Outcomes	Points
2 heads	1 for Player A
2 tails	1 for Player B
1 head and 1 tail	1 for Player C

1. Compare your results with the results of other groups who played this game. In each group, did Player A, Player B, or Player C win the most games?

2. Combine the results for all of the games played in your class. Which player won the most games overall?

3. Discuss whether or not one player has a better chance of winning the "Cup of Coins" game. Explain why or why not.

4. Talk about the rules for the "Cup of Coins" game. Do you think the rules make the game fair for each player? Explain why or why not.

THINKING IT THROUGH

1. Place your hands palms down. Then place your hands palms up. Then place your left hand palm down and your right hand palm up.

   • Is there another way to show that one hand is palm down and the other hand is palm up? Explain.

   • Talk about how this activity is related to the outcomes for the "Cup of Coins" game.

2. There are different ways to write rules for the "Cup of Coins" game to make it fair for each player. Find different ways to assign points in the game. For each way that you find, write a set of rules that makes the game fair.

3. Make up a "Cup of Coins" game that uses three pennies. Investigate the outcomes of your game. Write a set of rules that makes your game fair.

Frequency Tables

In a game, Kevin used this spinner 30 times. The 3 possible outcomes are red, yellow, and blue. The chance, or **probability,** of the spinner stopping on red is 1 out of 3, or $\frac{1}{3}$.

Kevin used a table and **tally marks** to record the spins. Then he added the tally marks to show how often each outcome occurred. The **frequency** for the color red was 8.

Color	Tally	Frequency
red	~~HHt~~ |||	8
yellow	~~HHt~~ ~~HHt~~	10
blue	~~HHt~~ ~~HHt~~ ||	

| means 1 tally mark
~~HHt~~ means 5 tally marks

▶A frequency table shows how often each possible outcome occurs.

CLASSWORK

Use the frequency table above to answer each question.

1. What was the frequency for the color yellow?

2. What was the frequency for the color blue?

3. Which color had the highest frequency?

4. Which color had the lowest frequency?

Jack made a frequency table to record the results of tossing a letter cube.

FREQUENCY TABLE		
Letter	Tally	Frequency
A	~~HHt~~ II	7
B	~~HHt~~ ~~HHt~~	10
C	~~HHt~~ IIII	9
D	~~HHt~~ ~~HHt~~ II	12
E	~~HHt~~ ~~HHt~~ I	11
F	~~HHt~~ ~~HHt~~ I	11

Use the frequency table to answer each question.

1. How many possible outcomes are there?

2. What are the possible outcomes?

3. Which letter had the highest frequency?

4. Which letter had the lowest frequency?

5. What was the frequency of the outcome B?

6. What was the frequency of the outcome C?

7. How many times did Jack toss the letter cube?

8. What is the probability of the letter cube landing with the letter A up?

9. Is the probability the same for each letter?

★ 10. If you tossed the letter cube 30 times, what would you expect the frequency of each letter to be?

APPLICATION

Michelle tossed a coin 20 times.

Results of 20 Tosses
heads, heads, tails, tails, tails, heads, heads, tails, heads, heads, tails, heads, tails, tails, heads, heads, tails, heads, heads, tails

11. Make a frequency table showing the results of the 20 tosses.

12. Which outcome had the highest frequency?

13. Toss a coin 20 times. Record your results in a frequency table. Compare your results with Michelle's results.

★ 14. What would you expect the frequency of heads to be if you tossed a coin 100 times?

363

Problem Solving

SKILLS AND STRATEGIES REVIEW Hobbies

The Youth Club held a 10-mile BIKE–A–THON around the park. It was to raise money for the Children's Hospital. The table shows the distance each member rode.

Name	Number of Miles
Andrea	ЖЖ ЖЖ
Adam	ЖЖ II
Michael	III
Lucille	ЖЖ II
Danielle	ЖЖ III
Scott	ЖЖ ЖЖ

1. How many miles did Lucille ride?

2. How many more miles did Danielle ride than Michael?

3. How many miles in all did the club members ride?

4. Who completed the BIKE–A–THON?

5. Adam had pledges for each mile he rode. His pledges were $.50, $.20, $1.00, and $.37. How much was the total pledge per mile? How much did Adam earn?

6. Two other members of the Youth Club, Anita and Burt, earned $35 in pledges. Anita earned $7 more than Burt did. How much did she earn?

7. Danielle had pledges of $.13, $1.25, $.20, and $.50 per mile. How much did she earn?

8. Andrea, Michael, Lucille, and Scott earned a total of $64. What was the average amount earned by each?

9. The members wore either their blue, yellow, or green club shirt. What is the probability that Scott wore his green shirt?

★ 10. Andrea's math teacher pledged 1¢ the first mile, 2¢ the second, and 4¢ the third mile. The pattern would continue for each mile Andrea rode. How much did her math teacher pay?

Solve.

11. Vic collects coins. He had $3 worth of quarters. How many quarters did he have?

12. Vic had 4 more dimes than nickels. He had a total of 48 dimes and nickels. How many of each coin did Vic have?

13. Evangeline, Tony, and Mabel went fishing. By noon Evangeline had caught 8 fish. Tony had caught 14 fish, and Mabel had caught 12 fish. Which two people caught a total of 22 fish?

14. Mandy has 4 stamps, one each from China, Argentina, the United States, and England. She is putting them in a row on an album page. How many different ways can she arrange them?

You are cooking dinner for your family. It is to be served at 6:00 P.M. The menu and preparation times are shown in the table.

Menu	Preparation Time
Vegetable Soup (canned)	15 minutes
Roast Chicken	$1\frac{1}{2}$ hours
Baked Potatoes	1 hour
Broccoli (steamed)	12 minutes
Salad	25 minutes
Sliced Cantaloupe	10 minutes

15. What time should you start the chicken to have it ready by 6:00 P.M.?

16. The chicken and potatoes must be ready at the same time. What time should you start baking the potatoes?

17. What time should you begin preparing the salad?

18. What time should you start heating the soup?

19. List the order in which to prepare each dish.

Estimate and measure each length to the nearest inch and nearest $\frac{1}{2}$ inch. pages 346–347

1. ▭▭▭▭▭▭▭▭▭▭▭

2. ▭▭▭▭▭▭▭

Choose the best answer for each. pages 348–351

3. A piano is about ___ high.

   a. 4 ft   **b.** 3 yd   **c.** 5 in.

4. Your math book weighs about ___.

   a. 10 oz   **b.** 2 lb   **c.** 20 lb

Complete. pages 348–353

5. 2 ft = ___ in.

6. 15 ft = ___ yd

7. 3 lb = ___ oz

8. 3 pt = ___ c

9. 12 qt = ___ gal

10. 18 pt = ___ qt

Write each Fahrenheit temperature. pages 354–355

11.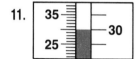

12.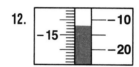

13.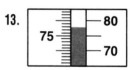

Use the spinner to answer each question. pages 358–363

14. How many possible outcomes are there?

15. What are the possible outcomes of a spin?

16. What is the probability of the spinner stopping on red?

17. What is the probability of the spinner stopping on green?

Use the frequency table to answer each question. pages 362–363

18. What is the frequency of the color black?

19. What color has the highest frequency?

Color	Tally	Frequency
black	ⅢⅢ ⅢⅢ	
orange	ⅢⅢ |||	8
purple	ⅢⅢ ⅢⅢ ||	12

Solve. pages 356–357, 364–365

20. A rug has 9 stripes. The first stripe is red and the second is white. If the pattern is repeated, what color is the eighth stripe?

21. Mrs. Cohen wants 2 gallons of juice. The juice comes in quart bottles. How many bottles of juice does Mrs. Cohen want?

Measure each length to the nearest inch and nearest $\frac{1}{4}$ inch.

1. ━━━━━━━━━━━━━━━━ 2. ━━━━━━━━

Choose the best answer for each.

3. A baseball bat is about ___ long.

   a. 1 ft   **b.** 1 yd   **c.** 1 in.

4. An apple weighs about ___.

   a. 2 lb   **b.** 5 oz   **c.** 1 T

Complete.

5. 36 in. = ___ ft

6. 4 yd = ___ ft

7. 32 oz = ___ lb

8. 4 qt = ___ pt

9. 2 gal = ___ qt

10. 12 c = ___ pt

Write each Fahrenheit temperature.

11.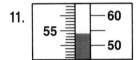

12.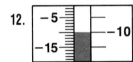

13.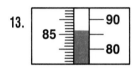

Use the spinner to answer each question.

14. How many possible letter outcomes are there?

15. What are the possible letter outcomes of a spin?

16. What is the probability of the spinner stopping on B?

Use the frequency table to answer each question.

17. What is the frequency of the color yellow?

18. Which color has the highest frequency?

Color	Tally	Frequency
pink	卌 卌 I	11
brown	卌 卌	10
yellow	卌 IIII	

Solve.

19. John wrote the pattern 20, 15, 11, 8, ___. Find the next number in his pattern.

20. How many 8-ounce servings are there in 2 pounds of meat?

Rachel is $5\frac{1}{2}$ feet tall. How many inches is this?

SPINNERS

You can find the frequency of an outcome. Make your own spinner and try this experiment.

This is what you need:

- a piece of white paper, 8 inches square
- red, blue, green, and yellow crayons
- a large paper clip
- a pencil

This is what you do:

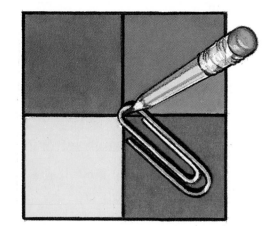

1. Fold the white paper in half along its length. Then fold it in half along its width.

2. Open the paper. You should see four squares.

3. Use the crayons to make each square a different color.

4. Copy this table.

Color	Tally Marks	Frequency
red		
blue		
green		
yellow		

5. Use the paper clip as a spinner. Hold it in place with the pencil point.

6. Spin the spinner 40 times and use tally marks to show the results.

What is the frequency of each outcome?

Compare your results with a classmate's results.

MARBLE MYSTERY

There were 10 marbles in a bag. A marble was picked from the bag and then returned. The color of the marble was recorded in the table. This was repeated 50 times.

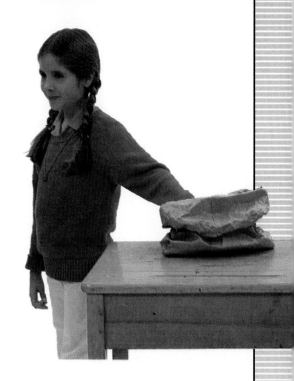

FREQUENCY TABLE		
Color	Tally	Frequency
blue	HHT HHT HHT	15
green	HHT HHT HHT HHT	20
red	HHT HHT	10
white	HHT	5

The frequency of blue was 15. You can use the table to estimate the probability of picking blue.

$$\frac{\text{frequency of blue}}{\text{total number of picks}} = \frac{15}{50} \longleftarrow \text{estimated probability}$$

Estimate the probability of picking

1. a green marble.   2. a red marble.   3. a white marble.

How many blue marbles do you think are in the bag? Use the estimated probability to help you make a good guess.

$\frac{15}{50} = \frac{3}{10}$, so 3 out of the 10 marbles are probably blue.

Guess that 3 marbles are blue.

4. How many marbles do you think there are of each color?

There is a better chance that there are more green marbles in the mystery bag. But until you see all the marbles you cannot be sure.

MAINTAINING SKILLS

Choose the correct answer. Write A, B, C, or D.

1. $\$7.00 - \$1.63 = \square$

   A $6.00   C $8.63

   B $5.37   D not given

2. $413 \div 4 = \square$

   A 103 R1   C 13 R1

   B 100 R13   D not given

3. $3.9 + 8.76 = \square$

   A 9.15   C 91.5

   B 4.86   D not given

4. Estimate.
$12 \times 58 = \square$

   A 600   C 500

   B 100   D not given

5. $169 \div 43 = \square$

   A 4 R9   C 4 R3

   B 3 R40   D not given

6. $\frac{3}{4} = \frac{3 \times 6}{4 \times 6} = \frac{\square}{24}$

   A 12   C 18

   B 6   D not given

7. What is the mixed number for $\frac{17}{6}$?

   A 2   C $2\frac{5}{6}$

   B 3   D not given

8. $1\frac{5}{8} + 1\frac{7}{8}$

   A $3\frac{1}{2}$ C $2\frac{1}{2}$

   B $2\frac{4}{8}$ D not given

9. $\frac{1}{2} + \frac{3}{4} = \square$

   A $1\frac{1}{2}$ C $\frac{1}{4}$

   B $1\frac{1}{4}$ D not given

10. Which unit would you use to measure the weight of a table?

   A ounce   C pound

   B ton   D not given

11. What is the chance of drawing a red marble from a bowl of marbles that has 1 red, 1 blue, 1 green?

   A 1 out of 3   C 2 out of 3

   B none   D not given

Solve.

12. John digs a hole for a fence post in 30 minutes. How far apart are the fence posts on this model?

   A 1 foot   C 5 feet

   B 4 feet   D not given

13. There was a road sign every $\frac{1}{2}$ mile for a distance of 3 miles. How many road signs were there?

   A 6   C 5

   B 7   D not given

Theme: Crafts

Space Figures

Daryl made a robot of papier-mâché.
Parts of the robot are shaped
like **space figures**.

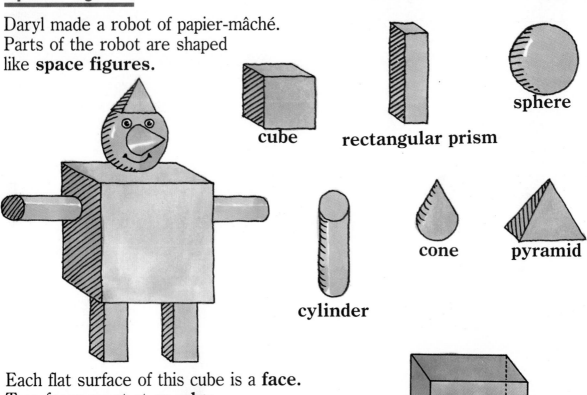

cube

rectangular prism

sphere

cylinder

cone

pyramid

Each flat surface of this cube is a **face**.
Two faces meet at an **edge**.
Edges meet at a **vertex**.

A cube has 6 faces, 12 edges, and 8 vertices.

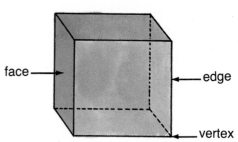

face

edge

vertex

CLASSWORK

Name the space figure suggested by each object.

1.

2.

3.

4.

Name the part shown by the arrow.

5.

6.

7.

8.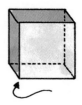

Name the space figure suggested by each object.

1.

2.

3.

4.

5.

6.

7.

8.

Copy and complete.

	Figure	Number of Faces	Number of Edges	Number of Vertices
9.		6		
10.				
11.				

Write _true_ or _false_ for each.

★ **12.** A sphere has no flat surfaces.

★ **13.** A cylinder and a cone have only curved surfaces.

APPLICATION

Daryl made this model of a town from papier-mâché.

14. What two space figures were used to make the town hall?

★ **15.** How many more vertices does the model of the town hall have than the model of the apartment building?

Polygons

Lee Ann dipped the sides of sponges into paint and printed these shapes. These shapes are examples of **plane figures.**

square

rectangle

triangle

A closed plane figure with straight sides is a **polygon.**
A polygon has 3 or more sides.
Two sides meet to form a vertex.

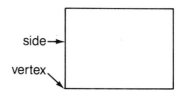

side→
vertex↘

A square has 4 equal sides and 4 vertices.
A rectangle has 4 sides and 4 vertices.
A triangle has 3 sides and 3 vertices.

Here are some other kinds of polygons.

quadrilateral
4 sides
4 vertices

pentagon
5 sides
5 vertices

hexagon
6 sides
6 vertices

octagon
8 sides
8 vertices

CLASSWORK

Name each polygon. How many sides does it have? How many vertices?

1.

2.

3.

4.

Name each polygon. How many sides does it have? How many vertices?

1.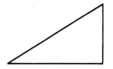

2.

3.

4.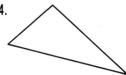

5.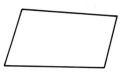

6.

7.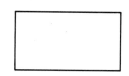

8.

9.

10.

11.

★ 12.

★ 13. A heptagon is a 7-sided plane figure. How many vertices does it have?

APPLICATION

14. Lee Ann used sponge printing to make a polygon. It had 4 sides and 4 vertices. What names could the polygon have?

★ 15. Lee Ann used sponge printing to make a 10-sided plane figure called a decagon. Draw a decagon. How many vertices does it have?

=== VISUAL THINKING ===

Joe cut out this pattern. He folded it along the dotted lines to make a space figure.

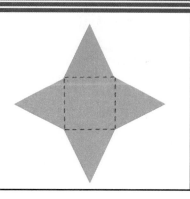

1. How many faces are triangles?

2. What other kind of polygon is a face?

3. How many faces does the space figure have?

4. What space figure did Joe make?

Points, Lines, and Line Segments

Maurice's kite shows some **geometric figures.** He attached the kite string at **point** A. He attached the kite tail at point C.

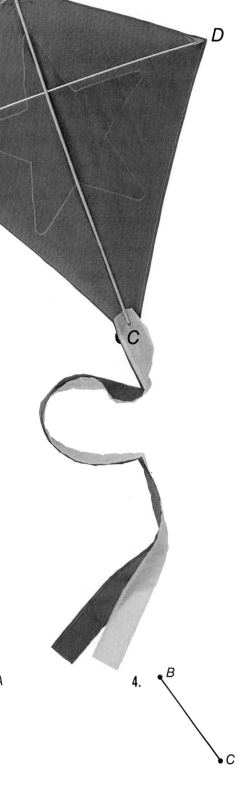

The kite frame is made of wood. One piece of the frame has **endpoints** B and D.

This drawing shows a **line segment** with endpoints B and D. A line segment is straight. It has 2 endpoints.

- read   line segment *BD* or line segment *DB*

- write $\overline{BD}$ or $\overline{DB}$

A **line** is also straight. It has no endpoints. A line goes on and on in both directions.

- read   line *AC* or line *CA*

- write $\overleftrightarrow{AC}$ or $\overleftrightarrow{CA}$

CLASSWORK

Name each figure.

1.

2.

3. • A

4.
B
↘
•C

376

Name each figure.

1. C   D

2. F   G

3. Q
    P

4. V
    W

5. • S

6. L   M

7. J
    K

8. T
    U

★ 9. How many line segments are there in this figure? Name the segments.

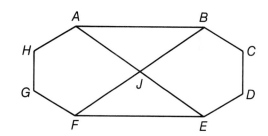

APPLICATION

Use the kite diagram on page 376.

10. Name all the line segments.

★ 11. Line segments *AC* and *BD* cross. They are **intersecting line segments.** Suppose point *E* is the point of intersection. How many more line segments can you name now?

═══ CALCULATOR ═══

Mr. Sumara walked from home to the bookstore, then to the laundry. Next he walked to the shoe store, to the grocery, and then back home.

1. How many line segments are used to draw the route he took?

2. How far did he walk in all?

3. Did he walk more or less than 1 kilometer?

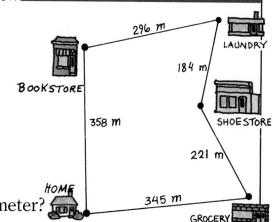

Rays and Angles

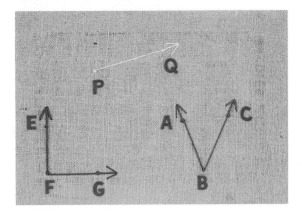

Craig used pins and yarn in his art project to show different geometric figures.

A **ray** is part of a line with one endpoint. It goes on and on in one direction. Name the endpoint first.

- read   ray *PQ*
- write $\overrightarrow{PQ}$

Two rays with the same endpoint form an **angle**.

- read   angle *ABC* or angle *CBA*
- write   ∠*ABC* or ∠*CBA*

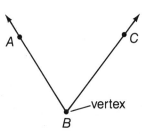

The endpoint of the two rays is the **vertex**. The vertex of ∠*ABC* is *B*.

An angle that forms a square corner is a **right angle**. In Craig's art project, ∠*EFG* is a right angle.

CLASSWORK

Name each figure.

1.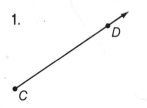

2.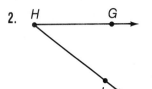

3.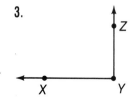

4.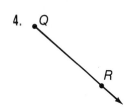

378

Name each figure.

1.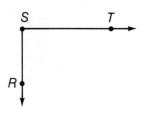

2.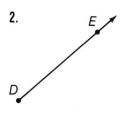

3.

4.

5.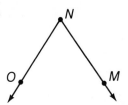

6.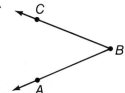

7.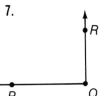

8.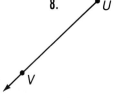

Use the figure to name each.

9. one line

10. four rays

11. two right angles

★ 12. five angles with vertex *B*

Write *true* **or** *false* **for each.**

13. The one-dollar bill has four right angles.

14. The stop sign has no right angles.

15. The clock has two right angles.

APPLICATION

16. Carolyn drew a square.

How many right angles does it have?

★ 17. Draw ray *XY*. Using endpoint *X* draw ray *XZ*. What figure have you drawn? Name it.

Congruent Figures

Gino is helping his mother make a pillow cover. He cuts out two pieces of material. The pieces are the same size and shape.

Congruent figures have the same size and shape. The figures in each pair are congruent.

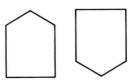

Congruent line segments have the same length.

To check whether two figures are congruent, trace one. Place your tracing over the other figure. Congruent figures will match exactly.

CLASSWORK

Are the two figures congruent? Write *yes* or *no*.

1.
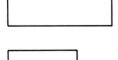

2.

3.

Are the two figures congruent? Write *yes* or *no*.

1.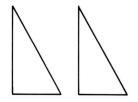

2.

3.

4.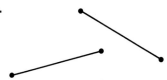

5.

6.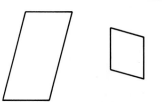

7. **Two of these figures are congruent.**
   Write the letters for the congruent figures.

a.   b.    c.   d. 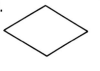   e.

Are all the sides of the polygon congruent?
Trace line segments to help you answer.

8.

9.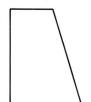

★ 10.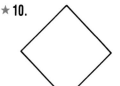

★ 11.

APPLICATION

=== VISUAL THINKING ===

Imagine that you cut each pattern and
folded it along dotted edges. Which patterns
make a cube with 6 congruent faces?

a. 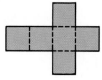   b. 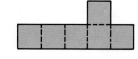   c.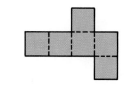

Symmetry

Some students folded paper, then cut designs to make decorations. The fold divides each design into two matching parts.

A **line of symmetry** divides a figure into two congruent parts.

A shape can have more than one line of symmetry.

Trace each figure. Fold it along any dotted line. The two parts match. Each of these dotted lines is a line of symmetry.

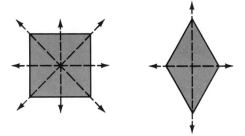

CLASSWORK

Is the dotted line a line of symmetry? Write *yes* or *no*.

1.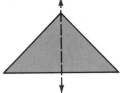

2.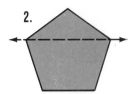

3.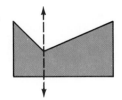

4.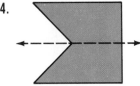

Is the dotted line a line of symmetry?

1.

2.
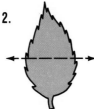

3.
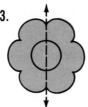

How many lines of symmetry does each figure have? Trace the figure. Then fold to help find the answer.

4.

5.

6.

7.

8.

9.

10.

★11.

★12.

APPLICATION

13. Lew cut out these letters from folded paper. What message did they spell when he unfolded the letters?

★14. Which letters in the message have more than 1 line of symmetry?

1. $\begin{array}{r} 379 \\ 481 \\ +65 \\ \hline \end{array}$

2. $\begin{array}{r} 8{,}023 \\ -479 \\ \hline \end{array}$

3. $\begin{array}{r} 631 \\ \times85 \\ \hline \end{array}$

4. $\begin{array}{r} \$32.95 \\ -16.89 \\ \hline \end{array}$

5. $\begin{array}{r} \$41.75 \\ +33.68 \\ \hline \end{array}$

6. $\begin{array}{r} \$9.65 \\ \times7 \\ \hline \end{array}$

7. $308 \div 7 = \square$

8. $640 \div 90 = \square$

9. $\$75.21 \div 3 = \square$

10. $16.3 + 8.4 = \square$

11. $9 - 0.75 = \square$

12. $279 \div 29 = \square$

13. $8.7 + 3.61 = \square$

14. $5.4 - 2.95 = \square$

15. $\frac{2}{7} + \frac{4}{7} = \square$

16. $\frac{8}{9} - \frac{2}{9} = \square$

17. $\frac{3}{4} + \frac{2}{4} = \square$

Problem Solving

FINDING ANOTHER WAY

Some problems can be solved in more than
one way. No matter how you solve it,
your answer should be the same.

Lynn made 3 shell necklaces. For each
one she used 2 pink shells and 4 white shells.
How many shells did she use in all?

One Way

Make a drawing to
show the necklaces.
Count the shells.

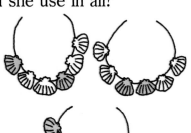

She used 18 shells.

Does each necklace have 2
pink shells and 4 white shells?
Yes. Check to see if you counted correctly.
Your answer is correct.

Another Way

Add to find the total number of shells
on each necklace.
Multiply by the number of necklaces.

Step 1 $2 + 4 = 6$ **Step 2** $3 \times 6 = 18$

She used 18 shells.

Are your answers the same? Check by finding
the sum of the number of pink shells and the
number of white shells she used.

Step 1 $3 \times 2 = 6$ pink shells   **Step 2** $12 + 6 = 18$ shells
$3 \times 4 = 12$ white shells

You solved the problem two different ways.
You checked the problem using a third way.
The answers are all the same.

Solve each problem in more than one way.

1. Ellen made 4 beaded bracelets. For each one she used 3 blue beads and 6 red beads. How many beads did she use in all?

2. Tom made 9 baskets. Three of them had handles. Four of them had tops. The rest were plain. How many were plain?

3. To make a jar of orange pottery glaze, Chris used 1 cup of red glaze and 2 cups of yellow glaze. How many cups of glaze does she need to make 4 jars of orange glaze?

4. Ellen ordered 6 packages of felt pieces. One package contained 2 green pieces and 4 blue pieces. How many pieces of felt did she order?

5. Chris expected to use 150 pounds of clay for a project. She used an average of 20 pounds per day for 6 days. How much more clay does she still have to use?

6. Ellen had a piece of wood 32 inches long. She cut off an 11-inch piece. How many 3-inch pieces can she make from the piece that is left?

★ 7. Tom worked on a leather belt for 30 minutes each morning and 45 minutes each evening. How long did he work on the belt each week?

★ 8. Clara made a quilt with 5 rows of flowers. The first row had 6 flowers and the second row had 7 flowers. The pattern is repeated. How many flowers are on the quilt?

═══ CREATE YOUR OWN PROBLEM ═══

The picture shows beaded necklaces. Write a problem that can be solved in more than one way. Solve the problem.

Circles

Rita and Dan painted the scenery for the class play. For the sun, they drew a circle. Rita found a point for the center of the circle. She held the string there with a thumbtack while Dan drew the circle.

All the points on a **circle** are the same distance from its center. A circle is named by its **center**.

▶ A **radius** is a line segment with one endpoint on the circle. The other endpoint is at the center.

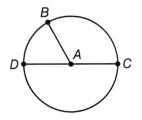

▶ A **diameter** is a line segment with both endpoints on the circle. A diameter always passes through the center of the circle.

A is the center of the circle. Points C, B, and D are on the circle.
$\overline{AB}$ is a radius.
$\overline{CD}$ is a diameter.

You can use a compass to draw a circle.

Step 1 Put the compass tip at a point to be the center.

Step 2 Open the compass to the length of the radius.

Step 3 Turn the compass to draw a circle with the attached pencil.

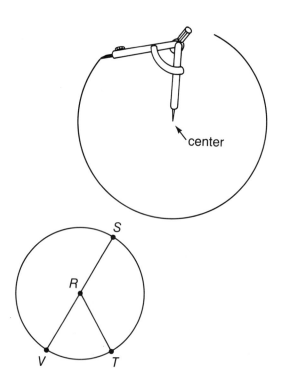

center

CLASSWORK

Use the drawing at the right.

1. Name the center of this circle.

2. Name a radius.

3. Name a diameter.

PRACTICE

Use the drawing at the right for 1-4.

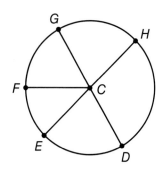

1. Name the center of this circle.

2. Name 4 points on the circle.

3. Name a radius of the circle.

4. Name a diameter of the circle.

Complete. Use the drawing at the right for 5-10.

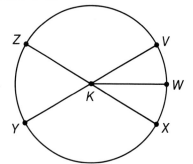

5. Line segment *KW* is a ____ .

6. Point *K* is the ____ of the circle.

7. Line segment *ZX* is a ____ .

8. Line segment *ZK* is a ____ .

9. Points *Y* and *V* are the endpoints of a ____ of the circle.

10. Points *K* and *X* are the endpoints of a ____ of the circle.

Write *true* or *false*.

11. The center of a circle is the same distance from any point on the circle.

12. A radius has both endpoints on the circle.

★ 13. All the radii of a circle are the same length.

APPLICATION

14. Use a ruler. Draw a line segment 3 cm long. Put your compass point on one endpoint. Open the compass so the pencil reaches the other endpoint. Draw a circle without moving the compass point.

15. Is the 3-cm line segment a radius or a diameter?

★ 16. Draw another radius of your circle. How long is it? Measure to check.

★ 17. Draw a diameter of your circle. How long is it? Measure to check.

Perimeter and Area

Juanita wants to put a frame of yarn around her picture. The picture is a rectangle 50 centimeters long and 30 centimeters wide. How much yarn does Juanita need for the frame?

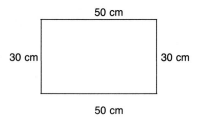

▶The distance around a polygon is called the **perimeter.**

▶To find the perimeter, add the lengths of the sides.

30 + 50 + 30 + 50 = 160

The perimeter is 160 centimeters.

Juanita needs 160 centimeters of yarn for the frame.

Juanita will display her picture on a bulletin board. What is the area of the board?

▶The **area** of the region is the number of square units needed to cover it.

Count the square units to find the area of the bulletin board. There are 15 square units.

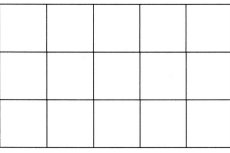

3 × 5 = 15 square units

You can find the area of a rectangle by multiplying. There are 3 rows. Each row has 5 square units.

▶Area = length × width

CLASSWORK

Find the perimeter and area of each polygon.

1.
3 m · 3 m · 3 m · 3 m

2.
4 cm · 2 cm · 2 cm · 4 cm

3.
2 m · 3 m · 3 m · 2 m

Find the perimeter of each polygon.

1.

2.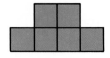

3.

Find the area any way you like.

4.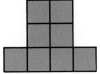

5.

6.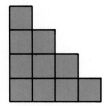

APPLICATION

7. Ivan made two rectangular pictures. What is the difference in perimeters? Solve using any method you like.

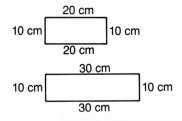

⋆ 8. Dolores used cellophone to cover her art project. The project is shaped like a square. Each side is 26 centimeters long. What is the area of the square?

⋆ 9. The sides of a triangle are 30 centimeters, 25 centimeters, and 150 millimeters long. What is the perimeter of the triangle?

MENTAL ARITHMETIC

If all sides of a polygon have the same length, you can find the perimeter by multiplying.

There are 10 sides.
Each side is 12 cm long.
$10 \times 12 = 120$

The perimeter is 120 cm.

Use mental arithmetic to find each perimeter.

1. 9 m

2. 7 cm

389

Understanding Volume

Work in a group. Each group member should make a different model for a cubic unit.

Use grid paper. Draw 5 identical squares of any size like the pattern shown at the right.

Cut your pattern out of oaktag or thin cardboard. Fold along the dashed lines. Tape the dotted edges together to make a cube.

Experiment.

1. Collect some empty containers of different sizes for your group to share.

2. Estimate the number of cubic units each container can hold. Record your estimates.

3. Fill your cubic unit model with beans. Empty it into a container. Repeat until the container is full. Keep track of the number of cubes full of beans each container holds. Record this number to show the measured volume of each container. Use Workmat 3, if you wish.

SHARING YOUR THINKING

Discuss these questions with your group. Use your data.

1. For which container was your estimate closest to the measured volume? Why do you think that estimate was closest?

INVESTIGATING VOLUME		
Container	Estimated Volume in Cubic Units	Measured Volume in Cubic Units
Paper cup		
Soup can		
Milk carton		
Jar		
Box		

2. Write a sentence to explain what the word volume means.

3. Choose a container that every student has filled. Compare the measured volumes. Are the numbers for the volume the same? Is the volume the same? Why or why not?

4. Each student selects a different container and tells the number of cubic units recorded. Can you use these results to order the containers from least to greatest volume? Explain why or why not.

THINKING IT THROUGH

1. Trace and cut this pattern out of oaktag or thin cardboard. Fold up along the dashed edges. Tape the dotted edges together.

   This cube is a model for a cubic inch.

2. Work as a group. Use the containers you collected for the activity on page 390.

   - Estimate how many cubic inches you think each container will hold. Make a list of your estimates.

   - Now measure the number of cubic inches one of your containers will hold. Use your model and some beans. Record the measured volume to check your estimate.

   - Do you want to change any of your estimates based on the results of filling one container? What changes will you make?

   - Measure and record in cubic inches the volume for each of your containers. Use your data to solve the problem of ordering the containers from least to greatest volume. Record your ordering.

Exploring Volume

WORKING TOGETHER

1. Work in a group. Use cubes to build each space figure. Find and record each volume.

a.

b.

c.

2. Investigate: Can different space figures have the same volumes? Show and explain.

3. Use the dimensions in the table below to build rectangular prisms. Find and record each volume. Use Workmat 4, if you wish.

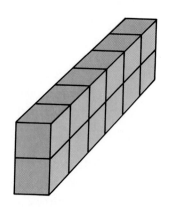

Length in Units	Width in Units	Height in Units	Volume in Cubic Units
1	6	2	
1	3	4	
1	12	1	
2	3	2	

4. Build rectangular prisms of your own. Record the dimensions and the volume for each of your space figures.

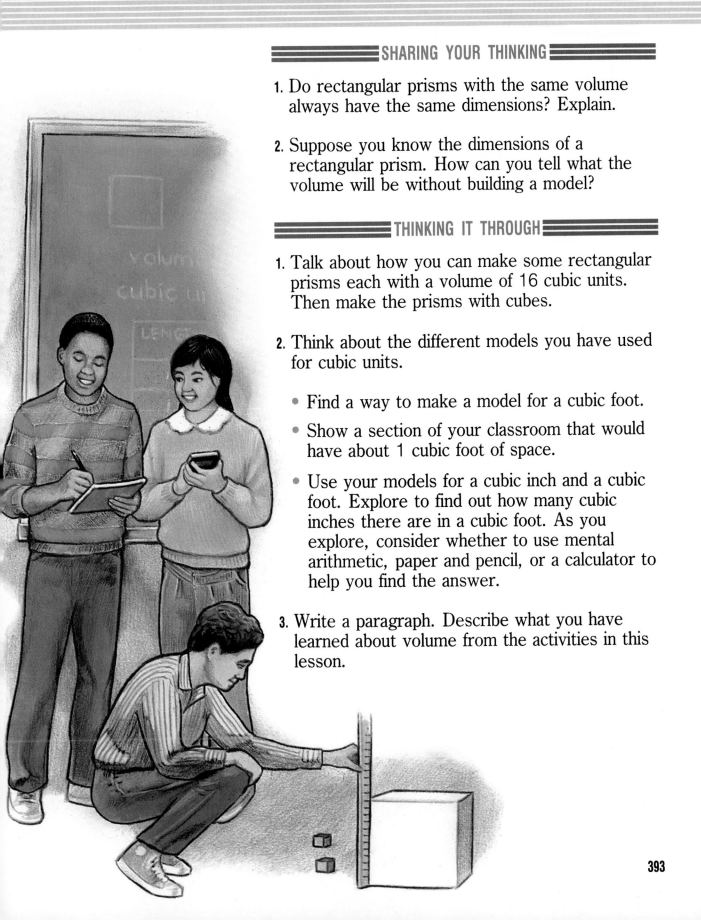

1. Do rectangular prisms with the same volume always have the same dimensions? Explain.

2. Suppose you know the dimensions of a rectangular prism. How can you tell what the volume will be without building a model?

THINKING IT THROUGH

1. Talk about how you can make some rectangular prisms each with a volume of 16 cubic units. Then make the prisms with cubes.

2. Think about the different models you have used for cubic units.

   • Find a way to make a model for a cubic foot.

   • Show a section of your classroom that would have about 1 cubic foot of space.

   • Use your models for a cubic inch and a cubic foot. Explore to find out how many cubic inches there are in a cubic foot. As you explore, consider whether to use mental arithmetic, paper and pencil, or a calculator to help you find the answer.

3. Write a paragraph. Describe what you have learned about volume from the activities in this lesson.

Ordered Pairs

Joe made this game board. He used an **ordered pair** of numbers to locate a point.

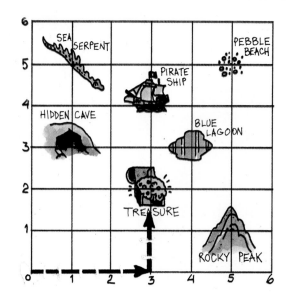

Follow these steps to locate a point with the ordered pair (3,2).

- Start at 0.
- Move 3 spaces to the right.
- Move 2 spaces up.

The ordered pair (3,2) locates the treasure.

To locate the hidden cave, start at 0. Move 1 space to the right. Then move up 3 spaces.

The ordered pair for the hidden cave is (1,3).

More Examples

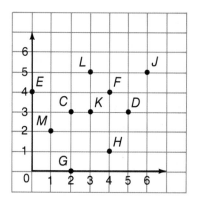

a. To locate the point at (3,3), start at 0. Move 3 spaces to the right. Then move up 3 spaces. The ordered pair (3,3) locates point *K*.

b. To locate point *G*, start at 0. Move 2 spaces to the right. The ordered pair for point *G* is (2,0).

CLASSWORK

Use the grid above to answer each question.
What point does each ordered pair locate?

1. (3,5)   2. (5,3)   3. (2,3)   4. (0,4)

Give an ordered pair to name each point.

5. *M*   6. *J*   7. *F*   8. *H*

394

Use the grid at the right to answer 1–9. What point does each ordered pair locate?

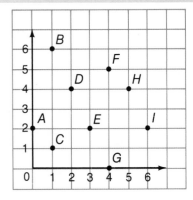

1. (1,6)   2. (2,4)   3. (6,2)

4. (1,1)   5. (5,4)   6. (4,5)

7. (3,2)   8. (4,0)   9. (0,2)

Use the grid at the right to answer 10–20. Give an ordered pair to name each point.

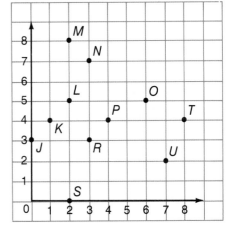

10. L   11. R   12. N

13. P   14. K   15. T

16. M   17. S   18. J

Complete.

★ 19. The ordered pair (__,5) locates a vowel.

★ 20. The ordered pair (7,__) locates a vowel.

APPLICATION

Use the game board on page 394 to answer each question.

21. Janet moved to (4,3). Where did she land?

22. Simon moved to (5,1). Where did he land?

23. Ruth wants to reach the Pirate Ship. What ordered pair locates the ship?

★ 24. Joe wanted to locate the Sea Serpent. He moved 5 spaces to the right. Did he choose the correct ordered pair?

MATH HISTORY

René Descartes was the first person to locate a point by using an ordered pair. In his honor the numbers used to locate a point are called **Cartesian coordinates.** Find three facts about René Descartes.

Graphing Ordered Pairs

To begin her fabric painting, Lila made a simple design on graph paper. She found the point located by each ordered pair. Then she connected the points in order to show her design.

A (2,5), *B* (4,1), *C* (6,5), *D* (4,9)

Follow these steps to graph the point for the ordered pair (2,5).

- Start at 0.
- Count 2 spaces to the right.
- Then count 5 spaces up.
- Make a dot.
- Write the letter *A* to name the point.

Another Example

Graph the point for the ordered pair (4,1).

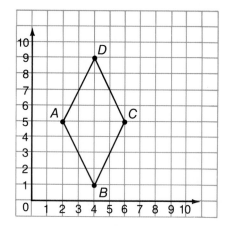

- Start at 0.
- Count 4 spaces to the right and 1 space up.
- Make a dot.
- Write the letter *B* to name the point.

CLASSWORK

Graph each point on graph paper.

1. *E* (2,2)   2. *F* (2,6)   3. *G* (6,6)   4. *H* (6,2)

5. Connect points *E*, *F*, *G*, and *H* in order. What polygon is formed?

Graph each point on graph paper. For each exercise, connect the points in order.

1. J (2,2)
   K (2,7)
   L (6,2)

2. M (1,1)
   N (2,8)
   O (6,1)
   P (7,8)

3. W (2,5)
   X (5,1)
   Y (8,5)

4. R (1,0)
   S (1,6)
   T (3,3)
   U (5,6)
   V (6,0)

Follow each rule. Write the ordered pairs.

Rule: Move 1 space up
      on the grid.

	Input	Output
★ 5.	(3,2)	
★ 6.	(7,4)	
★ 7.	(8,0)	

Rule: Move 1 space to the
      right on the grid.

	Input	Output
★ 8.	(4,1)	
★ 9.	(2,0)	
★ 10.	(0,3)	

APPLICATION

11. Graph each point.

A (2,1)   B (8,1)   C (9,2)   D (1,2)   E (5,8)
F (5,5)   G (5,2)   H (7,2)   J (2,2)

12. Connect point A to B. Connect point B to C. Connect point C to D. Connect point D to A.

13. Connect point E to F and F to G. Connect point E to J. Connect point E to H.

14. What is the completed design?

★ 15. Write 4 ordered pairs that form a rectangle when connected.

════ LOGICAL THINKING ════

1. Points A and B name a horizontal line segment. Is the first or second number the same in each ordered pair?

2. Points B and C name a vertical line segment. Is the first or second number the same in each ordered pair?

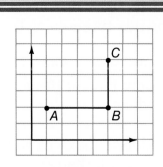

Problem Solving

SKILLS AND STRATEGIES REVIEW Crafts Fair

Toni is making dolls to sell at the crafts fair. The yarn used for the hair is either brown, black, or yellow. The dresses come in pink, blue, flowers, or stripes.

1. If Toni picked yarn for the hair without looking, what are the chances she would pick brown yarn?

2. If Toni picked a dress without looking, what are the chances she would pick a flowered dress?

3. How many different kinds of dolls can Toni make?

4. If Toni added red hair to the choices, how many different kinds of dolls could she make?

Sam uses square tiles to make a trivet. He starts with a red square in the center. Each tile around the red square is yellow. Each tile around the yellow square is blue.

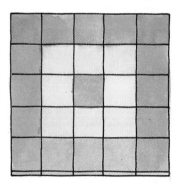

5. How many tiles of each color does Sam use for this three-color trivet?

6. Gladys ordered a four-color trivet. How many tiles of the fourth color are needed?

★7. Jean ordered a six-color trivet. How many tiles will the trivet have in all?

398

Problem Solving

WHAT IF . . .?

Jane makes red, white, and yellow flowerpots. She plants either tulip, daffodil, or crocus bulbs in each of the pots.

1. How many different pot-and-flower combinations can she make?

What if Jane adds green pots to her stock?

2. How many more pot-and-flower combinations can she make?

What if each of the 4 different colored pots comes in 2 sizes?

3. How many different combinations can Jane make now?

Crocus bulbs cost Jane 37¢ each. Daffodils cost her 40¢ each. Tulips cost her 50¢ each. Each small pot costs her 85¢ to make.

4. How much does it cost to plant 6 crocus bulbs in a small pot?

5. How much does it cost to plant 4 daffodil bulbs in a small pot?

What if Jane bought 25 of each kind of bulb?

6. How much would the tulips cost?   ★ 7. What would be the total cost?

What if Jane plants 8 of each kind of bulb in a large ceramic pot that costs her $1.25 to make?

8. How much does it cost Jane to make one pot of tulips?

9. How much does it cost Jane to make a pot of daffodils?

What if Jane sold each of these pots for $8.50?

★ 10. How much profit does Jane make on a pot of crocus?

★ 11. How much profit does Jane make if she sells 6 pots of tulips?

Name each figure. pages 372–379

1.

2.

3.

4.

5.

6.

7.

8.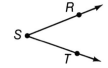

Tell if the two figures are congruent. pages 380–381

9.

10.

Tell if the dotted line is a line of symmetry. pages 382–383

11.

12.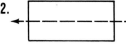

Use the circle to answer 13–15. pages 386–387

13. Name the center of the circle.

14. Name a radius.

15. Name a diameter.

Find the perimeter. pages 388–389

16.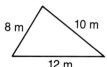
8 m   10 m   12 m

Find the area in square units. pages 388–389

17.

18.

Count the cubic units to find the volume. pages 390–393

19.

20.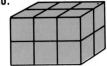

What point does each ordered pair locate? pages 394–397

21. (3,1)

22. (1,3)

Solve. pages 384–385, 398–399

23. Paige bought 6 round and 6 square beads. Each bead costs $.16. What was the total cost?

24. A square measures 3 centimeters on each side. What is the perimeter of the square?

Name each figure.

1.

2.

3.

4.

5.

6.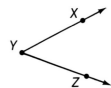

Are the two figures congruent?
Write *yes* or *no.*

7.

Is the dotted line a line of
symmetry? Write *yes* or *no.*

8.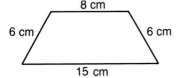

Find the perimeter.

9.

Find the area in square units.

10.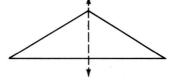

Count the cubic units
to find the volume.

11.

Give an ordered pair
to name each point.

12. *A*

13. *B*

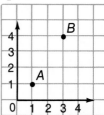

Solve.

14. Eve put 3 squares and 4
    triangles in each of 5
    rows. How many polygons
    did she use in all?

15. A triangle measures 6 centimeters
    on each side. What is the
    perimeter of the triangle?

The area of a rectangle is 12 square centimeters.
The length is 6 centimeters. What is the width?

MAKING SPACE FIGURES

Make your own model space figures.

This is what you need:

- tracing paper
- a pencil
- a ruler
- scissors
- construction paper
- transparent tape

This is what you do:

1. Trace these patterns on tracing paper. Use a ruler as a guide.

2. Cut out your tracings.

3. Use the tracings as patterns to cut the same shapes out of construction paper.

4. Tape the tracings to the cut-out construction paper.

5. Fold along the dotted lines so that the construction paper is on the outside.

6. Tape the edges together.

With these patterns, you can make a cube and a rectangular prism. Find examples of these shapes in your home and in school. Make a list of the objects you find.

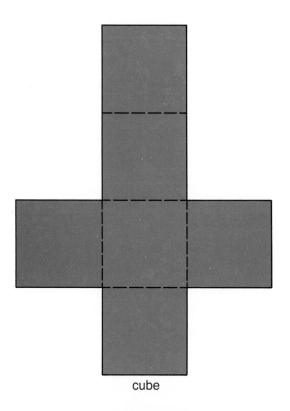
cube

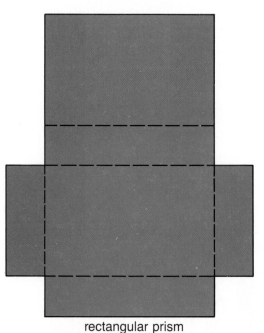
rectangular prism

GEOMETRIC DESIGNS

This design was created by an artist and mathematician named Maurits Cornelis Escher. His design is made up of one repeated shape.

Geometric designs can be made with one shape by using slides, flips, or turns.

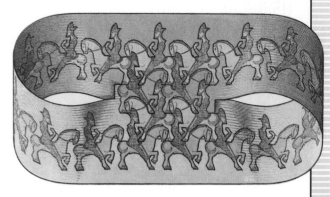

© M. C. Escher Heirs c/o Cordon Art, Baarn, Holland. Collection Haags Gemeente-museum, The Hague.

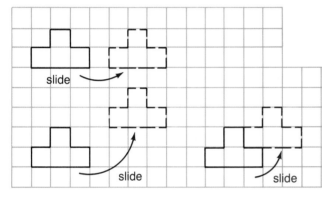

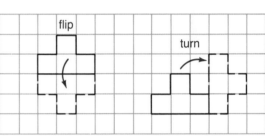

Here is a design using a △ and slides, flips, and turns.

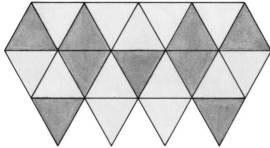

Choose one of the shapes below. Make a design of your own, using slides, flips, and turns. Use the shape as many times as you can to fill the paper. Then color your design.

USING BASIC

The computer can be used as a tool to solve problems. It will do computations over and over, quickly and accurately.

Find the perimeter of each rectangle.

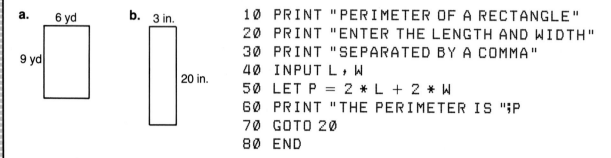

a. 6 yd, 9 yd

b. 3 in., 20 in.

```
10  PRINT "PERIMETER OF A RECTANGLE"
20  PRINT "ENTER THE LENGTH AND WIDTH"
30  PRINT "SEPARATED BY A COMMA"
40  INPUT L , W
50  LET P = 2 * L + 2 * W
60  PRINT "THE PERIMETER IS ";P
70  GOTO 20
80  END
```

Trace through the program to see how it finds perimeter.

Find the area of each rectangle.

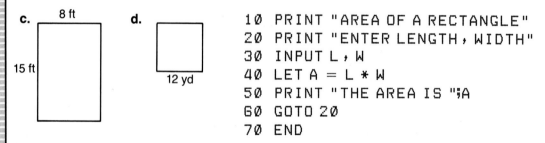

c. 8 ft, 15 ft

d. 12 yd

```
10  PRINT "AREA OF A RECTANGLE"
20  PRINT "ENTER LENGTH , WIDTH"
30  INPUT L , W
40  LET A = L * W
50  PRINT "THE AREA IS ";A
60  GOTO 20
70  END
```

Trace through the program to see how it finds area.

Use the two programs above. Tell what the output will be after entering the measurements shown in a–d. Then tell what the output will be for each of the following.

1. Rectangle: length = 2 miles
                width = 1 mile

2. Rectangle: length = 10 feet
                width = 5 feet

3. Square: side = 3 inches

4. Square: side = 15 yards

Find the volume of each figure.

e.

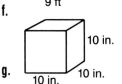

f.

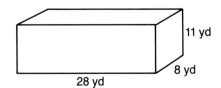

g.

11 yd

8 yd

28 yd

```
10  PRINT "VOLUME OF A RECTANGULAR PRISM"
20  PRINT "ENTER LENGTH, WIDTH, HEIGHT"
30  INPUT L, W, H
40  LET V = L * W * H
50  PRINT "THE VOLUME IS ";V
60  GOTO 20
70  END
```

Trace through the program
to see how it finds volume.

**Use the program above. Tell what the output
will be after entering the measurements shown
in e–g. Then try these.**

5. Rectangular prism: length = 6 in.,
width = 4 in., height = 18 in.

6. Rectangular prism: length = 29 ft,
width = 21 ft, height = 10 ft

═══ AT THE COMPUTER ═══

1. Enter and RUN the programs on pages 404 and 405. Use the
measurements given in the figures and in the exercises.

2. Compare the computer output with your answers.

3. On Your Own: Find three rectangular prisms.
Measure each with a ruler.
Enter the measurements in the program
above to find each volume.

Choose the correct answer. Write A, B, C, or D.

1. What fact is related to
   $16 - 9 = 7$?

   A $9 - 7 = 2$ C $9 + 7 = 15$

   B $7 + 9 = 16$ D not given

2. Compare. 9,125 ● 9,152

   A $>$ C $=$

   B $<$ D not given

3. What is the value of 4 in
   548,027?

   A 40,000   C 400

   B 4,000   D not given

4.   867
     + 75

   A 792   C 942

   B 832   D not given

5. Estimate.
   $113 + 555 = \square$

   A 600   C 500

   B 700   D not given

6. $4,000 - 976 = \square$

   A 3,024   C 3,100

   B 4,976   D not given

7. $5 \times 4 = \square$

   A 25   C 1

   B 9   D not given

8.   9
    $\times 7$

   A 63   C 2

   B 16   D not given

9. $72 \div 8 = \square$

   A 8   C 9

   B 64   D not given

10. What time will it be in 2 hours
    40 minutes?

    A 6:30   C 5:50

    B 6:50   D not given

11. What is the value of 1 ten-dollar
    bill, 1 quarter, 1 dime, 1 nickel,
    1 penny?

    A $10.36   C $10.41

    B $10.56   D not given

12. On a pictograph each 📖
    stands for 10 books. How much
    is 📖 📖 📖 ?

    A 3   C 30

    B 25   D not given

13. $6 \times 600 = \square$

    A 360   C 36,000

    B 3,600   D not given

14. $3 \times 276 = \square$

    A 279   C 828

    B 273   D not given

Choose the correct answer. Write A, B, C, or D.

15. $29.65
$\times$ 4

| A $118.60 | C $7.41 |
| B $29.61 | D not given |

22. Choose the best unit to measure a building's height.

| A meter | C kilometer |
| B centimeter | D not given |

16. 9)936

| A 114 | C 124 |
| B 105 | D not given |

23. What kind of day would it be at 5°C?

| A hot | C warm |
| B cold | D not given |

17. $76.32 ÷ 8 = □

| A $9.50 | C $8.04 |
| B $9.54 | D not given |

24. 34 × 74 = □

| A 108 | C 2,526 |
| B 2,516 | D not given |

18. What is the average of 96, 72, and 90?

| A 83 | C 86 |
| B 84 | D not given |

25. Estimate. 25 × 59 = □

| A 1,000 | C 1,800 |
| B 1,200 | D not given |

19. What decimal is twenty-one and nine hundredths?

| A 21.90 | C 21.9 |
| B 21.09 | D not given |

26. 63 × $.95 = □

| A $59.85 | C $1.58 |
| B $58.85 | D not given |

20. Compare. 27.4 ● 24.7

| A > | C = |
| B < | D not given |

27. Estimate. 28)222

| A 6 | C 8 |
| B 9 | D not given |

21. 79.13 − 10.1 = □

| A 89.23 | C 69.03 |
| B 69.12 | D not given |

28. $5.60 ÷ 16 = □

| A $.25 | C $.35 |
| B $1.30 | D not given |

Choose the correct answer. Write A, B, C, or D.

29. What fraction is equivalent to $\frac{4}{12}$?

A $\frac{1}{12}$ C $\frac{1}{3}$

B $\frac{2}{4}$ D not given

35. 12 ft = ___ yd

A 3   C 4

B 1   D not given

30. Compare. $\frac{1}{4}$ ● $\frac{1}{2}$

A >   C =

B <   D not given

36. 32 oz = ___ lb

A 2   C 3

B 1   D not given

31. What mixed number is shown?

A $1\frac{3}{4}$ C $1\frac{1}{4}$

B $2\frac{1}{4}$ D not given

37. What are possible outcomes of one spin?

A red, blue   C blue, green

B red, blue, green   D not given

32. $\frac{1}{6} + \frac{4}{6} = \square$

A $\frac{3}{6}$ C $1\frac{1}{6}$

B $\frac{5}{6}$ D not given

38. Name the figure.

A cube   C cylinder

B cone   D not given

33. $\frac{3}{5} - \frac{1}{5} = \square$

A $\frac{2}{5}$ C $\frac{4}{5}$

B $\frac{1}{5}$ D not given

39. Are the figures congruent?

A no   C maybe

B yes   D not given

34. $8\frac{1}{3} + 7\frac{1}{3} = \square$

A $16\frac{2}{3}$ C $1\frac{1}{3}$

B $15\frac{2}{3}$ D not given

40. What is the perimeter?

12 cm

4 cm

A 48 cm   C 32 cm

B 28 cm   D not given

Choose the correct answer. Write A, B, C, or D.

Use the picture.

41. Scott bought 1 box of crayons and 1 box of pencils. How much did he spend?

A $4.25 C $3.25

B $3.50 D not given

Use the table.

TICKETS SOLD FOR GAMES	
Friday	45,682
Saturday	54,908

45. How many tickets were sold on Friday and Saturday?

A 109,510 C 100,590

B 99,580 D not given

Choose the operation and solve.

42. Pencils come 10 to a pack. Carolyn bought 4 packs. How many pencils did Carolyn buy?

A divide; 4 C multiply; 40

B add; 14 D not given

Tell what information is missing.

43. George and Becky spent $2.38 apiece. How much change did George get?

A amount he gave C what he bought

B amount Becky paid D not given

Tell what information is extra.

44. Jean read 116 pages. Her sister Lou read 105 pages. How many more pages did Jean read?

A Lou is Jean's sister C pages Jean read

B pages Lou read D not given

Use the list.

46. Henry worked 3 days and then was off 2 days. He started on Monday. Find the last day he worked in 15 days.

On	3	3	3
Off	2	2	2

A Monday C Friday

B Saturday D not given

Solve.

47. Denise bought 45 pink roses. She had 30 white roses. To get 84 roses altogether, how many more roses does she need?

A 68 C 82

B 9 D not given

48. Bill had 40 lilies in one area. He took 12 of them out. He added 8 new lily plants. How many lilies are in the area now?

A 36 C 32

B 20 D not given

Choose the correct answer. Write A, B, C, or D.

Use a drawing to solve.

49. Ray stands just in front of Joel. Marsha stands just behind Cindy and in front of Ray. Who is last in line?

   A Ray   C Marsha

   B Joel   D not given

Use guess and test to solve.

50. Teresa has 9 coins that have a total sum of 79¢. What coins does she have?

   A 1 quarter,   C 2 quarters,
      2 dimes,   2 dimes,
      1 nickel,   1 nickel,
      4 pennies   4 pennies

   B 2 quarters,   D not given
      1 dime,
      5 nickels,
      1 penny

51. Which two numbers have a sum of 47 and a difference of 13?

   A 23 and 24   C 20 and 27

   B 34 and 12   D not given

Use a model to solve.

52. A shrub is to be planted every 3 meters around the base of a statue, except in the front. Each side of the base is 6 meters long. How many shrubs are needed?

   A 5   C 7

   B 8   D not given

Choose the way to complete each pattern.

53. 60, 62, 64, 66, ____, ____, ____

   A 70, 72, 74   C 68, 70, 72

   B 64, 62, 60   D not given

54. □, △, ○, □, △, ____, ____, ____, ____

   A ○, □, ○, △   C ○, □, △, ○

   B △, ○, □, △   D not given

Choose the two ways to solve the problem.

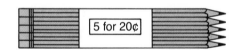

5 for 20¢

55. Marian bought 5 pencils. She got 80¢ change for $1.00. Was her change correct?

   A add; then   C guess and
      subtract   test; subtract

   B get facts from   D not given
      a picture;
      subtract

SET 1 Find each sum.

pages 2–3

1. 2	2. 5	3. 6	4. 5	5. 4	6. 2	7. 9
+3	+1	+4	+3	+4	+1	+6

8. 4	9. 6	10. 3	11. 6	12. 8	13. 4	14. 4
+1	+2	+9	+7	+7	+9	+5

15. $3 + 3 = \square$ **16.** $1 + 9 = \square$ **17.** $3 + 7 = \square$ **18.** $9 + 7 = \square$

SET 2 Add.

pages 4–5

1. 8	2. 1	3. 6	4. 4	5. 9	6. 7	7. 3
+1	+8	+4	+6	+7	+9	+0

8. 3	9. 8	10. 7	11. 0	12. 7	13. 1	14. 4
+4	+0	+2	+4	+0	+6	+9

15. $0 + 1 = \square$ **16.** $5 + 2 = \square$ **17.** $5 + 0 = \square$ **18.** $6 + 2 = \square$

SET 3 Add.

pages 6–7

1. 1	2. 8	3. 5	4. 3	5. 2	6. 2	7. 2
3	0	2	4	7	0	4
+4	+7	+6	+5	+1	6	1
					+1	+3

8. $2 + 1 + 4 = \square$ **9.** $5 + 8 + 6 = \square$ **10.** $4 + 1 + 2 + 5 = \square$

SET 4 Find each difference.

pages 8–9

1. 8	2. 4	3. 3	4. 9	5. 10	6. 11	7. 8
−3	−1	−2	−5	− 7	− 4	−2

8. 14	9. 12	10. 13	11. 15	12. 7	13. 17	14. 16
− 8	− 8	− 8	− 9	−3	− 8	− 9

15. $9 - 2 = \square$ **16.** $8 - 5 = \square$ **17.** $12 - 9 = \square$ **18.** $16 - 8 = \square$

SET 1 Subtract. Check by adding.
pages 10–11

1. 9
    −1

2. 5
    −3

3. 10
    − 5

4. 8
    −0

5. 9
    −2

6. 16
    − 7

7. 11
    − 5

8. 13
    − 8

9. 6
    −3

10. 12
    − 4

11. 15
    − 7

12. 6
    −0

13. 14
    − 9

14. 12
    − 6

15. 10 − 6 = □   16. 9 − 0 = □   17. 8 − 8 = □   18. 11 − 9 = □

SET 2 Find each missing number.
pages 12–15

1. 4 + 2 = □   2. 8 + □ = 13   3. □ + 6 = 15   4. □ + 3 = 10

   2 + 4 = □   5 + 8 = □   9 + 6 = □   3 + 7 = □

   6 − 4 = □   13 − □ = 5   15 − □ = 6   □ − 3 = 7

   6 − 2 = □   □ − 5 = 8   15 − 6 = □   10 − □ = 3

5. 6 + 3 = □   6. 5 + □ = 12   7. □ + 4 = 12   8. 7 + □ = 15

SET 3 Give the value of the digit 8.
pages 18–19

1. 285   2. 982   3. 538   4. 832   5. 768

Write each number in standard form.

6. 1 hundred 33

7. six hundred seventy-six

8. five hundred forty-one

9. eighty-seven

SET 4 Give the value of the digit 2.
pages 20–21

1. 2,680   2. 7,423   3. 5,052   4. 4,266   5. 9,821

Write each number in standard form using commas.

6. 3 thousand 42

7. five thousand eight hundred

8. one thousand nine hundred five

9. two thousand forty

SET 1 Give the value of the digit 9.   pages 22–23

1. 76,932   2. 95,347   3. 905,072   4. 389,645

Write each number in expanded form.

5. 20,345   6. 36,594   7. 839,272   8. 257,945

SET 2 Compare. Use >, <, or = for ●.   pages 24–25

1. 27 ● 28   2. 184 ● 148   3. 96 ● 96

4. 129 ● 219   5. 60 ● 65   6. 539 ● 139

7. 3,467 ● 3,647   8. 6,039 ● 6,039   9. 5,184 ● 5,084

10. 12,857 ● 12,785   11. 35,621 ● 32,611   12. 20,439 ● 20,439

13. 37,234 ● 37,235   14. 99,889 ● 99,898   15. 66,439 ● 66,397

SET 3 Round 1–4 to the nearest ten.   pages 26–29
Round 5–8 to the nearest hundred.

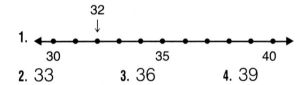

1.   5.
2. 33   3. 36   4. 39   6. 105   7. 162   8. 170

Round to the nearest thousand dollars.

9. $1,368   10. $1,527   11. $1,740   12. $14,420   13. $29,804

SET 4 Give the value of the digit 6.   pages 30–31

1. 16,370,425   2. 691,000,030   3. 63,100,987

Write each number in expanded form.

4. 8,204,371   5. 19,006,850   6. 127,932,000

SET 1 Add. Check by adding up.

pages 44–45

1. 47	2. $31.15	3. 8,705	4. 93	5. 66
+632	+ 56.50	+1,294	+19	+88

6. 276 + 423 = ☐   7. $5.85 + $62.14 = ☐   8. 52 + 1,832 = ☐

9. 45 + 75 = ☐   10. 26 + 83 = ☐   11. 79 + 89 = ☐

SET 2 Add and check.

pages 46–49

1. 41	2. 8	3. 37	4. 41	5. 98
16	25	24	89	7
+32	+15	+59	16	64
			+33	+12

6. 47	7. 381	8. 728	9. 975	10. $5.98
+609	+319	+862	+338	+ 9.94

11. 668	12. 293	13. 778	14. 17	15. 594
95	116	959	290	663
+747	+866	+594	+643	+975

SET 3 Estimate each sum.

pages 50–51

1. 48	2. 35	3. 83	4. 77	5. 8
+38	+72	+56	+563	+94

6. 856	7. 635	8. 425	9. 908	10. 749
+283	+670	+549	+166	+693

11. 58 + 140 + 78 = ☐ 12. 374 + 62 + 223 = ☐ 13. 36 + 8 + 41 = ☐

SET 4 Add. Estimate to be sure each answer makes sense.

pages 52–53

1. 5,628	2. 6,749	3. $385.66	4. 46,177	5. 45,944
+2,390	+7,538	+ 879.56	94,345	10,529
			+ 8,610	+58,363

6. 445 + 7,288 + 66 = ☐   7. 6,592 + 7,149 = ☐

SET 1 Subtract. Check by adding.

pages 56–61

1. $\begin{array}{r} 57 \\ -36 \end{array}$

2. $\begin{array}{r} \$89 \\ -\ 47 \end{array}$

3. $\begin{array}{r} 583 \\ -403 \end{array}$

4. $\begin{array}{r} 9,796 \\ -\ \ \ \ 34 \end{array}$

5. $\begin{array}{r} \$37.95 \\ -\ 25.44 \end{array}$

6. $4,568 - 1,302 = \square$ 7. $\$91.65 - \$91.50 = \square$ 8. $7,382 - 242 = \square$

9. $\begin{array}{r} 45 \\ -\ 9 \end{array}$

10. $\begin{array}{r} 73 \\ -28 \end{array}$

11. $\begin{array}{r} 32 \\ -19 \end{array}$

12. $\begin{array}{r} 85 \\ -77 \end{array}$

13. $\begin{array}{r} 61 \\ -34 \end{array}$

14. $\begin{array}{r} 576 \\ -148 \end{array}$

15. $\begin{array}{r} 914 \\ -387 \end{array}$

16. $\begin{array}{r} 658 \\ -299 \end{array}$

17. $\begin{array}{r} \$832 \\ -\ 796 \end{array}$

18. $\begin{array}{r} \$4.75 \\ -\ 3.98 \end{array}$

19. $55 - 28 = \square$ 20. $38 - 19 = \square$ 21. $92 - 25 = \square$ 22. $71 - 32 = \square$

23. $385 - 196 = \square$ 24. $763 - 484 = \square$ 25. $\$615 - \$536 = \square$

SET 2 Subtract and check.

pages 62–63

1. $\begin{array}{r} 508 \\ -153 \end{array}$

2. $\begin{array}{r} 900 \\ -676 \end{array}$

3. $\begin{array}{r} 401 \\ -228 \end{array}$

4. $\begin{array}{r} 900 \\ -398 \end{array}$

5. $\begin{array}{r} \$5.00 \\ -\ 2.15 \end{array}$

6. $\begin{array}{r} 100 \\ -\ 93 \end{array}$

7. $\begin{array}{r} 605 \\ -435 \end{array}$

8. $\begin{array}{r} 700 \\ -647 \end{array}$

9. $\begin{array}{r} 808 \\ -449 \end{array}$

10. $\begin{array}{r} 205 \\ -180 \end{array}$

11. $302 - 188 = \square$ 12. $400 - 94 = \square$ 13. $\$6.06 - \$3.19 = \square$

SET 3 Estimate each difference.

pages 64–65

1. $\begin{array}{r} 88 \\ -34 \end{array}$

2. $\begin{array}{r} 62 \\ -25 \end{array}$

3. $\begin{array}{r} 49 \\ -17 \end{array}$

4. $\begin{array}{r} 31 \\ -\ 8 \end{array}$

5. $\begin{array}{r} 54 \\ -48 \end{array}$

6. $\begin{array}{r} 77 \\ -16 \end{array}$

7. $\begin{array}{r} 543 \\ -365 \end{array}$

8. $\begin{array}{r} 730 \\ -\ 76 \end{array}$

9. $\begin{array}{r} 326 \\ -118 \end{array}$

10. $\begin{array}{r} 929 \\ -\ 65 \end{array}$

11. $\begin{array}{r} 884 \\ -249 \end{array}$

12. $425 - 85 = \square$ 13. $671 - 590 = \square$ 14. $981 - 54 = \square$

SET 4 Subtract. Check by adding.

pages 66–67

1. $\begin{array}{r} 1,000 \\ -\ \ \ \ 82 \end{array}$

2. $\begin{array}{r} 3,288 \\ -1,079 \end{array}$

3. $\begin{array}{r} 5,409 \\ -\ \ 318 \end{array}$

4. $\begin{array}{r} 5,591 \\ -2,602 \end{array}$

5. $\begin{array}{r} 9,070 \\ -1,100 \end{array}$

SET 1 Multiply.

pages 76–79

1. $\begin{array}{r} 2 \\ \times 8 \\ \hline \end{array}$
2. $\begin{array}{r} 3 \\ \times 4 \\ \hline \end{array}$
3. $\begin{array}{r} 2 \\ \times 2 \\ \hline \end{array}$
4. $\begin{array}{r} 2 \\ \times 7 \\ \hline \end{array}$
5. $\begin{array}{r} 3 \\ \times 5 \\ \hline \end{array}$
6. $\begin{array}{r} 3 \\ \times 7 \\ \hline \end{array}$

7. $\begin{array}{r} 4 \\ \times 3 \\ \hline \end{array}$
8. $\begin{array}{r} 5 \\ \times 2 \\ \hline \end{array}$
9. $\begin{array}{r} 4 \\ \times 8 \\ \hline \end{array}$
10. $\begin{array}{r} 5 \\ \times 4 \\ \hline \end{array}$
11. $\begin{array}{r} 4 \\ \times 9 \\ \hline \end{array}$
12. $\begin{array}{r} 5 \\ \times 5 \\ \hline \end{array}$

13. $3 \times 3 = \square$
14. $8 \times 3 = \square$
15. $9 \times 2 = \square$
16. $1 \times 2 = \square$

17. $4 \times 2 = \square$
18. $7 \times 5 = \square$
19. $6 \times 4 = \square$
20. $8 \times 5 = \square$

SET 2 Multiply.

pages 80–81; 86–87

1. $\begin{array}{r} 0 \\ \times 3 \\ \hline \end{array}$
2. $\begin{array}{r} 1 \\ \times 1 \\ \hline \end{array}$
3. $\begin{array}{r} 1 \\ \times 6 \\ \hline \end{array}$
4. $\begin{array}{r} 0 \\ \times 4 \\ \hline \end{array}$
5. $\begin{array}{r} 0 \\ \times 1 \\ \hline \end{array}$
6. $\begin{array}{r} 0 \\ \times 7 \\ \hline \end{array}$

7. $0 \times 9 = \square$
8. $1 \times 5 = \square$
9. $1 \times 3 = \square$
10. $0 \times 5 = \square$

Find each missing factor.

11. $\square \times 8 = 24$
12. $4 \times \square = 28$
13. $\square \times 1 = 6$
14. $\square \times 9 = 27$

15. $\square \times 6 = 36$
16. $8 \times \square = 16$
17. $9 \times \square = 63$
18. $\square \times 3 = 15$

SET 3 Multiply.

pages 82–85

1. $\begin{array}{r} 6 \\ \times 7 \\ \hline \end{array}$
2. $\begin{array}{r} 6 \\ \times 2 \\ \hline \end{array}$
3. $\begin{array}{r} 7 \\ \times 5 \\ \hline \end{array}$
4. $\begin{array}{r} 7 \\ \times 1 \\ \hline \end{array}$
5. $\begin{array}{r} 6 \\ \times 9 \\ \hline \end{array}$
6. $\begin{array}{r} 7 \\ \times 7 \\ \hline \end{array}$

7. $\begin{array}{r} 8 \\ \times 2 \\ \hline \end{array}$
8. $\begin{array}{r} 9 \\ \times 7 \\ \hline \end{array}$
9. $\begin{array}{r} 8 \\ \times 6 \\ \hline \end{array}$
10. $\begin{array}{r} 9 \\ \times 3 \\ \hline \end{array}$
11. $\begin{array}{r} 9 \\ \times 9 \\ \hline \end{array}$
12. $\begin{array}{r} 8 \\ \times 7 \\ \hline \end{array}$

13. $6 \times 6 = \square$
14. $7 \times 3 = \square$
15. $6 \times 8 = \square$
16. $7 \times 8 = \square$

17. $9 \times 4 = \square$
18. $8 \times 1 = \square$
19. $8 \times 8 = \square$
20. $9 \times 8 = \square$

SET 4 Find each quotient.

pages 90–91

1. $10 \div 2 = \square$
2. $12 \div 3 = \square$
3. $8 \div 2 = \square$

4. $2\overline{)12}$
5. $3\overline{)18}$
6. $2\overline{)4}$
7. $2\overline{)16}$
8. $3\overline{)27}$

SET 1 Find each quotient. pages 90–91; 98–99

1. $14 \div 2 = \square$ 2. $12 \div 2 = \square$ 3. $12 \div 3 = \square$ 4. $15 \div 3 = \square$

5. $16 \div 2 = \square$ 6. $0 \div 3 = \square$ 7. $3 \div 1 = \square$ 8. $0 \div 10 = \square$

9. $3\overline{)18}$ 10. $2\overline{)18}$ 11. $3\overline{)21}$ 12. $3\overline{)6}$ 13. $2\overline{)6}$

14. $2\overline{)10}$ 15. $3\overline{)27}$ 16. $2\overline{)8}$ 17. $3\overline{)9}$ 18. $3\overline{)24}$

19. $1\overline{)3}$ 20. $3\overline{)3}$ 21. $2\overline{)0}$ 22. $1\overline{)2}$ 23. $2\overline{)2}$

SET 2 Divide. pages 92–93

1. $36 \div 4 = \square$ 2. $30 \div 5 = \square$ 3. $24 \div 4 = \square$ 4. $20 \div 5 = \square$

5. $4 \div 4 = \square$ 6. $45 \div 5 = \square$ 7. $28 \div 4 = \square$ 8. $32 \div 4 = \square$

9. $5\overline{)25}$ 10. $4\overline{)20}$ 11. $5\overline{)10}$ 12. $4\overline{)16}$ 13. $5\overline{)35}$

14. $4\overline{)8}$ 15. $5\overline{)40}$ 16. $4\overline{)32}$ 17. $5\overline{)15}$ 18. $4\overline{)12}$

SET 3 Find each quotient. pages 94–95; 98–99

1. $24 \div 6 = \square$ 2. $21 \div 7 = \square$ 3. $48 \div 6 = \square$ 4. $12 \div 6 = \square$

5. $6 \div 6 = \square$ 6. $0 \div 7 = \square$ 7. $6 \div 1 = \square$ 8. $63 \div 7 = \square$

9. $7\overline{)49}$ 10. $7\overline{)14}$ 11. $6\overline{)30}$ 12. $7\overline{)28}$ 13. $6\overline{)36}$

14. $7\overline{)42}$ 15. $6\overline{)18}$ 16. $7\overline{)56}$ 17. $6\overline{)54}$ 18. $7\overline{)35}$

SET 4 Find each quotient. pages 96–97

1. $36 \div 9 = \square$ 2. $72 \div 8 = \square$ 3. $45 \div 9 = \square$ 4. $18 \div 9 = \square$

5. $81 \div 9 = \square$ 6. $32 \div 8 = \square$ 7. $64 \div 8 = \square$ 8. $27 \div 9 = \square$

9. $8\overline{)24}$ 10. $9\overline{)72}$ 11. $8\overline{)56}$ 12. $9\overline{)27}$ 13. $9\overline{)54}$

14. $8\overline{)40}$ 15. $8\overline{)8}$ 16. $9\overline{)63}$ 17. $8\overline{)48}$ 18. $9\overline{)9}$

SET 1 Write the time using numbers.

pages 114–117

1. 10 minutes after 6 **2.** half past 4 **3.** quarter to 2

Choose A.M. or P.M.

4. Dinner at 5:30 **5.** Wake-up at 7:00 **6.** School's out at 3:00

Tell how much time has passed.

7. start 3:05 P.M. **8.** start 5:20 A.M. **9.** start 2:00 P.M.
    end 8:05 P.M.   end 6:45 A.M.   end 2:15 P.M.

10. start 2:00 A.M. **11.** start 4:10 P.M. **12.** start 1:00 P.M.
     end 5:00 A.M.   end 6:00 P.M.   end 1:30 P.M.

SET 2 What day and date is it? Use the calendar on page 118.

pages 118–119

1. 2 days before March 14 **2.** 7 days before March 29

3. 9 days after March 18 **4.** 5 days after March 19

5. 1 day before March 10 **6.** 10 days after March 2

7. 14 days after March 3 **8.** 12 days before March 31

9. 2 days after March 31 **10.** 2 days before March 1

SET 3 Write the value.

pages 120–121

1. 1 half-dollar
   2 dimes
   4 pennies

2. 1 half-dollar
   1 quarter
   2 nickels

3. 1 one-dollar bill
   5 dimes
   6 pennies

4. 3 quarters
   7 dimes
   4 nickels

5. 1 five-dollar bill
   1 one-dollar bill
   3 pennies

6. 1 ten-dollar bill
   1 five-dollar bill
   2 half-dollars

SET 1 Subtract to find the change.

pages 122–125

	1.	2.	3.	4.	5.	6.
Cost	$ .26	$4.05	$2.65	$1.63	$3.24	$ 4.90
Amount Paid	$1.00	$5.00	$5.00	$5.00	$5.00	$10.00

SET 2 Use the pictograph to answer each question.

pages 128–129

1. What does this symbol mean: ▯ ?

2. How many books did Rose read?

3. How many more books did Kelly read than Kim?

4. How many books did Jake read?

5. Did Anthony or Kim read more books?

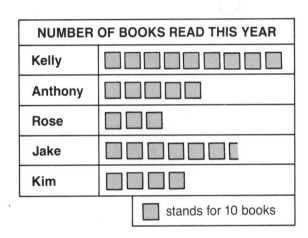

SET 3 Use the bar graph to answer each question.

pages 130–131

1. How many days did it rain in May?

2. Which month had the greatest number of rainy days?

3. Which months had the same number of rainy days?

4. Which months had fewer than 6 rainy days?

5. Which month had the least amount of rain?

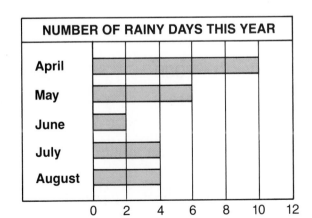

SET 1 Use the line graph to answer each question.

pages 132–133

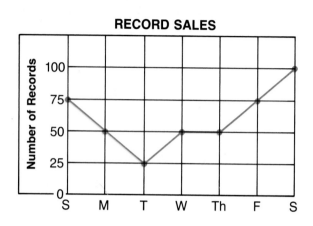

1. How many records were sold on Monday?

2. On which day were the fewest records sold?

3. On which three days were the sales the same?

4. On which days were fewer than 75 records sold?

5. Did the number of sales increase or decrease from Sunday to Monday?

SET 2 Use the circle graph to solve each problem.

pages 134–135

1. Does Julie sleep half the time or less?

2. Does Julie spend more time at play or on homework?

3. Does Julie spend more or less than $\frac{1}{2}$ of her time at school?

4. On what activity does Julie spend the least time?

5. What does "other" mean?

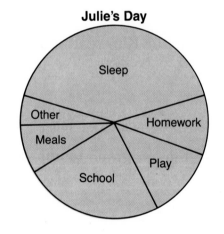

SET 3 Find each product.

pages 144–145

1. 30×6

2. 70×5

3. 200×8

4. 900×7

5. 500×4

6. 300×6

7. 200×5

8. 900×9

9. 200×3

10. 800×8

11. $6 \times 4 = \square$

12. $6 \times 40 = \square$

13. $6 \times 400 = \square$

14. $9 \times 1,000 = \square$

15. $7 \times 8,000 = \square$

16. $5 \times 6,000 = \square$

SET 1 Multiply.

pages 146–151

1. $\begin{array}{r} 23 \\ \times\ 3 \\ \hline \end{array}$
2. $\begin{array}{r} 34 \\ \times\ 2 \\ \hline \end{array}$
3. $\begin{array}{r} 21 \\ \times\ 4 \\ \hline \end{array}$
4. $\begin{array}{r} 24 \\ \times\ 2 \\ \hline \end{array}$
5. $\begin{array}{r} 33 \\ \times\ 3 \\ \hline \end{array}$
6. $\begin{array}{r} 44 \\ \times\ 2 \\ \hline \end{array}$

7. $3 \times 31 = \square$
8. $2 \times 41 = \square$
9. $3 \times 22 = \square$

10. $2 \times 40 = \square$
11. $3 \times 21 = \square$
12. $4 \times 22 = \square$

13. $2 \times 32 = \square$
14. $4 \times 21 = \square$
15. $3 \times 33 = \square$

SET 2 Multiply.

pages 146–151

1. $\begin{array}{r} 26 \\ \times\ 2 \\ \hline \end{array}$
2. $\begin{array}{r} 18 \\ \times\ 3 \\ \hline \end{array}$
3. $\begin{array}{r} 17 \\ \times\ 4 \\ \hline \end{array}$
4. $\begin{array}{r} 19 \\ \times\ 5 \\ \hline \end{array}$
5. $\begin{array}{r} 13 \\ \times\ 7 \\ \hline \end{array}$
6. $\begin{array}{r} 38 \\ \times\ 2 \\ \hline \end{array}$

7. $\begin{array}{r} 25 \\ \times\ 3 \\ \hline \end{array}$
8. $\begin{array}{r} 13 \\ \times\ 6 \\ \hline \end{array}$
9. $\begin{array}{r} 12 \\ \times\ 8 \\ \hline \end{array}$
10. $\begin{array}{r} 29 \\ \times\ 3 \\ \hline \end{array}$
11. $\begin{array}{r} 35 \\ \times\ 2 \\ \hline \end{array}$
12. $\begin{array}{r} 16 \\ \times\ 4 \\ \hline \end{array}$

13. $5 \times 15 = \square$
14. $6 \times 12 = \square$
15. $7 \times 14 = \square$
16. $3 \times 24 = \square$

SET 3 Find each product.

pages 146–151

1. $\begin{array}{r} 48 \\ \times\ 3 \\ \hline \end{array}$
2. $\begin{array}{r} 24 \\ \times\ 7 \\ \hline \end{array}$
3. $\begin{array}{r} 56 \\ \times\ 6 \\ \hline \end{array}$
4. $\begin{array}{r} 39 \\ \times\ 9 \\ \hline \end{array}$
5. $\begin{array}{r} 87 \\ \times\ 5 \\ \hline \end{array}$
6. $\begin{array}{r} 48 \\ \times\ 4 \\ \hline \end{array}$

7. $\begin{array}{r} 72 \\ \times\ 8 \\ \hline \end{array}$
8. $\begin{array}{r} 65 \\ \times\ 3 \\ \hline \end{array}$
9. $\begin{array}{r} 98 \\ \times\ 2 \\ \hline \end{array}$
10. $\begin{array}{r} 77 \\ \times\ 4 \\ \hline \end{array}$
11. $\begin{array}{r} 59 \\ \times\ 6 \\ \hline \end{array}$
12. $\begin{array}{r} 18 \\ \times\ 9 \\ \hline \end{array}$

13. $7 \times 33 = \square$
14. $4 \times 59 = \square$
15. $8 \times 67 = \square$

16. $5 \times 79 = \square$
17. $8 \times 36 = \square$
18. $6 \times 95 = \square$

SET 4 Find each product.

pages 152–153

1. $\begin{array}{r} 253 \\ \times\ \ \ 3 \\ \hline \end{array}$
2. $\begin{array}{r} 117 \\ \times\ \ \ 8 \\ \hline \end{array}$
3. $\begin{array}{r} 137 \\ \times\ \ \ 6 \\ \hline \end{array}$
4. $\begin{array}{r} 456 \\ \times\ \ \ 2 \\ \hline \end{array}$
5. $\begin{array}{r} 379 \\ \times\ \ \ 2 \\ \hline \end{array}$

6. $\begin{array}{r} 189 \\ \times\ \ \ 5 \\ \hline \end{array}$
7. $\begin{array}{r} 208 \\ \times\ \ \ 3 \\ \hline \end{array}$
8. $\begin{array}{r} 447 \\ \times\ \ \ 2 \\ \hline \end{array}$
9. $\begin{array}{r} 118 \\ \times\ \ \ 7 \\ \hline \end{array}$
10. $\begin{array}{r} 328 \\ \times\ \ \ 3 \\ \hline \end{array}$

11. $4 \times 243 = \square$
12. $5 \times 158 = \square$
13. $6 \times 129 = \square$

EXTRA PRACTICE

SET 1 Find each product.

pages 156–157

1. 502
× 3

2. 627
× 5

3. 243
× 9

4. 418
× 7

5. 896
× 6

6. 539
× 3

7. 952
× 8

8. 176
× 7

9. 358
× 4

10. 731
× 9

11. $8 \times 815 = \square$

12. $6 \times 379 = \square$

13. $4 \times 948 = \square$

14. $7 \times 436 = \square$

15. $9 \times 578 = \square$

16. $5 \times 857 = \square$

SET 2 Estimate each product.

pages 158–159

1. 56
× 8

2. 81
× 7

3. 18
× 4

4. 64
× 6

5. 45
× 5

6. 483
× 7

7. 652
× 9

8. 164
× 4

9. 818
× 6

10. 546
× 3

11. $8 \times 341 = \square$

12. $9 \times 95 = \square$

13. $3 \times 749 = \square$

SET 3 Multiply. Estimate to be sure each answer makes sense.

pages 160–161

1. 1,588
× 5

2. 2,736
× 2

3. 3,675
× 3

4. 1,724
× 9

5. 2,561
× 8

6. 5,643
× 6

7. 8,937
× 7

8. 6,192
× 9

9. 9,458
× 8

10. 7,394
× 5

11. $4 \times 8,519 = \square$

12. $6 \times 7,185 = \square$

13. $7 \times 9,062 = \square$

SET 4 Multiply.

pages 162–163

1. $.47
× 6

2. $.89
× 4

3. $5.35
× 8

4. $12.40
× 7

5. $9.91
× 6

6. $21.98
× 4

7. $8.76
× 9

8. $61.45
× 5

9. $78.34
× 6

10. $49.18
× 3

11. $7 \times \$2.99 = \square$

12. $9 \times \$.56 = \square$

13. $5 \times \$37.60 = \square$

SET 1 Divide. Check by multiplying.

pages 178–179

1. $7 \div 7 = \square$
   $70 \div 7 = \square$
   $700 \div 7 = \square$

2. $72 \div 8 = \square$
   $720 \div 8 = \square$
   $7,200 \div 8 = \square$

3. $45 \div 9 = \square$
   $450 \div 9 = \square$
   $4,500 \div 9 = \square$

4. $9\overline{)1,800}$
5. $7\overline{)2,100}$
6. $5\overline{)4,000}$
7. $6\overline{)5,400}$

8. $3\overline{)1,800}$
9. $8\overline{)640}$
10. $9\overline{)810}$
11. $2\overline{)1,400}$

12. $4\overline{)1,600}$
13. $6\overline{)300}$
14. $8\overline{)5,600}$
15. $3\overline{)2,700}$

SET 2 Divide. Check by multiplying.

pages 174–181

1. $3\overline{)17}$
2. $4\overline{)26}$
3. $2\overline{)19}$
4. $5\overline{)18}$
5. $3\overline{)29}$

6. $4\overline{)31}$
7. $6\overline{)59}$
8. $9\overline{)80}$
9. $9\overline{)26}$
10. $8\overline{)53}$

11. $7\overline{)24}$
12. $5\overline{)49}$
13. $6\overline{)22}$
14. $8\overline{)21}$
15. $9\overline{)31}$

16. $39 \div 5 = \square$
17. $23 \div 8 = \square$
18. $49 \div 9 = \square$

19. $61 \div 7 = \square$
20. $52 \div 6 = \square$
21. $79 \div 8 = \square$

SET 3 Divide. Check by multiplying.

pages 174–181

1. $2\overline{)31}$
2. $3\overline{)35}$
3. $5\overline{)73}$
4. $2\overline{)95}$
5. $6\overline{)95}$

6. $4\overline{)55}$
7. $3\overline{)88}$
8. $7\overline{)99}$
9. $8\overline{)91}$
10. $4\overline{)78}$

11. $96 \div 6 = \square$
12. $92 \div 5 = \square$
13. $81 \div 7 = \square$

14. $37 \div 2 = \square$
15. $67 \div 4 = \square$
16. $98 \div 3 = \square$

SET 4 Divide. Check by multiplying.

pages 182–183

1. $2\overline{)477}$
2. $6\overline{)851}$
3. $4\overline{)969}$
4. $5\overline{)722}$
5. $8\overline{)900}$

6. $7\overline{)847}$
7. $4\overline{)590}$
8. $8\overline{)975}$
9. $2\overline{)711}$
10. $6\overline{)755}$

11. $751 \div 4 = \square$
12. $855 \div 6 = \square$
13. $674 \div 5 = \square$

SET 1   Divide. Check by multiplying.

pages 182–183

1. $4\overline{)339}$
    2. $3\overline{)260}$
    3. $5\overline{)491}$
    4. $2\overline{)147}$
    5. $6\overline{)533}$

6. $5\overline{)395}$
    7. $2\overline{)183}$
    8. $8\overline{)778}$
    9. $6\overline{)479}$
    10. $9\overline{)860}$

11. $7\overline{)517}$
    12. $4\overline{)210}$
    13. $9\overline{)440}$
    14. $6\overline{)271}$
    15. $8\overline{)693}$

16. $255 \div 9 = \square$
    17. $689 \div 7 = \square$
    18. $475 \div 7 = \square$

SET 2   Divide. Check by multiplying.

pages 186–187

1. $5\overline{)538}$
    2. $3\overline{)623}$
    3. $2\overline{)701}$
    4. $9\overline{)905}$
    5. $7\overline{)846}$

6. $4\overline{)723}$
    7. $8\overline{)876}$
    8. $6\overline{)65}$
    9. $7\overline{)762}$
    10. $5\overline{)854}$

11. $3\overline{)928}$
    12. $9\overline{)980}$
    13. $4\overline{)807}$
    14. $8\overline{)966}$
    15. $6\overline{)652}$

16. $904 \div 5 = \square$
    17. $864 \div 8 = \square$
    18. $941 \div 2 = \square$

SET 3   Divide. Check by multiplying.

pages 188–189

1. $7\overline{)9,163}$
    2. $5\overline{)7,367}$
    3. $2\overline{)8,758}$
    4. $6\overline{)5,894}$

5. $9\overline{)9,538}$
    6. $4\overline{)2,103}$
    7. $3\overline{)8,811}$
    8. $8\overline{)5,946}$

9. $4\overline{)9,238}$
    10. $7\overline{)8,736}$
    11. $8\overline{)8,645}$
    12. $9\overline{)7,753}$

13. $6,693 \div 7 = \square$
    14. $5,944 \div 9 = \square$
    15. $6,518 \div 6 = \square$

SET 4   Divide. Check by multiplying.

pages 190–191

1. $3\overline{)\$4.38}$
    2. $5\overline{)\$16.85}$
    3. $8\overline{)\$92.64}$
    4. $6\overline{)\$54.42}$

5. $4\overline{)\$.36}$
    6. $9\overline{)\$48.96}$
    7. $3\overline{)\$87.24}$
    8. $7\overline{)\$75.32}$

9. $9\overline{)\$8.01}$
    10. $6\overline{)\$96.54}$
    11. $7\overline{)\$65.10}$
    12. $2\overline{)\$91.64}$

13. $\$4.55 \div 7 = \square$
    14. $\$58.24 \div 8 = \square$
    15. $\$86.40 \div 8 = \square$

SET 1 Find each average.   pages 192–193

1. 6, 9, 15   2. 24, 8, 58   3. 67, 45

4. $.45, $.18, $.33   5. 763, 511   6. 437, 966, 748

7. 98, 56, 77   8. $38.75, $92.61   9. 287, 859

10. 83, 49, 71, 65   11. 411, 850, 563, 228

SET 2 Write each decimal.   pages 204–207

1. 5 tenths   2. 3 and 2 tenths   3. 1 tenth

4. 6 and 9 tenths   5. four and eight tenths   6. 5 and 5 tenths

7. 6 out of 10 trees   8. 8 out of 10 spoons   9. 4 out of 10 cars

SET 3 Write each decimal.   pages 204–207

1. 3 hundredths   2. 14 hundredths   3. 8 and 7 hundredths

4. 6 and 45 hundredths   5. seventeen hundredths   6. 2 and 8 hundredths

7. thirty-three hundredths   8. 50 out of 100   9. 86 out of 100

10. 3 and 27 hundredths   11. 47 and 47 hundredths   12. 95 out of 100

SET 4 Compare. Use >, <, or = for ●.   pages 206–211

1. 0.37 ● 0.3   2. 0.89 ● 1.2   3. 6.7 ● 6.70

4. 0.11 ● 0.12   5. 13.50 ● 13.05   6. 0.01 ● 0.10

7. 78.40 ● 78.4   8. 81.54 ● 81.53   9. 23 ● 23.02

List in order from least to greatest.

10. 2.43, 2.3, 2.4   11. 0.58, 0.60, 0.52   12. 7.01, 7.0, 7.10

EXTRA PRACTICE

SET 1 Add. Check by adding up.

pages 208–215

1. $\begin{array}{r}0.7\\+0.2\\\hline\end{array}$	2. $\begin{array}{r}2.3\\+3.4\\\hline\end{array}$	3. $\begin{array}{r}7.5\\+1.5\\\hline\end{array}$	4. $\begin{array}{r}4.9\\+7.3\\\hline\end{array}$	5. $\begin{array}{r}6.6\\+8.4\\\hline\end{array}$
6. $\begin{array}{r}0.04\\+0.08\\\hline\end{array}$	7. $\begin{array}{r}3.06\\+4.07\\\hline\end{array}$	8. $\begin{array}{r}4.85\\+2.15\\\hline\end{array}$	9. $\begin{array}{r}7.96\\+0.15\\\hline\end{array}$	10. $\begin{array}{r}3.64\\+5.77\\\hline\end{array}$

11. $3.2 + 9.8 = \square$ 12. $7.62 + 3.47 = \square$ 13. $15.45 + 6.87 = \square$

SET 2 Subtract. Check by adding.

pages 208–215

1. $\begin{array}{r}7.5\\-4.3\\\hline\end{array}$	2. $\begin{array}{r}9.2\\-6.5\\\hline\end{array}$	3. $\begin{array}{r}28.4\\-\ \ 5.9\\\hline\end{array}$	4. $\begin{array}{r}34.3\\-\ \ 8.6\\\hline\end{array}$	5. $\begin{array}{r}72.1\\-24.2\\\hline\end{array}$
6. $\begin{array}{r}6.47\\-5.12\\\hline\end{array}$	7. $\begin{array}{r}4.92\\-1.35\\\hline\end{array}$	8. $\begin{array}{r}10.57\\-\ \ 7.69\\\hline\end{array}$	9. $\begin{array}{r}35.16\\-23.07\\\hline\end{array}$	10. $\begin{array}{r}54.68\\-25.89\\\hline\end{array}$

11. $4.6 - 2.7 = \square$ 12. $80.15 - 9.06 = \square$ 13. $8.03 - 7.68 = \square$

SET 3 Add or subtract.

pages 208–215

1. $\begin{array}{r}7.54\\-3.2\\\hline\end{array}$	2. $\begin{array}{r}0.28\\+0.43\\\hline\end{array}$	3. $\begin{array}{r}7.4\\-2.26\\\hline\end{array}$	4. $\begin{array}{r}0.5\\+3.58\\\hline\end{array}$	5. $\begin{array}{r}8.97\\+2.4\\\hline\end{array}$
6. $\begin{array}{r}31.7\\-17.68\\\hline\end{array}$	7. $\begin{array}{r}52\\-11.3\\\hline\end{array}$	8. $\begin{array}{r}79.3\\+\ \ 8.95\\\hline\end{array}$	9. $\begin{array}{r}0.8\\-0.45\\\hline\end{array}$	10. $\begin{array}{r}36.09\\+46.7\\\hline\end{array}$

11. $4.28 + 6.7 = \square$ 12. $0.2 - 0.01 = \square$ 13. $48 - 5.5 = \square$

SET 4 Complete.

pages 218–221

1. $1 \text{ cm} = \underline{\quad} \text{ mm}$ 2. $3 \text{ m} = \underline{\quad} \text{ cm}$ 3. $500 \text{ cm} = \underline{\quad} \text{ m}$

4. $900 \text{ cm} = \underline{\quad} \text{ m}$ 5. $4 \text{ km} = \underline{\quad} \text{ m}$ 6. $\underline{\quad} \text{ km} = 8{,}000 \text{ m}$

7. $11 \text{ km} = \underline{\quad} \text{ m}$ 8. $14 \text{ km} = \underline{\quad} \text{ m}$ 9. $6{,}000 \text{ m} = \underline{\quad} \text{ km}$

SET 1 Complete. pages 222–225

1. 4,000 g = __ kg
2. 8,000 g = __ kg
3. 9 kg = __ g

4. 10 kg = __ g
5. 15 kg = __ g
6. 11,000 g = __ kg

7. __ L = 9,000 mL
8. 3,000 mL = __ L
9. 8 L = __ mL

10. 4 L = __ mL
11. 5 L = __ mL
12. 11 L = __ mL

SET 2 Find each product. pages 240–243

1. $\begin{array}{r} 46 \\ \times 10 \\ \hline \end{array}$
2. $\begin{array}{r} 55 \\ \times 40 \\ \hline \end{array}$
3. $\begin{array}{r} 70 \\ \times 60 \\ \hline \end{array}$
4. $\begin{array}{r} 32 \\ \times 20 \\ \hline \end{array}$
5. $\begin{array}{r} 61 \\ \times 30 \\ \hline \end{array}$
6. $\begin{array}{r} 74 \\ \times 50 \\ \hline \end{array}$

7. $\begin{array}{r} 828 \\ \times 90 \\ \hline \end{array}$
8. $\begin{array}{r} 340 \\ \times 10 \\ \hline \end{array}$
9. $\begin{array}{r} 435 \\ \times 80 \\ \hline \end{array}$
10. $\begin{array}{r} 597 \\ \times 40 \\ \hline \end{array}$
11. $\begin{array}{r} 908 \\ \times 20 \\ \hline \end{array}$
12. $\begin{array}{r} 364 \\ \times 60 \\ \hline \end{array}$

13. 40 × 10 = □
14. 50 × 62 = □
15. 709 × 70 = □

SET 3 Find each product. pages 244–245

1. $\begin{array}{r} 16 \\ \times 23 \\ \hline \end{array}$
2. $\begin{array}{r} 73 \\ \times 45 \\ \hline \end{array}$
3. $\begin{array}{r} 31 \\ \times 56 \\ \hline \end{array}$
4. $\begin{array}{r} 60 \\ \times 84 \\ \hline \end{array}$
5. $\begin{array}{r} 97 \\ \times 33 \\ \hline \end{array}$
6. $\begin{array}{r} 83 \\ \times 94 \\ \hline \end{array}$

7. $\begin{array}{r} 44 \\ \times 78 \\ \hline \end{array}$
8. $\begin{array}{r} 53 \\ \times 11 \\ \hline \end{array}$
9. $\begin{array}{r} 60 \\ \times 29 \\ \hline \end{array}$
10. $\begin{array}{r} 49 \\ \times 18 \\ \hline \end{array}$
11. $\begin{array}{r} 37 \\ \times 49 \\ \hline \end{array}$
12. $\begin{array}{r} 74 \\ \times 55 \\ \hline \end{array}$

13. 68 × 50 = □
14. 27 × 72 = □
15. 92 × 86 = □

SET 4 Estimate each product. pages 248–249

1. $\begin{array}{r} 48 \\ \times 18 \\ \hline \end{array}$
2. $\begin{array}{r} 31 \\ \times 40 \\ \hline \end{array}$
3. $\begin{array}{r} 55 \\ \times 72 \\ \hline \end{array}$
4. $\begin{array}{r} 39 \\ \times 91 \\ \hline \end{array}$
5. $\begin{array}{r} 74 \\ \times 65 \\ \hline \end{array}$
6. $\begin{array}{r} 84 \\ \times 15 \\ \hline \end{array}$

7. $\begin{array}{r} 423 \\ \times 53 \\ \hline \end{array}$
8. $\begin{array}{r} 596 \\ \times 62 \\ \hline \end{array}$
9. $\begin{array}{r} 374 \\ \times 10 \\ \hline \end{array}$
10. $\begin{array}{r} 861 \\ \times 78 \\ \hline \end{array}$
11. $\begin{array}{r} 142 \\ \times 87 \\ \hline \end{array}$
12. $\begin{array}{r} 670 \\ \times 12 \\ \hline \end{array}$

13. 54 × 67 = □
14. 50 × 31 = □
15. 428 × 62 = □

SET 1 Multiply. Estimate to make sure each answer makes sense.

pages 250–251

1. 284
× 21

2. 675
× 37

3. 158
× 76

4. 743
× 55

5. 396
× 94

6. 485
× 86

7. 419
× 79

8. 347
× 18

9. 400
× 67

10. 664
× 49

11. 782
× 52

12. 961
× 85

13. 23 × 374 = ☐

14. 70 × 563 = ☐

15. 92 × 468 = ☐

16. 50 × 680 = ☐

17. 71 × 700 = ☐

18. 99 × 111 = ☐

SET 2 Multiply.

pages 252–253

1. $.67
× 42

2. $.87
× 20

3. $.34
× 75

4. $.46
× 54

5. $.77
× 38

6. $.51
× 63

7. $2.89
× 71

8. $3.62
× 83

9. $7.12
× 37

10. $4.23
× 30

11. $9.82
× 64

12. $6.48
× 93

13. 87 × $.70 = ☐

14. 50 × $6.94 = ☐

15. 62 × $5.43 = ☐

16. 39 × $3.67 = ☐

17. $7.48 × 65 = ☐

18. 87 × $6.27 = ☐

SET 3 Find each quotient. Check by multiplying.

pages 262–263

1. 16 ÷ 4 = ☐
   160 ÷ 40 = ☐

2. 14 ÷ 2 = ☐
   140 ÷ 20 = ☐

3. 27 ÷ 3 = ☐
   270 ÷ 30 = ☐

4. 360 ÷ 60 = ☐

5. 360 ÷ 40 = ☐

6. 540 ÷ 90 = ☐

7. 720 ÷ 80 = ☐

8. 810 ÷ 90 = ☐

9. 400 ÷ 50 = ☐

10. 10)80

11. 20)160

12. 50)250

13. 70)490

14. 70)630

15. 60)300

16. 40)320

17. 50)250

18. 10)50

19. 80)160

20. 70)350

21. 40)240

SET 1 Divide. Check by multiplying.

pages 264–265

1. $20\overline{)68}$
2. $10\overline{)45}$
3. $30\overline{)100}$
4. $50\overline{)256}$

5. $40\overline{)375}$
6. $60\overline{)310}$
7. $80\overline{)177}$
8. $30\overline{)231}$

9. $20\overline{)175}$
10. $70\overline{)490}$
11. $90\overline{)753}$
12. $30\overline{)155}$

13. $387 \div 40 = \square$
14. $400 \div 60 = \square$
15. $280 \div 80 = \square$

16. $800 \div 90 = \square$
17. $115 \div 20 = \square$
18. $370 \div 70 = \square$

19. $248 \div 50 = \square$
20. $456 \div 70 = \square$
21. $266 \div 60 = \square$

22. $399 \div 60 = \square$
23. $350 \div 40 = \square$
24. $483 \div 80 = \square$

25. $468 \div 70 = \square$
26. $269 \div 80 = \square$
27. $267 \div 40 = \square$

SET 2 Estimate each quotient.

pages 266–267

1. $28\overline{)60}$
2. $18\overline{)70}$
3. $61\overline{)370}$
4. $73\overline{)300}$

5. $21\overline{)93}$
6. $89\overline{)550}$
7. $92\overline{)432}$
8. $34\overline{)177}$

9. $52\overline{)395}$
10. $22\overline{)138}$
11. $19\overline{)49}$
12. $70\overline{)225}$

13. $650 \div 81 = \square$
14. $430 \div 55 = \square$
15. $460 \div 90 = \square$

16. $706 \div 94 = \square$
17. $348 \div 78 = \square$
18. $675 \div 88 = \square$

SET 3 Divide. Check by multiplying.

pages 268–269

1. $18\overline{)69}$
2. $11\overline{)57}$
3. $10\overline{)74}$
4. $19\overline{)89}$

5. $21\overline{)149}$
6. $28\overline{)248}$
7. $41\overline{)379}$
8. $21\overline{)193}$

9. $36\overline{)243}$
10. $45\overline{)352}$
11. $57\overline{)439}$
12. $75\overline{)652}$

13. $613 \div 89 = \square$
14. $298 \div 31 = \square$
15. $820 \div 91 = \square$

EXTRA PRACTICE

SET 1   Divide.

pages 272–275

1. $24\overline{)43}$ 2. $62\overline{)365}$ 3. $84\overline{)649}$ 4. $51\overline{)201}$

5. $55\overline{)112}$ 6. $35\overline{)75}$ 7. $23\overline{)142}$ 8. $28\overline{)174}$

9. $39\overline{)196}$ 10. $33\overline{)221}$ 11. $72\overline{)211}$ 12. $49\overline{)198}$

13. $290 \div 43 = \square$ 14. $79 \div 39 = \square$ 15. $615 \div 67 = \square$

SET 2   Divide. Check by multiplying.

pages 276–279

1. $20\overline{)468}$ 2. $35\overline{)467}$ 3. $84\overline{)900}$ 4. $63\overline{)777}$

5. $43\overline{)712}$ 6. $57\overline{)692}$ 7. $78\overline{)935}$ 8. $26\overline{)452}$

9. $18\overline{)510}$ 10. $46\overline{)589}$ 11. $25\overline{)\$2.50}$ 12. $30\overline{)\$8.40}$

13. $\$6.00 \div 15 = \square$ 14. $\$8.25 \div 75 = \square$ 15. $\$5.40 \div 27 = \square$

SET 3   Write the fraction that tells what part is blue.

pages 292–295

1. 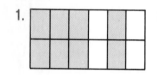   2. 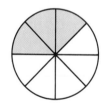   3. 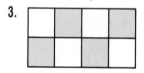   4.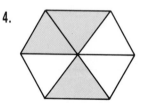

5. 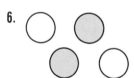   6.    7. 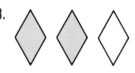   8.

SET 4   Complete. Write the equivalent fraction for each.

pages 296–299

1. $\dfrac{1}{3} = \dfrac{1 \times 4}{3 \times 4} = \dfrac{\square}{12}$ 2. $\dfrac{3}{5} = \dfrac{3 \times 2}{5 \times 2} = \dfrac{\square}{10}$ 3. $\dfrac{1}{4} = \dfrac{1 \times 4}{4 \times 4} = \dfrac{\square}{16}$

4. $\dfrac{2}{7} = \dfrac{2 \times 3}{7 \times 3} = \dfrac{6}{\square}$ 5. $\dfrac{1}{2} = \dfrac{1 \times 4}{2 \times 4} = \dfrac{4}{\square}$ 6. $\dfrac{3}{4} = \dfrac{3 \times \square}{4 \times \square} = \dfrac{12}{16}$

SET 1 Write each fraction in lowest terms.   pages 300–301

1. $\frac{2}{4}$ 2. $\frac{5}{15}$ 3. $\frac{10}{12}$ 4. $\frac{6}{8}$ 5. $\frac{4}{6}$

6. $\frac{8}{10}$ 7. $\frac{20}{24}$ 8. $\frac{11}{22}$ 9. $\frac{20}{30}$ 10. $\frac{4}{18}$

11. $\frac{10}{20}$ 12. $\frac{22}{33}$ 13. $\frac{9}{27}$ 14. $\frac{28}{36}$ 15. $\frac{6}{18}$

16. $\frac{75}{100}$ 17. $\frac{8}{10}$ 18. $\frac{30}{90}$ 19. $\frac{5}{45}$ 20. $\frac{2}{32}$

21. $\frac{11}{33}$ 22. $\frac{6}{36}$ 23. $\frac{3}{24}$ 24. $\frac{10}{55}$ 25. $\frac{15}{45}$

SET 2 Write < or > for ●.   pages 304–305

1. $\frac{2}{3}$ ● $\frac{1}{3}$ 2. $\frac{3}{4}$ ● $\frac{3}{5}$ 3. $\frac{2}{6}$ ● $\frac{5}{6}$ 4. $\frac{1}{4}$ ● $\frac{2}{3}$

5. $\frac{3}{5}$ ● $\frac{2}{4}$ 6. $\frac{2}{9}$ ● $\frac{1}{3}$ 7. $\frac{3}{7}$ ● $\frac{5}{7}$ 8. $\frac{3}{4}$ ● $\frac{3}{8}$

9. $\frac{4}{5}$ ● $\frac{7}{8}$ 10. $\frac{2}{3}$ ● $\frac{3}{6}$ 11. $\frac{4}{5}$ ● $\frac{7}{10}$ 12. $\frac{2}{4}$ ● $\frac{6}{8}$

13. $\frac{5}{7}$ ● $\frac{9}{14}$ 14. $\frac{4}{6}$ ● $\frac{13}{18}$ 15. $\frac{2}{3}$ ● $\frac{7}{12}$ 16. $\frac{2}{6}$ ● $\frac{1}{5}$

SET 3 Complete.   pages 306–307

1. $\frac{1}{6}$ of 18 = ☐   2. $\frac{2}{3}$ of 24 = ☐   3. $\frac{3}{8}$ of 32 = ☐

4. $\frac{1}{2}$ of 30 = ☐   5. $\frac{3}{4}$ of 16 = ☐   6. $\frac{4}{7}$ of 28 = ☐

Find $\frac{2}{7}$ of each amount.

7. 28   8. 21   9. 14   10. 49   11. 70   12. 56   13. 35

Find $\frac{5}{8}$ of each amount.

14. 16   15. 40   16. 32   17. 64   18. 96   19. 48   20. 72

SET 4 Write a mixed number or a whole number for each fraction.   pages 308–311

1. $\frac{18}{3}$ 2. $\frac{7}{7}$ 3. $\frac{17}{5}$ 4. $\frac{20}{9}$ 5. $\frac{7}{6}$ 6. $\frac{23}{2}$

7. $\frac{10}{4}$ 8. $\frac{32}{8}$ 9. $\frac{11}{2}$ 10. $\frac{12}{12}$ 11. $\frac{37}{7}$ 12. $\frac{40}{6}$

SET 1 Write a decimal for each fraction or mixed number.

pages 312–313

1. $\frac{3}{10}$ 2. $\frac{64}{100}$ 3. $2\frac{31}{100}$ 4. $4\frac{7}{10}$ 5. $3\frac{1}{100}$

6. $\frac{2}{10}$ 7. $5\frac{17}{100}$ 8. $\frac{9}{100}$ 9. $1\frac{5}{10}$ 10. $7\frac{98}{100}$

Write a fraction or mixed number for each decimal.

11. 0.40 12. 0.08 13. 12.06 14. 7.75 15. 38.23

16. 4.39 17. 0.03 18. 3.72 19. 9.6 20. 0.1

SET 2 Add. Write each sum in lowest terms.

pages 322–327

1. $\frac{1}{3} + \frac{1}{3} = \square$ 2. $\frac{2}{7} + \frac{1}{7} = \square$ 3. $\frac{1}{5} + \frac{3}{5} = \square$ 4. $\frac{4}{8} + \frac{3}{8} = \square$

5. $\frac{7}{12} + \frac{1}{12}$ 6. $\frac{5}{9} + \frac{3}{9}$ 7. $\frac{2}{6} + \frac{3}{6}$ 8. $\frac{2}{4} + \frac{1}{4}$ 9. $\frac{3}{10} + \frac{5}{10}$ 10. $\frac{6}{11} + \frac{4}{11}$

11. $\frac{1}{6} + \frac{2}{6}$ 12. $\frac{3}{8} + \frac{3}{8}$ 13. $\frac{1}{9} + \frac{2}{9}$ 14. $\frac{5}{12} + \frac{4}{12}$ 15. $\frac{1}{4} + \frac{1}{4}$ 16. $\frac{3}{13} + \frac{5}{13}$

SET 3 Write each sum as a whole number or a mixed number.

pages 322–327

1. $\frac{2}{3} + \frac{1}{3} = \square$ 2. $\frac{4}{6} + \frac{4}{6} = \square$ 3. $\frac{4}{5} + \frac{3}{5} = \square$ 4. $\frac{3}{4} + \frac{1}{4} = \square$

5. $\frac{9}{12} + \frac{3}{12}$ 6. $\frac{8}{10} + \frac{5}{10}$ 7. $\frac{5}{8} + \frac{4}{8}$ 8. $\frac{4}{7} + \frac{3}{7}$ 9. $\frac{5}{6} + \frac{2}{6}$ 10. $\frac{5}{9} + \frac{6}{9}$

SET 4 Subtract. Write each difference in lowest terms.

pages 326–327

1. $\frac{6}{7} - \frac{2}{7} = \square$ 2. $\frac{10}{12} - \frac{9}{12} = \square$ 3. $\frac{7}{8} - \frac{1}{8} = \square$ 4. $\frac{3}{4} - \frac{3}{4} = \square$

5. $\frac{4}{5} - \frac{3}{5}$ 6. $\frac{2}{3} - \frac{2}{3}$ 7. $\frac{6}{10} - \frac{1}{10}$ 8. $\frac{7}{9} - \frac{4}{9}$ 9. $\frac{5}{7} - \frac{2}{7}$ 10. $\frac{5}{6} - \frac{3}{6}$

SET 1 Add or subtract. Write each answer in lowest terms. pages 330–331

1. $3\frac{1}{7}$
$+\ \frac{5}{7}$

2. $6\frac{4}{5}$
$-4\frac{1}{5}$

3. $4\frac{1}{4}$
$+2\frac{1}{4}$

4. $5\frac{10}{12}$
$-3\frac{7}{12}$

5. $9\frac{2}{10}$
$+2\frac{3}{10}$

6. $4\frac{5}{6}$
$-\ \frac{3}{6}$

7. $8\frac{7}{8} - 4\frac{6}{8} = \square$

8. $7\frac{5}{9} + 6\frac{2}{9} = \square$

9. $5\frac{1}{5} + \frac{2}{5} = \square$

SET 2 Add. Write each sum in lowest terms. pages 332–333

1. $\frac{1}{3}$
$+\frac{5}{9}$

2. $\frac{1}{2}$
$+\frac{1}{4}$

3. $\frac{2}{6}$
$+\frac{1}{3}$

4. $\frac{3}{10}$
$+\frac{2}{5}$

5. $\frac{4}{12}$
$+\frac{1}{6}$

6. $\frac{3}{4}$
$+\frac{1}{8}$

7. $\frac{1}{10}$
$+\frac{1}{2}$

8. $\frac{2}{3}$
$+\frac{1}{4}$

9. $\frac{1}{6}$
$+\frac{1}{2}$

10. $\frac{1}{2}$
$+\frac{1}{3}$

11. $\frac{5}{9}$
$+\frac{1}{3}$

12. $\frac{3}{8}$
$+\frac{1}{4}$

13. $\frac{1}{3}$
$+\frac{2}{5}$

14. $\frac{5}{12}$
$+\frac{1}{3}$

15. $\frac{1}{6}$
$+\frac{3}{4}$

SET 3 Subtract. Write each difference in lowest terms. pages 334–335

1. $\frac{7}{8}$
$-\frac{1}{2}$

2. $\frac{8}{10}$
$-\frac{2}{5}$

3. $\frac{5}{6}$
$-\frac{2}{3}$

4. $\frac{2}{3}$
$-\frac{2}{9}$

5. $\frac{5}{6}$
$-\frac{3}{12}$

6. $\frac{1}{2}$
$-\frac{1}{3}$

7. $\frac{8}{12}$
$-\frac{1}{2}$

8. $\frac{2}{3}$
$-\frac{1}{4}$

9. $\frac{3}{4}$
$-\frac{2}{5}$

10. $\frac{4}{5}$
$-\frac{1}{3}$

11. $\frac{3}{4}$
$-\frac{2}{3}$

12. $\frac{7}{8}$
$-\frac{2}{3}$

13. $\frac{4}{5}$
$-\frac{2}{3}$

14. $\frac{7}{12}$
$-\frac{3}{6}$

15. $\frac{8}{12}$
$-\frac{2}{9}$

EXTRA PRACTICE

SET 1 Measure to the nearest inch and $\frac{1}{2}$ inch.

1.

2.

Measure to the nearest $\frac{1}{4}$ inch and $\frac{1}{8}$ inch.

3.

4.

SET 2 Choose *foot, yard,* or *mile* to measure.

pages 348–349

1. the distance to the sun

2. the height of a car

Complete.

3. 3 yd = ___ ft

4. 3 ft = ___ in.

5. 2 yd = ___ ft

6. 60 in. = ___ ft

7. 72 in. = ___ yd

8. 12 ft = ___ yd

9. 5 yd = ___ in.

10. 3 mi = ___ yd

11. 216 in. = ___ yd

12. 5 yd = ___ ft

13. 4 ft = ___ in.

14. 7,040 yd = ___ mi

SET 3 Complete.

pages 350–351

1. 4 lb = ___ oz

2. 10,000 lb = ___ T

3. 80 oz = ___ lb

4. 4 T = ___ lb

5. 8 lb = ___ oz

6. 7 T = ___ lb

7. 96 oz = ___ lb

8. 18,000 lb = ___ T

9. 8,000 lb = ___ T

Compare. Write >, <, or = for ●.

10. 7,000 lb ● 4 T

11. 112 oz ● 6 lb

12. 8 lb ● 144 oz

SET 4 Complete.

pages 352–353

1. ___ c = 4 pt

2. ___ qt = 12 pt

3. ___ gal = 20 qt

4. ___ pt = 10 c

5. ___ pt = 1 qt

6. ___ qt = 2 gal

7. ___ c = 3 pt

8. ___ qt = 6 pt

Compare. Use >, <, or = for ●.

9. 4 qt ● 2 gal

10. 5 pt ● 8 c

11. 2 qt ● 4 pt

12. 3 gal ● 16 qt

SET 1   Write the temperature or letter.

pages 354–355

1. C   2. G   3. H   4. B

5. 68°F   6. 52°F   7. 76°F   8. 30°F

Complete. Rule: Subtract 12°.

	9.	10.	11.	12.
Input	67°F	100°F	12°F	33°F
Output				

SET 2   You spin the spinner once. Answer each question.

pages 358–359

1. How many possible outcomes are there?

2. List all the possible outcomes.

3. What is the chance of landing on 0?

4. What is the chance of landing on M?

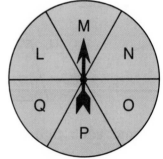

SET 3   Use the spinner to answer each question.

pages 362–363

1. How many possible outcomes are there?

2. What is the probability of landing on 5?

3. What is the probability of landing on an even number?

4. What is the probability of landing on a number less than 3?

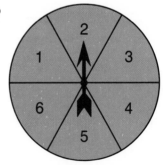

SET 4   Use the frequency table.

pages 362–363

1. What are the possible outcomes?

2. Which shape had the highest frequency?

3. Which shape had the lowest frequency?

4. What was the frequency for the △?

FREQUENCY TABLE		
Shape	Tally	Frequency
□	ℋℋ /	6
△	ℋℋ ///	8
○	ℋℋ ℋℋ	10
▭	ℋℋ	5
⬡	ℋℋ ///	8

SET 1 Name the space figure suggested by each object. pages 372–375

1.
2.
3.
4.

5.
6.
7.
8.

Name each polygon. Tell how many sides and vertices each has.

9.
10.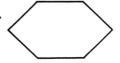
11.
12.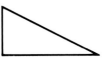

13.
14.
15.
16.

SET 2 Name each figure. pages 376–379

1.  *A* *B*
2. *C* *D*
3. *E* *F*
4. *H* *G* *I*

5. *J* *K*
6. *L* *M*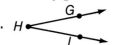
7. *N* *P* *O*
8. *Q*

9. *T* *S* *R*
10. *U* *V*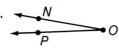
11. *W* *X*
12. *Y* *Z*

Name each figure.

13. *AB*
14. *CD*
15. *FE*
16. *AFE*
17. *CF*
18. *FB*

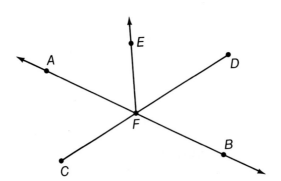

SET 1 Are the two figures congruent? Write *yes* or *no.* pages 380–383

1.

2.

3.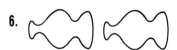

4.

5.

6.

Is the dotted line a line of symmetry? Write *yes* or *no.*

7.

8.

9.

10.

11.

12.

13.

14.

SET 2 Use the drawing to answer each question. pages 386–393

1. Name a diameter of this circle.

2. Name 4 points on the circle.

3. Name a radius of the circle.

4. Name the center of the circle.

5. Which diameter has *R* as an endpoint?

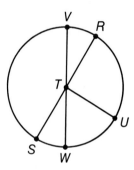

Find the perimeter of each polygon.

6.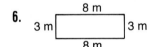

7.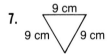

8.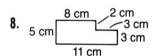

Find the area. Each ▨ is one square unit.

9.

10.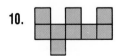

11.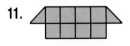

Multiply to find the volume.

12.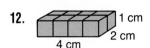

13.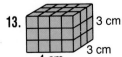

14.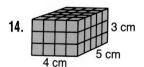

SET 1   Use the grid to find the ordered pair for each point.   pages 394–397

1. *A*

2. *B*

3. *C*

4. *D*

5. *E*

6. *F*

7. *G*

8. *H*

9. *I*

10. *J*

11. *K*

12. *L*

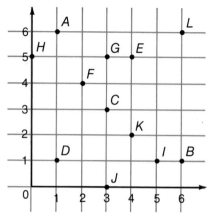

Graph each point on graph paper. For each exercise connect the points in order.

13. *F* (1,3)

14. *S* (1,0)

15. *B* (2,4)

16. *V* (1,1)

   G (2,5)

   T (2,1)

   C (3,1)

   W (2,2)

   H (3,4)

   U (3,2)

   D (4,0)

   X (3,3)

   V (4,3)

   E (6,3)

   Y (3,2)

   Z (3,1)

SET 1 Use the picture to answer the questions. pages 16–17

1. How many people can sit at the table in all?

2. How many people are seated?

3. How many more people can sit at the table?

4. How many more children than adults are there at the picnic?

SET 2 Use the picture to answer the questions. pages 32–33

1. How many children are at the game booth in all?

2. Robyn scored 175 points. What type of prize did she win?

3. How many more boys than girls were at the game booth?

4. Sam scored 75 points, 35 points, and 90 points. What type of prize did he win?

SET 3 Tell which operation to use. Then solve each problem. pages 54–55

1. Sally scored 74 points in a dart game. George scored 48 points, and Harvey scored 32 points. How many points were scored by George and Harvey together?

2. Carrie ran 52 yards and gave the baton to Patti. She ran 17 yards and gave the baton to Jean. Jean ran 28 yards with the baton. How many yards did the baton travel?

3. Ron kicked the ball 100 feet. Fay kicked it 67 feet. Gerry kicked it 102 feet. What was this total distance?

4. Albert passed the football to Bob 15 times. Bob caught it 7 times. How many times was the pass incomplete?

SET 1 Tell which operation to use. Then solve each problem. pages 68–69

1. Sue spent $2.75 at the Country Store. She gave the clerk $5.00. How much change did she get?

2. Sue had 17 bird stickers, 9 heart stickers, and 42 cartoon stickers. How many stickers did she have?

3. During one week the Country Store sold 39 stickers and 85 puzzles. How many more puzzles than stickers were sold?

4. Pens cost $.39 at the store, and notebooks cost $1.29. How much would 1 notebook and 2 pens cost?

SET 2 Tell what fact is missing in each problem. pages 88–89

1. Cathy had 27 books on her shelf. She received more books for her birthday. How many books does she have now?

2. Pat went to the flower shop. She bought 6 pansies for each of her flower boxes. How many flowers did she buy in all?

3. Mr. Anderson made 47 whistles. He gave one to every student in Mrs. Anderson's class. How many does he have left?

4. Marla and Jack read books over the vacation. Marla read 6 more books than Jack. How many books did Marla read?

SET 3 Use the menu to solve 1–5. pages 102–103

1. Mollie ordered spaghetti and juice for lunch. How much did she spend?

2. A sandwich costs $.98. How much more expensive is a salad than a sandwich?

3. If the price of rolls increased by $.25, would it be the same price as juice?

4. Harold bought a sandwich and juice. Did he spend more than a $1.50?

5. Eli ordered spaghetti, salad, roll, and juice. What did he pay?

TODAY'S MENU	
Spaghetti	$1.00
Roll	$ .25
Juice	$ .59
Salad	$1.37
Sandwich	$ .98

6. A bag contains 18 rolls. How many baskets of 3 rolls each can Tina serve from the bag?

7. Lisa waits on 6 tables. Each table seats 4 people. How many people does she wait on if all her tables are full?

SET 1 Tell which fact is extra. Then solve each problem. pages 126–127

1. Joan spelled 25 words correctly in the spelling bee. Gene had 17 right, and Pat spelled 21 correctly. How many more words did Pat spell correctly than Gene?

2. Mrs. Price sold bananas for $.35 each. Brett bought 2 bananas. Wes bought 4 bananas. How much did Brett spend for bananas?

3. Randi ate breakfast. Then she walked 3 blocks to David's house. She and David walked 6 more blocks to school. How far is school from Randi's house?

4. Ellen's class traveled 23 miles to the museum. They stayed at the museum for 2 hours. Then they drove 23 miles home. How far did the class travel on their trip?

SET 2 Use the graph to answer each question. pages 136–137

1. On which day are the most hot lunches sold?

2. On which day are more hot lunches sold, Monday or Thursday?

3. On which 2 days are the same number of hot lunches sold?

4. How many more hot lunches must be sold on Tuesday to equal the number sold on Thursday?

NUMBER OF HOT LUNCHES	
Monday	☐☐☐☐
Tuesday	☐
Wednesday	☐☐☐☐
Thursday	☐☐
Friday	☐☐☐☐☐☐
☐ = 25 Hot Lunches	

5. How many hot lunches were served on Friday? on Wednesday? How many more were served on Friday?

SET 3 Team games are played with a certain number of players. A basketball team has 5 players. A volleyball team and hockey team each have 6 players. There are 11 players on a soccer team. A baseball team has 9 players. pages 154–155

1. Make a table to show the facts.

2. What two teams have 6 players?

3. What game has the most players?

4. What team has the least players?

5. How many soccer players are on the field when the game begins?

6. A basketball league has 5 teams. How many players are needed?

SET 1 Use the table to answer each question.

pages 164–165

SLEEPING BAGS			
Model	Length	Width	Weight
Polar Bag	80 inches	33 inches	5 pounds, 14 ounces
Camp Bag	60 inches	30 inches	4 pounds, 8 ounces
Cabin Bag	76 inches	33 inches	4 pounds, 8 ounces
North Wood Bag	91 inches	32 inches	6 pounds, 2 ounces

1. How much wider is the Cabin Bag than the Camp Bag?

2. How much would 2 North Wood Bags weigh?

3. How much longer is the Polar Bag than the Camp Bag?

4. How much lighter is the Cabin Bag than the Polar bag?

5. Alice is 63 inches tall. How many extra inches will she have in a Polar Bag?

6. If Alice goes on a weekend hike, which of the four sleeping bags should she select?

SET 2 Make a list to help solve each problem.

pages 184–185

1. You have 1 penny, 1 dime, and 1 quarter. What different amounts can you make using any combination of coins?

2. Lee is painting the letters of the alphabet. He made A blue, B red, C green, and started the pattern over. What colors will he paint P and Y?

3. Adam, Sara, and Una are tennis players. They play in pairs. How many different ways can they pair off to play?

4. Jamie also plays tennis. They want to play doubles, or two players on each team. How many different ways can they make 2-person teams to play each other?

5. Nioki, Avi, Tim, and Scott had a chess tournament. Each played each of the others 1 time. How many games did they play?

6. A school bus can carry 55 children. The bus picks up 1 child at the first stop, 2 at the second, 3 at the third, and so on. At which stop will the bus be filled?

SET 1 Make a table to solve each problem.

pages 194–195

1. Hue High School lost to Smith High School in a football game 0–12. How many various ways could Smith High have scored 12 points? Points: touchdown 6; safety 2; extra point 1; field goal 3.

2. A tour bus with 53 people makes two stops. At the first stop 17 people get off and 19 get on. At the second stop 28 people get off and 23 get on. How many people are now on the bus?

3. It takes 7 lemons to make 2 liters of lemonade. How many lemons are needed to make 8 liters of lemonade?

4. Theresa bought pears at 10¢ each and plums at 12¢ each. She spent $1.00 in all. How many of each kind of fruit did she buy?

SET 2 Solve each problem.

pages 216–217

1. Fran has two dogs and two cats. Each dog eats 1 can of dog food a day. The cats share 1 can a day. How many cans do Fran's pets eat each week?

2. Jennifer pays $.21 for each newspaper and sells each one for $.30. If she has 50 customers on her paper route, how much money does she earn in one day?

3. Adam bought 3 pounds of apples and 6 oranges. Apples sell for 59¢ per pound, and oranges are 3 for 69¢. What change will Adam receive from $10.00?

4. Lois bought 8 cans of apple juice for 40¢ a can. She paid for it with a five-dollar bill. How much change should she receive?

SET 3 Use the graph to solve each problem.

pages 228–229

1. On which two days is the sum of the children absent equal to 13?

2. How many more children were absent on Monday than on Wednesday?

3. How many total absences were there for the week?

4. Which number of absences is the only one not divisible by 2?

NUMBER OF CHILDREN ABSENT														
M	X	X	X	X	X	X	X	X	X	X				
T	X	X	X	X	X	X								
W	X	X	X	X	X	X	X							
Th	X	X	X	X	X	X	X	X	X	X	X	X		
F	X	X	X	X	X	X	X	X	X	X	X	X	X	X
	1	2	3	4	5	6	7	8	9	10	11	12	13	14	15

EXTRA PRACTICE

SET 1   **Make a drawing to help solve each problem.**   pages 246–247

1. The sailors saw 5 whales. They saw 3 times as many dolphins. How many dolphins did they see?

2. The sailors saw 15 whales. They saw 3 times as many jellyfish. How many jellyfish did they see?

3. The bass is larger than the bluegill. The perch is smaller than the bluegill. The size of the trout is between the bluegill and the perch. Which fish is the largest?

4. Sue, Jan, and Meg live next to each other. One is an artist, one is an engineer, one is a teacher. Jan lives in the middle. When Meg is away, the artist feeds her dog. The engineer knocks on Sue's wall when the radio is too loud. What is the occupation of each girl?

SET 2   **Use the table to solve each problem.**   pages 254–255

Magnets	Cost
Horseshoe	$7
Disc	$5
Bar	$4

1. You have $35. You buy 3 disc magnets and 2 bar magnets. How many horseshoe magnets can you buy?

2. Can you buy 3 of each magnet for $50?

3. Disc prices go up to $10 and bars to $8. How many discs can you buy with $35 if you buy 2 horseshoes?

4. At the new prices, would 4 of each magnet cost more than or less than $95? How much more or less?

SET 3   **Use guess and test to solve each problem.**   pages 270–271

1. Luke and his brother, Hugh, picked 24 bags of apples. Luke picked twice as many bags as Hugh. How many bags did Hugh pick?

2. Mr. Cain sold 36 new cars during the month of April. He sold six more 2-door cars than 4-door cars. How many of each did he sell?

3. Mary, Beth, and Sue ate a box of 48 crackers. Mary ate $\frac{1}{2}$ as many as Beth and $\frac{1}{3}$ as many as Sue. How many crackers did each girl eat?

4. Joel, Matt, and Roy ate 14 apples. Matt ate twice as many as Roy and four times as many as Joel. How many apples did each boy eat?

SET 1   Make a drawing to help solve each problem.

pages 280–281

1. Ria, Luke, Pilar, and Juan live on the same block. Pilar lives next to Juan. Luke lives next to Pilar. Juan and Ria are neighbors. In what order are their homes?

2. Ten coins are stacked in a pile. Three are 2 millimeters thick, two are 4 millimeters thick. The rest are 3 millimeters thick. How high is the stack of coins?

3. A pendulum swings 10 meters to the right, then 9 meters to the left, then 8 meters to the right. Each swing decreases by 1 meter. How far to the right of its starting point is the pendulum after its third swing to the left?

4. Nan has a 5-room apartment. The bedroom is next to the kitchen. The living room is between the kitchen and the dining room. The den is the farthest from the bedroom. Which room is in the middle?

SET 2   Experiment to solve each problem.

pages 302–303

1. The Music Theatre has 90 seats. Count the number of seats in your classroom. How many fewer seats does your classroom have?

2. Tickets to a piano recital cost $5 each. If each person in your family attends, what will be the total cost?

3. Camp Mohawk's rubber raft is about $\frac{1}{2}$ the length of a canoe. Is the length of your desk more or less than $\frac{1}{2}$ the length of your teacher's desk?

4. A racquetball racket is about $\frac{2}{3}$ the height of a tennis racquet. What can you find in your classroom that is $\frac{2}{3}$ the height of the chalkboard?

SET 3   Make a table to help solve each problem.

pages 314–315

1. Mr. Simms works in a carpentry shop. He makes stools with 3 legs and tables with 4 legs. One day he used a total of 31 legs. How many of each could he have made?

2. In a small village in Kenya it takes 2 elephants to haul a load of wood that would build $\frac{1}{5}$ of a house. How many elephants are needed to build a house if each elephant makes only one trip to the house?

3. Joyce has 18 plants. She uses $\frac{1}{6}$ can of water for each plant. How many full cans of water would she use on her plants?

4. The average American family has 2 children. What is the average number of children in all the families in your class?

<u>SET 1</u> **For a safety report, Sam and Sanya gathered facts**
            about street signs in their neighborhood.   pages 328–329

1. Sam kept a log of yield signs. He saw 1 about every 5 minutes. Sanya saw 2 stop signs about every 6 minutes. When they finished, they had recorded 16 signs in all. How many of each type did they find? How long did they look?

2. A stop sign has 8 sides. Each side is $10\frac{1}{2}$ in. long. The sign is supported by a post 48 in. high. At one of the stop signs, Sam and Sanya stopped to watch a spider. It climbed up the post from the ground, around the edge of the sign, and back down to the ground. To the nearest foot, how far did the spider travel?

3. A yield sign has 4 sides. Each side is 14 inches. What is the total length of all the sides?

4. If Sam and Sanya started their survey at 3:15 P.M., what time did they finish it?

<u>SET 2</u> **Solve each problem.**   pages 336–337

1. Cara spent $9.70 on flowers. Roses were $2.50 each, daisies were $1.10 each. Lilies were $1.80 each. How many of each type of flower did she buy?

2. Dan, Eva, and Josh baked cookies. Dan made 38. Josh made 29. The average number of cookies baked by each person was 30. How many cookies did Eva bake?

3. Sy and Dana collect stamps. Sy has 170 more stamps than Leslie. Together they have 982 stamps. How many stamps does each have?

4. David can deliver 72 newspapers in 1 hour. Amy can deliver 61 newspapers in 1 hour. How many whole hours must each work to deliver a total of 460 papers?

<u>SET 3</u> **Complete each pattern.**   pages 356–357

1. 54, 48, 42, ___, ___, ___, ___

2. B, C, D, F, G, ___, ___

3. 12, 21, 30, ___, ___, ___, ___

4. $\frac{1}{2}$, $\frac{2}{3}$, $\frac{3}{4}$, $\frac{4}{5}$, ___, ___

SET 1 **Complete the charts to solve the problems.** pages 364–365

1. Kristi and Lynn started reading their library books today. If Kristi reads 8 pages each day and Lynn reads 5 pages, what page will Lynn be reading when Kristi is reading page 56?

Kristi		
Day	1	2
Page	8	16

Lynn		
Day	1	2
Page	5	10

2. Forty-five wheels were used to build 19 bicycles and tricycles. How many bicycles and tricycles were built?

Bicycles	1	2	3
Wheels	2	4	6
Tricycles	1	2	3
Wheels	3	6	9

3. Joe walked 13 kilometers in two hours to improve his fitness level. How many kilometers could he walk in 6 hours?

kilometer	13	
hours	2	

4. A pet shop has 3 dogs for every 2 cats. How many cats do they have for every 33 dogs?

dogs	3	
cats	2	

SET 2 **Solve each problem.** pages 384–385

1. Jenny bought a silver ring that costs more than $20 but less than $30. It cost her the same number of $1 bills as $5 bills to buy it. How much did the ring cost?

2. Marcy bought a copper ring for 29¢. She gave the clerk a $1 bill and received 5 coins in change. What five coins did she receive?

3. Marty bought a dart board at the County Fair. He told Missy that he had scored 75 points with 4 darts. How did he do it?

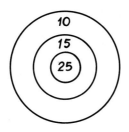

4. Below is the pattern of Fay's embroidery tape. It has a total of 42 circles, triangles, and squares. How many of each shape will there be?

SET 3 **Complete each pattern.** pages 398–399

1. 1, 8, 2, 9, ___, ___, ___, ___

2. 2, 6, 18, ___, ___, ___, ___

3. 17, ___, 31, 38, ___, ___, ___

4. 72, ___, 56, ___, ___, ___, ___

Glossary

addends The numbers that are added.
Example: 7 + 8 = 15
    The addends are 7 and 8.

addition An operation on two or more numbers to find the sum.
Example: 4 + 2 + 3 = 9
    The sum is 9.

angle Two rays with a common endpoint.
Example:

area The number of square units needed to cover a region.

average The sum of the addends divided by the number of addends.

bar graph A graph with bars of different lengths to show information.

BASIC A computer language.

central processing unit (CPU) The unit in a computer where calculations are performed.

circle A closed plane figure. All the points of a circle are the same distance from a point called the center.

circle graph A graph that shows how a total amount has been divided into parts.

cone A space figure with one circular flat surface and one vertex.

congruent figures Figures that have the same size and shape.

cube A space figure with six square faces, twelve edges, and eight vertices.

customary system A measurement system that measures length in inches, feet, yards, and miles; capacity in cups, pints, quarts, and gallons; weight in ounces, pounds, and tons; and temperature in degrees Fahrenheit. *See* Table of Measures.

cylinder A space figure with two bases that are congruent circles.
Example:

data Information that is gathered.

decimal A number with one or more places to the right of a decimal point.
Examples: 0.7, 1.8, 2.06

degree Celsius (°C) A unit for measuring temperature in the metric system.

degree Fahrenheit (°F) A unit for measuring temperature in the customary system.

denominator The number below the fraction bar in a fraction.
Example: $\frac{2}{5}$
    The denominator is 5.

diameter A line segment that passes through the center of a circle and has both endpoints on the circle.

difference The answer in subtraction.
Example: 9 − 4 = 5
    The difference is 5.

digit Any of the symbols used to write numbers: 0, 1, 2, 3, 4, 5, 6, 7, 8, and 9.

dividend The number to be divided.
Example: $6\overline{)36}$ or 36 ÷ 6
    The dividend is 36.

divisible A number is divisible by another number if the remainder is zero after dividing.

division An operation on two numbers that results in a quotient.

divisor The number by which another number is to be divided.
Example: $7\overline{)28}$ or 28 ÷ 7
    The divisor is 7.

edge The segment where two faces of a space figure meet.
Example: edge

END The last line in a BASIC computer program.

endpoint   A point at the end of a line segment or ray.

ENTER   The key that causes the computer to accept and process information. It is also called a RETURN key.

equivalent fractions   Fractions that name the same number. *Example:* $\frac{1}{2}$ and $\frac{2}{4}$

estimate   To give an approximate rather than an exact answer.

even number   A whole number that is divisible by 2.

expanded form   A number written as the sum of the values of its digits. *Example:* $200 + 80 + 7$ is the expanded form for 287.

face   A flat surface of a space figure.

factors   The numbers that are multiplied to give a product. *Example:* $3 \times 5 = 15$ The factors are 3 and 5.

flowchart   A diagram that shows a step-by-step way to solve a problem.

fraction   A number that names part of a group or part of a region. *Examples:* $\frac{1}{2}$, $\frac{2}{3}$, $\frac{6}{6}$

graph   A drawing used to show information.

greater than ($>$)   The symbol used to compare two numbers when the greater number is written first. *Examples:* $7 > 3$, $9 > 6$

grouping property of addition   The way in which numbers are grouped does not change the sum. *Example:* $2 + (4 + 5) = (2 + 4) + 5$

grouping property of multiplication   The way in which numbers are grouped does not change the product. *Example:* $2 \times (3 \times 5) = (2 \times 3) \times 5$

hexagon   A polygon with six sides and six vertices.

input   The numbers and commands entered in a calculator or a computer. A computer keyboard is an input device.

intersecting lines   Lines that cross at one point.

less than ($<$)   The symbol used to compare two numbers when the lesser number is written first. *Examples:* $3 < 7$, $6 < 9$

LET   A statement in a BASIC computer program that assigns a value to a memory location named by a letter.

like fractions   Fractions that have the same denominator. *Example:* $\frac{3}{4}$ and $\frac{1}{4}$

line   The collection of points along a straight path that goes on and on in opposite directions. A line has no endpoints.

line graph   A graph used to show changes over a period of time.

line of symmetry   A line that divides a figure into two congruent parts. *Example:*

line segment   A part of a line having two endpoints.

lowest terms   A fraction is in lowest terms when 1 is the only number that divides both the numerator and the denominator. *Example:* $\frac{1}{4}$ and $\frac{3}{5}$ are in lowest terms.

metric system   A measurement system that measures length in millimeters, centimeters, meters, and kilometers; capacity in milliliters and liters; mass in grams and kilograms; and temperature in degrees Celsius. *See* Table of Measures.

mixed number   A number written as a whole number and a fraction.
Example: $3\frac{4}{5}$

multiple   The product of a whole number and any other whole number.
Examples: 0, 3, 6, 9, and so on, are multiples of 3.

multiplication   An operation on two or more numbers, called factors, to find a product.
Example: 4 × 5 = 20
The product is 20.

number line   A line that shows numbers in order.
Example:

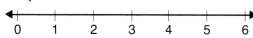

number sentence   A fact written in horizontal form.
Example: 3 × 4 = 12

numerator   The number above the fraction bar in a fraction.
Example: $\frac{2}{5}$
The numerator is 2.

octagon   A polygon with eight sides and eight vertices.

odd number   A whole number that is not divisible by 2.

order property of addition   The order in which numbers are added does not change the sum.
Example: 9 + 3 = 3 + 9

order property of multiplication   The order in which numbers are multiplied does not change the product.
Example: 3 × 2 = 2 × 3

ordered pair   A pair of numbers used to locate a point in a plane.

ordinal number   A number used to tell order or position.
Examples: first, fifth

outcome   A possible result in a probability experiment.

output   The answer given by a computer or a calculator. A computer monitor is an output device.

parentheses ( )   A symbol that shows grouping.
Example: (2 × 3) × 4 = 24
6   × 4 = 24

pentagon   A polygon with five sides and five vertices.

perimeter   The distance around a polygon.

period   A group of three digits of a number, separated by a comma.

pictograph   A graph that shows number information by using picture symbols.

place value   The value of a digit determined by its position in a number.
Example: In 562, 5 means 5 hundreds,
6 means 6 tens,
2 means 2 ones.

plane   A flat surface extending endlessly in all directions.

point   An exact location in space.

polygon   A closed plane figure with straight sides, called line segments.

prime number   A whole number greater than 1 with only two factors, itself and 1.
Examples: 5, 7, 11, and 13 are prime numbers.

PRINT   A command to the computer to show information on the screen.

prism   A space figure with two parallel and congruent bases.

probability   The relation of favorable outcomes to possible outcomes of an experiment.

product The answer in multiplication.
Example: $4 \times 8 = 32$
The product is 32.

program A list of instructions for the computer.

property of one The product of any number and 1 is that number.

pyramid A space figure whose base is a polygon and whose faces are triangles with a common vertex.

quadrilateral A polygon with four sides and four vertices.

quotient The answer in division.

Example: $24 \div 3 = 8$ or $3\overline{)24}^{\,8}$
The quotient is 8.

radius A line segment with one endpoint on the circle and the other endpoint at the center.

ray A part of a line that has one endpoint and goes on and on in one direction.

rectangle A polygon with four sides and four right angles.

rectangular prism A space figure whose faces are all rectangles.

regroup To use 1 ten to form 10 ones, 1 hundred to form 10 tens, 12 ones to form 1 ten 2 ones, and so on.

related facts Facts using the same numbers.
Example: $2 + 3 = 5$ $5 - 3 = 2$
$3 + 2 = 5$ $5 - 2 = 3$

remainder The number that is left over after dividing.
Example: $42 \div 8 = 5$ R2
The remainder is 2.

right angle An angle that has the shape of a square corner.
Example:

Roman numerals Symbols that the Romans used for numbers: I, V, X, L, C, D, and M.

rounding Expressing a number to the nearest ten, hundred, thousand, and so on.
Example: 43 rounded to the nearest ten is 40.

RUN An instruction that tells the computer to follow instructions one line at a time.

space figure A geometric figure whose points are in more than one plane.

sphere A space figure shaped like a round ball.

square A polygon with four equal sides and four right angles.

subtraction An operation on two numbers to find the difference.
Example: $15 - 3 = 12$
The difference is 12.

sum The answer in addition.
Example: $8 + 7 = 15$
The sum is 15.

triangle A polygon with three sides and three vertices.

unlike fractions Fractions that have different denominators.
Example: $\frac{1}{2}$ and $\frac{2}{3}$

vertex The point where two rays meet. The point of intersection of two sides of a polygon. The point of intersection of three edges of a space figure.

volume The number of cubic units that fit inside a space figure.

zero property of addition The sum of any number and 0 is that number.
Example: $3 + 0 = 3$

zero property of multiplication The product of any number and 0 is 0.
Example: $5 \times 0 = 0$

TABLE OF MEASURES

Metric

Length

1 centimeter (cm) = 10 millimeters (mm)
1 meter (m) = 100 centimeters
1 kilometer (km) = 1,000 meters

Mass/Weight

1 kilogram (kg) = 1,000 grams (g)

Capacity

1 liter (L) = 1,000 milliliters (mL)

Time

1 minute (min) = 60 seconds (s)
1 hour (h) = 60 minutes
1 day (d) = 24 hours
1 week (wk) = 7 days
1 month (mo) = 28 to 31 days, or
about 4 weeks
1 year (yr) = 12 months, or 52 weeks,
or 365 days

Customary

Length

1 foot (ft) = 12 inches (in.)
1 yard (yd) = 36 inches, or 3 feet
1 mile (mi) = 5,280 feet, or 1,760 yards

Weight

1 pound (lb) = 16 ounces (oz)
1 ton (T) = 2,000 lb

Capacity

1 pint (pt) = 2 cups (c)
1 quart (qt) = 2 pints
1 gallon (gal) = 4 quarts

Money

1 nickel = 5 cents (¢)
1 dime = 10 cents, or 2 nickels
1 quarter = 2 dimes and 1 nickel
1 half-dollar = 2 quarters
1 dollar ($) = 4 quarters

SYMBOLS

=	is equal to	65¢	sixty-five cents	$\overleftrightarrow{AB}$	line AB
>	is greater than	$2.10	two dollars and ten cents	$\overline{AB}$	line segment AB
<	is less than	°C	degree Celsius	$\overrightarrow{AB}$	ray AB
. . .	and so on	°F	degree Fahrenheit	$\angle ABC$	angle ABC

FORMULAS

$P = a + b + c + d$ Perimeter of a quadrilateral
$A = l \times w$ Area of a rectangle
$V = l \times w \times h$ Volume of a rectangular prism

Index

CREDITS

Design by Silver Burdett & Ginn

Contributing Design by Taurens Associates

Cover: Computer Art/Ron Morecraft and Bob Nicoll

All photographs by Silver Burdett & Ginn unless otherwise noted

All line art by Peter Krempasky and Mario Ferro, unless otherwise noted

Sports equipment provided by Fitzgerald Sporting Goods Company, Morristown, N.J.

D E F G H I J—RRD—96 95 94 93 92 91 90 89